THE NEW BOOK OF KNOWLEDGE ANNUAL

THE
NEW BOOK
OF
KNOWLEDGE
ANNUAL

The Young People's Book of the Year

Grolier Incorporated, Danbury, Connecticut

2001

Highlighting Events of 2000

ISBN 0-7172-0636-X

ISSN 0196-0148

The Library of Congress Catalog Card Number: 79-26807

 COPYRIGHT © 2001 BY GROLIER INCORPORATED

Copyright © in Canada 2001 by GROLIER LIMITED

—————— STAFF ——————

CONTENTS

10 In the Pages of This Book. . .

12 THE WORLD IN 2000
14 The Year at a Glance
18 January
20 February
22 March
24 April
26 May
28 June
30 July
32 August
34 September
36 October
38 November
40 December
42 The Battle for the White House
50 Let the Good Times Roll!
52 Turmoil in Africa
56 Around the World
64 Newsmakers

68 ANIMALS
70 Chameleons: Quick-Change Artists
74 Dino-Mite News
76 How Animals Protect Their Young
82 Hungry Plant. . .Poor Ant
86 Stars of the Sea
88 Parrots: Personality Plus
92 Raining Cats and Dogs!

96 SCIENCE
98 Biodiversity: A Tapestry of Life
102 The Human Genome: A Blueprint of You
104 Frankenfoods?
108 The Hayden Planetarium: A Trip Through the Universe
110 Score One for the Lefty
114 Space Briefs
120 Rhythms of Life
124 Battle of the Bugs
126 Earth Watch
130 Auroras: Mysterious Sky Shows

134 MAKE & DO
136 Wild Cards!
138 Stamp Collecting
142 It's Game Time. . .
144 Round Trip: The Flight of the Boomerang
150 Site-Seeing
152 Many Friends Cooking
154 Popular Crafts
158 Coin Collecting

160 SPORTS
162 The 2000 Summer Olympic Games
174 Baseball
177 Little League Baseball
178 Basketball
181 Football
184 Golf
185 Hockey
188 Ice Skating

188 Skiing
189 Track and Field
190 Tennis

192 **LIVING HISTORY**
194 The Counting of America
198 Fireworks: Showers of Light
202 The Vietnam War: 25 Years Later
206 The Hanover World's Fair
208 Capturing Time
212 The Vikings Are Here!
216 A Birthday for the White House

220 **SPOTLIGHT ON YOUTH**
222 WWW.CoolSites
224 Careers in Finance
232 Kid Stuff
238 JASON: The Ultimate Field Trip

242 **CREATIVITY**
244 Good-bye, Charlie Brown
248 2000 Academy Awards
250 Glowing Gems of the Sea
256 People, Places, Events
264 Movie Time!
268 2000 Emmy Awards
270 The Music Scene
276 The Internet Music Mall

278 **FUN TO READ**
280 Rikki-tikki-tavi
290 Poetry

292 Looking at Books
296 World of Tomorrow
308 Little Wildrose

315 **THE NEW BOOK OF KNOWLEDGE—2001**
316 Video Games
318 Inuit
323 Emotions
325 Middle Ages
332 Avalanches and Landslides
334 Elk and Moose
335 Reindeer and Caribou
336 World War I
352 World War II

379 **SUPPLEMENT**
380 Deaths
384 Independent Nations of the World
390 The United States
394 Canada

396 **INDEX**

414 **ILLUSTRATION CREDITS AND ACKNOWLEDGMENTS**

CONTRIBUTORS

ATKINS, Dale
Avalanche Researcher, Colorado Avalanche Information Center
(Reviewer) AVALANCHES AND LANDSLIDES

AUSUBEL, Herman
Former Professor of History, Columbia University; Author, *The Making of Modern Europe; Historians and Their Craft*
WORLD WAR I

BAUM, Rex L.
Research Geologist, U.S. Geological Survey
AVALANCHES AND LANDSLIDES

BERGER, Cynthia
Science Writer
ELK AND MOOSE
REINDEER AND CARIBOU

COOPER, Kenneth S.
Professor of History, George Peabody College for Teachers, Vanderbilt University; Author, *World Ways; The Changing Old World; Modern History*
MIDDLE AGES

EISENHOWER, John S. D.
Brigadier General, U.S. Army (Ret.); Former Member, White House Staff; Author, *The Bitter Wood; Allies*; Editor and Researcher, *The White House Years* by Dwight D. Eisenhower
(Reviewer) WORLD WAR II

HACKER, Jeffrey H.
Freelance Writer; Author, *Franklin D. Roosevelt; Carl Sandburg; Government Subsidy to Industry; The New China*
WORLD OF TOMORROW

HART, David L.
External Relations Manager, San Diego Supercomputer Center; Coauthor, *Mac OS 8 Web Server Cookbook*
VIDEO GAMES

KING, Bryan H., M.D.
Professor of Psychiatry and Pediatrics, Dartmouth Medical School; Director of Child and Adolescent Psychiatry, Dartmouth-Hitchcock Medical Center
EMOTIONS

MARSHALL, S. L. A.
Brigadier General, U.S. Army (Ret.); Former Chief Combat Historian, Central Pacific; Chief Historian, European Theater of Operations; Author, *Illustrated History of World War I*

WORLD WAR II

PASCOE, Elaine
Author, *South Africa: Troubled Land; Neighbors at Odds: U.S. Policy in Latin America; Racial Prejudice; The Horse Owner's Preventive Maintenance Handbook; Freedom of Expression: The Right to Speak Out in America*

AROUND THE WORLD

SMITH, Derek G.
Associate Professor of Anthropology and Sociology, Carleton University (Ottawa); Author, *Natives and Outsiders*

INUIT

TESAR, Jenny
Author, *Endangered Habitats; Global Warming; Scientific Crime Investigation; The Waste Crisis; Shrinking Forests; The New Webster's Computer Handbook; What on Earth Is a Meerkat?; Spiders*

SPACE BRIEFS

VAN RYZIN, Robert
Managing Editor, *Numismatic News*, Krause Publications; Author, *Striking Impressions: A Visual Guide to Collecting U.S. Coins*

COIN COLLECTING

WERSTEIN, Irving
Author, *1914–1918: World War I; 1776: The Adventure of the American Revolution Told with Pictures; The Many Faces of the Civil War*

WORLD WAR I

IN THE PAGES OF THIS BOOK . . .

How closely did you follow the events of 2000? Do you remember the people who made news during the year? What about the trends—what was in and what was out? Who won in sports? What were the top songs, films, and television shows? What important anniversaries were celebrated? All these helped make up your world in 2000—a year that was like no other.

Here's a quiz that will tell you how much you know about your world—about what took place during the past year and about other things, as well. If you're stumped by a question, don't worry. You'll find all the answers in the pages of this book. (The page numbers after the questions will tell you where to look.)

On January 1, worldwide celebrations marked the arrival of the year 2000. The first country to welcome in the new year was the Pacific island nation of (Kiribati/ Papua New Guinea/Fiji). (*19*)

On November 2, history was made in space when the first permanent crew of American astronauts and Russian cosmonauts entered the_____. (*114*)

At the 2000 Academy Award ceremonies, which film won the Oscar for best motion picture? (*248*)

In the November 7 U.S. presidential election, the winner was decided by the 25 Electoral College votes of (Oregon/New Mexico/Florida). (*42*)

A dinosaur named Willo made headlines in the science world. Willo's fossilized remains included the first dinosaur _____ ever found. (*75*)

Which team won the National Hockey League (NHL) championship by defeating the Dallas Stars? (*185*)

Whimsical fiberglass statues popped up in cities all across the country during the summer. If you had visited Cincinnati, Ohio, you would have spotted (cows/moose/pigs) frolicking all over town. (*256*)

One of the worst wildfire seasons in 50 years occurred in what part of the United States? (*127*)

In October, the U.S. navy destroyer *Cole* was attacked while it was refueling in a Middle Eastern country. What was the name of that country? (*36, 60*)

Sports fans in New York City received a rare treat when the New York Yankees faced the New York (Jets/Mets/Nets) in the World Series. (*174*)

Young British actor Daniel Radcliffe landed the role of a lifetime when he was picked to play _____, the wizard hero of the most popular children's books ever, in an upcoming movie. (*232*)

Which TV shows won Emmy Awards in 2000 for best comedy and drama series? (*268*)

On April 15, President Bill Clinton announced the creation of Giant Sequoia National Monument in (California/ Oregon/Washington). (*25*)

Boy bands were the top pop music wave, and the group _____ was riding at its crest. Its album *No Strings Attached* sold an amazing 2.41 million copies in its first week. (*272*)

Americans celebrated the 200th birthday of the White House—the official residence of the president of the United States. Who was the first president to live there? (*217*)

Hillary Rodham Clinton made history by becoming the first First Lady to be elected to public office. She won a U.S. Senate seat in (Arkansas/Illinois/New York). (*65*)

The 27th Summer Olympic Games were held in _____, Australia. (*36, 162*)

On Mother's Day, May 14, some 750,000 moms (and dads and kids, too) took part in the Million Mom March in Washington, D.C. What was this rally calling for? (*27*)

Preliminary results of the 2000 U.S. census put the population of the United States at about (175/275/375) million people. (*194*)

Quiz shows were a TV craze in 2000. And the show that sparked the new viewer frenzy was _____. (*263*)

The year 2000 marked the 1,000-year anniversary of the arrival of the first Europeans in North America. Who were these bold explorers? (*212*)

One of the most suspenseful action films of the year told the story of some fishermen who were caught in a terrific gale that raged along the New England coast. The name of the film was (*Vertical Limit/The Perfect Storm/Across the Sea of Time*). (*265*)

Pope John Paul II made a historic pilgrimage in March when he became the first pope to make an official visit to the country of _____. (*23*)

A new Russian tennis star burst onto the scene when he upset American champ Pete Sampras in the U.S. Open in September. What was his name? (*191*)

Singer-guitarist (Eric Clapton/James Taylor/Carlos Santana) swept the Grammy Awards, walking off with top honors in eight categories. (*275*)

President Kim Dae Jung of _____ won the Nobel Peace Prize in October. (*37, 56*)

In June, the United Nations reported that two-thirds of the people infected with HIV, the virus that causes AIDS, live on what continent? (*54*)

More fighting between Israel and the (Palestinians/Egyptians/Syrians) ended hopes for a Middle East peace agreement during the year. (*36, 61*)

Best-selling author _____ helped start a reading revolution when he published two books—*Riding the Bullet* and *The Plant*—in electronic form. (*260*)

In September, scientists announced that for the first time in more than 200 years, a member of the primate family had become extinct. What was this African monkey called? (*35*)

Teen sensation (Christina Aguilera/Macy Gray/Britney Spears) won a Grammy Award in February as best new artist. Later in the year she released her first Spanish-language album, *Mi Reflejo.* (*271*)

The Los Angeles Lakers won their first National Basketball Association (NBA) title since 1988. The Lakers were led by their dominating 7-foot, 1-inch center _____. (*178*)

Early in the year, a court battle involving the custody of a Cuban boy put a spotlight on the tensions that exist between the United States and Cuba. On June 28, the boy returned home to Cuba. What was his name? (*29*)

A parade of tall ships sailed into New York Harbor for OpSail 2000 on July 4. One ship that drew much attention was the schooner (*America/Amistad/Amity*), a hand-built replica of a famous slave ship of the 1800's. (31)

On December 6, 2000, two _____ arrived at the National Zoo in Washington, D.C., from China. (40)

THE WORLD IN 2000

Republican George W. Bush, the governor of Texas and son of former President George Bush, was named the winner in the 2000 U.S. presidential election. In one of the closest and most disputed presidential races ever, Bush lost the popular vote to Vice President Al Gore, the Democratic candidate. But after a five-week court fight, he carried the Electoral College, which in the U.S. system decides the presidency. Bush thus became only the second son of a U.S. president to follow his father to the White House. The first was John Quincy Adams in 1824.

THE YEAR AT A GLANCE

The year 2000 got off to an exciting start. Around the world, celebrations and magnificent fireworks displays greeted the beginning of a new millennium—a thousand-year period. And as the year unfolded, events provided plenty of additional excitement, as well as many memorable moments.

IN THE UNITED STATES

The U.S. presidential election produced enough heat, smoke, and noise to rival any fireworks display. After a yearlong campaign, the November 7 vote

was so close that it took more than a month before a winner was declared. Vice President Al Gore, the Democratic candidate, received more votes nationwide. But Texas Governor George W. Bush, the Republican candidate, could claim a majority in the Electoral College if he won the state of Florida. And in Florida, the outcome was disputed. Both sides went to court. It wasn't until mid-December that a U.S. Supreme Court ruling handed the victory to Bush.

A disputed presidential election is a rarity in the United States, and the drama kept people glued to news broadcasts. But the election was just one of many concerns for Americans during 2000.

It was a census year, so in April the government conducted a head count of all 275 million people in the United States. In May, the Million Mom March brought about 750,000 mothers (and other family members) to Washington, D.C., to show support for stricter gun-control laws. Summer saw one of the worst wildfire seasons on record in the West. In the fall, Americans celebrated the 200th birthday of the White House—even as they wondered who the next tenant would be.

For most Americans, 2000 was a good year. They were enjoying the longest economic boom in U.S. history. The economy had been growing steadily for nine years, and that had helped many Americans achieve a better standard of living. But by year's end, there were clear signs that economic growth was slowing down. Sliding stock prices had investors worried. And people in the United States, along with people in Canada and Europe, faced sharp increases in the cost of oil and gasoline.

Abroad, a U.S. Navy ship was the target of a serious terrorist attack in October. The USS *Cole* was at port in Yemen, on the Arabian Peninsula, when a small boat packed with explosives pulled alongside and blew a hole in the ship's side. The blast killed 17 sailors and injured 39 others. Yemeni authorities arrested several people who had links with Islamic terrorist groups.

Президент России

WORLD CONCERNS

The United States wasn't the only country to hold important elections in 2000. Canada's Liberal Party scored a victory in national elections on November 27, ensuring that Liberal Party leader Jean Chrétien would remain prime minister. Earlier in the year, in March, Vladimir V. Putin bested ten other candidates in a presidential election in Russia. Putin was already Russia's acting president, and his victory had been expected. But with the election behind him, Putin faced a difficult job. Russia had been struggling for years with growing crime, corruption, and economic troubles, as well as a rebellion in the province of Chechnya.

Yugoslavia also voted in a new president in 2000, and events there made the U.S. election look tame. In 1998, the world had been outraged by President Slobodan Milosevic's brutal treatment of ethnic Albanians in Kosovo, a region in southern Yugoslavia. The United States and European nations had stepped in, and Kosovo was placed under United Nations control. And in 2000, Yugoslavian voters decided they had had enough of Milosevic's dictatorial rule. On September 24, they elected Vojislav Kostunica, a lawyer and opposition leader, as their new president. Milosevic tried to rig the vote and at first refused to step down. But he was finally forced to go.

Elections were on the horizon for Israel, where Prime Minister Ehud Barak handed in his resignation in December. The troubled story of Israel and the Palestinian Arabs was in the news throughout the year. The Palestinians and Israelis have been at odds ever since 1948, when Israel was founded. Early in 2000, it seemed that the two sides might reach a peace accord at last. But it wasn't to be. New violence erupted in the fall, and by December more than 300 people, mostly Palestinians, had been killed.

Peace seemed far away in parts of Africa, too. Some of the bloodiest fighting took place in Congo. This conflict, which was being called Africa's "first world war," involved six outside nations and several rebel groups, all fighting for their own reasons. And United Nations troops were in the West African nation of Sierra Leone, trying to stop a civil war that had been running for nine years. Several African nations were also struggling with an epidemic of AIDS (acquired immunodeficiency syndrome).

U.S. President Bill Clinton visited Africa in August. Among his stops was Nigeria, where he expressed support for the country's democracy, and Tanzania, where he observed the signing of a peace agreement to end a seven-year-old civil war in Burundi. In October, Clinton also visited Vietnam, becoming the first U.S. president to go to that Southeast Asian country since the Vietnam War.

The year 2000 marked the 25th anniversary of the end of that war, in which the United States supported non-Communist South Vietnam against Communist North Vietnam. After years of fighting and more than a million casualties, the war ended with the reunification of Vietnam under a Communist government. Clinton's visit was a sign that the United States and Vietnam were finally ready to put the past behind them.

South and North Korea, enemies since the 1950–53 Korean War, seemed almost ready to forget the past, too. In June, South Korean President Kim Dae Jung and North Korean President Kim Jong Il met in Pyongyang, North Korea, in the first summit meeting ever between the two nations. Later in the year, Kim Dae Jung won the Nobel Peace Prize for his efforts to bring democracy to South Korea and improve relations with North Korea.

AMAZING SCIENCE

There was plenty of exciting science news in 2000. Researchers broke new ground in fields that were science fiction only a few years ago. The world's first clones of an adult pig arrived—five piglets named Millie, Christa, Alexis, Carrel, and Dotcom, all exact copies of an adult female named Destiny. And in June scientists announced that they had completed a working draft of the human genome—the blueprint of a human being. The genome project involved cataloguing tens of thousands of genes, tiny bits of hereditary material inside body cells. The achievement was hailed because knowledge of the human genome may lead to new treatments for disease and other benefits. But it prompted debate about how this knowledge should be used.

A new chapter in space travel began in November, when the first permanent crew moved into the *International Space Station (ISS)*. American William Shepherd and Russians Yuri Gidzenko and Sergei Krikalev planned to spend four months on the station, orbiting some 240 miles (386 kilometers) above Earth's surface. The year also saw the 100th flight of the U.S. space shuttle. The shuttle is playing a big role in constructing the *ISS,* which is being built in stages by sixteen countries.

Scientists worldwide expressed growing concern about global warming in 2000. Late in the year, a U.N. report predicted that average temperatures may rise anywhere from 2.7°F to almost 11°F (1°C to 3.5°C) in the next century, with serious effects worldwide. This global warming has been blamed on a build-up of carbon dioxide and other heat-trapping gases in the atmosphere. The United States and more than 100 other countries have signed an agreement aimed at reducing these gases, which are produced when oil and other fossil fuels are burned. But they haven't been able to agree on how to do it.

Alarm bells also sounded over a sharp decline in biodiversity, or the variety of living things on Earth. Scientists warned that Earth is going through a period of extinction, in which many species are dying out. Because living things—plants, animals, fungi, tiny microorganisms—all depend on each other, every loss puts other living things at risk. Scientists urge people to protect habitats and ecosystems, so that the variety of living things can be preserved.

WINNERS ALL

From sports to art, people found many ways to enjoy life in 2000. The sports event of the year was the 27th Summer Olympic Games, held in Sydney, Australia, in September. Some 11,000 athletes from 200 countries competed in 300 events. U.S. athletes won the most medals (97), followed by Russia and China. Among the highlights were victories by U.S. runners Marion Jones and Maurice Greene. Their gold medals in the women's and men's 100-meter races earned them the titles of "world's fastest woman" and "world's fastest man."

In the music world, young stars ruled. Teen singers such as Christina Aguilera, Britney Spears, and the "boy bands" 'N Sync and the Backstreet Boys topped the pop music charts. More and more young listeners were downloading music from the Internet, rather than buying CD's. But two Internet music services, MP3 and Napster, were sued for copyright violations during the year.

Moviegoers lined up for action films such as *Mission Impossible 2,* serious dramas such as *Erin Brockovich,* comedies such as *Galaxy Quest,* and animated features such as *Chicken Run.* A Jack Russell terrier stole the show in *My Dog Skip,* one of the year's most popular films. Readers young and old were spellbound by the latest adventures of *Harry Potter.* J. K. Rowling's fourth book about the young wizard-in-training, *Harry Potter and the Goblet of Fire,* was a best-seller even before it hit bookstores in July.

Art took to the streets in the summer, with outdoor exhibits of whimsical fiberglass statues—pigs in Cincinnati, Ohio; rabbits in Grand Rapids, Michigan; cows in New York City; even Mr. Potato Head in Rhode Island. Summer also brought OpSail 2000, in which ships from all over the world visited East Coast ports. Some 300 vessels, including 26 tall ships, sailed into New York Harbor on July 4 in a grand procession.

Sleek racing scooters were the fad of the year. Time capsules were popular, too, as a way to mark the millennium. People made their own personal time capsules, filled with mementos of the year. And there were major time capsules, such as the National Millennium Time Capsule at the National Archives in Washington, D.C. In years to come, when these sealed containers are opened, people of the future will know what life was like in the year 2000.

JANUARY

1 As the year 2000 began, almost all computers around the world continued to function normally. Many people had feared that a glitch called the Y2K ("Year 2000") bug might cause computers to crash when their internal clocks rolled over to 1/1/00—leading to power failures, transportation disasters, and other catastrophes. Though some minor computer problems were reported, the bug proved to be far less serious than predicted—largely because businesses and governments had spent billions of dollars to reprogram their computers to get rid of the bug.

10 America Online (AOL), the world's largest provider of Internet services, announced that it would merge with Time Warner, one of the world's largest media companies. If the merger takes place, it will be one of the largest mergers in history.

27 President Bill Clinton gave his final State of the Union address to Congress. He said that America was starting the 21st century in excellent shape, with the country strong and at peace. He reported that the economy was growing and crime was down. Clinton also proposed a series of tax cuts, increased spending for education, and stricter gun-control laws.

Government changes in January: In national elections in **Chile,** Ricardo Lagos Escobar was elected president. He succeeded Eduardo Frei Ruíz-Tagle, who had been president since 1994. . . .Following national elections in **Dominica,** Roose-

President Bill Clinton delivers his last State of the Union address. In his speech, the president said, "the state of our union is the strongest it has ever been."

IN GOD WE TRUST

New York City: Revelers in Times Square cheer as the famous crystal ball drops at midnight.

Welcoming the Millennium

On January 1, worldwide celebrations marked the arrival of the year 2000. The tiny Pacific island nation of Kiribati, which lies on the international date line, was the first to see the new year and the new millennium. From there, the global party moved westward as the Earth revolved and the calendar changed in Asia, Africa, Europe, and America.

In Sydney, Australia, a million people gathered in the city's harbor area to watch a phenomenal display of fireworks. In Hong Kong, China, festivities included a concert by American singer Whitney Houston and performances by other leading film and pop music stars. On a snowy street in Moscow, Russia, people danced to a disco beat.

As the ancient pyramids in Giza, Egypt, glowed beneath laser beams, people listened to a new high-tech opera. In Rome, Italy, Pope John Paul II blessed the crowd in St. Peter's Square, wishing them "a year filled with serenity and happiness." In London, England, Big Ben chimed in the new year as fireworks raced along the Thames River.

Rio de Janeiro, Brazil, was among the first places in the Americas to welcome the new year, with some 5 million people lining the city's beaches to welcome the dawn. In the United States, nearly 2 million people tossed confetti in New York City's Times Square as a huge crystal ball blazing with strobe lights and hundreds of bulbs descended at the stroke of midnight.

The happiness, sizzle, and glitter, were echoed in places large and small. It was definitely a night to remember!

velt Douglas became prime minister. He succeeded Edison James, who had been prime minister since 1995. . . .In **Ecuador,** President Jamil Mahuad Witt, who took office in 1998, was overthrown in a military coup. He was succeeded by Gustavo Noboa Bejarano. . . .Following national elections in **Guatemala,** Alfonso Portillo Cabrera became president. He succeeded Alvaro Arzu Irigoyen, who had been president since 1996. . . .In **South Korea,** Park Tae Joon was named premier. He succeeded Kim Jong Pil, who had been premier since 1998.

FEBRUARY

7–9 Hackers—people who use the Internet to gain unauthorized access to computer systems—attacked Yahoo.com and about a dozen other popular Web sites, knocking out service for hours. Visitors to these sites were greeted with a blank screen until the companies fixed the problem. Internet security experts call this type of attack "denial of service"—users were unable to use the Web sites' services. Hacking is a crime, and the Federal Bureau of Investigation (FBI) was called in to track down the people responsible for the attack.

11 Britain suspended the ten-week-old provincial government in Northern Ireland and returned rule of the province to officials in London. Catholics and Protestants had shared power in the new government, and it had been hoped that this would bring an end to 30 years of violence between the two groups. The self-rule administration was suspended because the Irish Republican Army (IRA), the region's largest Catholic paramilitary group, failed to begin disarming. (On May 6, the IRA proposed to place its weapons "beyond use" and allow weapons inspections. The proposal was accepted by Northern Ireland's largest Protestant party, leading to restoration of the government.)

22 The U.S. space shuttle *Endeavour* completed an eleven-day mission. Its objective was to map most of Earth's surface, using radar to gather data to create the most detailed global map ever. The crew consisted of Dominic Gorie, Janet Kavandi, Kevin Kregel, Janice Voss, Mamoru Mohri of Japan, and Gerhard Thiele of Germany.

In Northern Ireland, graffiti calls on the IRA to keep its weapons. The failure of the IRA to disarm led to the suspension of the new government.

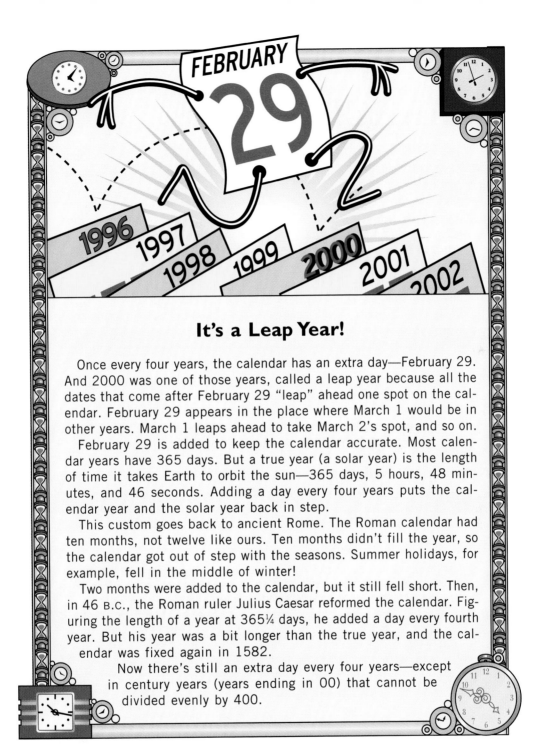

It's a Leap Year!

Once every four years, the calendar has an extra day—February 29. And 2000 was one of those years, called a leap year because all the dates that come after February 29 "leap" ahead one spot on the calendar. February 29 appears in the place where March 1 would be in other years. March 1 leaps ahead to take March 2's spot, and so on.

February 29 is added to keep the calendar accurate. Most calendar years have 365 days. But a true year (a solar year) is the length of time it takes Earth to orbit the sun—365 days, 5 hours, 48 minutes, and 46 seconds. Adding a day every four years puts the calendar year and the solar year back in step.

This custom goes back to ancient Rome. The Roman calendar had ten months, not twelve like ours. Ten months didn't fill the year, so the calendar got out of step with the seasons. Summer holidays, for example, fell in the middle of winter!

Two months were added to the calendar, but it still fell short. Then, in 46 B.C., the Roman ruler Julius Caesar reformed the calendar. Figuring the length of a year at 365¼ days, he added a day every fourth year. But his year was a bit longer than the true year, and the calendar was fixed again in 1582.

Now there's still an extra day every four years—except in century years (years ending in 00) that cannot be divided evenly by 400.

Government changes in February: Following national elections in **Austria,** Wolfgang Schüssel became chancellor. He succeeded Viktor Klima, who had been chancellor since 1997. . . .In national elections in **Finland,** Tarja Halonen was elected the nation's first woman president. She succeeded Martti Ahtisaari, who had been president since 1994. . . .Following national elections in **Guinea-Bissau,** Kumba Yala became president. He succeeded Malan Bacai Sanha, who had been president for less than a year.

MARCH

5 The world's first clones of an adult pig were born at the Virginia-Maryland College of Veterinary Medicine in Virginia. The five piglets—named Millie, Christa, Alexis, Carrel, and Dotcom—were exact copies of their "parent," an adult female pig named Destiny. Each piglet was created from a cell taken from Destiny; there was no mating or mixing of genetic material. The procedure was similar to the one used to produce the sheep named Dolly in 1996.

25 U.S. President Bill Clinton completed a week-long visit to India and Pakistan, South Asia's two most important nations. Throughout his trip, Clinton called on the two countries to settle their bitter dispute over Kashmir, a region on the India-Pakistan border that both claim. He also urged them to give up or at least limit their nuclear weapons.

31 By the end of March, Ugandan officials reported that more than 900 deaths had been linked to a religious cult called the Movement for the Restoration of the Ten Commandments of God. The deaths were being treated as murder, making the tragedy the worst mass killing in the history of modern religious cults.

Government changes in March: In **Nepal,** Girija Prasad Koirala became premier. He succeeded Krishna Prasad Bhattarai, who resigned after less than a year in office. . . .In **Norway,** Kjell Magne Bondevik, who had been premier since 1997, resigned. He was succeeded by Jens Stoltenberg. . . .In

These five little piglets, born in March, are look-alikes because they are clones of an adult female pig. A clone is produced using genetic material from only one "parent." And the clone's genes are exactly like those of the parent.

Pope John Paul II begins his historic trip to the Holy Land atop Mount Nebo, in Jordan.

Pope John Paul II in the Holy Land

Cheering crowds welcomed Pope John Paul II to the Middle East in March. The pope, head of the Roman Catholic Church, was on a pilgrimage to the biblical sites of the Holy Land. It was the first visit by a pope to the Holy Land in 36 years, and the first time a pope made an official visit to the country of Israel.

The pope's journey was a key event in what the Church called a Holy Year, in recognition of the 2,000th anniversary of the birth of Jesus. The trip had another goal, too. The pope hoped to ease tensions among Christians, Muslims, and Jews in the Middle East. Many places he visited are considered holy by all three religions, but there is a long history of conflict among these groups.

The pope's six-day trip began in Jordan on March 20. He prayed at Mount Nebo, where Moses was said to have looked out over the Promised Land. Next he traveled to Israel and Palestinian-controlled territories, to visit sites where Jesus lived, preached, and died. His stops included Bethlehem, Galilee, Nazareth, and Jerusalem. Wherever the pope went, he brought a message of peace and reconciliation. "We all know how urgent is the need for peace and justice, not for Israel alone but for the entire region," he said.

national elections in **Russia,** Vladimir Putin was elected president. He had been acting president since the end of 1999, when Boris Yeltsin—who had been president since 1991—resigned. . . .In national elections in **Senegal,** Abdoulaye Wade was elected president. He succeeded Abdou Diouf, who had been president since 1981. . . .In **Taiwan,** Chen Shui-bian was elected president. He succeeded Lee Teng-hui, who had been president since 1988. Chen named Tang Fei to be premier, succeeding Vincent Siew, who had held office since 1997.

APRIL

3 A federal court in Washington, D.C., ruled that Microsoft was a monopoly that violated antitrust laws. The ruling came in a suit brought by the U.S. Department of Justice and nineteen states. The court said that Microsoft had stifled competition by "bundling" its Windows operating system with its Internet Explorer Web browser, so that the two products couldn't be sold separately. Microsoft had also required computer manufacturers whose machines ran on Windows to install only Microsoft's programs on the machines. (On June 7, the federal court issued its final decision in the case, concluding that Microsoft's actions were illegal. To end the monopoly, the court said that the company should be split in two. Microsoft planned to appeal the ruling.)

12 The South Carolina Senate passed a bill that would lower the Confederate flag from atop the State House and place a smaller Confederate flag elsewhere on the State House grounds. The legislation was a compromise between people who wanted to keep the flag, calling it a symbol of Southern heritage, and civil rights groups and African Americans, who said the flag was a reminder of slavery and a symbol of racial prejudice. (A similar plan was later approved by the South Carolina House of Representatives, and was signed into law by Governor Jim Hodges. On July 1, the Confederate flag was lowered from the State House.)

In April, a federal court ruled that Microsoft was a monopoly that violated antitrust laws. This political cartoon, based on the popular board game Monopoly, shows Microsoft chairman Bill Gates being restrained by Uncle Sam.

Protecting the Giant Sequoia

On April 15, President Bill Clinton announced the creation of Giant Sequoia National Monument. Giant sequoias, found only in central California, are the world's biggest trees. The new national monument protects 34 groves of giant sequoias from logging. Mining and development will also be banned on the monument's 328,000 acres (132,737 hectares) of land.

Giant sequoias once grew in wide areas of western North America. Today they grow only on the western slopes of California's Sierra Nevada mountains. There are only about 70 groves of these ancient trees. Most of the groves that aren't within the new national monument are within national parks, so they were already protected.

Giant sequoias are close relatives of the redwoods, which grow near the coast in the Pacific Northwest. The world's tallest known tree is a redwood that's 368 feet (112 meters) tall. But giant sequoias are stouter than redwoods, and that makes them the *biggest* trees. As President Clinton said, "They grow taller than the Statue of Liberty, broader than a bus."

A forest supervisor shows President Clinton seeds from the protected trees in Giant Sequoia National Monument, in California.

18   The U.S. Food and Drug Administration (FDA) approved a new antibiotic, Zyvox, to combat deadly bacteria that had become resistant to standard antibiotics. Zyvox was the first entirely new type of antibiotic in 35 years. Experts stressed that Zyvox should be used to treat only the worst infections; otherwise, bacteria would soon develop a resistance to it, making the new antibiotic useless.

Government changes in April: In **Italy,** Giuliano Amato became premier. He succeeded Massimo D'Alema, who had been premier since 1998. . . .In **Japan,** the premier, Keizo Obuchi, suffered a severe stroke. Obuchi, who took office in 1998, was succeeded as premier by Yoshiro Mori. . . .In **Rwanda,** Paul Kagame was named president. He succeeded Pasteur Bizimungu, who had been president since 1994.

MAY

1–5 In Sierra Leone, a West African nation torn by civil war since 1991, more than 500 members of a United Nations peacekeeping force were kidnapped by rebel forces. (On May 17, the leader of the rebels was captured. By May 29, all the peacekeepers had been freed.)

3–4 A computer virus attached to an e-mail message saying "ILOVEYOU" spread rapidly around the world, jamming e-mail systems and destroying data on thousands of computers. Investigators traced the virus, dubbed the Love Bug, to the Philippines.

15 More than 25,000 residents returned to Los Alamos, New Mexico, and nearby areas after a raging wildfire had forced them from their homes. The National Park Service had purposefully set the fire on May 4 at a nearby wilderness area. The fire was supposed to be a "controlled burn" that would prevent future wildfires—by removing fuel that could feed them. But dry conditions and strong winds sent the blaze out of control. The fire destroyed more than 400 homes and also threatened the Los Alamos National Laboratory, a U.S. government center for nuclear weapons research.

24 Israel completed the withdrawal of its military forces from southern Lebanon. This ended 22 years of occupation that began in 1978 after a series of deadly attacks on Israel by Palestinian guerrillas based in Lebanon.

Firefighters wait for water as a house goes up in flames in Los Alamos, New Mexico.

The Million Mom March

On Mother's Day, May 14, about 750,000 moms (and dads and kids, too) rallied on the National Mall in Washington, D.C., in support of gun control. Thousands more marched in local demonstrations in about 70 other cities. Their message to Congress: We want stricter laws to control the sale of guns.

The Million Mom March was organized as a reaction to the alarming number of school shootings that had grabbed national headlines. People were disturbed by the fact that the youngsters involved in these shootings were able to get guns so easily.

The march participants wanted a national system that would require all handguns to be registered and licensed; they also wanted safety locks on all handguns. But not all mothers supported the goals of the demonstrators. Gun control remained controversial as some people opposed restrictions on gun ownership.

However, the huge turnout for the Million Mom March sent a clear signal. As one marcher said, "You can't mess with a million mothers trying to protect their families."

29 The U.S. space shuttle *Atlantis* completed a ten-day mission. The purpose was to repair the *International Space Station* (*ISS*). The crew consisted of James Halsell, Jr., Susan Helms, Scott Horowitz, James Voss, Mary Ellen Weber, Jeffrey Williams, and Yuri Usachev of Russia.

Government changes in May: In national elections in the **Dominican Republic,** Hipólito Mejía Dominguez was elected president. He succeeded Leonel Fernandez Reyna, who had been president since 1996. . . .In **South Korea**, Lee Han Dong was chosen premier. He succeeded Park Tae Joon, who had been premier since January. . . .In **Turkey,** Ahmet Necdet Sezer was chosen president. He succeeded Suleyman Demirel, who had been president since 1993.

JUNE

15 Leaders of South and North Korea completed a three-day meeting in Pyongyang, North Korea. It was the first summit meeting ever between the two nations, which had been bitter enemies since the 1950–53 Korean War. South Korean President Kim Dae Jung and North Korean President Kim Jong Il signed a pact agreeing to work for peace and unity.

29 President Clinton nominated Norman Y. Mineta to succeed William M. Daley as Secretary of Commerce. Daley had resigned to become chairman of Vice President Al Gore's presidential campaign. (On July 21, the Senate confirmed the nomination, making Mineta the first Asian-American member of a president's cabinet.)

In eastern Indonesia, an overloaded ferry carrying nearly 500 people sank in stormy seas. About 490 passengers lost their lives.

Government changes in June: In Hungary, Ferenc Madl was chosen president. He succeeded Arpád Goncz, who had been president since 1990. . . .In **Jordan,** Ali Abu al-Ragheb was named prime minister. He succeeded Abdoul Raouf al-Rawabdeh who had been in office since 1999. . . .In **Syria,** President Hafez al-Assad, who headed the nation since 1971, died. He was succeeded by his son, Bashar al-Assad.

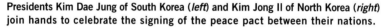

Presidents Kim Dae Jung of South Korea (*left*) and Kim Jong Il of North Korea (*right*) join hands to celebrate the signing of the peace pact between their nations.

Elián Goes Home

On June 28, Elián González returned home to Cuba, ending a seven-month stay in the United States that was marked by family disputes and court battles.

In November 1999, 5-year-old Elián left Cuba with his mother, headed for Florida. They planned to make a new life in the United States. But their boat sank, and Elián's mother died along with ten other passengers. Elián floated in the ocean in an inner tube for two days before he was rescued on Thanksgiving Day and taken to relatives in Miami, Florida.

Elián's parents were divorced. His father, Juan Miguel González, was still in Cuba and wanted Elián sent back to him. But Elián's Miami relatives wanted him to stay with them. Elián quickly became a symbol of the tension that has existed between the United States and Cuba since the 1950's, when Fidel Castro took power in Cuba and set up a Communist government. Castro accused the United States of kidnapping Elián, and Cubans demonstrated in the streets to demand his return. Meanwhile, lawyers for Elián asked that the United States grant him political asylum, so he could stay.

On January 5, 2000, U.S. immigration officials decided that Elián should go back to his father. But his relatives in Florida appealed the decision. As the case worked its way through the courts, Juan Miguel arrived in the United States. Then, on April 22, U.S. immigration agents forced their way into the relatives' Miami home. They took Elián and flew him to Washington, D.C., where his father was waiting.

On June 28, the U.S. Supreme Court refused final appeals by the Miami relatives to keep Elián in the United States and grant a political asylum hearing for him. Hours later, Elián and his father boarded a plane and returned to Cuba (photo above).

JULY

10 U.S. President Bill Clinton chose Hershel W. Gober as Acting Secretary of Veterans Affairs. Gober succeeded Togo D. West, Jr., who resigned.

23 In Okinawa, Japan, the leaders of the eight major industrial nations ended their annual summit meeting on world economic issues. The countries represented were Britain, Canada, France, Germany, Italy, Japan, Russia, and the United States. The participants agreed to help poor nations reduce their debts and to improve their access to better education, health care, and computer technology.

For the second year in a row, American Lance Armstrong won the Tour de France. This is the world's greatest and most grueling bicycle race, lasting up to 25 days and covering about 2,300 miles (3,700 kilometers).

25 Middle East peace talks at Camp David, the presidential retreat in Maryland, ended without an agreement. The summit meeting involved President Bill Clinton, Israeli Prime Minister Ehud Barak, and Palestinian leader Yasir Arafat. After fifteen days of intense negotiations, the talks broke down over the status of Jerusalem, which both Israelis and Palestinians claim. Although the summit was unsuccessful, both Barak and Arafat pledged to continue efforts to resolve the issues that have divided their people since Israel became a nation in 1948.

American cyclist Lance Armstrong, after winning the Tour de France for the second year in a row.

A Parade of Tall Ships

Ships from all over the world sailed into New York Harbor for OpSail 2000 on July 4. Led by the American three-masted bark *Eagle,* a procession of 300 vessels from nearly 20 nations—including 26 tall ships—moved majestically through the harbor and up the Hudson River. They passed the Statue of Liberty and the aircraft carrier *John F. Kennedy,* where President Bill Clinton spoke of the meaning of Independence Day and the importance "not only to welcome people to our borders but to welcome people into our hearts."

Accompanying the ships were fireboats spraying red, white, and blue water into the air. Military jets streaked through the sky above. People watched and waved from pleasure boats, piers, shoreside parks, and apartment balconies.

The U.S. frigate *The Rose*

One of the ships that drew much attention was a sleek black sailing ship making its maiden voyage. The ship was the schooner *Amistad,* a hand-built replica of a famous slave ship that sailed in the 1800's. It was built at Mystic Seaport, Connecticut, to be a floating classroom, teaching people about the struggle for freedom.

After the parade, many of the antique ships dropped anchor at piers around New York, during a week-long stay. Then the tall ships sailed on to New London, Connecticut. Other ports visited by OpSail 2000 during the summer included San Juan, Puerto Rico; Miami, Florida; Norfolk, Virginia; Baltimore, Maryland; Philadelphia, Pennsylvania; and Portland, Maine.

Government changes in July: In **Fiji,** Ratu Josefa Iloilo became president. He succeeded Kamisese Mara, who had been president since 1993. . . .In **Israel,** Moshe Katsav was chosen president. He succeeded Ezer Weizman, who had been president since 1993. . . .In national elections in **Mexico,** Vicente Fox Quesada was elected president. He succeeded Ernesto Zedillo Ponce de León, who had been president since 1994 and whose Institutional Revolutionary Party had held the presidency since 1929.

AUGUST

3 The Republican Party ended its four-day national convention, held in Philadelphia, Pennsylvania. George W. Bush, Governor of Texas, accepted the party's nomination for president. The party's nominee for vice president was Richard B. Cheney, a former Secretary of Defense under President George Bush.

12 During military maneuvers in the Barents Sea off the northern coast of Russia, the Russian navy submarine *Kursk* sank to the bottom. Despite more than a week of rescue efforts, including assistance by Britain and Norway, all 118 crew members died. Officials announced that the accident was caused by two explosions that breached the submarine's hull. The source of the explosions remained unknown.

17 The Democratic Party ended its four-day national convention, held in Los Angeles, California. Vice President Al Gore accepted the party's nomination for president. The party's nominee for vice president was Joseph I. Lieberman, a Senator from Connecticut.

25 In India, torrential rains caused widespread flooding. At least 400 people lost their lives, and thousands of homes and farms suffered heavy damage. (In September, a further deluge took the lives of more than 1,000 people in India and neighboring Bangladesh.)

The Republican and Democratic National Conventions. Left: (*Left to right*) Laura and George W. Bush, Dick and Lynne Cheney. Below: (*Left to right*) Tipper and Al Gore, Joseph and Hadassah Lieberman.

In the harbor of Charleston, South Carolina, a giant crane raises the Confederate submarine *H. L. Hunley* from its watery grave.

Raising a Confederate Submarine

On August 8, thousands of people on hundreds of boats gathered in the harbor of Charleston, South Carolina. They watched as a giant crane raised the Confederate submarine *H. L. Hunley* from its watery grave 30 feet (9 meters) below the ocean's surface.

The *Hunley* was the first submarine to sink an enemy warship. At the start of 1864, as the U.S. Civil War was nearing the end of its third year, more than 600 Union vessels were strangling the Confederacy with a blockade of Southern ports. One of the Union ships, the USS *Housatonic,* was stationed off the coast of Charleston.

On the night of February 17, 1864, the *Housatonic*'s officers saw what they thought was a giant porpoise heading toward them. It wasn't a porpoise; it was the *Hunley.* The submarine rammed the *Housatonic,* and its crew shoved an explosive charge into the damaged hull. Within three minutes, the *Housatonic* sank to the bottom of the harbor.

The *Hunley* thus became the first submarine to sink a ship in battle. Despite this claim to fame, the *Hunley* was an unlucky ship. With its crew of nine men, it had itself sunk several times during testing, killing many of its crew, including inventor H. L. Hunley. On February 17, the *Hunley*'s luck deserted it again. Moments after the *Housatonic* sank, the submarine followed it to the bottom.

The *Hunley* was discovered in its watery resting place in 1995. With its raising in 2000, the sub will undergo several years of conservation. It will then be placed on display at the Charleston Museum.

Government changes in August: In **Somalia,** Abdiqassim Salad Hassan became president. He was Somalia's first president since 1991, when civil war erupted and the country plunged into chaos.

SEPTEMBER

6–8 Leaders from more than 150 countries met at United Nations headquarters in New York City. They took part in the U.N. Millennium Summit, the largest meeting of world leaders ever held. The leaders discussed the major challenges facing the world at the start of the 21st century. The Summit ended with the signing of a Millennium Declaration, a document pledging to solve the world's most pressing problems—from pollution to poverty to war.

19 The U.S. Senate voted 83 to 15 to end restrictions on trade with China. Since 1974, Congress had extended U.S.-Chinese trade relations a year at a time. The idea was to use the threat of trade restrictions to get China to improve its record in human rights and other areas. But the yearly threats didn't accomplish much. In exchange for permanent trading relations, China agreed to end many of its own restrictions on foreign goods and services.

20 The U.S. space shuttle *Atlantis* completed a twelve-day mission. The purpose was to prepare the *International Space Station (ISS)* for occupancy by its first full-time crew. The mission members included Scott Altman, Daniel Burbank, Edward Lu, Rick Mastracchio, Terrence Wilcutt, and Yuri Malenchenko and Boris Morukov of Russia.

An independent prosecutor announced the end of the six-year, $52-million Whitewater investigation against President Bill Clinton and First Lady Hillary Rodham Clinton, clearing them of any criminal wrong-

The United Nations Millennium Summit: the largest gathering of world leaders in history.

Primates in Danger

In September, scientists announced that for the first time in more than 200 years, a member of the primate family had become extinct: A type of African monkey called Miss Waldron's red colobus (pictured below) had died out. These long-tailed, red-cheeked monkeys once lived in the rain forests of Ghana and the Ivory Coast. But they hadn't been seen since the 1970's. Scientists searched long and hard, but none could be found.

The primate family includes humans and our closest relatives: apes, monkeys, and lemurs. Some of these primates may soon disappear too. Of the more than 600 different kinds of primates, nearly 120 are in danger of dying out.

The list of endangered primates includes a number of apes. For example, only about 320 mountain gorillas still live in their African home. Several thousand orangutans live in parks and reserves in Indonesia; but some of the reserves are being logged, destroying the orangutans' homes. Gibbons from China and Indonesia also are threatened.

Monkeys from many parts of the world are also endangered, including tamarins from Brazil, langurs from Vietnam, and mangabeys from Africa. And several kinds of lemurs are on the list. Lemurs live only on Madagascar, an island country off the eastern coast of Africa.

Scientists say that if Miss Waldron's red colobus had been better protected in reserves, the animal might still be around. They are hoping that the disappearance of this monkey will prompt people to act in time to save other animals from dying out.

doing. The investigation was named for a failed Arkansas real-estate venture that the Clintons had taken part in during the 1980's. The inquiry then expanded to pursue other issues, including the president's relationship with White House intern Monica Lewinsky. This led to Clinton's 1999 impeachment trial, in which he was acquitted.

Government changes in September: Following national elections in **Mauritius,** Anerood Jugnauth became premier. He succeeded Navinchandra Ramgoolam, who had been premier since 1995.

OCTOBER

1   The 27th Summer Olympic Games ended in Sydney, Australia, after sixteen days of competition. U.S. athletes won the most medals (97), followed by Russia (88), and China (59).

12   A small boat filled with explosives blew an enormous hole in the side of the U.S. Navy destroyer USS *Cole,* as the destroyer was at a refueling station in Aden, Yemen. The blast killed seventeen sailors and injured 39 others. It appeared to be a deliberate act of terrorism.

17   Missouri Governor Mel Carnahan was killed when the small airplane in which he was traveling crashed south of St. Louis. He was succeeded by Lieutenant Governor Roger Wilson.

24   The U.S. space shuttle *Discovery* completed a thirteen-day mission—the 100th flight in the space shuttle program. The primary purpose of the mission was to attach a new docking port and a large framework to the *International Space Station* (*ISS*). The crew consisted of Leroy Chiao, Brian Duffy, Michael Lopez-Alegria, William McArthur, Jr., Pam Melroy, Jeff Wisoff, and Koichi Wakata of Japan.

31   During October, fighting between Israelis and Palestinian Arabs killed more than 100 people, mostly Palestinians. The fighting all but ended hopes for a peace agreement between the two peoples anytime soon.

The USS *Cole*, after being severely damaged by a terrorist bombing in Aden, the capital of Yemen. Seventeen sailors died in the attack.

South Koreans read that President Kim Dae Jung won the Nobel Peace Prize.

The 2000 Nobel Prizes

Chemistry: Alan J. Heeger and Alan G. MacDiarmid of the United States and Hideki Shirakawa of Japan, for discovering that thin films of certain plastics can be made to conduct electricity. The new plastics have been used to improve television and computer screens and photographic film.

Economics: James J. Heckman and Daniel L. McFadden of the United States, for developing methods to analyze and explain complicated individual behavior. Their methods have helped explain how people decide where to work, where to live, how to travel, and what to buy.

Literature: Gao Xinjian, a Chinese-born Frenchman, for his novels and plays, which blend traditional Chinese and modern Western writing techniques. He was the first Chinese writer to win the Nobel.

Peace: President Kim Dae Jung of South Korea, for his "moral strength," his lengthy efforts to bring democracy to South Korea, and his work in improving relations with North Korea.

Physics: Jack S. Kilby of the United States, Herbert Kroemer, a German-born American, and Zhores I. Alferov of Russia, for work that's at the core of computers, cell phones, and other electronic devices. Kilby helped develop the integrated circuit, or chip, that drives computers. Kroemer and Alferov did work that led to faster electronic circuits and the small lasers used in CD players, bar code readers, and fiber optics.

Physiology or Medicine: Paul Greengard of the United States, Eric R. Kandel, an Austrian-born American, and Arvid Carlsson of Sweden, for research on how brain cells send signals to each other. Their work has shed light on how the brain works and on learning and memory.

Government changes in October: In **Luxembourg,** Crown Prince Henri became Grand Duke. He succeeded his father, Jean, who had been head of state since 1964. . . .Following disputed national elections in the **Ivory Coast,** Laurent Gbagbo became president. He succeeded Robert Gueï, who had seized power in a military coup in December 1999. . . .In **Taiwan,** Chang Chun-hsiung was chosen premier. He succeeded Tang Fei, who resigned after less than five months in office. . . .In national elections in **Yugoslavia,** Vojislav Kostunica was elected president. He succeeded Slobodan Milosevic, who had been president since 1989.

NOVEMBER

7 In elections in the United States, the presidential race was so close that Americans waited for weeks to find out who was elected. It was the first time in more than a century that the outcome of a presidential election was so unclear for so long. In the U.S. Senate, Democrats gained four seats, resulting in a 50–50 split. In the House of Representatives, Democrats picked up two seats for a total of 212, Republicans had 221, and Independents had 2.

11 In Austria, fire broke out in a crowded cable car that had stalled inside a mountain tunnel en route to a ski run above the village of Kaprun. It was Austria's worst Alpine disaster, killing 155 people.

19 U.S. President Bill Clinton completed a three-day visit to Vietnam. Clinton was the first U.S. president to go to Vietnam since 1969, during the Vietnam War. He made the trip to advance political and business relations between the two nations.

Government changes in November: In national elections in **Haiti,** Jean-Bertrand Aristide was elected president. He succeeded René Préval, who had been president since 1996. . . .In national elections in **Palau,** Tommy Remenge-

On November 16, America's first high-speed electric passenger train—Amtrak's Acela Express—made its debut, traveling from Washington, D.C., to New York and on to Boston. This new train cruises at 135 miles (217 kilometers) per hour and hits top speeds of 150 miles (241 kilometers) per hour. It is powered by two electric locomotives—one at the front and one at the rear. A special computer-controlled hydraulic system allows it to tilt as it speeds around curves, for a safe and smooth ride.

After November elections, Prime Minister Jean Chrétien remained Canada's leader.

Elections in Canada

In national elections on November 27, the Liberal Party won a significant victory. Thus the party's head, Jean Chrétien—first elected in 1993—remained prime minister. The Liberals won 172 seats in the 301-seat Parliament, a gain of 17 seats since the last election, in 1997. The main challenger, Stockwell Day and his conservative Canadian Alliance, won 66 seats. Smaller opposition parties won the remaining seats. It was the first time since 1945 that a Canadian party won three consecutive majority governments.

Chrétien called the election in October, a year-and-a-half ahead of schedule, hoping to take advantage of high approval ratings. (An election must be held every five years.) But only 63 percent of the country's 20 million eligible voters went to the polls, a record low. (In 1997, 67 percent of eligible voters went to the polls.)

Regional divisions were a major issue in the days leading up to the election. The Bloc Québécois ultimately wants the province of Quebec to be an independent nation, and had hoped to win 50 of Quebec's 75 seats in Parliament. Also, western provinces have charged that they don't receive equal treatment. But the Liberal Party picked up 10 seats in Quebec, for a total of 36, winning more votes than the separatists for the first time since 1980. Most of the seats in the west, however, went to the Canadian Alliance (formerly called the Reform Party). Nonetheless, the Liberal Party's strong showing at least momentarily quieted concerns about the prospects for Canadian unity.

sau was elected president. He succeeded Kuniwo Nakamura, who had been president since Palau became an independent nation in 1994. . . .In **Peru,** Valentin Paniagua was named president. He succeeded Alberto Fujimori, who had been president since 1990. . . .Following national elections in **Tanzania,** Amani Karume became president. He succeeded Benjamin Mkapa, who had been president since 1995.

DECEMBER

4 President Bill Clinton created the largest nature preserve in the United States, setting aside 84 million acres (34 million hectares) underwater around the northwestern Hawaiian Islands. The preserve, named the Northwestern Hawaiian Islands Coral Reef Ecosystem Reserve, contains almost 70 percent of the coral reefs in the United States.

6 Two giant pandas on a ten-year loan from China arrived at the National Zoo in Washington, D.C. The 2-year-old female, Mei Xiang ("Beautiful Fragrance"), and the 3-year-old male, Tian Tian ("More and More"), moved into the same habitat occupied by the zoo's previous pair of pandas—Ling-Ling and Hsing-Hsing. The panda residence received a $1.8 million dollar makeover for the newcomers. Giant pandas are extremely rare—there are only about 1,100 in the world. In the wild, they are found only in China.

11 The space shuttle *Endeavour* completed an eleven-day mission. The primary purpose of the mission was to deliver and attach the world's largest set of solar wings to the *International Space Station* (*ISS*). This would provide additional electrical power to the station. The crew consisted of Michael Bloomfield, Brent Jett, Carlos Noriega, Joseph Tanner, and Marc Garneau of Canada. After attaching the solar wings, the crew visited the first crew to live in the *ISS,* in residence since early November.

13 Democrat Al Gore conceded to Republican George W. Bush in the U.S. presidential election. Gore's concession ended a five-week-long

Mei Xiang and Tian Tian eat bamboo inside the newly renovated panda residence at the National Zoo in Washington, D.C. The two giant pandas are on loan from China for the next ten years.

. . .and Looking Ahead to 2001

Here are a few of the many anniversaries that will be celebrated in 2001:

● The 125th anniversary of the first telephone message on March 10, 1876, delivered by Alexander Graham Bell. Bell phoned his assistant, saying, "Mr. Watson, come here. I want you."

● The 100th anniversary of the first Nobel Prizes, given for the most important work in six categories—physics, chemistry, physiology or medicine, literature, peace, and economics.

● The 75th anniversary of the first airplane flight over the North Pole, on May 9, 1926, by American aviators Richard E. Byrd and Floyd Bennett. They flew nonstop from Spitzbergen (islands in the Arctic Ocean) to the Pole and back in 15½ hours.

● The 75th anniversary of Robert H. Goddard's launch of the first rocket propelled by liquid fuel, on March 16, 1926. The rocket reached an altitude of 184 feet (56 meters).

● The 25th anniversary of the Mars landings by *Vikings I* and *II* in 1976. These U.S. spacecraft were the first spacecraft ever to land on a planet other than Earth.

court battle over election results in Florida. The U.S. Supreme Court ended the dispute on December 12 by ruling 5–4 to stop all recounting of votes in Florida.

Government changes in December: In **Israel,** Prime Minister Ehud Barak resigned, forcing new elections in February 2001. . . .In a run-off election in **Romania,** Ion Iliescu was elected president. He succeeded Emil Constantinescu, who had been president since 1996. (Iliescu had previously been president from 1990 to 1996.)

THE BATTLE FOR THE WHITE HOUSE

The 2000 presidential election was one of the closest, strangest, and most suspenseful in U.S. history. For weeks after the November 7 vote, Americans still didn't know who had won. It was the first time in more than a century that the outcome of a presidential election had been so unclear for so long.

It wasn't until December 13 that Texas Governor George W. Bush, the Republican candidate, was declared the winner. His victory came after a court fight waged by Vice President Al Gore, the Democratic candidate. And it was the result of a controversial U.S. Supreme Court ruling, marking the first time the nation's highest court had ever played a role in a presidential election.

The election involved a twist that has happened only a few times in U.S. history. On Election Day, Gore actually got over half a million more votes than Bush. But, by a margin of one vote, Bush claimed a majority in the Electoral College. In the U.S. system, each state has a set number of electoral votes. And it's the electoral votes that determine who will be president.

The closeness of the election and the bitter fight over the result left deep divisions between Republicans and Democrats. Bush had scored a narrow and controversial victory. He would have to work hard to gain the confidence and support of the many Americans who didn't vote for him.

CHOOSING THE CANDIDATES

The election began like any other, with the Democrats and Republicans choosing their candidates for president. The parties did this in the same basic way. In each state, they held primaries (direct elections) or caucuses (party meetings) to choose delegates pledged to one presidential hopeful or another. The delegates then went to the parties' national conventions, where the presidential and vice-presidential candidates were named.

The Primaries. The early primaries featured plenty of competition. Half a dozen Republicans sought their party's nomination. Bush started with a clear edge—he was the son of former President George Bush, and he had raised far more money for campaigning than any other presidential hopeful. Bush's strongest opponent was Senator John McCain of Arizona. McCain beat Bush in the first primary, held on February 1 in New Hampshire. But in the weeks that followed, Bush pulled ahead in the race for delegates. Conservatives and Republican loyalists rallied to his camp. McCain appealed to independent voters, but that wasn't enough to win.

Gore, a former senator who had served two terms as vice president under Bill Clinton, was the leading Democratic candidate. Bill Bradley, a former senator from New Jersey, made a strong challenge. But by mid-March, it was clear that Gore would have enough votes to get the Democratic nomination.

The Conventions. The Republican National Convention was held in Philadelphia, Pennsylvania, July 31 to August 3. Delegates formally nominated Bush and his choice for vice president, Dick Cheney. Cheney had been Secretary of Defense under Bush's father, who served from 1989 to 1993. The delegates also approved a party platform, or set of positions, on key issues such as taxes, health care, defense, and education. The platform was designed to appeal to conservatives, who are important to the Republican Party, and to those with more moderate views.

In his acceptance speech, Bush said it was time for Republicans to "seize this moment of American promise." He presented himself as the best leader for the country and said the Republican Party had become "the party of ideas and innovation."

The Democratic National Convention was held in Los Angeles, California, August 14 to 17. The Democratic delegates formally nominated Gore and his choice for vice president, Senator Joseph Lieberman of Connecticut. Lieberman, who had served eleven years in the U.S. Senate, thus became the first Jewish vice-presidential candidate of a major party.

In their platform, the Democrats set out their stands on the issues and their goals for a Gore administration. The platform outlined the successes achieved during President Bill Clinton's eight years in office and promised to build on them, securing "prosperity, progress, peace and security for all."

Most political candidates rely on professional speechwriters. But Gore brought delegates to their feet with an acceptance speech he had mostly written himself. In it, he promised to work for all Americans, "especially those who need a voice, those who need a champion, those who need to be lifted up so they are never left behind."

HOW THE COUNTRY VOTED
(The numbers are each state's Electoral College votes—270 were needed to win.)

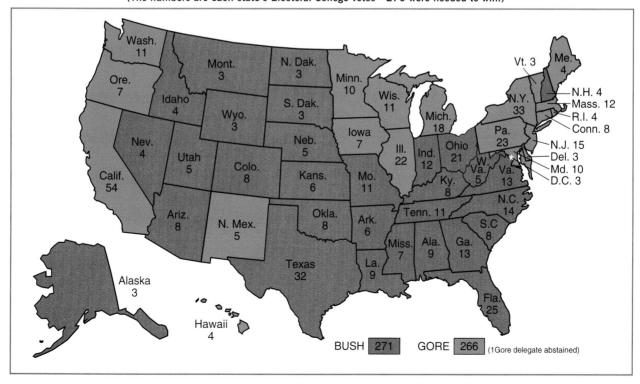

The vice-presidential candidates: Republican Dick Cheney (*above*) served as Secretary of Defense under former President George Bush. Joseph Lieberman (*right*), Democratic Senator from Connecticut, was the first Jewish vice-presidential candidate of a major party.

THE ISSUES

With the conventions behind them, each candidate set out to make his case to the voters. There were clear differences between Bush and Gore on many important issues.

Budget and Taxes. For many years, the U.S. government spent more money than it took in. It borrowed money to make up the difference, and all that borrowing led to a national debt of trillions of dollars. But in 1999, the government took in more money than it spent. There was money left over—a budget surplus for the year. If the U.S. economy stays strong, experts say, surpluses will grow in years to come. The candidates had different ideas about how to use the money.

Bush proposed $1.3 trillion in tax cuts over ten years. Income-tax rates would be reduced across the board, so people who earned the most and paid the most taxes would get the biggest cuts. He also supported increased spending on defense, education, and health programs.

Gore proposed $500 billion in tax cuts, mostly targeted to middle- and low-income families. Tax deductions would encourage people to save for education and retirement. He also proposed increased spending on health, education, the environment, and other programs, and he said he would pay off the national debt by 2013.

Campaign Finance Reform. U.S. politicians raise and spend huge amounts of money campaigning for election. That creates suspicion: Do those individuals or businesses who put up the money gain influence over the officials they help elect? Gore supported public funding for presidential and congressional campaigns. He also backed a ban on "soft money" donations—unregulated donations to political parties. Bush opposed public campaign financing. He proposed bans on "soft money" donations from unions and corporations but not from individuals.

Education. Bush supported a school-voucher plan: If public schools were failing, public money would be given to low-income parents for private-school tuition. He also said states should set educational standards, with students tested yearly to see if the standards were met. Gore supported national education standards. And he opposed the use of vouchers for private schools, saying this would take funding away from public schools. He proposed plans to help schools hire more teachers and improve teaching.

Environment. Gore supported stronger enforcement of anti-pollution laws. He proposed new measures to create parks and reduce the use of fossil fuels such as oil and gasoline. He opposed oil drilling in the Arctic National Wildlife Refuge and logging in undeveloped national forests. And he supported the 1997 Kyoto agreement, under which nations would limit emissions of the gases responsible for global warming. Bush opposed the Kyoto global warming agreement. He said states, rather than the federal government, should have more say in environmental issues. And he supported opening the Arctic National Wildlife Refuge to oil exploration and drilling.

Gun control. Both candidates supported stronger enforcement of current gun laws. Bush opposed mandatory registration of guns, and he said people should be allowed to carry concealed guns. Gore proposed stricter regulations for gun sales. He said handgun buyers should get a photo license, like a driver's license, and guns should have mandatory child-safety locks.

Health care. Some 45 million Americans have no health insurance, mostly because they can't afford it. Gore supported a step-by-step approach to solving the problem. The first step would be to make sure all children have health insurance by 2004. Coverage for all Americans would follow. Bush supported private and state reforms, rather than federal actions, as the best way to fix the health-care system.

Social Security. Social Security provides benefits for elderly and disabled people. These

The Electoral College: How It Works

When voters cast their ballots in a U.S. presidential election, they're not electing the president directly. The names of the presidential candidates are on the ballot. But the votes go to choose electors—members of the Electoral College—who are pledged to those candidates. It's the Electoral College that actually picks the president and vice president.

The founders of the United States set up the Electoral College for several reasons. In their day, with no radio or television, it was hard for people to learn about candidates outside their own states. The founders thought voters should choose electors who would learn about the candidates and make the decision for them.

The Electoral College was also set up to protect the interests of small states. Every state gets one electoral vote for each of its U.S. senators and one vote for each U.S. representative. The number of a state's representatives is based on its population. But the number of senators is not—all states have two. Thus small states have a slightly bigger

voice in the Electoral College than they do in the popular vote. No state has less than three electoral votes.

The electors vote weeks after the election, in December. (December 18 was the date in 2000). To win, a candidate must get 270 electoral votes, out of the total of 538. If no candidate gets a majority, the House of Representatives picks the president, and the Senate picks the vice president.

These days the electors are no longer supposed to make up their own minds when they cast their ballots. They are supposed to follow the wishes of the people who voted for them. It's rare for a "faithless elector" to break ranks and switch his or her vote. In nearly all states, the candidate who wins a majority of the popular vote gets all that state's electoral votes. Maine and Nebraska are the only states in which the electoral vote is sometimes divided among candidates. The winner-takes-all rule means that a candidate who narrowly loses the popular vote can still win in the Electoral College.

Presidential candidates George W. Bush and Al Gore met in a series of three televised debates, in October.

benefits are paid for by taxes on wages and salaries. Bush proposed changing Social Security so that some of the money would go into personal retirement accounts. Gore opposed the plan because it would reduce the amount of money available for payments to people currently receiving benefits.

THE CAMPAIGN

From the start, opinion polls showed that this would be a close election. Bush and Gore crisscrossed the country, spending a lot of time in key states whose electoral votes would be important in the outcome. They appeared on television talk shows. In October, they also met in three televised debates. That gave voters a chance to compare them side by side and see how their positions differed.

But the candidates' positions weren't the only factors that voters weighed. Personality and qualifications also played a role. Bush, whose only government experience was his six years as governor of Texas, tried to overcome the impression that he was less qualified than Gore. If elected, he promised, he would surround himself with top advisers. For his part, Gore struggled to overcome the impression that he was stiff and artificial in public appearances.

As Election Day neared, however, no candidate seemed to have sparked the kind of widespread enthusiasm that would lead to a sure victory. Polls showed the race too close to call.

Candidates from minor political parties also played a role in the 2000 campaign. The most important of these "third party" candidates was Ralph Nader of the Green Party. Nader, a consumer-rights activist, focused on universal health care, environmental and consumer protection, campaign-finance reform, and labor rights. Democrats worried that he might draw support from Gore.

THE VOTE

More than 100 million people (51 percent of eligible voters) voted on November 7, and they split almost equally between Gore and Bush. In the final count, Gore led nationally by 540,000 votes—a narrow margin, but a close one nonetheless. He won most of the Northeast, North Central, and Pacific states. He carried large states with big cities—California, New York, Pennsylvania, Michigan, Illinois. Bush won in the South and West. He did well in smaller, more rural states. Nader won about 2,656,000 votes (less than 3 percent).

But Gore's edge in the popular vote wasn't enough. To win, he needed a majority of the electoral votes. And as returns came in on election night, it became clear that he might not get it. The outcome hinged on the state of Florida (where Jeb Bush, George W.'s brother, was governor). If Gore won Florida, he would have more than enough electoral votes. But if Bush won Florida, the state's 25 electoral votes would push his total to 271—one more than needed to win the presidency.

The Florida vote was so close that a statewide recount of the ballots was ordered. It showed Bush with a lead of a few hundred votes. But there were problems. In Palm Beach County, voters said they had been confused by misleading ballots. And automated vote-counting machines had failed to count many ballots. Gore refused to concede until Florida's results were clear. And it took more than a month for that to happen.

THE FIGHT FOR FLORIDA

Calling for a "full and fair count," Democrats asked for hand recounts of the ballots in three Florida counties—Palm Beach, Broward, and Miami-Dade—where machine counts of punch-card ballots had been questioned. Voters were supposed to punch holes next to the names of the candidates they chose. Sometimes the punch left a flap—called a "hanging chad"—that kept machines from

A New Generation

George W. Bush, the son of former President George Bush, was born on July 6, 1946, in New Haven, Connecticut. But he grew up in Midland and Houston, Texas, and has remained a Texan at heart.

Bush received a bachelor's degree from Yale University and a master's in business administration from Harvard Business School. After serving in the Texas Air National Guard, he went to work in the Texas oil and gas industry.

In 1978, Bush ran for Congress but lost. Then, except for helping on his father's 1988 presidential campaign, he put politics aside. In the late 1980's he left the oil industry. He and a group of partners bought the Texas Rangers baseball franchise in 1989, and he was managing partner of the team. But in 1994 he returned to politics and ran for governor. This time, he won.

As governor, Bush worked to reform education, cut taxes, and put welfare recipients to work. He also worked to strengthen the state's criminal justice system.

The new First Lady, **Laura Welch Bush,** was born on November 6, 1946, in Midland, Texas. She graduated from Southern Methodist University with a degree in education and later earned a master's in library science at the University of Texas. She worked as a teacher and a librarian before she married George W. Bush in 1977. After he was elected governor, she became an advocate for early education and reading. She said she would make early childhood education one of her priorities as First Lady. The Bushes have twin daughters, Barbara and Jenna.

The new vice president, **Richard Cheney,** was born on January 30, 1941, in Lincoln, Nebraska. He graduated from the University of Wyoming in 1965 and later earned a master's degree in political science. In the 1970's, he was an assistant to President Gerald Ford and served as White House chief of staff. Cheney represented Wyoming in the House of Representatives from 1978 to 1989. In Congress, he gained a reputation for staunchly conservative views. As Secretary of Defense under George Bush, George W.'s father, he helped plan strategy during the 1991 Persian Gulf War.

Cheney went to work in the oil industry and lived in Texas during the 1990's. Because a president and vice president can't be from the same state, he moved back to Wyoming before the 2000 election. He and his wife, Lynne, have two daughters.

Coincidence Or . . .?

The 2000 election wasn't the first in which the winner of the popular vote didn't win the presidency. Three earlier presidents were elected that way: John Quincy Adams (1824), Rutherford B. Hayes (1876), and Benjamin Harrison (1888). And historians have noted some odd similarities with those earlier presidential elections:

Shades of 1876. The 2000 election was too close to call, and Florida's votes were the key. In 1876, the outcome was nearly the same! Republican Rutherford B. Hayes and Democrat Samuel J. Tilden fought a bitter campaign. Tilden pulled ahead, and on election night he went to bed thinking he had won.

Tilden had won the popular vote. But at the last minute, Republicans claimed the victory in Florida—and Florida would give Hayes the edge in the Electoral College. As in 2000, the results were contested. Each side accused the other of fraud. Each produced its own returns for Florida and two other Southern states.

Finally Congress set up a special commission to decide the election. The commission voted along party lines and gave the presidency to Hayes. He was promptly nicknamed "Rutherfraud." And he left office after one term.

Winning Is Relative. John Quincy Adams was the son of John Adams, the second U.S. president. Until 2000, he was the only son of a president to be elected to the office. Benjamin Harrison was the grandson of William Henry Harrison, the ninth president. He was the only grandson of a president to win the office. Both men won the Electoral College vote but not the popular vote. Both served one term and then were soundly defeated by the men they ran against four years earlier. Andrew Jackson came back to win a solid victory over Adams in the election of 1828. Grover Cleveland came back to beat Harrison in 1892.

Is there a parallel with the 2000 election? George W. Bush is the son of former president George Bush. Like John Quincy Adams and Benjamin Harrison, he didn't win the popular vote. Will his presidency also end after one term? We'll have to wait four years to find out.

reading the ballot. Sometimes the punch didn't go all the way through, leaving a "dimpled chad." Republicans asked state and federal courts to stop the vote recounts. But on November 21, the Florida Supreme Court ruled that the recounts could continue, and the results should be included in the statewide count.

The court set a deadline of November 26 for the final results. Only one county, Broward, completed the recount in time. Florida officials certified, or approved, their state's tally without the other recounts—but that wasn't the end.

The Gore campaign went to court to contest the results, saying that thousands of ballots hadn't been properly counted. On December 8, the Florida Supreme Court ruled for Gore. The court ordered hand recounts of untallied ballots in all Florida counties. But Republicans appealed to the U.S. Supreme Court. And on December 12, the U.S. justices voted 5–4 in Bush's favor.

The Supreme Court seemed to be as deeply divided as the rest of the country. The five members of the majority, all conservatives, said that Florida's hand recounts violated the U.S. Constitution because the standards for counting the ballots varied from county to county. Thus all votes wouldn't be treated equally. And, the majority said, the time for counting had run out. States were supposed to resolve challenges and pick their electors by December 12.

The four remaining justices disagreed. Several said that the Court shouldn't have ruled in the case because there was no violation of the Constitution—only state laws were at issue. Others said Florida should have been given time to come up with a uniform standard for the recounts. The Electoral College wasn't scheduled to meet and vote until December 18.

Several of the dissenters worried about the effects of the Court's divided ruling. By stopping the vote count, the Court left unanswered the question of who got more votes in Florida. Justice Stevens wrote: "Although we may never know with complete certainty the identity of the winner of this year's Presidential election, the identity of the loser is perfectly clear. It is the nation's confidence in the judge as an impartial guardian of the rule of law."

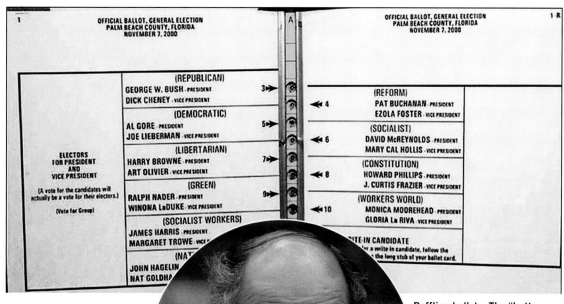

Despite these concerns, the Court's majority ruling closed the door on Gore's effort to win Florida and the presidency. On December 13, he conceded.

Baffling ballots: The "butterfly ballot" (*above*) used in Florida's Palm Beach County confused many voters. And machines—and even people (*left*)—couldn't read punch-card ballots that left "hanging chads" or "dimpled chads."

THE OUTCOME

The presidency wasn't the only office at stake on November 7. Voters chose all 435 members of the U.S. House of Representatives and 34 of the 100 U.S. Senators. Eleven state governorships and many other state offices were also on the line.

Republicans kept a slim majority in the House. Democrats picked up two seats for a total of 212. Republicans had 221, and independents had 2. The Senate was divided right down the middle—Democrats had 50 seats and Republicans had 50. First Lady Hillary Rodham Clinton made history by winning election to the Senate (from New York). No other First Lady had ever been elected to public office. Clinton was one of four women elected to the Senate in 2000, bringing the total number of female senators to a record thirteen.

What did the election of 2000 show? Neither Republicans nor Democrats could claim the support of a strong majority of voters, and the dispute over the election left bad feelings on both sides. To lead the country, the winner would first have to bring Americans together.

The election also highlighted some flaws in the U.S. election system. Voting methods varied widely across the country. Depending on where they lived, people used paper ballots, voting machines, the problem-plagued punch cards, ballots read by optical scanners, and computers. After the confusion in Florida, people called on the federal government to help towns and cities update their voting systems.

Some people also called for an end to the Electoral College system. The president, they said, should be chosen by popular vote. But it would take an amendment to the U.S. Constitution to change the system. And that seemed unlikely—an amendment would have to be passed by a two-thirds majority in Congress and approved by three-fourths of the states.

The close election of 2000 gave Americans a lesson in the workings of their political system. If there was one message that came through, it was this: Every vote matters.

The United States has been experiencing the longest economic boom in its history. But as the year ended, there were signs that the economy was cooling down.

LET THE GOOD TIMES ROLL!

"Let the good times roll!" That's how many Americans felt about the year 2000. The United States was enjoying the longest economic boom in its history. The good times began in April 1991 and were still rolling on, nine years later.

But as the U.S economy continued to grow during 2000, people began to wonder: How long could the boom last? And in fact, by year's end the boom seemed to be running out of steam.

NUMBERS TELL THE STORY

Numbers tell the story of the economic boom. During the years from 1991 to 2000, the value of goods and services produced in the United States grew by more than a third. About 20 million new jobs were created. Unemployment fell to about 4 percent—the lowest rate in more than 30 years. And personal incomes rose an average of 68 percent.

Several factors created this boom:

● U.S. businesses became more efficient during the 1990's, thanks to computers and other new ways of working. Increased efficiency made them more productive, allowing them to grow and increase their profits.

● Stock prices soared to unheard-of levels. And more Americans invested in stocks, profiting from the rising stock prices.

● As incomes rose, so did spending—on everything from food to cellular phones. This helped drive more economic growth.

● The Federal Reserve, a federal agency, got some credit. The "Fed" sets U.S. monetary policy. During the 1990's its policies kept inflation—increases in the cost of goods and services—low.

● Government leaders helped by ending huge federal budget deficits. Deficits had grown during the 1980's as the government spent more money than it took in. The government borrowed money to make up the difference, pushing the country deep into debt. Now the federal government expects to take in more money than it spends, resulting in budget surpluses.

LOOKING AHEAD

The benefits of economic growth weren't spread evenly. The boom made some people, especially those who invested in stocks of new Internet companies, fabulously rich. Others lost their jobs as companies adopted new ways of doing business. On the whole, the wealthiest fifth of U.S. families gained the most. The lowest fifth saw their incomes fall.

During 2000, economists also pointed to some clouds on the horizon:

• Early in the year, there were signs that inflation might be increasing. The Federal Reserve raised interest rates several times, to keep inflation in check. High interest rates tend to slow economic growth.

• Americans were saving very little money—less than 3 percent of personal income, compared to more than 8 percent in the early 1990's.

• The U.S. trade deficit grew, hitting record highs. This meant the country imported more goods than it sold overseas, and spent more abroad than it earned from exports.

• Stock prices, which helped create much new wealth, took some wild swings. Stocks of Internet and other technology companies, which had led the big increases, plunged in value in 2000.

Would these factors end the boom? No one could tell. By the end of the year, consumers and businesses alike were spending less, and the rate of economic growth was slowing. Some people said these signs meant the boom was over. Others hoped that the economy would keep growing at a slower, safer rate. Then the good times might just roll on.

Taxi drivers in Marseilles, France, go on strike, protesting the high cost of fuel.

The Rising Price of Oil

People in many countries were digging deeper into their pockets to put gas in their cars, pay their heating bills, and even buy airline tickets in 2000. The main reason was the price of crude oil, unrefined petroleum that's pumped out of the ground.

In mid-February 2000, the price of crude oil topped $30 a barrel, its highest level since 1991. And the price kept going up, reaching $35 a barrel in August. Crude oil is used to make many products—gasoline, kerosene, heating oil, jet fuel, diesel fuel, and more. Increased crude oil prices meant rising prices for all these products.

The crude-oil price hike didn't happen by chance. Most of the world's major oil-producing nations belong to a group called the Organization of Petroleum Exporting Countries (OPEC). OPEC members control nearly 80 percent of the world's known petroleum resources. In March 1999, OPEC members agreed to cut the amount of oil they produce. Cutting production limited oil supplies worldwide. And that caused prices to rise.

The soaring price of oil raised concern in the United States, Canada, and other nations that are major users of oil. They worried that price increases might contribute to inflation and other economic problems. European countries were especially hard hit by the price increases. In September, protestors in Britain, France, and other European nations staged demonstrations to protest the rising costs.

OPEC members responded to international pressure and agreed to increase oil production several times during 2000. But even so, prices stayed high. This was partly because reserves of oil were low worldwide, and partly because demand for gas and other petroleum products was high.

Refugees from Africa's "first world war" walk along a road in Congo. Seven African nations were involved in the conflict, which raged throughout the year.

TURMOIL IN AFRICA

In 1998, U.S. President Bill Clinton traveled to sub-Saharan Africa. He hailed "the beginning of a new African renaissance"—a period of rebirth for the nations south of the Sahara desert. The hope then was that reforms would bring better days to these nations.

In 2000, Clinton visited Africa again. On this trip, he went to Nigeria, which had a new democratic government. He also stopped in Tanzania. But except in Nigeria and a few other bright spots, it seemed that Africans were no closer to the hoped-for better days.

Africa has enormous potential, but it faces enormous problems. Most of the countries south of the Sahara were colonies of European nations until the 1960's. Hopes were high when they gained independence. But, despite natural resources that include oil, gold, and diamonds, many African nations rank among the world's poorest.

In some African countries, misguided economic policies are partly to blame. Corrupt officials have often helped themselves to national resources and aid provided by other countries, including the United States. Wars have drained many African countries. In 1999, eleven wars were fought in Africa. And during 2000, Africa's troubles showed no sign of lessening.

AFRICA'S "FIRST WORLD WAR"

Fighting raged throughout the year in Congo, in a conflict that was being called Africa's "first world war." Six outside nations and several rebel groups were involved in the war. All were fighting for their own reasons. And all were grabbing Congo's riches, which include diamonds, gold, uranium, timber, and oil.

Rather than a single war, this conflict was really a series of related wars. It grew out of ethnic conflict in Rwanda in 1994. There, fighting between Rwanda's two main ethnic groups, the Hutu and the Tutsi, resulted in terrible bloodshed. Hutu fighters killed at least 500,000 Tutsi. The Hutu fighters were eventually driven out, but they set up new bases in eastern Congo (then called Zaire) and continued to fight.

Zaire's ruler at the time, Mobutu Sese Seko, supported the Hutu. So Rwanda's Tutsi-led government threw its support to a rebellion against him. In 1997 the rebellion succeeded, and rebel leader Laurent Kabila became the new president. But once Kabila was in power, he cut his ties to the Rwandans. And they then backed new rebellions aimed at toppling *him*. Although the parties signed a cease-fire in 1999, it didn't stick. This was the situation in 2000:

• Three rebel groups controlled nearly half of Congo, mostly the north and east. With no government in this region, violence erupted between rival tribal groups.

• Troops from Rwanda and Uganda were in Congo, fighting in support of various rebel groups. Like Rwanda, Uganda was being attacked by Hutu fighters based in eastern Congo.

• Burundi also had troops in Congo, fighting Hutu militias. Burundi's Tutsi-led government has been waging a civil war with Hutu rebels for years. South African statesman Nelson Mandela brokered a peace agreement in that fight, and President Clinton went to Tanzania for the signing in August. But at the last minute, some of the parties refused to sign.

• On Kabila's side were the Hutu militias and the Mayi-Mayi, a Congolese group.

• Zimbabwe, Kabila's strongest ally, had thousands of troops in Congo to support him.

• Angola also backed Kabila. For more than 25 years, Angola has been fighting a civil war with a group called Unita. It sent troops into southern Congo mainly to stop Unita from launching attacks from that region.

• Namibia, a close ally of Angola, also sent troops to help Kabila.

• Zambia and Tanzania, two neighboring nations, sat out the conflict. But they were flooded with refugees from the fighting. And the fighting around them hurt their economies, affecting everything from trade to tourism.

From 1998 to mid-2000, about 1.7 million people died because of this war. Some were killed in the fighting; many more died of hunger and disease when they fled into the forests to escape the conflict. The United Nations proposed sending a force of 5,500 peacekeepers to Congo, and in August 2000, Kabila accepted the idea. But the fighting only intensified. Meanwhile, the U.N. was also involved in another African war, in Sierra Leone.

SIERRA LEONE

The West African nation of Sierra Leone was in the ninth year of a civil war in 2000. A rebel group led by Foday Sankoh had been fighting the government since 1991. The rebels used terror tactics, attacking civilians. Thousands of people were killed, and thousands more fled their homes to escape the fighting. The rebels financed their war by smuggling diamonds, one of the country's most important resources.

In July 1999, the United Nations helped work out a peace agreement. Under its terms, Sankoh was to be a member of the government. In exchange, the rebels were to give up their weapons and the diamond-rich territory they controlled to peacekeeping forces from the United Nations. But the rebels didn't live up to their promises.

By May 2000, the United Nations had about 8,700 lightly armed peacekeeping troops in Sierra Leone. Most of the peace-

African soldiers in Sierra Leone were part of a United Nations peacekeeping force. More than 500 peacekeepers were kidnapped in May.

keepers were from other African nations. Nigeria also had troops in Sierra Leone, supporting the government, but these stronger troops weren't part of the peacekeeping forces. As part of the peace agreement the Nigerians pulled out at the end of April. The rebels then launched new attacks and began seizing peacekeepers as hostages. By mid-May, about 500 peacekeepers had been taken. The rebels were advancing on Freetown, the capital. The situation looked grim. Then, in a twist of fate, Sankoh was captured.

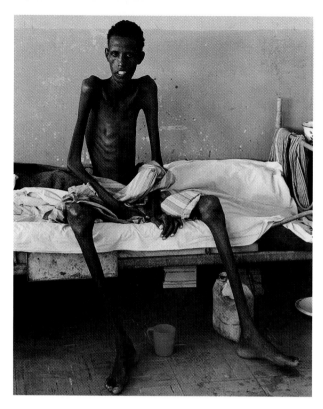

An Ethiopian suffering from malnutrition waits for aid at a medical station. Ethiopia's border war with Eritrea, along with a three-year drought, created fears of widespread famine in that country.

The U.N. sent more troops, increasing its force to 13,000. It also took steps to set up a war crimes tribunal to investigate charges of attacks on civilians.

MORE TROUBLES

Congo and Sierra Leone weren't the only hot spots in sub-Saharan Africa. Here are some other events of 2000.

Ethiopia and Eritrea. In June, Ethiopia and Eritrea agreed to end a two-year border war. Eritrea was once a province of Ethiopia, but it won independence in 1993 after a long struggle. However, the two countries didn't agree on an official border, and that led to war.

The cease-fire agreement came after Ethiopian forces pushed deep into Eritrea in May. The fighting caused hundreds of thousands of people to flee their homes. This crisis, along with a three-year drought, raised fears of famine. But a month later, both sides agreed to a cease-fire drafted by the Organization of African Unity. It called on troops to pull back to their prewar positions while U.N. mediators established an official border.

With Sankoh in custody, peace once again seemed possible. About half the U.N. hostages were released. But the rebels continued to fight. In July, U.N. troops attacked a rebel base in the eastern part of the country to free 233 peacekeepers.

AIDS in Africa

One of sub-Saharan Africa's biggest problems is an epidemic of AIDS (acquired immunodeficiency syndrome), a disease that destroys the body's ability to fight infection. Nearly two-thirds of the people infected with HIV, the virus that causes AIDS, live in Africa. In June 2000, the United Nations reported that HIV had infected more than one out of three people in Botswana, one out of four in Swaziland and Zimbabwe, and one out of five in South Africa.

The U.N. estimated that nearly two-thirds of all 15-year-olds in these hardest-hit nations would eventually die of AIDS.

Stopping the spread of this disease, and treating those who already have it, is a huge challenge. So far, there is no vaccine to prevent AIDS and no drug to cure it. Some drugs seem to keep the disease in check, at least for a time. But these drugs are very expensive. During 2000 the World Bank, aid groups, and drug companies all announced plans to help African nations set up programs to fight AIDS.

Zimbabwe. Zimbabwe celebrated its 20th anniversary of independence in 2000. But the year was marked by racial tensions in the country, the former British colony of Rhodesia. In February, former soldiers—veterans of the country's war for independence—began occupying land owned by white farmers. The veterans were supported by President Robert Mugabe. White farmers owned nearly 75 percent of the country's farmland, and Mugabe said he would redistribute the land to poor, landless blacks.

Ivory Coast. Ivory Coast was once an island of calm in Africa. Under President Félix Houphouët-Boigny, who led the small West African country for about 30 years, people of different ethnic and religious groups lived together peacefully. That began to change when Henri Konan Bédié took over as president in the early 1990's. Bédié fanned tensions between Muslims, who account for 40 percent of the population and live mostly in the north, and Christians like himself, in the south.

In 1999, General Robert Gueï seized power in a military coup. He also widened the divisions between northerners and southerners. Gueï agreed to hold presidential elections in October 2000, and he put himself forward as a candidate. But then he banned his two strongest rivals, including Alassane D. Ouattara, a Muslim. As a result, most Muslims refused to vote.

Even so, the election didn't go Gueï's way. It quickly became clear that his only serious opponent, Laurent Gbagbo, had out-polled him. On October 23, Gueï halted the vote count and declared himself the winner. But Ivoirians would have none of it. Tens of thousands of people took to the streets. They forced Gueï to flee, and Gbagbo was sworn in as president.

Ivory Coast's troubles weren't over. Muslims who supported Ouattara wanted a new election, and Gbagbo refused. Their supporters fought, and mosques and churches were attacked. By the end of October, the clashes had stopped. But many people still feared that the country was headed toward civil war.

Nigeria. The future looked brighter for Nigeria. In 1999, voters there chose a new

U.S. President Bill Clinton meets with President Olusegun Obasanjo of Nigeria during his visit to Africa.

president, Olusegun Obasanjo, in the country's first free elections in 16 years. In 2000, they watched to see how he would tackle Nigeria's many problems. Nigeria is the most populous country in Africa, with about 120 million people. It's the world's sixth largest oil producer. But years of civil war, corruption, and dictatorship have held this West African country back. Ethnic violence has become a serious problem. In 1999 and 2000, some 2,000 people were killed in clashes between Yoruba extremists and Hausas, who are mainly Muslims.

In many ways, Nigeria's problems mirror those of other African countries. The new president faced a difficult job. He would have to put Nigeria's economy on track, so that the country's people could all benefit from its great natural wealth. And he would have to gain the trust of all of Nigeria's groups, so they could work together. That wouldn't be accomplished quickly. But with an elected government in office once again, many Nigerians looked to the future with hope.

North and South Korea—divided for more than half a century—took steps toward peace in 2000. Here, a North Korean mother hugs the South Korean son she hasn't seen for 50 years.

AROUND THE WORLD

New leaders and historic steps toward peace made headlines during 2000. So did a flare-up of intense violence in the Middle East. Following is a rundown of some of the year's important events.

THE TWO KOREAS: STEPS TOWARD PEACE

Tall fencing topped with barbed wire slices through the middle of the Korean peninsula. Soldiers patrol the fence line. On one side of this border is North Korea. It's one of the world's last and most severe Communist countries. On the other side is South Korea. It's a fast-growing country with an elected government.

Korea was divided more than 50 years ago, when rivalry was growing between Communist and non-Communist countries. North Korea and South Korea then fought a bitter war. The United States and other nations fought on the side of South Korea. China and the Soviet Union backed North Korea. The war ended in a truce in 1953, but North Korea and South Korea remained enemies.

In 2000, however, leaders of the two Koreas took a daring step. In June, South Korean President Kim Dae Jung traveled to Pyongyang, the capital of North Korea. There he met with North Korean President Kim Jong Il. The two leaders talked about ways to reduce tension between their countries.

The division of Korea had split families as well as land. And among the actions the leaders planned were reunions for people who had relatives on opposite sides of the border. South Korea also promised to speed delivery of aid to North Korea. North Korea's economy has crumbled in recent years, and hunger is a major problem.

The South Korean president, who was elected in 1997, is a lifelong champion of human rights and democracy. He has made improving ties with North Korea a major goal of his presidency. For his progress toward that goal, Kim Dae Jung was awarded the 2000 Nobel Peace Prize.

It was too soon to tell if the June meeting and other contacts would lead to lasting peace. But there was cause for hope. North Korea also seemed ready to build better relations with the West.

In the past, North Korea has been a harsh critic of the United States and other Western nations. It has built missiles and is believed to be developing nuclear weapons. But in 2000 there were signs that North Korea might be persuaded to change course. U.S. Secretary of State Madeleine Albright visited North Korea in October. She made some progress in talks aimed at limiting North Korea's missile program, although no agreement was reached.

CHINA AND TAIWAN: SOME HISTORIC CHANGES

A presidential election brought historic change to Taiwan in 2000. For the first time, a new party took control of the government through a free, democratic vote. But the vote, held on March 18, also brought threats from China. China views Taiwan, an island off its coast, as a rebellious province and not as an independent country.

The winner of Taiwan's election was Chen Shui-bian, 49, leader of the Democratic Progressive Party. He succeeded President Lee Teng-hui. And his victory ended more than 50 years of rule by Lee's Nationalist Party. Nationalist rule began in 1949, at the end of China's civil war. Defeated by the Communists in that war, the Nationalists fled to the island of Taiwan and set up a government-in-exile there.

Today Taiwan's status is unclear. China has continued to declare that Taiwan is a part of China. Taiwan, however, carries on its affairs as if it were an independent country, even though it has never declared independence. And the United States has promised to defend the island if China ever attacks.

While they were in power, Nationalist leaders walked a fine line in their relations with China. They said they were willing to talk about reunification—but only on their own terms. Chen, in contrast, long supported independence for Taiwan. But in the months before the election, he stepped back from that position. No formal declaration of independence was needed, he said.

All the same, China's leaders feared that a victory by Chen might put Taiwan on a path to independence. And they tried to influence the vote—by threatening Taiwan. In February, they repeated warnings that any move toward independence would lead to war. And they added a new threat: If Taiwan didn't start negotiating terms for reunification soon, that could also lead to war.

Taiwanese voters seemed to ignore these alarming threats. And China was only one issue in the presidential election. Many voters felt that the Nationalists had been in power too long. They were upset about corruption in the government.

A split in the Nationalist Party turned the campaign into a three-way race. Chen, a lawyer and former mayor of Taipei (Taiwan's capital), won with 39 percent of the vote. James Soong, a former Nationalist who ran as an independent candidate, took 37 percent. Lien Chen, the official Nationalist candidate, was third with 23 percent.

With strong support, Chen Shui-bian (*inset*) was elected Taiwan's new president—ending 50 years of rule by the Nationalist Party.

This poster shows Putin, with the words "Honest, Intelligent, Firm, Active, Persistent." The first letters of the words in Russian make up the name "Putin."

Russia's New President

Vladimir V. Putin, Russia's new president, has spent most of his career out of the public eye. He's known for his intelligence and his calm manner. But he's a bit of a mystery to many people in the West.

Putin grew up in Leningrad (now St. Petersburg) and earned a law degree there. But instead of becoming a lawyer, he joined the KGB—the spy agency of the Soviet Union. He was posted to East Germany, where his job was to gather information on the political views of East Germans.

In 1989, as Communism was collapsing in Eastern Europe, Putin returned to Russia. After the breakup of the Soviet Union, he held several posts in the Russian government. He rose quickly, and in 1998 he became head of the Federal Security Bureau—the Russian equivalent of the old Soviet KGB. Later he was put in charge of internal security and national defense.

In August 1999, Russian President Boris Yeltsin named Putin prime minister. As prime minister, Putin sent troops into the province of Chechnya to put down a rebellion. Russians approved, and his popularity soared. Putin became acting president when Yeltsin resigned at the end of the year.

In his victory speech, Chen seemed to reach out to China. He promised to seek stronger economic ties and permanent peace with the mainland. But the new president faced big problems. The Nationalists still controlled the legislature. And in October, they began a drive to impeach the new president and turn him out of office. But it seemed unlikely that they would succeed.

Meanwhile, China and the United States started a new chapter in their relations. In September, the U.S. Senate voted to end restrictions on trade with China. Since 1974, Congress had extended U.S.-Chinese trade relations a year at a time. The idea was to use the threat of trade restrictions to get China to improve its record on human rights and in other areas. But the yearly threats didn't accomplish much. And meanwhile, American trade with China grew. Businesses of all kinds want a chance to reach China's huge markets. China is the world's most populous nation, and it has lots of customers for U.S. goods.

In exchange for permanent trade relations, the new agreement called on China to end many restrictions on foreign goods and services. These restrictions have kept U.S. companies from competing in China. Now it will be easier for them to do business there.

The agreement also paved the way for China to join the World Trade Organization (WTO). This international organization governs trade between member nations. Joining the WTO will make it easier for China to sell its products worldwide. And China will have to follow the same trade rules that the other 135 members follow.

A NEW LEADER FOR RUSSIA

Vladimir Putin won a clear victory in Russia's presidential election on March 26. His win was no surprise: Outgoing President Boris Yeltsin had named Putin, 47, as his successor and appointed him acting president on December 31, 1999. Russians, who had suffered years of growing crime and economic troubles, saw Putin as a leader who would take action and make Russia a world power once again. He outpolled his ten rivals in the March election.

But the new president had a lot of work ahead. The country's tax and banking systems needed reform. Its social services and military needed rebuilding. Bribery, kickbacks, and other forms of corruption were major problems throughout Russia. To curb corruption, Putin said he would use former secret-service agents to track down crooked politicians. And he promised to strengthen Russia's government and establish law and order.

However, many Westerners worried that Putin might also limit civil liberties, such as freedom of speech. Russians have enjoyed free elections and a free press for only a few years. Under the old Soviet system, they were ruled by a Communist dictatorship. Would Putin lead Russia toward greater democracy or back to dictatorship?

Another problem Putin faced was a fierce rebellion in the province of Chechnya. Russia had sent soldiers into Chechnya in September 1999, after Islamic militants based there staged terrorist attacks. In early February, the Russians captured Grozny, Chechnya's capital. But that didn't end the fighting, and Russian troops sparred with rebel bands throughout the year.

Meanwhile, concern about Chechen civilians grew worldwide. More than 200,000 people had fled their homes to escape the fighting. Chechens say that thousands of civilians have been killed in the Russian campaign. Most of Grozny was destroyed by weeks of Russian shelling. Still, by fall, about a third of Grozny's people had returned to the city. Most camped out in damaged buildings without water or electricity.

U.S. President Bill Clinton visited Russia in June, and Chechnya was one of the subjects he discussed with Putin. The two leaders also discussed arms control, pledging to work toward reducing stockpiles of nuclear weapons. But they didn't reach a new agreement.

Thousands of demonstrators at Yugoslavia's Parliament building demanded that President Slobodan Milosevic step down, after his defeat in September elections. Vojislav Kostunica (*inset*) became the country's new president.

A Deadly Attack

In one of the most serious terrorist acts in recent years, a small boat full of explosives blew an enormous hole in the side of a U.S. Navy destroyer on October 12, as the destroyer arrived in Yemen, on the southern tip of the Arabian peninsula. The blast killed 17 sailors and injured 39 others.

The destroyer, the USS *Cole*, was on its way to the Persian Gulf to join a naval battle group. It stopped to refuel in Aden, Yemen. The ship was at the refueling station when the blast occurred. Witnesses said a motorized skiff pulled alongside the Navy ship. Then two men in the skiff stood up, and their boat—packed with at least 440 pounds (200 kilograms) of high explosives—blew up. The explosion tore an 80-foot (24-meter) gash in the *Cole*'s side, right at the waterline. It was powerful enough to buckle the ship's deck and damage the engine room.

The injured sailors were flown to U.S. military hospitals in Germany while the rest of the crew struggled to pump out water and keep the ship afloat. Eventually, the ship was towed back to Norfolk, Virginia.

No one claimed responsibility for the explosion. Many U.S. officials suspected that Osama bin Ladin, a terrorist leader living in Afghanistan, was behind the attack. Bin Laden had masterminded terrorist bombings of U.S. embassies in Kenya and Tanzania in 1998. And he had ties to Islamic terrorist groups operating in Yemen.

The United States had been trying to improve relations with Yemen, despite that country's links to terrorists. Refueling stops like the *Cole*'s were part of the effort. American antiterrorist experts went to Yemen to help authorities there investigate the attack. In November, the Yemenis were reported to have made several arrests. U.S. officials weren't allowed to question the suspects, who were thought to be linked to a terrorist group called Islamic Jihad. The suspects had met several times with the bombers in the months leading up to the attack.

YUGOSLAVIA: A DICTATOR IS VOTED OUT

Slobodan Milosevic ruled the eastern European country of Yugoslavia as a dictator for many years. His years in office were marked by violence. But those years ended in 2000. On September 24, Milosevic lost a presidential election to Vojislav Kostunica, 56, a lawyer and opposition leader. Milosevic tried to rig the vote and refused to admit defeat. But, in a drama that had the whole world watching, he was finally forced to step down.

Milosevic first rose to power by fanning conflict between ethnic groups. In 1989, he became president of Serbia, one of the several republics that made up Yugoslavia at that time. There was growing friction between the Serbs and Yugoslavia's other ethnic groups. Milosevic encouraged Serbian nationalism, warning that Serbs might have to fight the other groups. Serbs rallied to his banner.

In the early 1990's, Yugoslavia broke apart. The republics of Slovenia, Croatia, and Bosnia-Herzegovina declared independence.

Milosevic became president of what remained of Yugoslavia—Serbia and the smaller republic of Montenegro.

Civil war soon broke out in the former Yugoslav republics. And Milosevic played a big part in it. He backed Serbian militias that fought to grab territory in Croatia and Bosnia. In Bosnia, Serb militias carried out a brutal campaign of "ethnic cleansing," killing thousands of civilians and driving them from their homes. Bosnia was divided into ethnic regions when the fighting ended in 1995.

In 1998, Milosevic again used ethnic conflict to boost his popularity. This time he turned on the ethnic Albanians of Kosovo, a region in southern Yugoslavia. But the plan backfired. The United States and European nations stepped in, using air strikes to stop Milosevic's forces. Kosovo was placed under United Nations control. And a U.N. tribunal charged Milosevic with crimes against humanity for his brutal campaign against the ethnic Albanians.

After years of war and growing poverty, many Serbians were fed up. And they showed their unhappiness in the September 2000 election. Kostunica beat Milosevic by better than 51 percent to 36 percent, according to international observers. But the Yugoslavian election commission, which was controlled by Milosevic, claimed that no candidate had won 50 percent. Under the election rules, that would require a runoff vote. However, it seemed clear that the commission's tally was faked.

Kostunica's supporters staged demonstrations and strikes, demanding that Milosevic step down. World leaders added their

calls to the chorus. On October 5, thousands of demonstrators poured into Belgrade, the capital, and took over the Parliament building. The police and the army did little to stop them. Even Yugoslavia's government-controlled television and radio threw their support to Kostunica.

On October 6, Milosevic finally admitted that he had lost. Kostunica was sworn in as president the next day. He promised to work to bring the people of this troubled country together. The United States and European nations responded immediately. They lifted bans on trade and other economic sanctions that had been applied to Yugoslavia during Milosevic's attacks on Kosovo. And they welcomed the start of a new era in Yugoslavia.

ISRAEL AND THE PALESTINIANS: MORE FIGHTING

Can Israel and the Palestinian Arabs ever find peace? That question was asked often in 2000. Hopes for a peace accord were high early in the year, but they went up in smoke when new violence broke out in the fall.

Ever since Israel was founded in 1948, it has been at odds with neighboring Arab states and with the Palestinian Arabs. Arab countries have fought three wars against Israel, hoping to wipe it from the map. The

Palestinian Arabs, who live in territory occupied by Israel, have long demanded an independent state of their own. For years, they have carried on a campaign of war and terrorism.

But in 1993, Israel and the Palestinians signed the Oslo accords. This agreement gave the Palestinians limited self-rule over land in the Gaza Strip and parts of the West Bank, territories occupied by Israel in a 1967 war. More talks were to decide the question of an independent Palestinian state. The two sides were supposed to reach a final agreement by May 4, 1999. But when that date came, there was no pact. The deadline was extended to September 13, 2000.

With an eye on that deadline, U.S. President Bill Clinton brought leaders from both sides to Camp David, Maryland, for top-level talks in July. But after two weeks of intense negotiations, Israeli Prime Minister Ehud Barak and Palestinian leader Yasir Arafat were far apart on several key issues.

The biggest stumbling block was the future of Jerusalem, the capital of Israel. That city is sacred to both Israelis and Palestinians. Israel said that Jerusalem must be its undivided capital. The Palestinians have said that the city's eastern sector must be the capital of their state.

The end of the summit left many people worried about the future. Israeli and Palestinian negotiators met again in August, and leaders of Egypt and Jordan offered help. But the talks stalled. And in late September, violence erupted.

The trigger seemed to be the visit of Ariel Sharon, an Israeli politician, to a holy site in Jerusalem. Sharon was known for his opposition to the Palestinians. He visited the Tem-

A New Leader for Syria

President Hafez al-Assad ruled Syria with an iron hand for 30 years. But the Syrian leader died on June 10, 2000. And as he had planned, the presidency passed to his son, Bashar al-Assad. Bashar, 34, was sworn in on July 17, after winning more than 97 percent of the vote in an election in which he was the only candidate.

Syria's new president had trained to become an ophthalmologist—an eye doctor. But his father picked him to become Syria's next leader. In the years before his father's death, Bashar al-Assad had led a campaign against corruption. That made him popular with Syrians. But he faced some difficult tasks as president. Syria's state-run economy was in bad shape. What Assad would do to revive the economy wasn't clear.

Nor was it clear whether Syria's relations with other countries, especially Israel, might change under the new president. No Arab nation has been more strongly opposed to Israel than Syria. In the past, Syria has fought wars with Israel and backed anti-Israeli terrorists. A major issue between the two countries is the Golan Heights, a high plateau along their border. Israel took control of the Golan from Syria during the Six-Day War of 1967. Syria wants it back, but talks broke down over this issue in January 2000. Would Bashar al-Assad make more progress? The world waited to see.

Iranian women wave flags and carry portraits of moderate President Mohammed Khatami during a pre-election rally.

ple Mount, a site holy to Muslims as well as to Jews, accompanied by television cameras and 1,000 armed policemen. Control of this site has been a big issue between Israelis, who are mostly Jews, and Palestinians, who are mostly Muslims. And Palestinians were outraged by Sharon's visit. Deep feelings of resentment flashed to the surface.

The violence began with riots. Young Palestinians threw rocks at Israeli security forces, and the Israelis struck back. The protests spread to other places, and soon armed Palestinian militants were involved. Rioting swept the West Bank, Gaza, and Arab towns in Israel.

With the violence spiraling out of control, world leaders called on both sides to stop. Barak and Arafat met in October and agreed to a cease-fire, but the fighting didn't stop. Arafat didn't seem able to rein in the Palestinian militants. And Barak didn't have strong support from Israelis. In fact, his support was so low that it seemed likely he might lose power.

By December, more than 300 people, mostly Palestinians, had been killed. Arafat called on the United Nations to send troops to protect Palestinian civilians. Barak said Israel would never accept such a force. Both leaders traveled separately to Washington, D.C., to meet again with Clinton. But the meetings didn't bring peace.

THE MODERATES WIN IN IRAN

The Islamic government of Iran has placed many restrictions on its people. The Muslim clerics who lead the government want Iran to be governed by religious law and kept free of Western influences. Under their rule, personal freedom has been greatly limited, especially for women. But in 2000, moderates were gaining a growing voice in the way the country was run. They promised to bring reform and greater freedom to the country.

In elections on February 18, moderates won a majority of seats in Iran's parliament. The vote showed that Iranians were increasingly unhappy with their government. Many were out of work and having trouble making ends meet. Young people played an important part in the Iranian election. Half of Iran's population is under 25, and the legal voting age is 16. Many young Iranians want more freedom and opportunity.

After a second round of voting in May, moderates controlled about 70 percent of the legislature. Iranian president Mohammed Khatami, who was elected in 1997, was also a moderate. But conservatives still had the upper hand. In the Iranian system, the most powerful person in the country was the spiritual leader, Ayatollah Ali Khamenei, a conservative Muslim cleric. And religious conservatives still controlled the Council of Guardians, which must approve all legislation passed by parliament.

The vote clearly showed that Iranians wanted more social and political freedom. However it wasn't so clear that these conservatives would go along with the moderates' plans for reform.

NEWSMAKERS

For the British royal family, 2000 was a big birthday year. On June 21, **Prince William,** who stands second in line for the throne, turned 18 and officially came of age. And on August 4, the **Queen Mother**—the mother of Queen Elizabeth II, Britain's reigning monarch—turned 100.

William is Queen Elizabeth's grandson. His father is Prince Charles, heir to the throne. Now that he's 18, tradition calls for him to be addressed as Royal Highness and greeted with bows and curtsies. But he has asked that those practices be put off until he finishes his education. William graduated from Eton, an exclusive secondary school, in 2000. He took a "gap year"—a year away from school, for traveling. Then he'll go on to the University of St. Andrews in Scotland to study art history.

Hillary Rodham Clinton made history in 2000. As a candidate for the U.S. Senate, she was the first First Lady in United States history to run for public office. And she won! Clinton, 53, ran for an open seat in New York State. She and her husband, President Bill Clinton, had bought a home there late in 1999. This was the first time Hillary Clinton, who is a lawyer, had run for office. But she had plenty of experience in campaigning with her husband. And she had worked alongside her husband throughout his long career in government. New York's Democratic Party nominated her enthusiastically. She campaigned hard throughout the state. And on November 7, Election Day, she won a solid victory over her Republican opponent, Congressman Rick Lazio.

During the French Revolution, King Louis XVI and his family were thrown in jail. In 1793 the king was executed. So was his queen, Marie Antoinette. But their 8-year-old son, who would be **Louis XVII,** remained in prison. What became of him? Officials said he died in jail in 1795. But others said the boy who died was someone else, and the real Louis escaped. In 2000, the mystery was finally solved. Scientists tested DNA from the preserved heart of the boy who had died in the French jail 205 years before. It matched DNA from a lock of Marie Antoinette's hair—proof that the boy had been the heir to the French throne.

Kathleen McGrath scored a first for women in the military in 2000. As captain of the guided-missile frigate USS *Jarrett,* she became the first woman to command a U.S. Navy warship at sea. It was a big step forward—no woman commanded a Navy ship of any kind until 1990, and women have been serving on Navy warships only since 1994. McGrath, 47, joined the Navy in 1981 on a whim. Years of training and experience on other ships prepared her to be captain. On its first voyage under her command, the *Jarrett* sailed "into harm's way": The ship spent six months patrolling the Persian Gulf, searching for smuggled oil. McGrath's crew included 259 men and 4 women. Her husband, a retired Navy officer, looked after their two adopted children while she was away.

In 1963, at the Lincoln Memorial in Washington, D.C., civil-rights leader **Martin Luther King, Jr.,** delivered his famous "I Have a Dream" speech (right). Now a memorial to King may rise nearby, between the Lincoln and Jefferson memorials. A site for the King memorial was approved late in 1999. It overlooks the Tidal Basin, famous for its flowering cherry trees. The picture below shows a proposed design.

Doris Haddock of Dublin, New Hampshire, walked across the United States for a cause she believed in. That trek of 3,200 miles (5,150 kilometers) would be a feat for anyone. But for Haddock—a 90-year-old great-grandmother—it was amazing. "Granny D," as she was called, made her journey to protest the U.S. campaign finance system, which lets special-interest groups contribute huge amounts of money to help candidates run for office. Many people, including Haddock, say that gives the special-interest groups a bigger voice in government than average people have.

To make the point, Haddock decided to walk from Pasadena, California, to Washington, D.C. She set out on January 1, 1999. Her route took her across twelve states, and she wore out four pairs of sneakers. When she hit snow-covered ground in Maryland, she strapped on cross-country skis and kept going. On February 29, 2000, she finally climbed the steps of the Capitol in Washington. "Wake up, America, recognize what is happening to your country, and do something about it," she said.

ANIMALS

When two chameleons come face to face on a log, the results can be very colorful. These fascinating lizards are famous for their ability to change color. Temperature, light, the animal's mood, and other factors may make a chameleon turn pale or "blush" with color. The changes help the chameleon attract mates, drive away rivals, and hide from enemies and prey.

The chameleon, a lizard whose name means "little lion," is best known for its ability to change colors. But this colorful behavior is just one of the tricks this animal magician has up its sleeve.

CHAMELEONS: QUICK-CHANGE ARTISTS

A small brown chameleon sits on a shady branch. The lizard blends in with the branch so well that you'd need very sharp eyes to spot it. Later, that same chameleon moves through sunlit leaves. Within minutes its skin turns a bright green. Once again it blends in with its surroundings.

The chameleon's ability to change color is probably its best-known feature. But contrary to what many people believe, a chameleon doesn't change color just to match its surroundings. Nor does it simply decide to put on a new hue. The lizard's color changes occur in response to temperature, light, the animal's mood, and other factors. The changes help the chameleon survive—by making it attractive to potential mates, threatening to rivals, and invisible to its enemies and to the insects it hopes to catch.

A COLORFUL ACT

The colors of chameleons—and the colors they can turn—vary from species to species. Most chameleons sport shades of green and brown most of the time. And since most of these lizards live in trees, those colors help them stay hidden. But chameleons may also display yellows, blues, reds, and black. The colors may be uniform over the chameleon's body. Or there may be colored patterns of spots or stripes.

Warmth and sunlight deepen and darken the chameleon's colors. Scientists think darker colors may help the animal absorb heat—just as a dark shirt absorbs more heat than a white one. Like other lizards, chameleons are cold-blooded. They depend on external warmth to maintain their body temperature. At night, when it's comparatively cool, they fade to a pale color.

Moods also affect a chameleon's hue. If a chameleon is frightened, it will change colors, becoming very drab. It will turn pale when it is ill and dark when it is angry. A male who wants to mate will change color to attract a female. Rival males face off in color wars, turning brilliant hues as each tries to scare the other away. And a female chameleon may become brightly colored just before she begins to lay eggs.

How do these lizards manage their quick changes? Chameleons are able to change their body color because of special color cells, called chromatophores, in their skin. These cells contain all the color pigments that an individual chameleon has. The cells are organized in layers. The outermost layer has red and yellow pigments. The deepest layer has melanin, a dark brown pigment. In between are layers that reflect light, appearing white or blue. These layers combine to produce all the chameleon's colors.

As a chameleon responds to a situation, nerve impulses are sent to the skin.

A chameleon's large, bulging eyes are almost completely covered by scaly lids. And the lizard can look in two different directions at the same time!

The nerve impulses produce changes in the pigment cells and the reflecting layers. For example, if a chameleon sits among green leaves, the melanin may contract into a small area of each cell, allowing other colors to dominate. The combination of yellow pigment cells and the blue reflecting layer may make the lizard look bright green. If the animal moves to a dark branch, the melanin may spread out, masking the brighter colors. The chameleon changes from green to brown.

HIDDEN IN TREES

There are about 90 species of chameleons. They belong to the lizard family *Chamaeleontidae*. Most live in southern Africa or Madagascar, but a few can be found along the Mediterranean and in Asia. None are natives of the Americas—although many people incorrectly call the American anole lizard a chameleon.

Chameleons have massive heads and flat, scaly bodies. Their bulging eyes are almost completely covered by scaly lids. Some spe-

Chameleons are the masters of color changing. These amazing lizards change color primarily as a physical reaction to temperature and light conditions. In the photos below, notice how a fern placed on a chameleon's back (*left*) leaves the light-green image of its cool shadow behind after it is removed (*right*).

Chameleons are well suited to living in trees. Their feet grip branches like hands. And they can appear invisible to their prey—or to enemies—by masquerading as a harmless twig or leaf swaying gently in the breeze.

cies have horns on the head, and many have a crest along the back or under the throat. Most chameleons grow to about a foot (30 centimeters) in length. But some pygmy chameleons are only 2 inches (5 centimeters) long when they are full grown. And the largest chameleons measure nearly 2 feet (60 centimeters) from snout to tail.

Although some species of chameleons make their homes on the ground, most live in trees and bushes. They are amazingly well adapted to life in the trees. They have feet that grip like hands, with three toes pointing

When a hungry chameleon wants to dine, it catches its meal with a special weapon—its tongue. The lizard can shoot its sticky-tipped tongue forward with lightning speed and grab hold of an insect.

in one direction and two toes pointing in the opposite direction. And they are the only lizards that have gripping tails.

Looking like a harmless leaf or part of a branch, a chameleon spends most of its time just lying in wait for prey. The chameleon even looks like a leaf when it walks. Unlike other lizards, which often move quickly, the chameleon walks slowly. Its body rocks gently with each step, like a leaf being swayed by the wind.

Chameleons are so perfectly suited to tree life that they rarely venture down to the ground. Usually they climb down only to move to another tree. The females of many chameleon species also climb down to the ground to dig nests for the eggs they lay. (A few chameleon species give birth to live young.) The female covers her eggs with soil and leaves them. Young chameleons hatch months later. They are on their own from the start.

"LITTLE LIONS"

Chameleons are extremely good hunters. In fact, they have been named for their hunting skills: The word "chameleon" comes from a Greek word meaning "little lion." The chameleon has two advantages when it comes to hunting—its eyes and its tongue.

A chameleon's large, bulging eyes can look in two directions at once. One eye can look forward, while the other swivels around like a gun turret to see what's behind. This means that the lizard can check out the entire neighborhood without moving and without giving itself away. But once an insect comes into view, the chameleon focuses both eyes on it. Slowly the chameleon creeps toward its prey. Once in range, it is ready to use its special weapon—its tongue.

Fully extended, a chameleon's tongue may be longer than its body, and it can be shot forward with lightning speed. The tip is covered with a sticky substance that catches and holds its prey. Powerful muscles controlling the

Lizard Lore

▲ More than 50 different kinds of chameleons live in Madagascar, an island nation off the eastern coast of Africa. They range from the tiny dwarf chameleon, no bigger than your thumb, to Oustalet's chameleon, the world's largest at nearly 2 feet (60 centimeters).

▲ The people of Madagascar have many beliefs about the chameleons that share their homeland. For example, some people think it's unlucky to walk under a branch where a chameleon is resting. And calling someone a "chameleon" is an insult—it means the person is ugly. (In North America, people sometimes use the term "chameleon" for someone who is fickle or changeable.)

▲ Madagascar's people also have about 90 proverbs and legends about chameleons. Here are two popular proverbs: "Don't be like the chameleon parading on a rock. It acts proud, even though it isn't beautiful." "Behave like the chameleon: Look forward and observe behind."

tongue draw it back with the prey attached. The chameleon gulps down its meal. The prehistoric-looking little lizard will then quietly lie in wait until another unsuspecting victim comes along.

Chameleons face many threats. In Madagascar and other areas where they live, the forests that are their homes are being cut down. And the chameleon's fascinating ability to change color has made it popular with people—as a pet. Hundreds of thousands are taken from the wild each year, and three out of four die before they reach pet stores.

Wildlife experts are worried about these colorful lizards. Today they are working to save the wild areas where chameleons live. And some researchers have begun breeding and raising rare chameleons, so these wonderful animals won't disappear.

A dinosaur named Sue—the largest, most complete, and best-preserved skeleton of a *Tyrannosaurus rex* ever discovered—went on display at Chicago's Field Museum of Natural History in 2000.

DINO-MITE NEWS

Dinosaurs disappeared 65 million years ago, but they made plenty of news in 2000. Sue—the largest and most complete *Tyrannosaurus rex* skeleton ever discovered—went on display at the Field Museum of Natural History in Chicago in May. A month earlier, another major dino-discovery—the fossilized heart of a dinosaur named Willo—had the scientific world buzzing.

SUPER SUE: THE TITANIC *T. REX*

Visitors to the Field Museum stop in their tracks when they catch sight of Sue. Crouched and looking ready to pounce, she stands 13 feet (4 meters) tall at the hips and stretches 42 feet (13 meters) from nose to tail. Her huge jaws bristle with teeth as long as your forearm. No wonder *T. rex* ranks among the most awesome meat-eating dinosaurs!

Sue was named for Sue Hendrickson, a fossil hunter who found the skeleton in 1990. Although the museum calls the fossil "her," scientists aren't completely sure this *T. rex* was a female. They do know that Sue roamed what are today the badlands of South Dakota about 67 million years ago.

Sue's skeleton is 90 percent complete, with more than 200 fossilized bones. Her massive skull, which weighs 600 pounds (272 kilograms), was too heavy to be mounted with the rest of the skeleton. It's displayed in a case nearby, and a lightweight cast takes its place on the skeleton.

The skeleton is teaching scientists a lot about *T. rex*. For example, studies of Sue's skull show that the dinosaur's olfactory bulbs, which control the sense of smell, were as big as grapefruits. They were bigger than its cerebrum, the "thinking" part of the brain. *T. rex* probably used smell to track down prey.

Sue's stomach contained bones of a duck-billed dinosaur—a sign that she probably gulped down her prey bones and all. Her skeleton also shows battle scars and signs of disease. Scientists think she had a hard life. She may even have died in a fight with others of her kind.

Scientists hope to learn a lot more from Sue. Meanwhile, Sue will remain part of the Field Museum's permanent exhibit. Thousands of lucky museum-goers will get a chance to meet this awesome *T. rex* face to face.

WILLO'S HEART OF STONE

A dinosaur nicknamed Willo also caused quite a stir in the world of science in 2000. In April, researchers reported that the fossil remains of this dinosaur included a heart. That was amazing—no one had ever found a fossilized dinosaur heart before. Even more surprising, the heart was more like the heart of a bird or a mammal than the heart of any modern reptile.

The discovery may help answer one of the big questions about dinosaurs: Were they cold-blooded, like modern reptiles, or warm-blooded, like birds and mammals? Cold-blooded animals need warm surroundings to maintain their body temperature. They slow down and become sluggish in the cold. Warm-blooded animals maintain their body temperature on their own. They stay active in the cold.

Willo was a *Thescelosaurus,* a plant-eating dinosaur that lived around 66 million years ago. About 13 feet (4 meters) long and weighing 665 pounds (300 kilograms), Willo was the size of a small short-legged pony. It had a long tail and a snout that resembled a parrot's beak. Like Sue, Willo was found in South Dakota, in 1993. The fossil is at the North Carolina Museum of Natural Sciences in Raleigh.

Willo is exceptionally well preserved. Even so, scientists were amazed to find the grapefruit-sized heart. Most dinosaur fossils are bones. They formed slowly, as minerals replaced bone tissue. Fossils of internal organs are hardly ever found because these organs decay quickly, before minerals can replace their tissues. Scientists think that Willo may have been covered by wet sand, perhaps sediment from a river, soon after death. The sediment sealed out air, preventing decay. That allowed the heart to turn to stone.

When researchers used computerized X rays to look inside the heart, they were amazed. The heart seemed to have four chambers, like the hearts of warm-blooded animals. Also like warm-blooded animals, Willo seems to have had a single aorta. The aorta is the main artery that takes blood from the heart to the rest of the body.

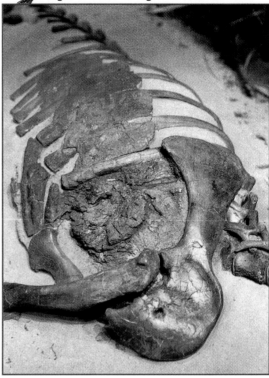

Left: A dinosaur named Willo probably looked like this. Below: The reddish-brown lump that's lodged in Willo's rib cage is its fossilized heart.

Cold-blooded animals have simpler hearts, with three chambers, and two aortas. They pump blood less efficiently. That's one reason many reptiles are sluggish. But with a four-chambered heart, Willo probably zipped around the underbrush of its prehistoric home. Speed would have helped it escape from giant meat-eating dinosaurs—like Sue.

Researchers were surprised to find that Willo may have been warm-blooded. Many scientists believe that birds descended from a group of dinosaurs called theropods. They would have expected a theropod to have had a four-chambered heart, as birds do. But Willo belonged to a completely different branch of the dinosaur family, the ornithischian branch.

Willo may change our ideas about dinosaurs. By the time this dinosaur lived, late in the Age of Reptiles, many dinosaurs may have been warm-blooded.

It isn't easy growing up in the wild. But a big hug from Mom makes everything okay for this cuddly baby monkey. Just like most other animal youngsters, it needs its parents' protection in order to survive.

HOW ANIMALS PROTECT THEIR YOUNG

Have you ever been buzzed by a songbird? If so, you've seen an animal parent in action.

The smallest bird will zoom down from a tree if it feels that its nest is in danger. With frantic shrieks and dashes, it can drive away prowling dogs and cats. Even tiny hummingbirds have made swift, dive-bombing passes at people who came too close to their nests.

This powerful urge to protect the young is found mainly among warm-blooded animals—birds and mammals. Most cold-blooded animals never see their offspring. They simply lay large numbers of eggs. Then they fly, crawl, or swim away, leaving the eggs to hatch by themselves. But there are plenty of exceptions. Some reptiles, frogs, fish, and insects will defend their helpless infants as fiercely as any mammal or bird.

Any animal can be dangerous when it's guarding its young. If approached too closely, it may attack suddenly and without warning, using its teeth, claws, horns, hoofs, or whatever weapon it has. And yet fighting is always a last resort. If given a chance, an animal parent will slip quietly away with its offspring. Whenever possible, it will keep its young out of harm's way.

SAFE AT HOME

For most animal parents, the first line of defense is a safe nursery. Baby animals have little to fear if they are tucked away in secret nooks and crannies, where enemies can't find them.

Down on the ground, a tangled clump of grass conceals the nest of a field mouse. She

made the nest quickly, weaving strands of grass into a hollow ball and then lining the ball with the softest cattail down. Inside this snug nursery, she hovers protectively over her pink, wrinkled infants.

At the edge of the woods, a skunk has hidden her babies in a hollow log. Sixty feet above the ground, a squirrel nurses her infants in the safety of a tree hole.

Even the biggest and most powerful animals hide their young. When a mother lion goes hunting, she leaves her small cubs in a sheltered cave, rock pile, or thicket. Sometimes she moves the cubs from one hiding place to another, carrying them one at a time by the scruff of the neck. After all the cubs have been taken to the new den, their mother will go back to the old one. She will sniff around carefully, as if making sure that none of her cubs has been left behind.

Wolves raise their cubs in underground dens, dug into hillsides. The small entrance hole is barely wide enough for the mother to squeeze through. Inside, a tunnel leads to the dark and secluded nursery chamber, where the wolf cares for her pups on a bare earth floor. She may have two or three other dens nearby. If the main den is disturbed, the mother will move her pups to one of her emergency dens.

Birds often seek out nesting sites that are hard to reach or hard to find. A pair of eagles might build their platform nest of sticks and twigs at the edge of an isolated cliff. In Africa, the long-legged secretary bird avoids enemies by placing its nest in the middle of a prickly thorn tree. In South America, cloud swifts nest on rocky ledges behind waterfalls. As

A mother lion may move her cubs from one hiding place to another, often carrying them in her mouth one by one to safety.

No, this red jungle fowl doesn't have eight legs. A bunch of babies are protected beneath the umbrella of Mom's feathers.

they bring food to their nestlings, they fly back and forth through a curtain of spray.

In the southeastern United States, the red-cockaded woodpecker chisels its nest in the trunk of a pine tree. Then it drills hundreds of tiny holes around the entrance to the nest. Sap oozes out of these holes. It surrounds the nest with a sticky barrier that traps insects and keeps prowling animals away.

Nests for developing eggs and young are also built by animals like cobras and alligators, by

A lamb has found the perfect hiding place: Mom! This mother and baby are mountain-dwelling Dall sheep.

certain tropical frogs and toads, and by a surprising number of fish. Other fish are called "mouthbrooders," because they offer their mouths as safe and secure nurseries. A male sea catfish swims about for weeks with a bulging mouthful of eggs the size of marbles. When the eggs hatch, the baby catfish stay put—they grow inside their father's mouth for a few more weeks, until they are big enough to take care of themselves.

DANGER SIGNALS

No matter how safe a nest or den may seem, there's always a chance that an enemy may show up at the door. When young animals are discovered and threatened, their parents must act quickly to save them.

One of the first lessons a bear cub learns is to quickly climb the nearest tree when its mother grunts sharply. If the cub hesitates, it gets cuffed. The next time mother grunts the signal to start climbing, the cub knows what to do.

Any sharp, sudden sound can be a danger signal. Monkeys bark, howl, or roar when they spot an enemy. Woodchucks whistle. Rabbits thump the ground with their hind feet. Beavers smack the water with their flat tails. The sounds differ, but the message is the same. Youngsters and grown-ups alike react instantly when they hear these sounds. They dash for cover or freeze on the spot.

Like many animals, prairie dogs have more than one danger signal. When one of them sees something suspicious, it gives a warning bark. At the sound, all prairie dogs within hearing range sit up and look around. If the bark becomes a rapid series of high-pitched whistles, it means that an eagle or hawk is overhead. And if the bark changes to a sharp yip, then the enemy is a land animal, like a coyote or fox. Now, every prairie dog scrambles into its underground burrow. The animals wait silently, then peek out to see if the enemy is still around. If all is well, they sound a loud, two-note "all-clear."

Danger signals can be silent, too. When a white-tailed deer is alarmed, it flicks up its tail. The underside of its tail is pure white—the only white patch on the deer's body. A raised tail is like a white flag that alerts all the deer in the herd.

Birds warn their young with calls and cries. When baby songbirds hear these calls, they crouch silently in their nests, making themselves as small as possible.

Young ground-nesting birds are able to run and hide when their parents sound the alarm. A mother hen screams harshly if she spots a hawk overhead. At that signal, her chicks scatter and dash for cover. But if an enemy approaches on the ground, the hen gives a different call—a loud cackling sound. Instead of running, the chicks stop in their tracks and freeze.

The chicks have a distress call of their own, a loud peeping that brings mother running to them. They peep in distress whenever they are lost, cold, or frightened.

ESCAPING FROM THE ENEMY

Baby crocodiles have a distress call, too. If they are alarmed, they croak loudly. As they sound off, their mother comes sloshing through the swamp heading toward them. She may actually take the babies in her toothy jaws and carry them to safety.

Animals of many kinds protect their young by carrying them away from danger. Monkeys leap like acrobats from tree to tree as infants cling tightly to their bellies or hips. For a baby monkey, a strong grip is as important as breathing. Dogs and cats carry youngsters the same way lions do, picking them up with their teeth by the scruff of the neck.

Squirrels use their teeth to pick up babies by the slack of the belly. A mother squirrel will carry her infants quite a distance if her nest is disturbed. She moves them one at a time, returning to the nest until all her young are safely evacuated. Each infant curls its legs and tail around its mother's neck as she races up tree trunks and runs along branches.

This mother crocodile isn't hurting her baby. Her powerful jaws can also be gentle enough to carry her young safely away from danger.

Some birds actually carry their chicks into the air when danger is near. When the ground nest of a woodcock is threatened, the mother may take off with a chick clasped firmly between her legs. Marsh hawks and chickadees hold their young in their beaks as they fly with them to safety. Red-tailed hawks carry their young in flight just as they carry captured prey—by grasping them with their claws.

Grebes swim around with their young on their backs. The chicks cling on tightly when their parent spots an enemy and crash-dives beneath the surface of the water.

Grebes are ducklike birds that swim about with one or more young on their backs. They are sometimes called "water witches" or "hell divers" because they can dive underwater and disappear in a flash. When a grebe spots an enemy, it crash-dives beneath the surface and swims underwater while the chicks on its back hang on.

Grazing animals depend on speed to escape their enemies. They live in the open and are constantly on the move as they search for new feeding grounds. Their calves and foals are born with open eyes and long legs. These young are too big to be carried, and for many there is no place to hide. A newborn calf must climb to its feet and follow its mother or lose its life.

On the plains of East Africa, it takes between five and ten minutes for a wildebeest calf to be born. Nudged by its mother, the calf struggles quickly to its wobbly legs. It runs a few steps, then falls to the ground as its legs collapse. But it gets up again and runs a few more steps. Within fifteen minutes the calf is galloping away at its mother's side. If it becomes separated from its mother in the vast herd, it may starve or be killed by an enemy.

FOOLING THE ENEMY

A ruby-throated hummingbird is an expert in the art of camouflage. She flies back and forth, adding bits of moss to the walls of her nest. By the time she is ready to lay her eggs, the nest blends perfectly with the tree that supports it. It looks like nothing more than a mossy growth on a branch.

A wild turkey scratches out a nesting hollow beneath the cover of a log or bush. She lines the nest with grass and leaves. Before going off to feed, she covers her spotted eggs with more grass and leaves. Then she flies directly into the air, leaving no tracks to reveal her camouflaged nest.

Marsh wrens build dummy nests. As the female prepares one nest for her eggs, the male dashes about the marsh and builds several decoy nests to distract attention from the real one. A mother deer takes advantage of natural camouflage when she hides her spotted fawn in a woodland thicket. White spots on the fawn's reddish-brown coat blend with sunlight and shadows filtering through the leaves. While its mother is away, the fawn lies absolutely still, like a sunspeckled bump on the forest floor. It has practically no body scent to betray its whereabouts. An enemy may pass within a few feet and never notice.

Some animals trick their enemies by luring them away from their young. A raccoon leads her cubs up the nearest tree when hunting dogs come sniffing around. Then she runs down the tree and takes off through the woods. The dogs chase her. She keeps running until she has thrown them off the trail. She then disappears among the trees and slips quietly back to her family.

Some birds act as though they are injured when an enemy approaches their young. A mother duck will flap awkwardly across a pond, as though she is trying to rise from the water and can't. But she stays one step ahead of the enemy chasing her. When she is far enough away from her ducklings, who are hiding along the shore, she flies safely into the air.

A plover performs the same act on land. She calls attention to herself by crying out and dragging a "crippled" wing. As the enemy tries to catch her, she moves farther from her nest, and then flies off in the nick of time. Many ground-nesting birds protect their chicks in this way. They can fool dogs, cats, snakes, and even people.

FIGHTING THE ENEMY

When all else fails, when helpless young are cornered and can't escape their enemies, their parents will come to their aid and fight.

A giraffe fights with her long front legs. She pushes her calf beneath her body, stands over it, and starts kicking. She aims her sharp hoofs at the enemy's head. With a single kick, she can crack open a lion's skull.

Buffalo are armed with stout, curved horns. When attacked by wolves, they form a circle around their calves. Then they lower their heads and dash forward to slash and tear at the enemy. Mountain goats use their long, slender horns as daggers. A mother doe whose kid is cornered will fight back recklessly. She can kill a marauding bear by stabbing it in the heart.

Dolphins will attack sharks that threaten their calves. One or two dolphins will swim out to attract the shark's attention. As the shark turns toward these decoys, other dolphins move in on either side. Then they charge swiftly, one after another, slamming their beaks into the shark's side and crushing its gills until it drowns.

Even the most timid animals will try to save their babies. Deer have come crashing out of the woods to kick and trample hunters who discovered their hidden fawns. Bats have been known to land on people who were carrying off their babies. Squirrels have climbed up the trousers of loggers who had taken their young from tree dens. They snatched their infants from the kidnappers' hands and dashed with them to safety.

Birds often attack enemies that are much bigger than they are. Geese will charge at people who are doing nothing more than admiring their goslings from the shore of a lake. The

When an enemy approaches, a mother deer hides her fawn in a woodland thicket. The white spots on the fawn's reddish-brown coat blend with sunlight and shadows, making the youngster look like nothing more than a bump on the forest floor.

goose and gander may join forces, beating their wings and lunging forward with menacing hisses and squawks.

They will take on any enemy that seems to threaten their goslings. Like so many animal parents, they will risk their lives so their young can live for another day.

The Venus's-flytrap is a rare carnivorous (meat-eating) plant. When an insect lands on one of its lobes, the two halves draw together and lock the insect inside.

HUNGRY PLANT...POOR ANT

Travelers in space have landed on a strange planet far from Earth. In single file, they walk warily through a jungle of unfamiliar plants with odd, twisted forms. Suddenly one of the party cries out in surprise—the tendrils of a vine have wrapped around his body and are pulling him into the brush! The others rush to help him, shouting in terror, "Man-eating plant!"

Small wonder that the characters in this make-believe scene are surprised and frightened. In nature as we usually think of it, animals eat plants—not the other way around. Plants draw nourishment from the soil and then convert it into energy with the help of sunlight, through a process called photosynthesis. Animals then get nourishment from plants. Horses and cows eat grass, for example, and you enjoy fruits and vegetables.

But did you know that right here on Earth, there are plants that turn the tables on this natural order and actually get most of their nourishment by eating animal life? It's true—but there's no need to be afraid. Most of these plants aren't large enough to devour anything much larger than a moth. A few of the largest species might manage a small frog or lizard, but even so, insects are their usual dinner.

These carnivorous (meat-eating) plants make up a very small portion of the plant life on Earth. Some of them are very rare. But others are more common—you might even find one in a bog or a swampy area near your home, because marshes are a carnivorous plant's usual habitat.

Scientists aren't sure why these plants have developed the ability to eat insects, but they have a theory. Plants must have certain nutrients, especially nitrogen, to thrive. In the marshy areas where these plants generally grow, the soil is often very poor in nutrients. But nitrogen and other nutrients are contained in the amino acids that form the proteins in animal tissues. Thus these plants may be getting the nutrients they need by trapping and digesting insects.

Of course, catching insects isn't all that easy—if you've ever tried to swat a buzzing fly, you know how difficult it can be. How does a plant, which is rooted to the ground, manage to do it? The various carnivorous plants have developed different methods, but the basic idea is the same: They lure the insect in with some sort of attractive bait, and then trap it so that it can't escape.

the sensitive hairs. If it touches one hair, nothing happens. But when it touches a second—SNAP! The lobes draw together, and their spines lock the fly inside like prison bars.

Tiny insects may be able to escape through the spines, but they have to do so quickly. In a few minutes the lobes slowly begin to press tighter and tighter together, crushing the insect. Then the plant begins to secrete digestive juices. Digestion may take anywhere from one to ten days. When the plant has finally finished its meal, the lobes open up again, ready for the next victim.

VENUS'S-FLYTRAP

The plant called Venus's-flytrap is one of the rarest of the carnivorous plants. It grows only in a few marshy spots along the coasts of North Carolina and South Carolina. Because these plants are such curiosities, people often want to dig them up and take them home. Now so few are left, conservationists are afraid the plant may die out.

The Venus's-flytrap is a small plant. It bears white flowers on a stalk about 12 inches (30 centimeters) tall. Branching out from the base of the flower stalk are leaves that may be 6 inches (15 centimeters) long. Every leaf ends in a pair of hinged lobes that face each other, like the two halves of a clamshell. (In fact, this shell-like appearance helped give the plant its name— a seashell was the symbol of the ancient Roman goddess Venus.) Each pair of lobes is rimmed with long, sharp spines; the inner surfaces of the lobes have six sensitive hairs, which tell the plant when an insect alights.

The lobes are the plant's fly-catching mechanism. They produce secretions that are very attractive to insects. When a fly or some other insect is lured by the secretions and lands on the lobes, it touches

The sundew's leaves bristle with reddish hairs, each one tipped with a blob of a sticky fluid. When an insect alights on the plant, it's trapped!

SUNDEWS

Sundews are relatives of the Venus's-flytrap; in fact, they belong to the same plant family, *Droseraceae.* There are 120 kinds of sundews. There are species on all the continents of the world, although sundews are most common in Australia and in southern Africa. The most common species in North America is the round-leaved sundew. It bears white flowers on stalks about 10 inches (25 centimeters) tall, and it has a cluster of round leaves that are about the size of small coins. (Some species of sundews have leaves

Attached to the underwater leaves of a bladderwort are tiny hollow "bladders"—which are the plant's insect traps.

that are teaspoon-shaped; still others have leaves that are 2 feet, or 60 centimeters, long.)

A sundew's leaves bristle with reddish hairs. Each hair is tipped with a blob of a sticky secretion. In the sunlight, these blobs glisten like dewdrops. When an insect is drawn to one of the leaves by the glitter, it is quickly trapped by the gluelike fluid on the hairs. Then the hairs on the edge of the leaf bend in over the unfortunate bug to make sure that it won't escape, and the leaf begins to secrete digestive juices that will break down its body tissues. When digestion is complete, the hairs unbend and begin to secrete more glittering glue.

BUTTERWORTS AND BLADDERWORTS

Butterworts grow in the swampy areas of most northern countries. They are small plants with attractive flowers—the common butterwort, which is found in North America, has violet blooms on tall stems. The plant's leaves lie close to the ground, form-

ing a cluster at the base of the flower stalk.

Like the sundews, butterworts use glue to catch their prey. The leaves are covered with a sticky secretion that draws insects to them. When the insect lands, the leaf curls up to trap it and digest it.

Although butterworts use the same trapping methods as sundews, they belong to a different plant family—*Lentibulariaceae,* the bladderwort family.

Most bladderworts are aquatic plants—they grow right in water. The common bladderwort, which is native to lakes and bogs in North America and Europe, is sometimes grown in garden ponds. It has spikes of showy yellow flowers that bloom above the water. Below the surface is the rest of the plant—a network of thin roots and stems and small, feathery leaves. Attached to the leaves are many tiny, hollow, balloon-shaped "bladders." The bladders help keep the plant afloat, and they're also the plant's insect traps.

Underwater insects and insect larvae are the bladderwort's prey. The mouth of each bladder is surrounded by sensitive hairs and covered by a trap door that will open only inward. When an insect brushes against the hairs, the walls of the bladder suddenly expand, creating suction that opens the door and pulls the insect inside. Then the door slams shut, and the insect is digested.

PITCHER PLANTS

Several species of pitcher plants grow wild in the swamps and bogs of North America. They range in height from 2 to 3 feet (60 to 90 centimeters) and carry purple or yellow flowers. And pitcher plants have yet another method of trapping their meals.

Shortly after the plant blooms each spring, it sprouts its pitchers—long tube-shaped leaves, sometimes with a flap arching over the opening at the top. The rim of each tube is streaked with color so that it resembles the petals of a flower, and it is baited with a sweet "nectar." When an insect comes to investigate and lands on the edge of the tube, it slips on the slick secretion, falls inside, and is trapped—the inner walls of the tube are covered with stiff hairs that point down, preventing the bug from crawling up and out. Gradually the insect slides deeper and deeper into the pitcher, until it falls into a pool of rainwater and digestive juices at the bottom.

Not all insects fall victim to the plant. One type of mosquito actually lives inside pitcher plants—it hovers about in a helicopter-like fashion without getting trapped in the hairs. A species of fly lays its eggs right in the trap. When the larvae hatch, they secrete enzymes that protect them from the plant's digestive juices, and they help themselves to the plant's dinner. And the larvae

A pitcher plant's tube-shaped leaves are baited with a sweet nectar—which lures unsuspecting insects inside.

of a certain type of moth can actually kill the plant. The moth larva enters the pitcher and spins a web across the opening, cutting off the plant's food supply. Then it begins to eat the plant. Finally it pupates in the withered plant, emerging as an adult moth.

But moths aren't the pitcher plant's greatest enemies—people are. Like the Venus's-flytrap, the pitcher plant has been collected because it is an oddity. And as marshes are drained to build roads and homes, the plant's habitat is being destroyed. In some areas, the plants have nearly died out, and several types are classified as endangered species. Now conservationists are working to protect these strange animal-eating plants that have successfully turned the tables on nature.

STARS OF THE SEA

There are stars in the sky. . .and stars in the ocean. Sea stars are among the most colorful and unusual ocean animals. They're found all over the world. Many kinds live in shallow waters near the coast. But some prefer the deeper ocean.

Sea stars are also known as starfish—but they aren't fish. They belong to a group of animals called echinoderms. "Echinoderm" means "spiny skinned." And sea stars are covered with little spines. Other echinoderms include sea urchins and sand dollars.

A sea star's body parts are in a balanced arrangement, with identical arms growing out from the center. This arrangement is called radial symmetry. Most sea stars have five arms. And most have five eyes—one at the tip of each arm! The eyes can sense light, but they don't give the sea star clear vision.

The sea star has hundreds of tiny tube feet on the undersides of its arms. Each foot has a tiny suction cup. The sea star uses its feet to

Sea stars come in many colors and are found all over the world. This page: Sea stars and anemones (*top*) live in tidal pools along the coast of Washington State. The blue sea star (*above*), from the coral reefs of the Solomon Islands, is dazzling. Opposite page: The candy cane star (*top left*), from the Red Sea in Egypt, is one of the most colorful sea stars. The five arms of the pincushion sea star (*top right*), from the Coral Sea off the coast of Australia, are so short and fat that they're hard to spot. The spiny sun star (*far right*) has thirteen arms.

pull itself along the ocean bottom as it hunts for food—clams and other shellfish. When it finds a tasty clam, the sea star wraps its arms around its prey and uses its suction feet to force the shell open. A sea star's mouth is in the middle of the underside of its body. When the sea star gets the shell open, it pushes its stomach through its mouth and right into the shell. The sea star digests its dinner in the shell!

Sometimes a sea otter or another hungry animal takes a bite out of a sea star. But a sea star can lose an arm—or several arms—and be no worse off. The sea star just grows new arms to replace the lost ones.

Parrots, like these masked lovebirds, have long fascinated people with their acrobatics, high intelligence, and dazzling beauty.

PARROTS: PERSONALITY PLUS

Parrots are the clowns of the bird world, a three-ring circus all in themselves. In the wild, they fly through the air in noisy flocks and clamber about like acrobats in the trees. In captivity, they are prized for their beauty and cleverness—including, sometimes, the ability to mimic human speech.

The parrots that are most familiar are the brightly colored birds often seen in pet stores. They range from common parakeets to exotic macaws and cockatoos. But these birds are just a few of the hundreds of different kinds of parrots that live in the wild. Many are rare, and some are in danger of dying out. Their popularity with people has increased their problems, since they are often captured and sold as pets.

PARROTS IN THE WILD

Parrots are found in warm regions all over the world, but they are most common in Central and South America, South Asia, the South Pacific, and Australia and New Zealand. Europe is the only continent with no native parrots, although fossil records show that parrots once lived there. One American type, the Carolina parakeet, once ranged as far north as Virginia and Ohio. But this bird is now extinct.

Parrots vary greatly in size—some are smaller than sparrows and some are as much as 3 feet (1 meter) long. Many are strikingly colored, although a few are dull green or even black. But all parrots share certain traits, the most distinctive of which is a powerful, sharply hooked beak. Some parrots can easily crack nuts with their beaks. And nearly all use their beaks as an aid in climbing, pulling themselves up tree trunks with this "third foot."

Parrots also have unusual feet. Most birds have three toes pointing forward and one toe pointing back, but parrots have two toes pointing in each direction. Their feet act like pincers, which also helps them climb. And unlike other birds, some parrots can use their feet like hands to hold food. But the odd toe configuration makes them wobble comically when they walk on the ground.

Some people believe that parrots are among the most intelligent birds. They are also highly sociable, gathering in pairs and flocks to roost and feed each day. They're noisy when they gather—their raucous calls fill the air and can be heard miles away.

While the flock is feeding, one parrot will often serve as a lookout, alerting the others with a scream if a predator approaches. Most parrots are vegetarians, eating fruits, nuts, seeds, flowers, grasses, and other plants. Many also eat insects. Parrots have fleshy tongues and appear to have a good sense of taste; they often test food before eating it.

Most parrots prefer to build their nests in cavities, such as a hole in a tree trunk. A few use burrows in the ground, and some Australian types dig nesting holes in termite mounds. Many kinds of parrots mate for life. They may breed once or twice a year, and both parents help care for the newly hatched chicks.

KINDS OF PARROTS

There are more then 300 different species (types) of parrots, and all belong to the family *Psittacidae*. Scientists have divided them into eight groups, or subfamilies:

● The **owl parrot** is in a group by itself. This bird is extremely rare—in fact, it's close to extinction. The owl parrot is unique in two ways: It's nocturnal (active at night), and it can't fly. Owl parrots are native to New Zealand. As the name suggests, their bristle-like feathers around the beak make them look more like owls than parrots.

● Another rare species, the **vulturine parrot**, takes after a different bird. With a ruff of feathers around its neck, this crow-sized parrot looks like a vulture.

● Like the owl parrot, the **kea** and its close relative the **kaka** live in New Zealand. These

Among the more than 300 species of parrots are the scarlet macaw (left), the rainbow lorikeet (*below, left*), and the pink cockatoo (*below, right*).

All parrots share certain traits. Unlike other birds, they have two toes pointing forward and two pointing back on each foot. And they have powerful hooked beaks that can easily crack hard nuts.

- The **pygmy parrots** of New Guinea live up to their name—some are no bigger than a man's thumb. The half dozen species have short, stiff tails that they use to brace themselves as they inch up and down tree trunks.
- **Cockatoos** are big birds, with large heads topped by crests of feathers. These birds can expand their crests like fans, for a spectacular display. There are sixteen different species, some white with pink or yellow crests and a few completely black. Found in Australia, New Guinea, and neighboring Pacific Ocean islands, cockatoos sometimes gather in flocks of thousands and can cause considerable damage to crops.
- **True parrots** are the largest group, with some two hundred different species found around the world. The most familiar are probably the **Amazon parrots,** square-tailed green birds that are often marked with yellow, red, or blue. True parrots also include the flashy **macaws,** long-tailed birds in hues that range from scarlet to brilliant greens, yellows, and blues. Macaws, which are found in Central and South America, are the largest parrots. And the great blue hyacinth macaw of Brazil is the largest macaw.

are large, aggressive birds with sharp beaks. The kea is unusual because it occasionally attacks sheep. But its usual diet is composed of insects and roots.

- The **lories** and **lorikeets** of Australia and the South Pacific include nearly 60 different species. They are small birds with brilliantly colored plumage, and they are among the most beautiful of all the parrots. They have relatively slender bills and use their tongues, which are rough and furry, to feed on the nectar of flowers.
- **Hanging parrots** are small birds with an unusual habit: They sleep hanging head down, like bats, from the branches of trees. (Although sleeping upside down is rare, some other parrot species like to hang head down to bathe.) Hanging parrots are native to Southeast Asia, and there are some ten species.

Parakeets are also part of the true parrot group. The most familiar parakeets belong to two Australian groups, the ground parakeets and the grass parakeets. Ground parakeets never roost in trees; they even build their nests on the ground. One of the grass parakeets, the **budgerigar,** is the familiar parakeet seen in pet stores.

Lovebirds, native to Africa, are still another kind of true parrot. These small birds earned their name from their habit of mating for life and spending much of their time cuddling up to each other. But it's likely that the birds are just preening each other, not showing true affection.

PARROTS AND PEOPLE

People have been fascinated by parrots for thousands of years, and these birds were among the earliest domesticated animals. They were brought from Asia to Europe in the time of Alexander the Great. The ancient Romans kept parrots as pets, although parrots also showed up as dinner at Roman banquets. Tame parrots were kept by Indians in South and Central America, too.

The birds' cleverness and bright colors account for some of their popularity with people. But what fascinates people most about parrots is probably their ability to mimic human speech. The African gray parrot is famous for its ability to "talk." Many other types, including Amazon parrots and even parakeets, have also been taught to repeat words and phrases. But most scientists think it's unlikely that parrots have any understanding of what they say—to parrots, the words are just sounds. Teaching a parrot to speak requires great patience because the words must be repeated over and over again.

Parakeets and lovebirds make fine pets, but larger parrots can be difficult. While many are docile, they can be noisy, unpredictable, and sometimes destructive. They can't be kept in small cages—they need room to stretch their wings. Like many other birds, parrots also carry psittacosis, a disease that can be transmitted to humans, and other diseases that can be spread to poultry. For that reason, every bird imported to the United States and Canada is inspected and held in quarantine.

Despite these difficulties, large parrots remain popular as pets. And that popularity has created other problems. Many species are becoming rare in their natural habitats. This is partly because many are captured and sold as pets, but even more because the tropical forests where they live are being destroyed as civilization advances.

Some types of parrots are bred for sale as pets. But other types are rare, and they sell for thousands of dollars in pet stores. A hyacinth macaw or a palm cockatoo, for example, can

Alex Is No Bird Brain!

Parrots are known to be smart birds. But Alex, a 23-year-old-African gray parrot, is something else! He can recognize and name 50 objects, count to six, and distinguish colors, shapes, and materials such as plastic and wood. What's more, Alex understands *concepts* such as bigger and smaller, same and different.

Alex belongs to Irene Pepperberg, a biologist at the University of Arizona who works with the parrot to explore his ability to learn and use language. Until Alex came along, most people thought that parrots could only "parrot" words. That is, they could mimic sounds but had no understanding of their meaning. But Alex knows what he says, and he says what he means.

Pepperberg's work with Alex has added fuel to the debate about animal intelligence and communication skills. When people communicate, they use words as symbols to express thoughts. Most scientists think that animals don't have abstract thoughts and aren't able to use symbols. Thus, they can't use language. But Alex's skills seem to show that at least some animals might use language.

cost as much as $6,000. It may not be possible to obtain a rare parrot at all, since many countries limit or forbid the capture and export of these birds. Still, the demand for parrots is so great that some people smuggle captured birds. The smuggled birds are often mistreated and many die. Others may be carrying disease. For these reasons, wildlife experts say that people shouldn't buy rare parrots or keep them as pets. These clever, colorful birds should be allowed to live free in the wild.

RAINING CATS AND DOGS!

Cayenne, the mother cat below, is an ordinary housecat. But **Jazz,** her male kitten, is anything but ordinary. Jazz is a rare African wildcat.

How can a housecat have a wildcat kitten? Through a laboratory method developed at the Audubon Institute, in New Orleans. The scientists there hope to use this method to help save endangered animals.

Jazz was a "test-tube" kitten. The scientists took eggs from a female African wildcat, and sperm from a male African wildcat. They used them to grow eight African wildcat embryos in an incubator for five days.

Then they froze the embryos and kept them on ice for a week. And then the embryos were thawed and placed in Cayenne's womb. Seven failed to grow—but the eighth was Jazz. Scientists say the same process could be used to save many kinds of endangered animals.

Cayenne turned out to be a good mother to her odd little kitten, who was born on November 24, 1999. "She thinks she has the ugliest baby in the world, but she takes care of it," said one of the researchers. The Audubon Zoo put Jazz on display in early 2000.

African wildcats are believed to be the ancestors of today's housecats. And when Jazz is full grown, he'll be about the size of a housecat, too. But this feisty little kitten made it clear from the start that he's all wildcat, spitting and swiping at anyone who came near.

Pajean's Wild Thang! You might expect a cat with that name to be a ferocious jungle predator. Not so. Pajean's Wild Thang is a fluffy blue and white Persian cat. Like most Persian cats, she's very gentle. Her owner, Pamela Bassett, says she's "a couch potato," "an excellent pet," and "queen of the shows." And on March 5, 2000, Pajean's Wild Thang walked away with best-in-show honors at the International Cat Show in New York City, a very important show. The judges chose her from among 1,000 other cats, representing 40 breeds.

Champion Salilyn 'N Erin's Shameless has nothing to be ashamed of. On February 15, 2000, she won the top award at the Westminster Kennel Club Dog Show, in New York City. Westminster is the top dog show in the country. So Samantha, as she's called, was the year's top dog! Samantha is a brown and white English springer spaniel. Springer spaniels belong to the sporting dog group. They are friendly, eager to please, and excellent hunters. The breed was originally developed for bird hunting. The Westminster judges chose Samantha from among 2,500 dogs, representing 156 breeds. She turned out to be quite a ham. After her victory, she kissed the camera operators who crowded around and even tried to jump in her silver trophy.

Gemma is a Persian cat from Australia. Whatever she lacks in beauty she more than makes up for in bravery. In 1998, Gemma was found stuffed in a pillowcase, in a tide pool at the beach. Her rescuers took her to the Royal Society for the Prevention of Cruelty to Animals (RSPCA) in Brisbane. She lost an eye, but she lived. Soon she was adopted by a new owner. And in May 2000 she led the Million Paws Walk in Brisbane, an event that raises money for the RSPCA. She received a special award—as the only cat brave enough to walk with 1,500 dogs!

"Every dog has its day," goes an old saying. And on April 7, 2000, **Ariel,** a 2½-year-old St. Bernard, had hers. She gave birth to 16 puppies! The litter was so big that the pups had to nurse in two shifts of eight. Ariel's owners, Gregg Howard and Renee Wendover, found homes for the pups. But for weeks, the pitter-patter of 64 puppy paws filled their Philmont, New York, home.

A dog that can drive a car—or look as if he can—would have to be a Hollywood star. **Enzo,** a 3-year-old Jack Russell terrier, made his screen debut in 2000 in the feature movie *My Dog Skip.* Based on a memoir by Willie Morris, the movie told the story of a shy and gawky boy (played by Frankie Muniz) growing up in Mississippi in the 1940's, during World War II. For his 9th birthday, he gets a puppy—Skip. Skip changes his life, helping him come out of his shell, make friends, and even learn to play football.

Enzo actually shared the role of Skip with five other Jack Russell terriers, including three puppies. But he was the dog on screen through most of the movie. Besides pretending to drive a car, he had to look sweet or fierce on cue, play baseball and football, and do all sorts of other stunts. Naturally, he and the other canine actors were given star treatment off camera, with plenty of pats between takes. They even had their own air-conditioned trailer.

Enzo was well-prepared for his challenging screen role. Animal trainer Matilde Decagney spent two months coaching the film's canine stars. And Enzo comes from a show-business family. His dad is Moose, a Jack Russell terrier who plays Eddie on the popular television sitcom *Frasier.* Moose had a scene in *My Dog Skip,* too, so father and son had a chance to work together. Near the film's end, when Skip is old, Moose stepped into the role.

SCIENCE

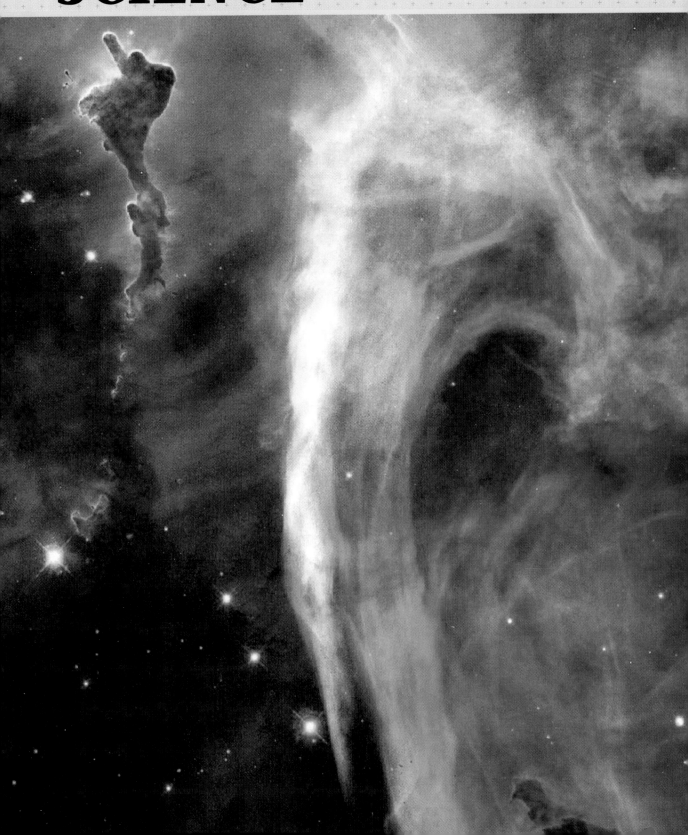

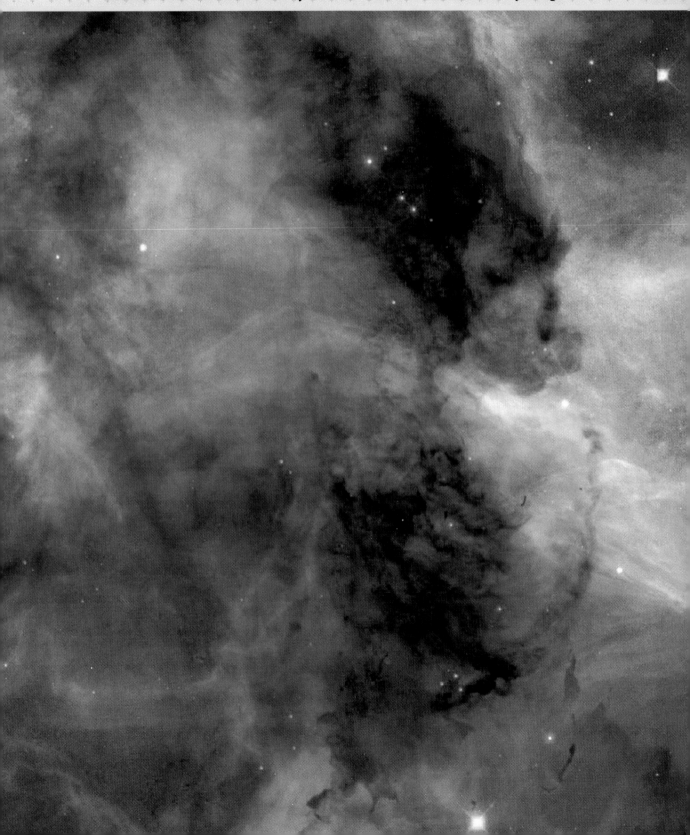

The year 2000 marked the tenth birthday of the Hubble Space Telescope (HST). Launched in 1990 , the HST orbits Earth, scanning the skies to uncover the mysteries of the universe. It has beamed back many incredible pictures, such as this view of swirling gas clouds in the Carina Nebula, 8,000 light-years from Earth. Information from the HST has helped astronomers learn that the universe may have formed as much as 12 to 14 billion years ago.

BIODIVERSITY: A TAPESTRY OF LIFE

In a distant sea, a crab scuttles across a coral reef. A parrot perches on a branch in a tropical rain forest, a splash of color against the green leaves. In the cool and quiet of a forest far to the north, a fungus slowly grows on a damp, rotting log. Zebras sprint across the African plains, escaping lions on the prowl. In a garden—perhaps yours—a spider spins a web among the flowers.

These are just a few snapshots of Earth's wonderful variety of life. The term for that variety is **biodiversity:** "bio" means life, and "diversity" is variety. And biodiversity is one of our planet's greatest treasures. All the millions of different living things—plants, animals, fungi, tiny microorganisms—form a tapestry of life. Each species, or kind of living thing, depends on others to survive.

When a species dies out, or becomes extinct, it's like pulling a thread from the tapestry. The fabric is weaker. If more threads are pulled, the fabric may tear. And right now, a lot of threads are being pulled. The Earth is going through a period of extinction, in which many species are dying out. Why is this happening? What can be done?

VARIETY PACK

When people talk about biodiversity, they're really talking about three ideas:

• **Diversity of Ecosystems:** The plants and animals that live together in a habitat, such as a tidal pool or a forest floor, are part of an ecosystem, or living community. They depend on each other and on the climate and other aspects of their habitat. Protecting a variety of ecosystems is important because individual species often aren't able to survive outside their communities.

• **Diversity of Species:** No one knows how many different kinds of plants, mammals, insects, fungi, bacteria, reptiles, birds, and other living things there are. Scientists have identified more than 1.4 million species, but they think there may be ten times that many.

• **Diversity of Genes:** Genes are hereditary material inside cells. They set traits ranging from the color of your eyes to the size of a sunflower. Genes determine what species living things belong to. They also make each member of a species slightly different from other members. Those slight differences help living things survive in a range of conditions. For example, a husky and a greyhound are both dogs. But the husky's genes give it a thick coat

Snapshots of Earth's greatest treasure—its wonderful variety of life. Above, left to right: a crab on a coral reef, a parrot in a rain forest, a fungus growing on a log, and a spider web in a garden.

that keeps it warm in the far north. The greyhound's short, sleek coat keeps it comfortable in warm climates.

It took millions of years for Earth's biodiversity to develop. For most of those years, life consisted of one-celled microbes floating in the sea. Then, about 600 million years ago, new forms of life began to blossom. Ever bigger and more complex plants and animals evolved. Over long stretches of time, millions of different species appeared.

Most of those species are no longer around. Many died out through natural causes—their food supply shrank, new predators moved in, a disease struck. It's normal for individual species to die out in these ways from time to time. In addition, Earth has seen five mass extinctions—times when many species suddenly disappeared. These events were triggered by disasters, such as asteroids striking the planet or extreme climate changes. Each time, new species developed to take the place of those that died out.

Now Earth seems to be going through a sixth mass extinction. No one knows how fast species are vanishing. But some scientists estimate that, on average, three species are dying out every hour—more than 20,000 a year. That's far more than the natural rate. And this time, there's no asteroid to blame for the increase. Species are disappearing because people are changing the planet in ways that make it hard for other living things to survive.

WHAT'S HAPPENING

There are about six billion people in the world today, and that number is expected to double in the coming century. The needs of that many people for food and shelter are putting tremendous pressure on the natural world.

People affect the natural world with just about everything they do. They cut down forests for timber and fuel and tear up prairies to make farms. They clear land and fill in wetlands to build homes, shopping centers, and roads. They dam streams to get water for irrigation and hydroelectric power. When this happens, habitats are destroyed, and wild plants and animals lose their homes.

Some ecologists (scientists who study the relationships between living things) say that people have already changed half of Earth's surface through their actions. Ecologists are especially worried about tropical rain forests. These forests are like species warehouses—they contain the greatest varieties of living things on Earth. And they are being cleared.

People upset the balance of natural ecosystems in other ways. They harvest huge numbers of fish and other ocean animals. Over-

People often upset the balance of nature. Left: A housing development in Florida's Everglades has harmed the wetland's fragile ecosystem. Above: A hillside cleared for farmland has destroyed a Malaysian rain-forest habitat.

fishing has vastly reduced the numbers of some species, such as cod and blue-fin tuna. Coral reefs are in trouble, too. Along some reefs, fishermen use cyanide to stun fish—killing the coral polyps that are the foundation of the reef ecosystem.

People also develop new varieties of plants and animals. And they take plants and animals to new parts of the world, often accidentally. Seeds can travel on clothing, for instance, and mice and insects may hitch rides on ships. In their new homes, the newcomers may crowd out native species.

Pollution from cars, factories, farms, and other sources has fouled the air, water, and land in many places, harming the wild things that live there. When the balance of an ecosystem is upset in any of these ways, the living things that are part of it begin to die.

WHY IT MATTERS

Everyone has seen pictures of adorable giant pandas, graceful cheetahs, and other beautiful animals that are endangered. Everyone worries about them. But it's just as important to worry about species that aren't so pretty—worms, insects, water plants, and other living things you might pass without noticing.

Many wild species benefit people directly. For example, they are sources of food and medicine. Many modern medicines contain ingredients from plants. Cures for cancer and other deadly diseases may be contained in rain-forest plants that have yet to be discovered. And microbes may provide new antibiotics.

Biodiversity is important for other, less obvious reasons. It's part of what keeps the web of life humming along. Since nearly every living thing depends on other living things, one extinction can lead to many more.

Diversity helps living things survive stress. For example, a swamp is filled with plant and animal life. Some animals eat the plants, and other animals prey on the plant eaters. If a drought strikes and the swamp starts to dry up, the plants will be stressed. If there are many kinds of plants, some will probably be tough enough to survive. Then some animals will survive, too. But if there are only a few plant species, they may all die. Then the animals that depend on them will also be gone. The swamp ecosystem will "crash."

Even the most humble living things play important roles in the web of life. Worms and microbes enrich the soil. Insects pollinate flowers, so that seeds and fruits can form. Without their help, plants couldn't grow. And all the living things that depend on plants—including people—would be in trouble.

WHAT'S BEING DONE

Around the world, many people are working to protect endangered plants and animals. The United States has a strong law, the Endan-

What You Can Do

Here are five steps you can take to protect the variety of life on Earth.

Protect Habitats. Let a corner of your yard become a habitat for wild plants and animals such as insects and birds. Help clean up and maintain habitats in parks and other places.

Let Wildlife Be. Enjoy wild animals and plants by watching them. Leave them in their natural setting—don't take them home.

Don't Let Pets Roam. Cats and dogs are predators. In the United States, cats kill an estimated 4.4 million songbirds a day.

Reduce, Reuse, Recycle. Buy only what you need. Reuse items—wear your brother's outgrown sweater.

Recycle Paper, Plastic, and Metal. You'll save energy and other resources, and you'll help protect the environment.

Volunteer. Find out what groups are working to protect biodiversity in your area.

Peregrine falcons are one of the many endangered species that people have helped save through captive-breeding programs and other protective measures.

gered Species Act. More than 160 other countries have also taken steps to protect endangered species. Through captive-breeding programs and other steps, some species have been helped. Gray wolves, peregrine falcons, whooping cranes, California condors, and bald eagles are among those whose numbers have increased.

Protecting individual species isn't enough, however. To keep the variety of life, people need to preserve habitats and protect entire ecosystems. Efforts to save or even restore wildlife habitats are under way in many places. Preserves have been set up in rain forests and in the last sections of the old growth forests that once covered much of the U.S. Pacific Northwest. Sections of prairie have been restored in the Midwest. The United States government also has programs that encourage private landowners to protect wildlife habitats.

So far these steps haven't been enough to stem the loss of habitats and species. Conservation is especially difficult in poor countries, where people are worried about their own survival. Even if poor people are concerned about other species, they may need to cut timber and clear land for farming. Poor countries often need financial help to encourage conservation.

Ecologists say that people everywhere need to do more to protect biodiversity. After all, people are part of the tapestry of life, too. If the fabric tears, *we* are affected.

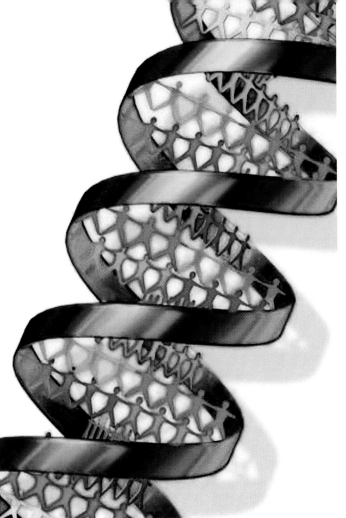

Scientists have completed a working draft of the human genome—the blueprint of a human being.

THE HUMAN GENOME: A BLUEPRINT OF YOU

In June 2000, scientists made a historic announcement. They had completed a working draft of the human genome—the blueprint of a human being. It was an amazing achievement, one that was compared to putting astronauts on the moon.

To assemble the draft, scientists catalogued tens of thousands of genes, tiny bits of hereditary material inside body cells. But what made their announcement so exciting was its promise for the future. Knowledge of the human genome may lead to new treatments for disease and other benefits. Still, there are questions about how this knowledge should be used.

GENES AND GENOME

All living things have genes. Genes determine whether an animal is a dog or a cat or a human being. They also determine individual traits, such as eye color and hair color. Genes do this by instructing cells to make proteins that build body tissues and control the way the body works. Some genes even affect behavior.

In all animals that reproduce sexually, offspring get half their genes from each parent. The offspring are unique—they have some traits of both parents, but they aren't identical to either. You have tens of thousands of genes, arranged in strings called chromosomes inside your cells. Together, all those genes make up your genome. Because you are unique, your genome isn't exactly the same as anyone else's. But the differences between any two people's genes are so small that scientists speak of "the human genome" as if there were only one.

The human genome is the body's master plan, a complete set of instructions for making a human being. It holds the keys to all the different types of body cells, and it guides the body through the life cycle, from growth to aging. Although every cell has a full copy of the genome, each type of cell uses only part of it. That why muscle cells and brain cells are built differently and work differently.

A CHEMICAL CODE

Individual genes are really segments of a chemical, DNA (deoxyribonucleic acid). In the chromosomes, double strands of DNA coil tightly around each other. Linking the double strands are compounds called nucleotide bases, arranged in pairs. A diagram of DNA looks like a twisted ladder, with pairs of bases forming the rungs between the strands. There are four bases: adenine, thymine, guanine, and cytosine. They are represented by the letters A, T, G, and C. Repeated over and over in various combinations, they form a set of coded instructions. It's the precise order of A's, T's, G's, and C's that makes you who you are.

There are more than 3 billion bases in the human genome. The letters that represent them would fill 200 books, each 1,000 pages long. It would take more than nine years to read all the letters out loud. Thus, compiling all the information that went into the rough draft of the genome was a huge effort, and many scientists took part.

A publicly funded program called the Human Genome Project drew on the work of top laboratories in the United States, Britain, and other countries. A private laboratory, Celera Genomics, worked on the genome separately. Using the latest laboratory and computer technology, the scientists mapped, or sequenced, about 85 percent of the 3 billion bases. The public and private labs completed their drafts at the same time. Within a few years, scientists hope to have a complete picture of the genome. It will take longer to understand what every gene does. But researchers are already focusing on the potential uses of this new knowledge.

BENEFITS AND RISKS

Knowledge of the genome holds great promise for medicine. Flawed genes cause or contribute to many diseases. With a blueprint of the genome, researchers will be able to nail down the role of genes in illnesses from diabetes to high blood pressure to cancer. They'll be able to develop treatments that counter genetic flaws. Someday personal genetic information will help doctors predict the diseases that an individual may develop. They'll be able to design personalized treatments to prevent the diseases and keep that individual healthy. Ultimately, doctors may be able to correct genetic flaws before birth.

As people learn more about the way genes work, it may even be possible to slow the aging process. Because genes are handed down from one generation to the next, researchers will be able to use genetic information to trace human history and evolution. And knowledge of the genome will give people a clearer sense

of their place in nature and their relationship to other living things. Researchers already know that people are closer to other animals, genetically, than you might think. The differences that separate animal species account for only a small percentage of the genome.

But knowledge of the genome is also raising questions. For example, should people have personal genetic testing? If so, who should have access to test results? Insurance companies might refuse to give health insurance—or even jobs—to people who might one day develop a certain genetic disease.

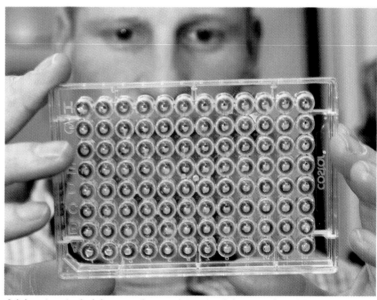

A laboratory technician examines a plate containing samples of DNA.

Who "owns" genes and other pieces of DNA? Drug manufacturers are eager to develop treatments based on genetic information. Commercial genetics labs want to charge fees for letting the drug manufacturers use the information. They would like to patent the sections of DNA they decode, so that others can't use them without paying.

Many scientists say that information about the genome should be public knowledge. After all, the genome belongs to all of us. Spreading information about it will encourage discoveries that improve life for people everywhere.

Demonstrators in Chicago, Illinois, protest against genetically modified (GM) foods. While many people believe that GM foods offer the promise of increased nutrition and other benefits, some worry that they are really "Frankenstein foods" that pose a danger to health and the environment.

FRANKENFOODS?

Corn plants that make their own pest-killing chemicals. A tomato that won't get mushy when it ripens. A pig that produces low-fat pork chops. Fish that grow to market size in half the usual time.

These amazing plants and animals don't exist in nature. But all either have been or are being developed by scientists, through a process called genetic modification. In genetic modification (or genetic engineering), scientists change the genes, or hereditary material, of a plant or animal. Changing the genes allows them to improve the taste and look of foods; to make plants naturally resistant to pests, disease, and frost; and to increase crop yields and livestock production.

Genetically modified (GM) plants and animals seem like a farmer's dream come true. Some GM crops—including tomatoes, corn, soy, and potatoes—are already widely grown and eaten in America. There may very well be GM corn in your tortilla chips, and GM soy in your fast-food shake!

But to some people, genetic modification seems more like a nightmare than a dream come true. They worry that GM foods will turn out to be "Frankenstein foods"—lab-created monsters that may harm health and the environment. As yet, there's no evidence that GM foods do any harm. Still, people are taking a close look at this new way of producing foods.

BETTER CROPS AND LIVESTOCK

Farmers have always tried to develop better crops and livestock. In the past, this was done through selective breeding. Farmers saved seeds from plants with the best characteristics for planting the following year. They bred only their best cows, sheep, and pigs. In this way, over generations, they slowly developed crops and livestock that had the traits they wanted. Unwanted traits were weeded out.

Selective breeding wasn't very scientific at first. But in the late 1800's, Gregor Mendel, an Austrian monk, saw that there was a predictable pattern to how certain traits were passed from parents to offspring. His work led to the science of genetics—the study of inheritance. Scientists learned that traits are passed from parents to offspring by genes—bits of the chemical deoxyribonucleic acid (DNA). The genes are arranged in strings called chromosomes in the nuclei of living cells. They occur in pairs, and one of each pair is contributed by each parent.

DNA provides the blueprint for every living thing, from apple trees to zebras. Different genes determine how a plant or animal grows and how it functions as a living organism. The texture of a tomato and the size of a salmon are determined, at least in part, by genes. Some characteristics are controlled by a single pair of genes, but often several pairs of genes work together to control one trait.

Understanding how genes control various characteristics has allowed scientists to help farmers improve selective breeding programs. But selective breeding is a slow process. It often takes a decade or more to develop a new variety of a crop such as corn, and even longer for livestock.

Genetic modification is a shortcut. Instead of breeding for certain traits and hoping that the genes for those traits will show up in the offspring, scientists insert the genes for the traits they want right into the chromosomes of the plant or animal.

JUGGLING GENES

In genetic modification, scientists remove a gene for a desired trait—such as rapid growth or resistance to disease—from one organism and then place it in another. The methods that allow them to do this have been around only since the 1980's. They are still being improved. But already genetic modification is widely used. Dozens of GM crops have been approved for sale in the United States. In 1999, American farmers planted 62 million acres (250 million hectares) of GM soybeans, potatoes, corn, cotton, and other crops.

Many of these crops have been altered to better resist pests and diseases. A GM corn plant, for example, produces its own pesticide. Some plants have been altered to resist weed-killing chemicals. This allows farmers to spray their fields with weed killers without harming

Using genetic modification, scientists have produced larger mice (*left,* shown next to a normal-sized mouse) and new varieties of larger corn (*below*).

their crops. Still other GM crops, such as the Flavr Savr tomato, have longer shelf life and better flavor.

Hundreds more GM crops are being developed by "biotech" companies, using genes that are "borrowed" from bacteria, viruses, insects, and even animals. Higher yields, better nutrition, and the ability to grow in harsh conditions are some of the goals. Some crops are even being modified to produce vaccines and medicines. One day, instead of an injection, vaccinations may be delivered in a delicious meal!

GM animals are also in the works. Researchers have developed Atlantic salmon that make extra growth hormone, so they grow to market size twice as fast as normal salmon. They're working on oysters that can withstand viruses, and the pig that produces a leaner pork chop. Also on the way is "Enviropig," a pig whose feces contain less phosphorus than usual and thus are less harmful to the environment.

THE GM DEBATE

Genetic modification seems to be a wonderful shortcut that may bring lots of benefits. But many people are worried about this new way of producing food. GM foods aren't well accepted in Europe, and the countries of the European Union have been slow to approve the sale of these foods. That has hurt some U.S. food exports. Now Americans, too, are taking a second look at GM foods. They are asking two important questions:

● Are GM foods safe for people to eat? The U.S. Food and Drug Administration (FDA) says yes. The GM foods approved for sale in the United States don't differ in safety from their non-GM counterparts, according to the agency. But critics of genetic modification say that more research should be done on these new foods.

● Are GM foods safe for the environment? So far, they haven't caused major problems. And many GM crops are good for the environment. When farmers plant pest-resistant GM crops, for instance, they don't have to use lots of pesticides. But some people are concerned that GM plants and animals may cause accidental harm. For example, one research study showed that pollen from a corn plant that had been genetically modified to produce its own pesticide could kill monarch butterflies along with corn pests.

What's Organic?

You're in the produce section of your local supermarket, looking at the apples. One bin is filled with Red Delicious apples. Next to it is another bin of Red Delicious, but these are labeled "organic." They look the same. What's the difference?

In March 2000, the U.S. Department of Agriculture proposed new rules for labeling products "100-percent organic." Organic (unprocessed) foods—such as apples, lettuce, sweet peppers and so on—must be grown without pesticides, synthetic fertilizers, or added hormones. They can't be bombarded with radiation (irradiated) to kill microbes. And they can't be genetically modified. Organic products are usually more expensive than standard products. Are they better? That's for you to decide. But the new rules ensure that you'll know what the label means.

Protestors dress as butterflies to draw attention to concerns that GM corn could be harmful to the monarch butterfly. Scientists have developed corn that is naturally resistant to insect pests. But some researchers found that when monarch caterpillars ate pollen from these corn plants, they died or didn't develop properly. However, a study by the Environmental Protection Agency found that GM corn posed little danger to monarchs.

Critics of genetic modification say there are other risks. What if GM plants or animals interbreed with wild varieties? Would their modified genes harm the wild species? Could a gene for producing pesticides or medicine be transferred to wild plants, so they produce these substances? Nothing like that has happened yet, but some people worry that it might.

ENSURING SAFETY

The concerns about GM foods have led governments and others to take steps that, they hope, will limit the risks. In January 2000, delegates from more than 130 nations adopted a treaty regulating GM products. The treaty allows countries to bar imports of GM seeds, microbes, animals, and crops that they think could pose a threat. Some people would like to see even stronger restrictions.

Meanwhile, food companies are responding to consumer worries. They are cutting back on purchases of GM foods. The fast-food chain McDonald's and snack-food maker Frito-Lay are among companies that have limited their use of GM foods. Although GM crops are often less expensive, these companies worry that customers may not want them. With less demand for GM crops, U.S. farmers cut back a bit on the amounts of these crops planted in 2000.

The U.S. government is also responding to concerns about GM foods. In May 2000, the government proposed new rules for these foods. The rules would require biotech companies to notify the FDA at least four months before releasing new GM ingredients for food and animal feed. Companies would also have to provide the agency with their research data. The FDA would review the safety data and post its conclusions on the Internet. The agency would also set standards for labeling products made with GM ingredients, although such labeling would be voluntary.

Genetic modification holds lots of promise. GM crops that are more nutritious and pest- and drought-resistant could even help end hunger and malnutrition in the world's poor nations. But for now, genetic modification isn't likely to replace older ways of improving crops and livestock. It's a new tool, but one that many scientists agree should be used very carefully.

Has an alien spaceship landed on Earth? No, it's the spectacular new Hayden Planetarium in New York City. And in the planetarium's Space Theater, visitors can take a breathtaking virtual-reality trip through the universe.

THE HAYDEN PLANETARIUM: A TRIP THROUGH THE UNIVERSE

Hear the rumbling of the sun's explosive fires. Journey into a black hole. See the most distant object ever detected in the universe. You can do that and more at the new Hayden Planetarium, which opened on February 19, 2000, at the American Museum of Natural History in New York City. For years, the old Hayden Planetarium was one of the museum's top attractions. But the old sky show was nothing compared to this one.

The planetarium is the main attraction at the museum's new Frederick Phineas & Sandra Priest Rose Center for Earth and Space. The Rose Center is housed in an addition that looks like something from science fiction—almost as if an alien spaceship had landed in Manhattan. The striking design features a giant globe that seems to float inside a huge glass-walled cube. Almost an acre of glass covers the outside of the cube, which is 95 feet (29 meters) tall. But the real excitement is inside.

THE HAYDEN SPHERE

The new Hayden Planetarium is inside the globe, which is called the Hayden Sphere. The high-tech Space Theater takes up the top half of the globe. Here visitors take off on a breathtaking virtual-reality trip.

Passport to the Universe is the name of the Space Theater's first show. It's narrated by actor Tom Hanks. Aboard a "spaceship" that seems to hurtle through space, viewers fly past Jupiter, through the Milky Way, and on to the farthest reaches of the universe. They zoom in for close views of planets and star fields. At the edge of the universe, they plunge into a black hole—and come out back on Earth.

The theater's powerful supercomputer and a one-of-a-kind projector produce three-dimensional images that are accurate as well as spectacular. The show draws on a database of more than 100,000 stars and computer models of 2 billion more. The setup is so good that scientists plan to use it for research after hours.

The planetarium's Big Bang Theater takes up the bottom half of the globe. Here visitors go back to the beginning of time and space for a dramatic laser show that re-creates the first moments of the universe. Actress Jodie Foster narrates this presentation. Visitors gather over a round screen, set in a well in the floor. Lasers, lighting effects, and an explosive sound track put them on the scene when the universe was born in a burst of radiant energy. They watch as the universe expands, cools, and takes the shape we know.

A WALK THROUGH SPACE AND TIME

Leaving the globe, visitors follow the Cosmic Pathway, a 360-foot-long (110 meters) spiral ramp that chronicles the history of the universe—all 13 billion years of it. At its start, visitors can measure the length of their stride and determine how many millions of years pass with each step. An average stride covers 75 million years.

Fascinating artifacts are displayed along the pathway—diamond dust formed before the solar system took shape; a meteorite that dates from the birth of the solar system; fossils of some of the earliest living things. The Age of Dinosaurs, which ended 65 million years ago,

is less than 2 feet (.6 meter) from the end of the Cosmic Pathway. The time of people on Earth takes up a space no wider than a strand of hair!

Another walkway hugs the glass walls of the Rose Center. Called the Scales of the Universe, this long path illustrates the vast range of sizes in the universe. Visitors learn about the relative sizes of galaxies, stars, planets, and atoms. Enormous models of planets, stars, and galaxies hang from the ceiling, over visitors' heads.

There's still more to see and do at the Rose Center. The Cullman Hall of the Universe, on the lower level, has permanent exhibits. It's divided into four zones that focus on the creation of planets, stars, galaxies, and the uni-

The Cosmic Pathway traces the entire history of the universe.

verse. The exhibits use 3-D images, interactive computers, and videos. There's even a mini-theater where visitors can experience the inside of a black hole. And they can step on digital scales to discover what they would weigh on Saturn, Jupiter, a neutron star, the sun, and other celestial bodies where gravity is stronger or weaker than it is on Earth.

Millions of visitors flocked to the center in its first year. They made it clear that the Rose Center is an out-of-this-world experience!

Is there something about lefties that draws them to the presidency? Former President Bill Clinton (*above, left*), former Vice President Al Gore (*above*), and former President George Bush (*left*) are all left-handed.

SCORE ONE FOR THE LEFTY!

There's "left-wing" politics and "right-wing" politics. But the best term for politics in the presidential election of 2000 may be "left-handed." As the campaigns got under way, four presidential hopefuls were "lefties"—even though nine out of ten Americans are right-handed! The lefties were Vice President Al Gore, former Senator Bill Bradley, Senator John McCain, and publisher Steve Forbes. George W. Bush, who won the race, is right-handed. But his father, former president George Bush, is a lefty. So is former president Bill Clinton.

Is this a coincidence, or is there something about lefties that draws them to the presi-dency? Researchers can't say. They do know that lefties are a select group. Most people use one side of the body—eye, hand, foot—more than the other. But usually, it's the right side. Certainly most people write and do almost everything best with the right hand. But nature isn't 100-percent consistent, and about one out of ten people does things better with the left hand. And two thirds of those are male.

WHAT DETERMINES HANDEDNESS?

"Handedness"—the preference for doing things with one hand instead of the other hand—is a trait that's inherited, or passed down from parents to children. Interestingly, many animals also show preferences for using one side of the body over the other. If you teach a dog to "shake hands" by offering a paw, for example, it will probably want to give you the same paw each time. But unlike people, animals are about evenly divided between preference for the left and the right.

The actual causes of right-handedness and left-handedness are found in the brain. Your brain is divided into two sides, or hemi-

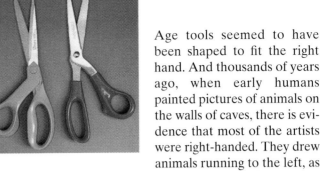

Left-handed scissors (orange) are shown next to a pair of right-handed scissors (red). Notice that the top blades are reversed.

spheres—right and left. The right hemisphere controls the left side of your body, and the left hemisphere controls the right side of your body. In most people, the left hemisphere is dominant. But in others, the right hemisphere is dominant. They're left-handed.

Although the two sides of the brain look nearly identical, researchers think the hemispheres work in slightly different ways. The left side of the brain is generally thought to be best at logical tasks, while the right is believed to be more creative. Does that mean that lefties have more creative ability? Researchers can't say. Some studies show a higher proportion of lefties among artists and intellectuals, but the link between handedness and creativity or other abilities isn't clear.

Lefties Notebook

Researchers have discovered that the brain of a lefty isn't as specialized as the brain of a right-hander. Many lefties seem to use more of the brain for certain tasks than right-handers do. For example, almost all right-handers use the left side to process language. But about half of lefties use both sides of the brain for language processing. This may explain why many left-handed children grow up to become ambidextrous adults—they can use both hands equally well for many tasks.

A SINISTER GROUP

As far back as history can be traced, most people have been right-handed. Even Stone Age tools seemed to have been shaped to fit the right hand. And thousands of years ago, when early humans painted pictures of animals on the walls of caves, there is evidence that most of the artists were right-handed. They drew animals running to the left, as right-handed people would draw them.

Since the right hand has always been stronger for most people, people in cultures all over the world—from Africa to Asia, from Europe to America—seem to have concluded that right is somehow better than left. Thus lefties have been viewed with suspicion and fear, and they have faced a great deal of prejudice over the years.

That prejudice is reflected in language. A "left-handed compliment," for example, is one that isn't sincere. And think about the word "sinister." It means evil or inauspicious—but it comes from *sinister,* the Latin word for left. By contrast, our word "dexterous," which

Lefties Keyboard

means clever or skillful, comes from the Latin *dexter,* the word for right. In other languages, terms for left have also picked up unpleasant meanings. The French word for left, *gauche,* also means tactless and clumsy. In Italian *mancino* also means crooked or maimed. The Spanish *zurdo* also means malicious. And the word "left" itself comes from an old Anglo-Saxon word, *lefte,* that meant weak or worthless.

Lefties Ruler

LEFTIES RULE!

Famous Lefties Throughout History

Left-handers have made their mark in many fields. Here are a few of the most famous:

Military Might: Famous left-handed generals include Alexander the Great and Julius Caesar. The French Emperor Napoleon was also a lefty. In his day, armies usually attacked from the left. Napoleon liked to attack from the right, to gain an element of surprise.

Kings and Queens: Louis XVI, who was beheaded in 1793 during the French Revolution, was left-handed. Another lefty, Queen Victoria of England (above), had better luck. She ruled for 63 years, longer than any other British monarch, and was greatly loved by her subjects. Britain is likely to have another left-handed monarch in the future: Prince William (right), who is in line for the throne after his father, Prince Charles.

Sports: Left-handed baseball greats include Babe Ruth (left), Lou Gehrig, Ty Cobb, Sandy Koufax, and current stars such as Dave Wells and Ken Griffey, Jr. Left-handed tennis players like Martina Navratilova, Jimmy Connors, and

The beliefs reflected in these words persisted well into the 20th century. In the early 1900's, some authorities even asserted that left-handedness was linked to dishonesty, criminal behavior, and insanity. There is, of course, no evidence whatsoever of this. Still, many people decided that left-handedness should be eliminated. Parents of left-handed children went to great pains to teach them to use the right hand. Sometimes they even tied the child's left hand down to force the change!

These efforts ended after researchers found that forcing a person to switch hands could lead to stuttering and other disorders. But many lefties were still taught to write with the left hand in an unnatural position, so that the writing would have the slant of right-handed script.

PROBLEMS FOR LEFTIES

Today lefties can be lefties—no one tries to force them to use the right hand. But that doesn't mean left-handed people don't have problems getting along in our right-handed world. For most lefties, life is a series of adjustments. Zippers, jar tops, can openers, corkscrews, most common tools, and countless other everyday objects are made to be used by right-handers. Lefties have to struggle with scissors designed to be held with the right hand. Most desk-and-chair combinations are built for right-handers; lefties have to twist their bodies around if they're unlucky enough to sit at one.

Right-handed parents struggle to teach left-handed children to tie their shoes. Left-

Monica Seles (left), put a wicked spin on the ball. Larry Bird and David Robinson are on the list of basketball lefties.

Art: Lefties can claim some of the greatest names in art, including modern painters such as Pablo Picasso and Paul Klee and Renaissance artists such as Raphael, Michelangelo, and Leonardo da Vinci (right)—who not only painted with his left hand but wrote backwards, in mirror script.

Entertainment: Famous left-handed entertainers include actors and actresses past (Charlie Chaplin, Greta Garbo, Marilyn Monroe, Sid Caesar) and present (Tom Cruise, Whoopi Goldberg, Goldie Hawn, Luke Perry, Robert Redford, Julia Roberts, Jerry Seinfeld, Bruce Willis). TV hosts Jay Leno and Oprah Winfrey (below, left) are lefties.

Music: Composers Ludwig van Beethoven and Cole Porter were left-handed. Left-handed singers and musicians include Judy Garland, Phil Collins, Jimi Hendrix, and two of the four Beatles—Paul McCartney and Ringo Starr.

Notoriety: The list of famous lefties includes many people who wound up on the wrong side of the law. Billy the Kid, the Boston Strangler, and Jack the Ripper were all reported to be left-handed.

U.S. Politics: A number of left-handers have been president—James Garfield, Herbert Hoover, Harry Truman, Gerald Ford, George Bush, and Bill Clinton.

handed knitters must figure out instructions written for right-handers. Left-handed violinists face special problems. In an orchestra, all violinists must use the bow with the right hand. A left-handed violinist seated next to a right-handed one could turn a concert into a sword fight!

In some sports, lefties need special gear. In golf they need clubs with heads that face the opposite way of those for right-handers. And in baseball they need mitts that fit on their right hands. But that hasn't stopped lefties from excelling. "Southpaws" (left-handed pitchers) are highly valued. And about half the hitters in the Baseball Hall of Fame are lefties. They seem to have an easier time hitting pitches from right-handers.

The list of successful lefties is long. It includes artists, military leaders, kings and queens, entertainers, musicians, and others. Maybe lefties succeed because they learn how to overcome obstacles! And today lefties are proud to belong to a select group. There are even organizations especially for lefties. One of the largest is Lefthanders International, based in Topeka, Kansas. It publishes a newsletter, "Lefthander Magazine," and sponsors an annual International Left-Handers Day (August 13).

There are stores and catalogs that cater to lefties, selling everything from rulers and notebooks to watches and guitars—all designed to be used with the left hand. So if you're a lefty, you've got a lot going for you!

Operators of Russia's Mission Control Center monitor the crew of the *International Space Station* as they float inside the living module, in November. The two cosmonauts and one astronaut joined hands in a show of unity.

SPACE BRIEFS

The start of the new millennium marked the beginning of a new era in space exploration, as people began living far beyond Earth's atmosphere in the *International Space Station.* The year 2000 also brought fascinating new knowledge about other bodies in the universe, from asteroids and planets in our solar system to objects thousands of light-years away.

LIVING IN SPACE

History was made on November 2, 2000, when the first permanent crew entered the *International Space Station* (*ISS*) to begin a four-month stay. The Expedition 1 crew, carried aloft in a Russian *Soyuz* spacecraft, consisted of American William Shepherd and Russians Yuri Gidzenko and Sergei Krikalev. Shepherd and Krikalev had trained for almost five years for the mission. Gidzenko joined them in 1997; he had previously spent almost six months in space aboard *Mir,* the first long-term space station, launched by Russia (then the Soviet Union) in 1987.

The three men got right to work in the *ISS,* activating equipment and unpacking supplies left behind by earlier missions. They started a water system and an oxygen generator, charged electric tools, hooked up the station's toilet, and checked communication links. And it wasn't long before they received their first visitors: On December 2, the space shuttle *Endeavour* and its five-member crew arrived and attached an enormous set of solar wings to the *ISS.* The blue and gold wings will provide additional power to the station.

The *ISS,* which orbits Earth some 240 miles (386 kilometers) above the planet's surface, is being built in stages by sixteen countries: the United States, Russia, Canada, Japan, and members of the European Space Agency. The first section to be placed in orbit was *Zarya* (which means "sunrise" in Russian), carried aloft by a Russian rocket in November 1998; it contains the space station's power and communications systems. A few weeks later, *Endeavour* took up the second module, *Unity,* which is the main point of attachment for additional modules. In July 2000, the *Zvezda* ("star") module from Russia—the third major module and the *ISS*'s command and living section—was launched and linked to the other modules. And in October, the shuttle *Discovery* attached a docking port and a huge framework (to hold the solar wings). Other shuttle missions during 2000 delivered tons of supplies.

When the Expedition 1 crew took up residence, the *ISS* weighed 81 tons and consisted of the three pressurized modules plus other segments. By the time additional modules and segments are attached and the *ISS* is completed—which is scheduled to occur in 2006—it will weigh 480 tons. Its solar panels will stretch over an area equal to two football fields. The interior will be about the size of a 747 jumbo jet. It will have six laboratories— more room for research than any previous spacecraft. Transport and assembly of the more than 100 components will require more than 40 space flights during the coming years, plus a combination of human space walks and robot technologies.

Space scientists anticipate that the *ISS* will be occupied continuously for at least fifteen years, with each crew of up to seven members spending three to six months there. Crew members will carry out long-term research in biology, chemistry, physics, ecology, and medicine. Some experiments will take place inside the *ISS*, while others will take place outside. It's hoped that this work will lead to a better understanding of how the space environment affects living things, and also to the development of new technologies and products— such as more effective drugs, better weather forecasting systems, stronger metals, and more powerful computer chips.

Crew-return vehicles will always be attached to the *ISS*, to ensure the safe return of crew members in the event of an emergency. Currently, a *Soyuz* capsule is present to provide the means of evacuation. But work is underway on development of a new

The 100th Space Shuttle Flight

When the space shuttle *Discovery* rocketed into orbit on October 11, 2000, it marked the start of the 100th shuttle flight. The United States launched the first space shuttle, *Columbia,* in 1981. Until that time, spacecraft were used only once. But *Columbia* returned safely to Earth, ready to be refitted and flown again.

Today the United States has a fleet of four shuttles: *Discovery, Columbia, Atlantis, and Endeavour.* A fifth shuttle, *Challenger,* flew nine missions but exploded on January 28, 1986, killing all seven astronauts aboard.

The shuttles are still the only craft that can fly mission after mission in space. They're launched like rockets. They orbit like spacecraft. And they glide back to Earth to land like airplanes.

In their first 100 flights, the shuttles carried 596 people and about three million pounds of cargo into space. Shuttle astronauts have retrieved satellites and repaired the Hubble Space Telescope. They have

launched unmanned probes that traveled to Jupiter, Venus, and the sun. They have also carried out hundreds of studies of the effects of space travel on plants, animals, and people. During the year 2000, the shuttle fleet's main job was building the *International Space Station.*

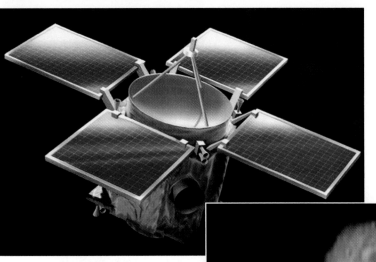

NEAR captures Eros's heart! The U.S. spacecraft NEAR (*drawing above*) snapped this picture of Eros (*right*) just in time for its Valentine's Day date with the asteroid, which was named for the Greek god of love. The picture reveals a heart-shaped depression about 3 miles (5 kilometers) long on the asteroid.

emergency crew-return ship. With the code name of X-38, this vehicle will also have a second function. Crew members will be able to use it to fly away from the *ISS,* perhaps to pick up a satellite and carry it back to the space station. "It's sort of a pickup truck for the space station," said the project manager.

SOLAR SYSTEM NEWS

High-powered instruments aboard spacecraft plus powerful telescopes in mountaintop observatories here on Earth gathered valuable information about the bodies that make up the solar system.

Encounter with Eros. For the first time ever, a spacecraft entered an orbit around an asteroid. On February 14, 2000, the U.S. spacecraft NEAR (Near Earth Asteroid Rendezvous) slowed down so that it could be captured by the weak gravity of Eros, a potato-shaped rock about 21 miles (34 kilometers) long and 8 miles (13 kilometers) wide. During the following weeks, NEAR's orbit slowly descended closer and closer toward Eros—a tricky maneuver because Eros is irregularly shaped and tumbles end over end. In late October, NEAR photographed Eros from a distance of only 4 miles (6.4 kilometers).

Tens of thousands of asteroids circle the sun, most of them in a region between Mars and Jupiter. Eros, however, is the largest of the near-Earth asteroids, which pass much closer to Earth. It was 160 million miles (257 million kilometers) away when NEAR began circling it. Eros is pitted with craters and grooves, and covered with numerous boulders and a deep layer of dust. NEAR's sensors detected minerals such as magnesium, aluminum, iron, and calcium in the asteroid.

A Double Asteroid. Astronomers used to believe that asteroids were lone objects. But in 1993 the U.S. spacecraft *Galileo* found a tiny moon orbiting the asteroid Ida. A second asteroid moon was observed in 1999, and a third in 2000. Even more surprising was the 2000 discovery that the asteroid Antiope isn't one body but two— the first known double asteroid. The two

The *Mars Global Surveyor* spacecraft photographed this gully on Mars. Was it carved by flowing water? Do the gullies indicate that liquid water may be near the surface?

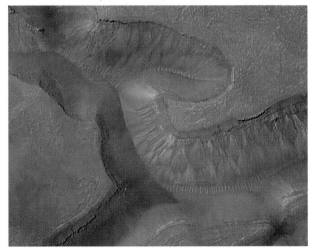

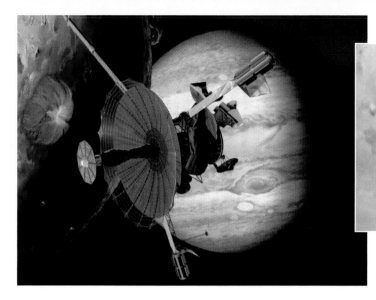

Left: A drawing of *Galileo* as it approaches Jupiter's moon Io. Above: *Galileo* took this image of a volcano on Io. You can see the brightly glowing lava.

bodies, which are separated by about 100 miles (160 kilometers), orbit each other as they orbit the sun.

Water on Mars? Scientists have long believed that the planet Mars is a vast red desert. But now they aren't so sure. Photos beamed back to Earth by the *Mars Global Surveyor* spacecraft, which has orbited Mars since 1997, show gullies and other features that could have been carved by flowing water. The gullies seem to have been formed in the recent past,

perhaps by flash floods. This suggests that Mars could have liquid water, maybe in underground reservoirs just below the surface. The idea of water on Mars is exciting because life as we know it depends on water. If Mars has liquid water near its surface, life could have developed there—and perhaps still exists.

Moon Leader. Which planet has the most moons? For a long time Saturn led with 18, followed by Uranus with 17. Then in 1999 four

The Dog-Bone Asteroid

For the first time, scientists working with the U.S. National Aeronautics and Space Administration (NASA) made radar images of one of the asteroids orbiting the sun between Mars and Jupiter. And they discovered something odd: The asteroid, 216 Kleopatra, looks like a giant dog bone! It is 135 miles (217 kilometers) long and about 58 miles (93 kilometers) wide. Its surface is covered with many small holes, rather like our moon's surface.

Kleopatra's existence has been known for more than 100 years. To learn its shape, NASA astronomers bounced radar signals off the asteroid to obtain radar echoes. Then they used computers to decode the echoes and change them into images.

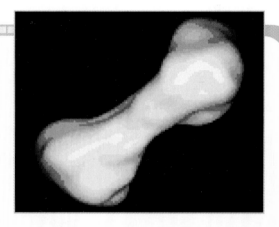

Scientists suspect that Kleopatra originally was two separate asteroids and that one of two things happened. The asteroids may have collided violently and become one. Or the two asteroids may have orbited around each other for such a long period of time that the space between them eventually filled in with debris from other collisions.

additional moons were discovered around Uranus, giving it 21. . .and the lead. But in 2000, astronomers using an Earth-based telescope reported finding four new moons of Saturn, all smaller than 30 miles (50 kilometers) across. Like the 1999 Uranus discoveries, the new Saturn moons are irregular satellites. That is, they are far from their planet and are believed to have been captured into orbit after the planet formed. Regular moons are closer to their planet and are thought to have formed from the same cloud of dust and gas that formed the planet.

Jupiter. The *Galileo* spacecraft has turned up many fascinating facts about Jupiter and its moons since it began orbiting the planet in 1995. In 2000, *Galileo* found an unusually pure cloud of ammonia ice on Jupiter—the first cloud of ammonia ice ever seen, although Jupiter is known to contain ammonia gas.

In January 2000, *Galileo* zoomed close to the surface of Jupiter's moon Europa to study magnetic disturbances. Scientists think these disturbances show that Europa contains a shell of electrically conducting material—such as a salty, liquid ocean. This is exciting because liquid water might support life.

Flybys of the moon Io—the solar system's most volcanically active body—detected extremely high temperatures inside some of its volcanoes. The volcano Pele, for example, had internal temperatures of about 2,700°F (1,500°C), much higher than found in Earth volcanoes.

In October, the U.S. spacecraft *Cassini* approached Jupiter on its way to its ultimate destination, Saturn. Images of Jupiter taken by *Cassini* will be used to study the planet's atmosphere and surface features such as the Great Red Spot, a storm as wide as two Earths and more than 300 years old.

Earth Snapshot. During an eleven-day mission in February, the crew of *Endeavour* bombarded Earth with radar signals. The signals bounced back to two antennas on the shuttle, one on the mast and one in the cargo bay. Data from the two antennas was used to produce the most detailed maps ever created of our planet.

Endeavour mapped almost 80 percent of Earth's landforms at least twice. Multiple images are needed to create precise and detailed maps. The mission even mapped places hidden by clouds, because radar can "see" through clouds. Besides landforms, the radar showed soil types, plant cover, and water.

The information produced by the mission will be used in many ways. Scientists will use it to study flooding, erosion, climate change, and other patterns and changes on Earth. Businesses may use it to find better locations for cell phone towers and other structures.

Left: This partially computer-generated picture shows how the space shuttle *Endeavour* bombarded Earth with radar signals to produce the most detailed maps ever created of our planet. Above: This radar image shows an area of the Andes Mountains in Ecuador.

Happy Birthday, Hubble!

On April 24, 2000, astronomers celebrated the tenth anniversary of the launch of the Hubble Space Telescope into orbit around Earth. This complex scientific instrument has a huge mirror that collects visible light from distant objects, as well as instruments that make infrared and ultraviolet observations. It has given us the clearest view yet of outer space.

Hubble has revolutionized astronomers' understanding of the universe. It showed that the universe probably formed 12 to 14 billion years ago. It provided pictures of young galaxies, formed within a billion years of the birth of the universe. It found brown dwarf stars, places where new stars are being born, and fragments of exploding stars. It gathered evidence that supermassive black holes are common in the center of galaxies.

Closer to home, Hubble's most dramatic pictures of events within our solar system

The Hubble Space Telescope (*above*) took this dazzling image (*left*) of a dying, sunlike star that scientists have nicknamed the Eskimo Nebula.

came in 1994, when it documented the collision of Comet Shoemaker-Levy and Jupiter. Shuttle missions visited Hubble in 1993, 1997, and 1999 to repair damage, replace worn parts, and install new instruments. It is expected that Hubble will continue to provide a front-row seat to the spectacular happenings in the universe for another ten years.

Everyone from hikers to the military will benefit from having more-detailed and more-accurate maps.

OUT IN THE UNIVERSE

Beyond our solar system lies vast numbers of stars and other matter. Their tremendous distances from Earth make these objects difficult to observe. Nevertheless, every year astronomers add to their knowledge of the cosmos.

Extrasolar Planets. The first planet known to orbit a star other than the sun was discovered in 1995. By late 2000, such extrasolar planets had been found around more than 40 stars. These planets cannot actually be seen, even by the most powerful telescopes. Astronomers know they are there because the stars that the planets are orbiting wobble—and astronomers can detect that wobble with telescopes.

The wobbling is caused by the enormous gravitational pull of the planets, which tug the stars first one way and then the other. By analyzing these effects, scientists can determine the size and orbits of the planets. All extrasolar planets found so far are huge hot balls of gas, at least as big as Jupiter or Saturn.

In 2000, astronomers announced the discovery of eighteen planet-sized gas balls in the constellation Orion, about 1,500 light-years from Earth. Unlike other known extrasolar planets, these objects weren't associated with a star. They appeared to be wandering through space like orphans. Since they lack a central star, they weren't formed like the planets in our solar system. In fact, it's debatable if they should be called planets, since the definition of a planet is "a round object that goes around a star."

JENNY TESAR
Author, *Global Warming*

RHYTHMS OF LIFE

Life is made up of rhythms. Animals sleep and wake according to set patterns. Flowers open and close their petals at certain times of the day. Birds migrate, and some animals hibernate, as the seasons change.

These are biological rhythms—activities that are regularly repeated or that fluctuate in time with changes in the environment. Even single-celled organisms have daily rhythms. And in people, hundreds of rhythms have been detected, from changes in blood pressure and body temperature to levels of alertness. In fact, biological rhythms are so widespread among plants and animals that a new branch of science has evolved: chronobiology, the study of biological rhythms (from *chrono*, which means "time," and *biology*, the "study of life.")

This new science asks important questions: How do these rhythmic changes affect living things? What purpose do they serve? And what causes them?

RHYTHMS FOR SURVIVAL

Biological rhythms serve an important purpose: They help plants and animals survive. Take the fiddler crab, which lives at the edge of the sea. The crab's activities are timed precisely to the 12.4-hour cycle of the tides. During low tide, the little creature scurries around the beach to feed. But just before the tide comes in, it digs a safe burrow. Fiddler crabs also change color during the day—their legs are darkest at midday and paler at night. The color change may help regulate their temperature or hide them from predators.

Daily rhythms such as this are called circadian rhythms, from the Latin words *circa* ("about") and *dies* ("day"). Many plants have circadian rhythms. Flowers open at certain times to attract certain pollinators—bees, birds, and butterflies during the day; moths and bats at night. The leaves of many plants curl or droop in "sleep" at night and perk up at dawn to catch sunlight, which the plants use to make food.

Annual rhythms, too, aid survival. The breeding cycles of birds and many animals are keyed to the seasons—newborn animals have a better chance of surviving if they're born in warm months. Ground squirrels and other animals that hibernate save energy during winter,

when temperatures are cold and food is scarce. And many birds fly south for the winter.

These and many other biological rhythms seem to be linked to outside factors, such as light, temperature, and ocean tides. But scientists have learned that these external factors can't, by themselves, explain the rhythms of life.

INTERNAL OR EXTERNAL?

The first clue came in 1729, when the French astronomer Jean Jacques d'Ortous de Mairan conducted an experiment with a mimosa plant. This type of plant opens its leaves each morning and closes them at night. De Mairan put his mimosa in a dark cellar. And he found that the leaves followed the same schedule—with no clues to the time of day.

Later scientists found that many biological rhythms are maintained when external factors such as changes in light and temperature are eliminated. Fiddler crabs, for example, keep up their cycles even when they're kept in constant light or darkness, in a laboratory that's far from the tides. Hibernating animals also keep to their cycles in the lab, without the changes in temperature and length of day that mark the change in seasons.

Scientists who kept migrating birds in cages under artificial light found that this rhythm, too, was maintained without external cues. As winter approached, the birds grew restless and perched on the south sides of the cages. In spring, they preferred northern perches.

Experiments such as these convinced many scientists that internal clocks play a major role in governing biological rhythms. But some scientists believed that there might be still other external factors that the experiments couldn't account for—factors such as changes in Earth's magnetic field or in atmospheric radiation.

To rule out those factors, scientists conducted an experiment in space. They sent aloft glass tubes of a fungus that produces spores at set intervals. In most of the tubes, the rhythm of spore production continued even when the spacecraft was beyond the range of the Earth's atmosphere and magnetic field. That was strong evidence that at least some biological rhythms are set by internal clocks.

A CELLULAR CLOCK

How do these internal clocks operate? One theory is that animals have a "time center." The pineal gland and a tiny section of the brain called the suprachiasmatic nucleus play a role in mammals. But fiddler crabs, plants, one-celled organisms, and many other living things don't have these organs. It seems that some biorhythms are controlled by individual cells—that every living cell has a tiny clock.

Researchers have discovered how this cellular clock works. Cells produce what might be called "clock proteins." These clock proteins steadily build up inside the cell. When they reach a certain concentration, they bond into pairs. The paired proteins have a distinct shape, and they cause the cell to switch off production of new clock proteins. Then, gradually, the paired proteins break down and disappear. And the cell once again begins to make clock proteins.

Cells of all kinds of living things, from fungi to mammals, show this cycle. The cycle takes 22 to 26 hours to complete—roughly the length of a day. It keeps running even when cells are kept in the lab, away from changes in light and temperature.

External factors, however, do play a part in biological rhythms. Most scientists now agree that internal clocks work best when combined with cues from the environment. In nature, changes in light and temperature act to reset the clocks and keep them running on time. And some rhythms are more affected by external factors than others. While some flowers seem to run on internal clocks, others won't open unless external conditions are right.

But the theory of internal clocks explains some biological rhythms that seem to be unrelated to the environment, including rhythms that run over periods much longer than a year. Most species of bamboo, for example, bloom every 15 years. One species blooms every 120 years—and all members of the species bloom at the same time, everywhere in the world.

YOU'VE GOT RHYTHM

"Early to bed and early to rise makes a man healthy, wealthy, and wise." That famous saying may have scientific truth behind it. Where people are concerned, biological rhythms affect many aspects of life, from moods to how well your body uses medicine to fight disease.

Some people are "larks" who rise early and go to bed early. Others are "owls" who have trouble getting up in the morning but stay up late at night. If you're an owl, you may be sleepy during the day and have trouble in school as a result. People who travel across time zones by jet suffer "jet lag" because the schedule in the new time zone doesn't fit their normal rhythm.

Researchers have shown that bright light can help people "reset" their internal clocks by as much as three hours. Depending on when it's applied, light can set the clock ahead or back. People don't even have to see the light for this to happen. In one experiment, researchers shined light on the backs of people's knees for three-hour periods and found that their biorhythms had changed!

Light has also been shown to help people who suffer the winter blues. Wintertime depression, called seasonal affective disorder (SAD), seems to be linked to seasonal rhythms. As scientists learn more about natural rhythms, they will likely discover more ways in which these fascinating patterns affect our lives.

Floral Clocks

Some flowers open and close their petals with such regularity that you can almost set your watch by them. In fact, flowers might *become* your watch—if you plant a clock garden.

The idea of a garden that keeps time isn't new. In the 1700's, the Swedish botanist Carolus Linnaeus noticed that certain flowers opened and closed at set times of the day, regardless of the weather. He used his observations to develop a floral clock, choosing for each daylight hour a plant that would open or close its blooms at that time. A person could tell the time simply by glancing at the garden to see which flowers were open.

Flower clocks aren't as precise as mechanical clocks and watches. The exact opening and closing times of the blooms can vary with the weather and the location of the garden. But a floral clock is a fun and unusual addition to any garden. By adding night-blooming plants, you can even extend the time-keeping hours past daylight. Here are some plants that you might include, with their approximate opening and closing times:

Morning
- 5:00—Tawny daylily, morning glory, blue flax open
- 6:00—Sundrop, waterlily open
- 8:00—Mouse-ear hawkweed, portulaca (moss rose) open
- 9:00—Lesser celandine opens
- 11:00—Star of Bethlehem opens

Afternoon
- 12:00—Passionflower opens; morning glory closes
- 1:00—Mouse-ear hawkweed closes
- 2:00—Blue flax closes
- 3:00—Prickly pear cactus opens
- 4:00—Portulaca closes
- 5:00—American starflower opens

Evening
- 6:00—Evening primrose, catchfly open
- 7:00—Iceland poppy closes
- 8:00—Tawny daylily closes
- 10:00—Moonflower opens
- 12:00—Night-blooming cactus opens

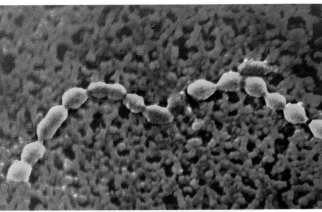

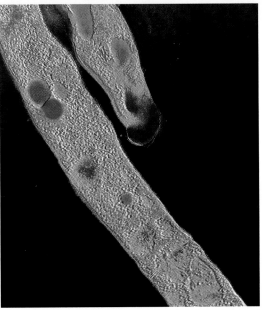

Clockwise from left: Staphylococcus, streptococcus, and tuberculosis are three of the most common disease-causing bacteria that have become increasingly resistant to standard antibiotics (*opposite page*).

BATTLE OF THE BUGS

You have an awful sore throat, but you're not worried. A trip to the doctor will soon have you feeling better. The doctor will prescribe medicine, probably an antibiotic to wipe out disease-causing bacteria. In a couple of days, your sore throat will be history—or so you hope.

But what if the medicine your doctor prescribes doesn't work? What if the bacteria in your throat are tougher than the medicine and able to resist it? A few years ago, such worries would have been dismissed as silly. No longer.

In June 2000, the World Health Organization (WHO) reported on a growing problem: drug-resistant microbes (microscopic organisms such as bacteria and molds). Drug resistance has made it much harder to treat bacterial illnesses ranging from ear infections to tuberculosis. Antibiotics that once knocked these infections out now fail in many cases. And health officials are calling on doctors and patients alike to join the fight against drug-resistant "bugs."

WONDER DRUGS

Just 100 years ago, something as simple as a small cut might turn out to be deadly. Bacteria would infect the cut, multiply, and spread unchecked. Then scientists found new weapons—antibiotics—to fight bacteria. And they found them in the microbe world. Antibiotics are natural substances produced by bacteria and molds to destroy other microbes.

Penicillin, the first widely used antibiotic, was discovered by accident in 1928. Alexander Fleming, a Scottish scientist, was growing bacterial cultures. One of the cultures was contaminated by bread mold—and the mold killed the bacteria. Fleming isolated the substance produced by the mold and named it penicillin. Penicillin was used to treat wounded soldiers in World War II. After the war, it became widely used.

Before long, many other antibiotics were developed. They were hailed as wonder drugs because they cured deadly infections such as tuberculosis, pneumonia, meningitis, and typhoid fever. Would science at last win the war against disease? It wasn't to be. By the late 1960's, new strains of bacteria were appearing—strains that could resist antibiotics.

HOW RESISTANCE DEVELOPS

Bacteria grow resistant to antibiotics as a result of changes in their genetic makeup. Bacteria often mutate, or undergo slight changes in their genes. Sometimes the change helps the bacteria—by making them better able to survive antibiotics.

Resistant strains of bacteria develop through natural selection. Here's how it works: When a patient takes an antibiotic to fight disease, the drug doesn't kill all the disease-causing bacteria at once. The weakest bacteria die first, and the most resistant are the last to go. If the drug doesn't do a thorough job, some of the strongest bacteria survive. They multiply, and all their offspring are just as resistant to the antibiotic as they are.

If that scenario is repeated, each generation of bacteria will be more resistant than the last. And bacteria can also pass genes from one to another. So genes that make one type of bacteria resistant to a drug can be passed along to another type of bacteria.

Not all bacteria are harmful. There are harmless and even helpful bacteria in your body right now. Some of them help to digest your food. But if those harmless bacteria develop a resistance to antibiotics, they may one day pass that resistance to harmful bacteria.

Drug resistance occurs naturally, but people have added to the problem:

Misuse. Sometimes people start an antibiotic, feel better, and stop the medication too soon. In poor nations, people often buy only as many pills as they can afford—and that may not be enough to kill all the bacteria. Either way, resistant bacteria may survive and multiply.

Overuse. Antibiotics are often given unnecessarily. For example, antibiotics don't work against colds and other diseases caused by viruses. But a doctor may prescribe antibiotics anyway, just to make sure a bacterial infection won't take hold. By some estimates, more than 30 percent of the antibiotics prescribed in the United States are unnecessary.

Use in Livestock. Farmers and ranchers feed antibiotics to chickens, cattle, and other farm animals as part of their regular diet. This helps the animals grow fast. But it also creates resistant bacteria—and it's possible for that resistance to "jump" into bacteria that can cause disease in humans.

FIGHTING BACK

Scientists have tried to defeat drug-resistant bacteria with new antibiotics. But bacteria have become resistant to those drugs, too. There are some "superbugs" that can resist multiple antibiotics. Now, while scientists continue to develop new drugs, they recognize that more is needed. In its report, the World Health Organization urged these steps:

● Make vaccinations more widely available, to prevent infection.

● Educate people about using medicine wisely.

● Reduce the use of drugs for livestock.

● Help poor nations get needed antibiotics. You can help, too:

● Don't pressure your doctor to prescribe antibiotics. These drugs should only be taken to fight specific diseases.

● Follow directions when your doctor does prescribe antibiotics. Take all the medication—don't save pills for a future illness.

● Wash your hands thoroughly, and keep dishes and household surfaces clean. This will help avoid infection. But avoid using antibacterial soaps and germ-killing household cleansers. Health officials say that these products are rarely necessary, and their growing use is helping to create resistant bacteria.

By following these steps, people can help win the battle of the bugs.

EARTH WATCH

Earth's climate affects all living things. That fact was underscored in 2000, as possible climate changes caused growing concern. The year also brought many reminders of the close ties between people and the natural environment.

Polar Meltdown? In the summer of 2000, tourists aboard a Russian icebreaker were startled to find a patch of open water at the normally ice-covered North Pole. Scientists say summertime gaps in the polar ice pack aren't unusual. But researchers who have studied the Arctic climate say the region may be warmer now than at any time in the past 400 years. And measurements taken by submarines show that about 40 percent of the ice cap has melted away since 1958. At the opposite end of the world, in Antarctica, ice is melting too.

The polar warm-up is part of a worldwide climate trend called global warming. Earth's climate has gone through many cycles of warming and cooling. But most scientists agree that this current warming doesn't fit any natural cycle. They say people are largely responsible for the trend. When people use gasoline, oil, coal, and other fossil fuels, carbon dioxide and other gases are released into the air. These gases act like the glass in a greenhouse, trapping heat from the sun. This "greenhouse effect" causes the atmosphere to warm.

The effects of global warming are being seen first at the poles, researchers say. Everything from wildlife to ocean currents is being affected. In the Far North, glaciers are melting. So is the permafrost, a frozen layer that lies just below the ground surface. Sinkholes and swamps are appearing in land that was once firm, swallowing entire sections of forest. In Hudson Bay, sea ice forms later and breaks up earlier, giving polar bears fewer weeks to roam the ice hunting for seals. The bears are thinner and have fewer cubs than they did just 20 years ago.

So far, few other parts of the world have seen any serious problems as a result of this climate change. Most Americans didn't seem to mind that the winter of 1999–2000 was the warmest one on record for the United States—and the third in a row to set records for warmth. But climate experts say that many areas may see big changes in years to come.

In a report released late in 2000, a United Nations scientific panel predicted that average temperatures may rise 2.7°F to almost 11°F (1°C to 3.5°C) in the next 100 years. That could have wide effects. Melting polar ice could release so much water that sea levels would rise, flooding coastal areas. Tropical diseases might increase. Forests and other wildlife habitats might be damaged, too.

In 1997 the United States and more than 100 other countries signed the Kyoto Protocol—an agreement aimed at reducing greenhouse gases. But most of the countries (including the United States) haven't ratified the treaty, so it hasn't taken effect. The countries haven't been able to agree on how to cut the levels of gases they produce. Negotiators met in November 2000 to try to firm up the agreement, but failed to reach a consensus.

A Hole in the Sky. You can't see it, but there's a hole in the sky. It's the "ozone hole"—a thinning of a special layer in the blanket of air that surrounds Earth. In 2000 the hole was getting bigger, and that had scientists worried.

Ozone is a gas found high in the atmosphere. The ozone layer is very important because it screens out a lot of ultraviolet (UV) radiation from the sun. Too much UV radiation can be harmful, causing health problems such as skin cancer and damage to crops.

But the ozone layer has been getting thinner and thinner since the 1970's. And in the 1980's, scientists first spotted the ozone hole, an area of drastic thinning over Antarctica. Since then, the ozone hole has formed there each year in September and October (spring in Antarctica). During 2000, it reached its peak earlier than ever. And it was bigger than ever. The hole covered 17.1 million square miles (27.5 million square kilometers)—an area greater than all of North America!

People have already taken some steps to protect the ozone layer. In the 1970's, scientists discovered that pollution was damaging the layer. The main culprits were chemicals called chlorofluorocarbons, or CFC's. When CFC's enter the air, they float high up in the atmosphere. There they destroy ozone. CFC's were used in refrigerators, air conditioners, aerosol cans, and solvents. Out of concern for the ozone layer, industries and governments have taken steps to end their use.

CFC's last a long time, so CFC's released in the past are still in the atmosphere. Even so, scientists were surprised by the size of the ozone hole in 2000. What was causing the hole to grow? Some scientists thought that global warming might be playing a role. The atmosphere is a complex system, and climate change might be speeding up the action of CFC's on ozone.

Wildfires in the West. The summer of 2000 brought one of the worst wildfire seasons in 50 years to the western United States. In forests throughout the West, hot,

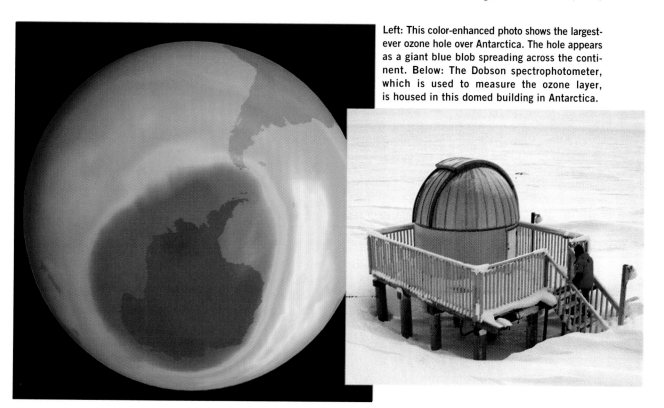

Left: This color-enhanced photo shows the largest-ever ozone hole over Antarctica. The hole appears as a giant blue blob spreading across the continent. Below: The Dobson spectrophotometer, which is used to measure the ozone layer, is housed in this domed building in Antarctica.

dry, windy weather fanned flames started by lightning or other causes.

By early September, the fires had burned more than 6.3 million acres (2.5 million hectares)—an area larger than the state of Vermont. That was nearly double the average for the date, and the fire season was far from over. More than 65 large wildfires were raging in a dozen states. Some of the worst fires were in Montana and Idaho. About 25,000 firefighters were on the job across the region.

Besides the hot, dry weather, forest management was also blamed for the raging fires. Wildfires are natural events in the West. For centuries, many small fires broke out in the forests there every year. The fires mostly burned out before they reached the size of this year's big blazes. But since 1900, people have stepped in to put out most forest fires. At the same time, big trees have been cut for timber. The result is that the forests have changed. They are crammed with dense brush and small trees—ideal fuel for big wildfires.

Since 1995 the U.S. government has tried to correct the problem, by thinning forests and

The worst wildfire season in 50 years brought devastating blazes to the western United States. Residents were grateful to the 25,000 firefighters who battled the flames.

sometimes by setting controlled fires. The idea is to take away the buildup of brush that would help a big fire get out of control. But these steps were too little and too late to prevent the fires of 2000. And they actually helped to cause one of the year's worst fires.

That fire forced more than 25,000 people to flee Los Alamos, New Mexico, and nearby areas in May. It started with a "controlled burn" in Bandelier National Monument, a wilderness area near Los Alamos. Park officials set the blaze to burn off brush and deadwood. But strong winds sent the flames racing through dry canyons toward Los Alamos. Firefighters couldn't stop it. On May 10, the entire town was ordered evacuated. The fire destroyed more than 200 homes and threatened the Los Alamos National Laboratory, a U.S. government center for nuclear weapons research.

The wildfire moved on, and finally calmer winds and lower temperatures helped firefighters get the upper hand. Meanwhile, Los Alamos slowly came back to life. And the government began an investigation into the setting of the fire.

De-oiled African penguins *(above)* make their way back to the sea after volunteers *(right)* helped to clean them. The birds had been coated with fuel oil from a ship that sank off the coast of South Africa.

Penguin Rescue! Nearly 1,000 volunteers pitched in to save thousands of African penguins from an environmental disaster in 2000. The penguin rescue was the largest effort of this kind ever attempted. And it was a great success.

The disaster started when a ship called the *Treasure* sank off the tip of South Africa in June. The ship released tons of fuel oil into the ocean, creating a giant oil slick that washed up on Robben Island and Dassen Island. These islands are home to about 60,000 African penguins, about a third of the total world population of the birds. The African penguin is also known as the jackass penguin because it makes a donkey-like braying noise. A hundred years ago, there were about 1.5 million of these birds. Today there are only 150,000 to 180,000.

The oil spill left thousands of African penguins coated with gooey oil. With oiled feathers, they couldn't stay warm or swim to catch food. So volunteers, knowing the birds would die without help, went into action.

Some 43,000 penguins were evacuated from Dassen and Robben islands. Those that were

oil free—about 20,000—were trucked to Port Elizabeth, almost 500 miles (805 kilometers) down the coast. There they were set free and allowed to swim home.

The first of the group returned to Robben Island about two weeks later, giving workers time to clean up the oil spill. Meanwhile, about 23,000 oil-soaked penguins were taken to centers in and around Cape Town. There volunteers fed them by hand. As soon as the penguins were strong enough, they were de-oiled—scrubbed and rinsed until their black and white feathers sparkled. Clean at last, the penguins were set free in their home territory. They waddled into the water without a backward glance, clearly happy to be home.

Mysterious lights flicker and glow in the night sky. These breath-taking celestial displays, known as auroras, are caused by storms on the sun. During 2000, an increase in solar storms caused auroras to appear over much wider areas than normal.

AURORAS: MYSTERIOUS SKY SHOWS

An eerie greenish glow appears in the night sky. The glow spreads, and the sky explodes in shimmering streamers and bands of light. Bursts of white, green, blue, and red pulsate and flicker high over Earth. Then the colors grow pale, and the light fades. The show is over.

This amazing natural fireworks display is an aurora. Auroras appear regularly around Earth's North Pole and South Pole. In the Northern Hemisphere, the eerie glow is called the *aurora borealis,* or northern lights. The South Pole version is the *aurora australis,* or southern lights.

The auroras are rarely sighted in other parts of the world. But in 2000, many more people had a chance to see these amazing lights. Chances of seeing auroras will be good through

2001. The reason is a burst of storms on the sun. Solar storms cause the auroras. And when solar storms increase, the auroras appear over much wider areas than they usually do.

FIRES IN THE AIR

In ancient times, people thought the auroras were omens or signs of supernatural events. Old manuscripts describe the northern lights as "fires in the air," spirit horsemen galloping through the sky, or torchlight flickering on angels' wings. To the Inuit, who live in the Arctic, the northern lights were the spirits of people who had died violent deaths. Other people thought the strange glow might be caused by ice particles high in Earth's atmosphere.

Richard Carrington, an English astronomer, was the first to make the connection between the auroras and the sun. In 1859, he observed a solar flare—a huge burst of hot gas ejected from the sun. Two nights later, the northern lights glowed over much of Europe. Carrington believed the events were linked. But it took other scientists many years to figure out exactly how solar activity produces the auroras.

Today scientists know that solar flares and similar eruptions send huge amounts of matter hurtling from the sun into space. This matter breaks up to form the "solar wind"—a stream of charged particles, or plasma. As the solar wind rushes past Earth, it strikes Earth's magnetic field.

The magnetic field is like an invisible shield around our planet. Most of the charged particles bounce off it. But some of the particles are trapped and are funneled toward the polar regions, where the magnetic field bends in toward Earth. The particles are pulled into the thin upper atmosphere. There they strike atoms of various gases, such as oxygen and nitrogen, producing the glowing colors and dancing lights of the auroras.

The auroras usually appear around Earth's magnetic poles. In fact, they're nearly always present around the poles—although they can't always be seen from the ground. The northern and southern auroras mirror each other exactly. Viewed from space, they look like rings of fire around the poles. The displays form high above the clouds, at altitudes of 60 to 600 miles (96 to 966 kilometers). The bands of light may stretch hundreds of miles high.

When they're seen from the ground, the lights may appear in arcs, streamers, veils, rays, beads, waves, curtains, or other shapes. They may waver, flicker, pulsate, or burst across the sky. Green is the most common color. But blue, purple, red, yellow, and even

Auroras are created as Earth is bombarded by charged particles from the sun.

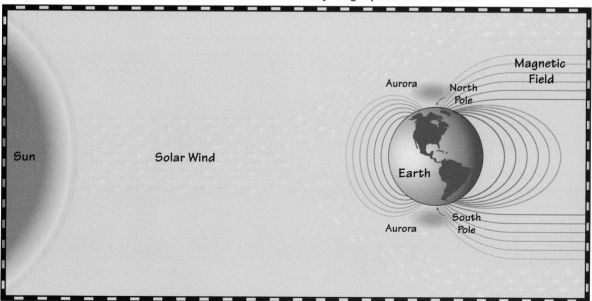

Auroras usually appear over Earth's magnetic poles. When an aurora is photographed from space, like this one was, it looks like a ring of fire around the pole.

pink lights may appear. The color depends on which gases are struck by the solar wind and how high in the atmosphere the aurora forms. Some people report hearing crackling or hissing noises as the light show plays. No one knows what causes the noises.

A RARE SIGHT

Most people never get a chance to see these mysterious natural fireworks. Perhaps under 5 percent of people have actually seen the auroras. Most of the lucky few live in northern regions, such as Alaska and northern Canada. During winter, people who live in the Arctic may see the northern lights almost every night. But the Arctic is horribly cold in winter, and very few people live there. No one lives around the South Pole, apart from scientists at research stations in Antarctica.

But every so often, events on the sun give more people a chance to see the show. The sun's storminess waxes and wanes in a cycle that lasts roughly eleven years. Scientists chart this activity by observing sunspots, cool spots on the sun's surface that are somehow linked to the cycle. As sunspots increase, so do bright patches known as faculae, solar flares, and other disturbances that send matter shooting into space. The increase in solar disturbances causes the auroras to spread much farther from the poles than normal—and to appear more colorful. The biggest solar storms can drive the auroras almost to the Equator.

The year 2000 saw a peak in the sunspot cycle. As a result, the strange, eerie lights of the auroras appeared over areas that normally don't see them. For example, on April 6, people as far south as Florida and Texas witnessed a rare and spectacular display of the northern lights. Other unusual fireworks shows were expected to continue to appear for a year or two after the sunspot peak, giving even more people a chance to see them.

On April 6, 2000, a luminous aurora was seen by people as far south as Texas and Florida. This photo was taken in Virginia.

How to Catch the Show

Scientists can often predict when and where unusual displays of the northern lights will appear. They do this by observing solar eruptions. They calculate the time it takes for solar particles produced by the eruption to cross the 93 million miles (149 million kilometers) of space between the sun and Earth.

Watch for news reports of aurora predictions in your area. Or check for predictions posted on the Internet. NASA posts predictions at **www.spaceweather.com**. The National Oceanic and Atmospheric Administration (NOAA) posts predictions at **www.sec.noaa.gov**. These sites also have satellite pictures and other information about the auroras.

Even with the increase in solar storms, the odds of seeing the northern lights are still best in northern regions. People in New York, for example, have more opportunities to catch the show than people in Florida.

The best time to search for the northern lights is on a clear, dark night with no moon. Look to the north. The light show is often most active around midnight. If you're awake then, and very lucky, maybe you'll get a chance to see the rare spectacle of the aurora.

A CHANCE TO LEARN MORE

The solar storms that create the auroras can have other effects, too. As solar particles rain down on Earth, they can disrupt radar, radio transmissions, and power grids. In the past, solar "superstorms" have caused widespread power blackouts and other problems. Some scientists think that the effects of solar wind may even influence Earth's weather.

Scientists are taking advantage of the increase in solar activity to learn more about the auroras and other effects of solar wind. A polar satellite placed in orbit by the National Aeronautics and Space Administration (NASA) in 1996 is one of the tools they are using to gather information. This satellite's camera can photograph ultraviolet light, which can't be seen by the human eye. It can detect the auroras even during the day, when sunlight masks them from view.

Image, a new NASA satellite launched in 2000, is also studying the auroras. It's the first satellite devoted to creating images of Earth's magnetic field. Scientists hope *Image* will help them understand how the solar wind disturbs the magnetic field and produces the auroras. This may also help people be better prepared for some of the harmful effects of these disturbances, including radar, radio, and power disruptions.

Thanks to scientific research, people no longer think the northern lights are strange omens from the spirit world. But these wonderful displays will always seem magical and mysterious when they appear in the night sky.

MAKE & DO

You've made or bought the perfect gift. Now present it in the perfect wrapping: a colorful bag decorated with cutouts, stickers, ribbons, and other materials. You can even match the design of the bag to its contents—such as felt flower cutouts for garden seeds or a construction-paper sailboat for a pair of deck shoes.

WILD CARDS!

Your friends and family might say you're wild 'n' wonderful when they see your handmade collage cards. A collage is a picture made of small pieces of cut paper or other small items glued onto a background. Almost anything can be used in a collage—bits of straw, scraps of cloth, cutouts from magazines and catalogs, dried flowers, coins, lace, stickers. . .even candy!

Create your cards to match the occasion, and include an appropriate message. The inside of this straw horse card might include a get-well greeting saying, "Quit horsing around and gallop back to good health!" A collage of sun, sand, surf, and cruise ships could say "Bon Voyage!" A collage of lace, flowers, hearts, and cupids is perfect for "Be My Valentine!" And a candy card could be enclosed in a decorated envelope saying "A Sweet for a Sweetie!"

1. To make this straw card, start by cutting a rectangle shape from a sheet of thin cardboard. Paint it with black acrylic paint. Let the paint dry.

2. Cut the straw into strips. Glue the strips onto the black cardboard to create a picture. When you're done, let the glue dry completely.

3. Brush acrylic varnish over the finished picture. When it's dry, glue it onto the front of a folded card that's a little bigger than your picture.

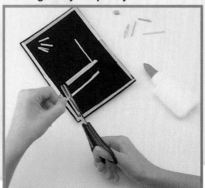

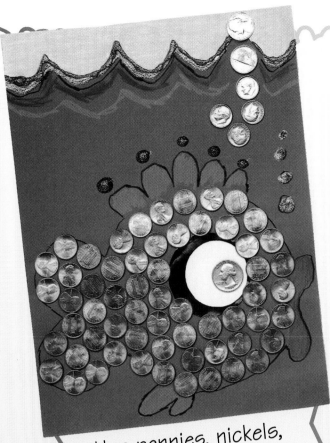

Use pennies, nickels, and dimes to create this fishy coin card. It would make a great "Good Luck" card.

1. To make this candy card, you will need small candies like candy corn and gumdrops. Arrange them on a graham cracker so they make a picture.

2. Make frosting "glue" by stirring a teaspoon of milk or water into 1/4 cup of powdered sugar.

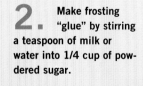

3. One at a time, lift the candies off the cracker. Dip the bottoms into the frosting. Set the candies back in place. Let dry thoroughly.

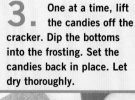

STAMP COLLECTING

What will the future be like? In 2000, children around the world shared their visions—on stamps. Kids under 12 from more than 25 countries took part in a stamp-design contest called Stampin' the Future. Each country issued stamps featuring its own winning designs.

In the United States, some 120,000 kids took part. The winning designs showed a family traveling through space in a rocket, astronauts, children with a heart-shaped Earth behind them, and a space dog on the moon.

Canada's winning designs showed people traveling to a distant planet by monorail, children of different races completing a puzzle map of Canada, and astronauts. Space themes were popular with kids in other countries, too. A stamp from Guernsey showed people traveling to a distant planet in a space bus. Other stamps from other nations showed floating cities, flying people, space aliens, and robots. The Stampin' the Future issues were a great opportunity for collectors. But collectors had plenty of other choices during 2000, too.

U.S. STAMPS

The U.S. Celebrate the Century stamp program came to a close in 2000 with thirty new 33-cent stamps. This program honored some of the most important people, places, events, and trends of the 20th-century. Fifteen stamps were issued for each ten-year period. For the stamps marking the 1950's and later decades, the public was asked to vote for subjects.

The fifteen subjects selected for the 1980's were Cabbage Patch Kids dolls, video games, the fall of the Berlin Wall, the Vietnam Veterans Memorial, the return of hostages from Iran in 1981, the movie *E.T. The Extra-Terrestrial,* television's *The Cosby Show,* the Broadway musical *Cats,* hip-hop culture, figure skating, the San Francisco 49ers football team, personal computers, compact discs, cable TV, and the space shuttle program.

Computer art and graphics, cellular phones, the movie *Titanic,* the Gulf War, the TV sitcom *Seinfeld,* and the recovery of endangered species were among the subjects chosen for the

2000 STAMPS FROM AROUND THE WORLD

1990's. Other 1990's subjects were the World Wide Web, the movie *Jurassic Park*, sport-utility vehicles, virtual reality, the Special Olympics, new baseball records, extreme sports, astronaut John Glenn's return to space at age 77, and improvements in education.

The U.S. Postal Service added to its series of Looney Tunes character stamps with a new 33-cent design featuring Wile E. Coyote and Road Runner. The stamp showed Wile E. Coyote face-down in the dirt after another failed attempt to catch Road Runner. Road Runner, perched on a mail box, holds out a letter with an image of the 1999 Looney Tunes stamp, which showed Daffy Duck.

A colorful 33-cent stamp highlighted the theme of Adoption Awareness. The stamp featured a design of stick figures holding hands. The idea of the stamp was to help raise awareness of how adoption can make a positive difference in the lives of children.

For the eighth time, the U.S. Postal Service joined the many countries that issued stamps honoring the Chinese New Year. The 33-cent stamp featured a flowing, stylized dragon—because 2000 was the Year of the Dragon in the Chinese lunar calendar. The dragon is the fifth of the twelve animals that govern the years in the lunar calendar cycle. People born in dragon years are said to be strong, energetic, confident, and curious.

STAMPS AROUND THE WORLD

In 1908, Canada's first rural mail delivery began. Horse-drawn wagons carried the mail, and people were asked to put up roadside mailboxes. In 2000, Canada celebrated that tradition with a colorful quartet of 46-cent stamps showing rural mailboxes. The boxes were decorated to look like barns, houses, a tractor, a cow, a goose—even a fish.

Halifax, Nova Scotia, hosted nearly 150 tall ships in 2000, and the event was commemorated with a pair of stamps. The sailing ships were taking part in Tall Ships 2000, a transatlantic race run in stages from April to August. The design for the two Canadian stamps ran from one to the other, with no border between. It showed the fleet of ships in Halifax Harbor, with all their white sails flying.

Each year the member countries of the Association of European Public Postal Operators put

together an omnibus issue—a group of stamps from many countries on the same theme. In 2000 the Europa stamps, as this issue is called, shared a common design as well as a common theme. The theme was united Europe. The design featured a column of stars, representing the European Community (EC). Children were shown approaching the column, carrying more stars, as a sign of the EC's future growth.

Twenty countries, from Ascension Island in the Atlantic Ocean to Uganda in Africa, took part in omnibus issues celebrating the 18th birthday of Prince William of Britain. Many of the stamps showed photographs of the popular prince as a young child, with family members. Jersey showed him enjoying favorite pastimes such as polo and skiing.

Malta joined the growing number of countries that issue greetings stamps each year. Malta's five designs were suited to various occasions, from birthday greetings to wedding congratulations. France, famous for fashion design, turned to one of its top fashion designers for a pair of love stamps. Yves Saint Laurent created two heart-shaped designs, one in

bright pink and orange and the other showing a woman's profile against a green background.

Switzerland featured its favorite souvenirs in a group of six stamps. Each stamp showed a snow globe, and inside each snow globe was a scene representing something Switzerland is famous for. The items included a clock, a pot of fondue, St. Bernard dogs, a man playing a huge Alpine horn, and grapes and wine jugs from the country's wine-making region.

Other interesting stamps from Europe included a group from Luxembourg showing musical instruments. Slovenia featured some alarming carnival masks on stamps in its folklore series. And when Slovenia's national soccer team qualified for the European championship, the country celebrated with a stamp that showed a chicken atop a soccer ball.

The United Nations continued its endangered species series with twelve new stamps showing animals. The stamps were issued in groups of four with different denominations—U.S. dollars, Swiss centimes, and Austrian schillings—for use by U.N. offices in different countries. Each group featured different ani-

A TOPICAL
COLLECTION OF
MILLENNIUM NEW YEAR
STAMPS

mals. The 33-cent stamps showed North American brown bears; the black-bellied bustard, an African bird; Chinese crocodile lizards; and a bonobo (pygmy chimpanzee) mother and baby. A sea otter, an emerald monitor lizard, Coscoroba swans, and hippopotamuses were on the 90-centime stamps. The 7-schilling stamps had a leopard, a killer whale, wading birds known as white spoonbills, and a huemal, a small deer found in the Andes mountains of Chile and Argentina.

Animals are always popular subjects for stamps, and several countries released animal stamps in 2000. The Caribbean nation of Dominica had some of the cutest designs. Six stamps featured puppies—basset hound, Jack Russell terrier, golden retriever, boxer, Shar Pei, and wire-haired terrier. Sixteen more stamps showed cats of various breeds, from the American shorthair to the Japanese bobtail.

Wonderful African animals turned up on a group of four stamps from Botswana. The stamps celebrated scenic rivers, but animals such as elephants and hippos stole the show. New Zealand showed mythical creatures in its Spirits and Guardians stamps. Among them were dragonlike sea serpents said to guard New Zealand's North Island and South Island.

Ghana reached back into history for a stamp marking the 2000 Summer Olympics held in Sydney, Australia. The Ghanaian stamp showed an ancient Greek chariot race. Armenia, Canada, Israel, and Sweden were among the many other nations that issued stamps honoring the Olympics. Most chose to depict modern sports.

Four island nations—Kiribati, Fiji, Samoa, and the Cayman Islands—took the children's TV show *Sesame Street* as a theme for stamps. Kiribati issued nine stamps showing characters from the show, including Bert and Ernie, Big Bird, Grover, and Cookie Monster.

A TOPICAL COLLECTION

New Year stamps are a great subject for a topical collection, a collection built around a single theme. And in 2000, the start of a new millennium brought a flood of special New Year stamps. Designs featured fireworks, streamers, and important events from the century that had passed. A collection of these stamps will capture an exciting moment in the world's history.

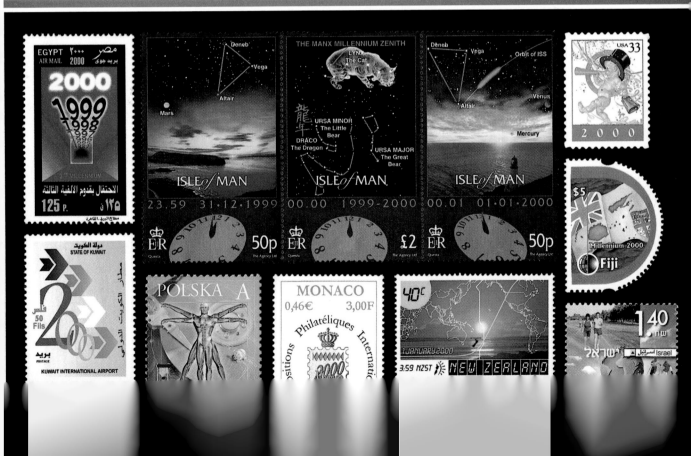

LIVING IN THE WHITE HOUSE

On November 1, 2000, Americans celebrated a special anniversary: 200 years earlier, a new mansion opened on Pennsylvania Avenue in Washington, D.C. Today known as the White House, it became the official residence of the president of the United States. It was significantly smaller than the building of today. Many additions and changes have been made during the past two centuries. But every president except one has lived and worked there.

To learn the name of the president who didn't live in the White House, you need a pencil and sheet of paper. Carefully follow the directions given below. Hint: It will be easier if you rewrite the complete words at each step. (The solution is on page 415.)

1. Print the words WHITE HOUSE. Leave the words separated.

2. Change the U to two N's.

3. Move the S to the beginning of the second word.

4. Find the second consonant from the left. Replace it with three G's.

5. Insert the letter that comes after H in the alphabet in front of the O.

6. Add an A to the beginning of the first word.

7. Move one of the G's between the I-O combination.

8. Place the vowel that comes before P in the alphabet between the two G's.

9. Move the T to the left of the O in the second word.

10. Locate the last vowel of the second word. Place it in front of the second vowel in the first word.

11. Take one of the N's and place it between the I-G combination.

12. Change the I in the first word to an R, then move the R to the other side of the G.

13. Reverse the first two letters of the first word and put them at the beginning of the second word.

The year 2000 was also the 200th anniversary of the building of the Capitol and the creation of the Library of Congress.

ANIMAL BEHAVIOR

People have all different kinds of behavior traits. And so do animals. In fact, traits associated with animals are often used to describe people. For instance, have you ever been told that you are as playful as a monkey? Or have you ever done something deceitful and been called a snake in the grass?

Below are 15 statements that use animal traits to describe the behavior of people. Complete each sentence by filling in the blank with the proper animal.

1. Ann is an enthusiastic worker. She's a real eager _____.

2. When Ben doesn't get his way, he can be as stubborn as a _____.

3. When someone tells Cindy a secret, she will _____ up rather than reveal it.

4. No matter how hard Harry tried, he couldn't _____ the secret out of Cindy.

5. Susan suspected something was up. She smelled a _____.

6. David got _____ bumps when he watched the scary movie.

7. Fred lifted the heavy weights. He's as strong as an _____.

8. Karla had a crush on her classmate and made _____ eyes at him.

9. Jim is very cunning. He's crazy like a _____.

10. When Jennifer studies at the library, she's as quiet as a _____.

11. Larry was furious. He was as mad as a _____.

12. Melissa, nervous about speaking before the class, had _____ in her stomach.

13. Vicki pretended to be sad and cried huge _____ tears.

14. Walter tried to cut into the movie line. He was told to hold his _____.

15. Sally, cheerful and laughing, is as happy as a _____.

a. beaver

b. butterflies

c. clam

d. cow

e. crocodile

f. fox

g. goose

h. hornet

i. horses

j. lark

k. mouse

l. mule

m. ox

n. rat

o. worm

ANSWERS: 1.a; 2.l; 3.c; 4.o; 5.n; 6.g; 7.m; 8.d; 9.f; 10.k; 11.h; 12.b; 13.e; 14.i; 15.j.

ROUND TRIP: The Flight of the Boomerang

We live in an age of high-tech entertainment—big-screen TV's, digital cameras, VCR's, laptop computers, and DVD players. Occasionally, however, people long for a simpler form of entertainment. And what could be simpler than tossing a piece of wood as far as you can, and then, lo and behold, watching in awe as it comes sailing right back to you? This round-trip object is a boomerang, a curved stick that originated in the Stone Age. When you learn to throw it correctly, you can play catch with yourself all day long.

It's believed that "rangs" were invented by the aborigines of Australia about 11,000 years ago and were probably first used for hunting. Those early "throw sticks" didn't return to the hunters who threw them. They weren't supposed to. But it is thought that the aborigines refined their throw sticks, making them lighter and carving them in smooth curves so that they would travel farther and faster. Eventually, and quite possibly by accident, a throw stick was fashioned in just the right shape. A hunter hurled the stick at a meaty bird; he

arms (like the letter Y), and some have four (like the letter X). "Pinwheel" boomerangs have six arms! Still other rangs are shaped like triangles, or like the letters H, S, or T. The important idea is that the arms—no matter how many or in what configuration—should be shaped like airplane wings: one side curved, one side flat.

Even though it seems like a simple object, and even though it was invented in prehistoric times, the boomerang relies on some fancy physical laws to achieve its pattern of flight. Because of the shape of its arms, a boom-

Once a Stone Age hunting tool, the boomerang has become a popular object for sport and play. Thrown correctly, it can never get lost—the boomerang will sail through the air on a perfect round-trip flight.

missed, but the weapon made a U-turn and came winging back to him. The boomerang was born.

SHAPED TO FLY

What is the "right" shape? We usually picture a boomerang as being in the form of a wide V with a gradual, smooth curve at the vertex, where the two arms meet. Each of the two arms, or blades, looks like an airplane wing, flat on the bottom and curved on the top.

But this basic shape can have many variations. The angle between the arms may be sharp. Or it may be a semicircle, so that the boomerang looks more like the letter U than a V. Some have three erang produces the same sort of lifting force that an airplane's wings do: The rang, or the plane, will rise in the direction of the curved side. This is why a well-thrown boomerang seems to sail. But the boomerang is spinning at the same time, the arms creating a circle as it flies. The boomerang's lift, the speed of its forward motion, and the spin of its arms all combine to cause the boomerang to turn and eventually come back.

THROWING PROPERLY

Throwing a rang so that it returns to you may not be easy at first. It takes some practice. Generally, though, if you can throw a baseball fairly well, you can become skillful at throwing a boomerang.

Begin with the proper grip. Hold the boomerang with your thumb and fingers wrapped around the end of one blade. The vertex of the "V" is pointed over your shoulder. The curved side of the blades is toward you, and the flat side is away from you.

The key to tossing a rang correctly is to throw overhand. Not sidearm, not even "three-quarters" (between sidearm and overhand), but directly overhand, as close to vertical as possible. You may be tempted to throw sidearm to launch the boomerang into a smooth, flat flight. Avoid this temptation. A boomerang isn't a Frisbee. Thrown sidearm, the rang will rise straight up and then quickly come down with a crash. If thrown properly overhand, though, the boomerang will eventually "flatten out" and sail smoothly, its arms more or less parallel to the ground, during the return trip.

Pitch the boomerang toward the horizon, and snap your wrist as you release it. This snap is important—it helps create the spin that makes the rang fly.

Boomerangs come in many different shapes. The most common rang has two arms that meet in a smooth curve. Some have arms that meet in a semicircle or a sharp angle. And still others have three or more arms.

Boomerang Builders

Professionally made boomerangs start out as strips of wood. Above: The strips are pressed and bent into the shape of a boomerang and glued together or laminated into a single block of wood strips. The block is then sliced into individual boomerangs. Above right: Sanding is an important part of the finishing process. Right: A stack of newly made three-armed boomerangs.

If you can't get the boomerang to return to you at first, keep at it. You may have to experiment with your technique, perhaps by slightly altering the direction in which you throw. In time, you'll get the hang of it.

A word of caution: Never throw a boomerang on a busy street. Stay away from houses and buildings. Find a broad, open field with few obstructions—you don't want to break any windows or accidentally harm someone who gets in the way of your rang. Also, calm days are better than windy ones for good throwing, although some throwers have learned to use a mild breeze to help get the boomerang to return to them. If the conditions are right, and you've learned the technique, you'll be all set for hours of fun—either alone or with friends who also enjoy boomerangs.

FUN AND GAMES

Here are some games and tricks that you can do with boomerangs just for the fun of it.

Distance. How far can you throw a rang? Unlike a baseball, a boomerang creates a lift—it defies gravity for at least part of its flight. Therefore you may expect to be able to throw a boomerang farther than you can hurl a baseball. In 1999, Manuel Schütz of

Making a Boomerang

Different types of wood are used to make boomerangs. In addition, toy manufacturers produce boomerangs out of plastic.

You can make the simple boomerang shown here out of cardboard. It isn't in the customary V shape, and its arms don't have a curved side. But it should fly and return fairly well.

Begin with a piece of stiff cardboard at least 8 inches (20 centimeters) wide. Using a ruler and a compass, draw a picture of exactly how the boomerang will look when completed. The small center circle should be about 1½ inches (4 centimeters) in diameter. The larger circle is about 3¼ inches (8 centimeters) in diameter. Measuring from the edge of the large circle, draw each arm of the boomerang about 3 inches (7.5 centimeters) long. The arms gradually increase in width.

When you're finished drawing your pattern, carefully cut out the boomerang. Remember to cut out the center circle, so there's a hole in the middle.

Cardboard boomerangs don't usually fly well outdoors because they're too light. Try throwing this one in a gymnasium, or in another indoor place where there's nothing breakable. Have fun!

Switzerland heaved a rang 260 yards (238 meters) before it turned around and came back. That's more than two and a half times the length of a U.S. football field. Top distance throwers regularly exceed 100 yards (91 meters). But you would be considered pretty good if you could make your boomerang travel 20 to 45 yards (18–41 meters).

Time Aloft. How long will your rang stay in the air? The more you practice, the longer you'll be able to keep the rang aloft. Many expert boomerangers are able to achieve flights of a minute or more. The world record is about 1 minute and 40 seconds.

Accuracy. How accurate are you? The winner of this game is the person who has to move the least to catch the returning boomerang. An expert can toss a rang and then haul it in without disturbing a blade of grass. Most people, however, usually have to do some moving to make the catch.

Making the Catch. Who's the best catcher? Grabbing a returning boomerang can be tricky. Don't expect to pluck it out of the air with one hand, the way some people catch a Frisbee. Beginners should learn the two-handed "sandwich" catch—as if each of your hands were a piece of bread and the boomerang a flying slice of salami. Keep your palms flat, and place them together above and below the rang as it returns.

Pretty Tricky. Boomerang throwers can be quite inventive with some of their tricks. One is "quantity tossing"—getting many rangs into the air simultaneously. Several boomerangers have put as many as ten aloft before the first one set down.

Another trick is to throw and catch one boomerang five times in the fastest possible time. The world record for this is just about fifteen seconds.

A similar trick is to see how many throws and catches can be made with one boomerang in five minutes. The world record for this difficult task is 80 catches.

Other expert tricks include behind-the-back catches; under-the-leg catches; throwing two boomerangs at the same time; and—this is a real tough one—tossing a boomerang so that it circles back to you, passes over your head, and circles back to you a second time.

MANY HAPPY RETURNS

Although the boomerang is strongly associated with Australia, the prehistoric throw

Many boomerang competitions are sponsored by the United States Boomerang Association. (You can find its interesting Web site at www.USBA.org.)

Today, competitions are also held in about 25 other countries. Boomerang throwing may never become an Olympic sport. But boomerang lovers were thrilled that a boomerang-throwing exhibition was a highlight of the 2000 Olympic Games in Sydney, Australia—the birthplace of the boomerang.

Boomerang lessons: Hold the boomerang with your thumb and fingers wrapped around the end of one blade and throw it directly overhand, snapping your wrist as you release it.

stick (the precursor of the rang) has been found in Europe, Asia, and Africa. Throw sticks were also used by the ancestors of certain Native American tribes of the American Southwest. Today, throwing the boomerang may be catching on as a sport worldwide.

Some people suggest that the popularity of the Frisbee—known for its own swirling flight patterns—has inspired people to rediscover the ancient boomerang. Whatever the reason, folks are flinging boomerangs in all directions, hoping for "many happy returns."

SITE-SEEING

When you visit a distant city, much of what you see may remind you of your home town. But other city sites are unique, and these are the things you don't want to miss: historical monuments, fairy tale palaces, beautiful parks.

Travelers will tell you that a trip to London isn't complete without watching the changing of the guard at Buckingham Palace. A trip to San Francisco must include a ride on one of the city's famous cable cars. And if you are going to Italy, ask someone to take your picture beside the Leaning Tower of Pisa.

The names of 25 famous sites are listed below (in the left column). Match each to its city and country (in the right column).

1. Alamo		**a.** Addis Ababa (Ethiopia)	
2. Big Ben		**b.** Agra (India)	
3. Brandenburg Gate		**c.** Athens (Greece)	
4. Chapultepec Park		**d.** Beijing (China)	
5. Chateau Frontenac		**e.** Berlin (Germany)	
6. Colosseum		**f.** Copenhagen (Denmark)	
7. Diamond Head		**g.** Honolulu (U.S.)	
8. Eiffel Tower		**h.** Jerusalem (Israel)	
9. EPCOT		**i.** St. Petersburg (Russia)	
10. Ginza		**j.** London (England)	
11. Graceland		**k.** Madrid (Spain)	
12. Hermitage		**l.** Mecca (Saudi Arabia)	
13. Kaaba		**m.** Memphis (U.S.)	
14. Kremlin		**n.** Mexico City (Mexico)	
15. Lion Park		**o.** Moscow (Russia)	
16. Little Mermaid		**p.** New York (U.S.)	
17. Parthenon		**q.** Orlando (U.S.)	
18. Prado		**r.** Paris (France)	
19. SkyDome		**s.** Quebec (Canada)	
20. Statue of Liberty		**t.** Rio de Janeiro (Brazil)	
21. Sugar Loaf		**u.** Rome (Italy)	
22. Taj Mahal		**v.** San Antonio (U.S.)	
23. Tiananmen Square		**w.** Tokyo (Japan)	
24. Wailing Wall		**x.** Toronto (Canada)	
25. White House		**y.** Washington, D.C. (U.S.)	

Next, go on a hunt. The names of all 25 city sites are hidden in this word-search puzzle. Try to find them. Cover the puzzle with a sheet of tracing paper. Read forward, backward, up, down, and diagonally. Then draw a neat line through each place as you find it.

B	S	T	A	T	U	E	O	F	L	I	B	E	R	T	Y
E	R	N	I	H	S	A	C	O	L	O	S	S	E	U	M
T	I	A	N	A	N	M	E	N	S	Q	U	A	R	E	C
U	N	O	N	E	H	T	R	A	P	G	B	L	E	W	A
A	G	E	J	D	I	O	E	V	A	C	I	T	W	E	N
D	I	G	A	N	E	P	D	R	L	T	G	A	O	F	E
A	N	A	K	L	C	N	L	A	T	I	B	J	T	L	T
E	Z	T	M	O	A	O	B	L	R	L	E	M	L	I	N
H	A	I	T	V	A	M	E	U	B	P	N	A	E	O	O
D	K	M	H	F	L	M	O	N	R	O	W	H	F	N	R
N	G	R	A	C	E	L	A	N	D	G	I	A	F	P	F
O	C	E	E	R	N	T	X	A	N	U	G	L	I	A	U
M	K	H	M	M	G	R	Y	I	U	Q	H	A	E	R	A
A	P	A	D	H	L	E	L	M	O	R	R	O	T	K	E
I	I	Z	A	W	H	I	T	E	H	O	U	S	E	E	T
D	M	I	N	B	A	J	N	E	M	O	D	Y	K	S	A
Y	S	T	O	W	A	O	K	R	L	H	U	R	A	I	H
C	H	A	P	U	L	T	E	P	E	C	P	A	R	K	C

MANY FRIENDS COOKING

MAPLE SNOW
from Canada

In the center of Canada's flag is a red maple leaf—a symbol of Canada's many maple trees. No wonder everyone likes to turn out in the early spring to help collect the sweet liquid from the sugar maples. The snow is still on the ground. The sap is gathered and boiled down into maple syrup. As a special treat, the hot syrup is poured over fresh snow. With cider and doughnuts, cups of sweet Maple Snow make festive refreshments at a sugaring-off party.

INGREDIENTS

1 cup clean snow or
1 tray of ice cubes
½ cup maple syrup

EQUIPMENT

pan or bowl   small paper
measuring   cups
cup   tablespoon
saucepan

HOW TO MAKE

1. Fill a pan or bowl with snow. Be sure the snow is clean. Have all your ingredients ready before you bring in the snow so it doesn't have time to melt. If there isn't any snow, make crushed ice. An easy way to do this is to wrap a few cubes of ice in a kitchen towel and pound them with a heavy object like a rolling pin. Put the crushed ice in a bowl. Continue until all the cubes are crushed.

2. Heat the maple syrup in the saucepan over low heat for about two minutes until it is warm. Remove it from the heat.

3. Fill each paper cup with enough snow or ice to make a rounded top.

4. Drop a tablespoon or more of maple syrup on top of the snow or ice.

This recipe serves 4 people.

COCONUT CHICKEN
from Indonesia

Have a *rijsttafel*—that means rice table—a unique Indonesian way of eating. Here's how Indonesians do it. First they make a pot of fluffy rice. Then they prepare an assortment of meats, vegetables, and relishes. Indonesian cooks vary the tastes between spicy and bland, hot and cold, crisp and soft, sweet and sour. When the foods are ready, each diner heaps the rice in the middle of the plate and carefully spoons other foods in a ring around the rice. You can begin your rice table with rice and coconut chicken.

INGREDIENTS

1 chicken (3 lbs.) cut into serving pieces
3 cups coconut milk
¼ teaspoon salt
⅛ teaspoon cayenne
5 mint leaves
1 medium onion

EQUIPMENT

paper towels
deep frying pan
paring knife
measuring spoons
measuring cups
baking pan
kitchen tongs

HOW TO MAKE

1. Wash the chicken and dry it with paper towels.
2. Place the chicken in the frying pan. Add the coconut milk, salt, cayenne, and mint leaves.
3. Cut up the onion into small pieces and add to the frying pan.
4. Bring the chicken and other ingredients to a boil. Then turn down the heat and simmer for 20 minutes or until the liquid is nearly gone and only thick sauce remains.
5. Preheat the broiler.
6. Remove the chicken from the frying pan and put it into the baking pan. Save the sauce.
7. Broil the chicken for 20 to 30 minutes. Use the kitchen tongs to turn the chicken while it cooks so that it doesn't burn.
8. When the chicken is done, transfer it to a platter and pour the sauce over it. Serve.

This recipe serves 6 people.

POPULAR CRAFTS

Making something with your hands is one of the most enjoyable and satisfying experiences. Whatever your level of skill—from beginner to expert—you'll find great pleasure in creating objects that are attractive and useful.

New crafts are constantly being introduced. But old favorites are popular, too. Here are four projects you'll want to try that combine new ideas and techniques with ones enjoyed by past generations.

A BRAIDED PAPER WREATH

Paper twist looks like strands of twisted cord. But when you untwist it, you have a flexible material that can be shaped in various ways to create many different kinds of interesting crafts.

To make this puffy braided wreath, you'll need a wire wreath frame and three colors of paper twist. Two of the colors are used for the woven backing; all three colors are braided together to make the wreath.

To make the backing, cut and untwist lengths of paper twist, and dampen them under a faucet. Thread the pieces through the bottom wire. Weave the lengths, alternating the colors. Wrap the ends of each piece around the wire, and hold them in place with clothespins until the paper is dry. Then remove the clothespins and glue all ends to the frame.

154

Make the braid from long lengths of untwisted, dampened paper. The braid should be somewhat longer than the circumference of the frame because it will shrink as it dries. When the braid is completely dry, glue it to the frame. For added puffiness, stuff small pieces of untwisted, dry paper into each of the "bumps" of the braid.

Now add a perky double bow. Make the lower bow from untwisted, dampened paper. Make the upper bow from dry paper twist—untwist only the ends, to form tiny florets. This country wreath will look wonderful in almost any room, and it will make a charming gift—if you can part with it.

PEARLY BUBBLES

Use your imagination and turn a pretty picture into a bubbly collage by adding pearls, beads, and other materials. The "Bubble Girl" picture at right shows you how easy this can be.

You can start out with a print purhased at a craft store. Glue the print onto a colored piece of mat board. Start adding items to create a 3-D effect. To add a rug, for example, outline the area to be covered on a piece of tracing paper. Then transfer this pattern to a sheet of white paper. Cut out the rug and glue it onto the picture.

In a similar fashion, use pieces of printed fabrics to create a layered effect on the tub, the sponge, the scrub brush, and the cat. Add bows and lace ruffles

as finishing touches. The fancy perfume bottles on the shelf over the bathtub are made with different shapes and colors of glass beads and gold-toned beads. Glue them one atop the other.

To make your picture burst with bubbles, apply lots and lots of small, medium, and large pearls around the tub. Dot the scrub brush with a few, and give the cat a couple to play with! The bubbles will seem extra soapy if you paint the pearls with iridescent glitter in glue.

Finally, place the finished collage in a shadowbox. Attach screw eyes and picture wire to the back of the box. You might want to hang your picture in the bathroom so you can see it while you relax in your own bubbly tub.

This imaginative collage is just bubbling over with glittery pearls—and other materials that give a 3-D effect.

A perpetual calendar like this one lasts forever—you'll never have to buy a paper calendar again.

The month and date blocks are made from basswood, too. Cut 12 month blocks and 31 date blocks. Lightly sand the edges so the blocks are smooth. Then press black transfer letters and numbers onto the blocks to create the months and dates.

Now you have to use your math skills. Divide the plaque so that there are six evenly spaced horizontal sections. Each section should be just slightly higher than the blocks—you want the blocks to remain in the tracks, but you don't want the fit to be so snug that the blocks get stuck.

Glue the narrow basswood strips onto the plaque. After the glue has dried, set the wider strips on top, positioning them so that tracks are formed. Let dry. Divide the space over the top strip into seven equal parts. Press black transfer letters for the days of the week in these spaces. As a final touch, decorate the plaque with stencils or stickers, perhaps with a country theme—apples, hearts, flowers.

At the beginning of each month, simply remove the prior month's blocks and put in the appropriate blocks for the current month. (Note: If a 31-day month starts on a Friday or Saturday, you'll need to begin your date blocks in the same section that's holding the month block.)

You now have something very special—a calendar that's perpetually accurate and perpetually beautiful.

GRANNY'S NOTE BOARD

Here's a perfect gift for a grandparent: a note board complete with pen and paper, and featuring a soft-sculpture Granny.

Begin with a base made from a piece of Styrofoam or thick cardboard. (You might ask your local fabric store for the cardboard insert from a fabric bolt.) Completely cover

THIS CALENDAR IS FOREVER

Do you buy a new paper calendar every year? If you make this perpetual calendar, you'll never have to buy a paper one again.

The calendar's base is a rectangular plaque with a beveled edge. But even a wooden cutting board can be used. Sand the base lightly and wipe it clean with tack cloth. Paint or stain the beveled edge.

Use basswood stripping, available in hobby and craft shops, to make the tracks that hold the month and date blocks. You'll need two pieces of basswood for each track: a narrow strip to be glued to the base and a wider strip to be glued on top of the narrow strip, thus forming a track in which to slide the blocks.

This delightful note board seems to be beckoning Granny to come over and jot down a few words.

the base with natural colored burlap. Now cut two pieces of red checked fabric. Glue one piece to the top of the burlap, the other to the bottom. Glue strips of rickrack over the edges.

To make Granny's head, stuff the toe of a knee-high stocking with fiberfill. Try to get a flat, circular shape, with a diameter about half the width of the base. When you're satisfied with the shape, use needle and thread to tie off the stocking at the bottom of the head. Stitch the excess stocking to the back of the head.

Make Granny's nose by covering a marble-sized piece of fiberfill with a small piece of stocking. Sew the nose to the center of the face. Add two black beads for eyes and some stitches of red embroidery thread for a V-shaped mouth. Pink blush, applied with a make-up brush, will give Granny rosy cheeks.

Use gold-colored wire to shape Granny's glasses, and stitch them to the face at the bottom and sides. Granny's hair is fiberfill, fluffed up and lightly glued around the face. Sew red pindot fabric to her bonnet, edge it with white lace, and firmly stuff it with fiberfill. Glue the completed head to the top of the burlap.

Make a notepad holder from a strip of fabric or a double thickness of rickrack. Glue the two edges to the burlap, making certain there's enough room between the glued ends to slip a notepad over the strip.

Place a red marker upside down next to the notepad, and glue the cap section to the burlap. Stick a few push-pins on the base, to hold notes. Finally, sew two plastic curtain rings to the back of the base for hanging—and Granny's note board is ready to take messages.

You can, of course, replace the face with an appropriate one for other family members or friends. How about Mom's Shopping List?

Adapted from articles appearing in
Crafts 'n Things magazine

COIN COLLECTING

People went crazy over quarters in 2000. New state quarters from the U.S. Mint were snapped up as quickly as they appeared, with an amazing four out of every ten Americans collecting the coins. Canada had similar success with new millennium quarters, one for each month of the year. Collectors had much else to choose from, too, with new issues from many countries.

formation, was teamed with the motto "Live Free or Die" on the New Hampshire quarter. Virginia showed the three ships that brought the first English settlers to Jamestown in 1607.

The Mint also issued a new dollar coin showing Sacagawea, one of the most famous American Indian women in history. Sacagawea served as guide and interpreter for the Lewis and Clark expedition, which explored

U.S. "state" quarters representing Massachusetts, Maryland, South Carolina, New Hampshire, and Virginia.

UNITED STATES

In its state quarter program, the U.S. Mint is releasing five new quarters a year through 2008, each highlighting a different state's history and culture. Honored in 2000 were Massachusetts, Maryland, South Carolina, New Hampshire, and Virginia. All the coins were readily available in pocket change or in collector sets from the Mint.

The Massachusetts coin showed a Revolutionary War Minuteman, in a design that was submitted by two Massachusetts grade-school students. Maryland's quarter showed the dome of the Maryland State House and carried the state nickname, "The Old Line State." South Carolina, "The Palmetto State," showed its state bird, the Carolina wren, and state tree, the cabbage palmetto. The Old Man of the Mountain, an unusual natural rock

U.S. "golden dollar" coin showing Sacagawea; and the bimetal coin marking the 200th anniversary of the Library of Congress.

the West in 1804–06. The coin showed her carrying her infant son, who was born during the journey. It was made of a mixture of brass, copper, and manganese. But because of its gold color, it was quickly nicknamed the "golden dollar."

The U.S. Mint also issued its first bimetal coin in 2000. This was a $10 gold coin with a platinum insert, issued to mark the 200th anniversary of the Library of Congress, in Washington, D.C. A silver $1 coin also marked the anniversary.

WORLD COINS

While U.S. collectors filled in holes in their state quarter albums, Canadians collected their own special 25-cent pieces. The Royal Canadian Mint released a new quarter each month, with designs created by Canadians who took part in the mint's "Create a Centsation" contest.

Each coin had a theme related to Canada's future: pride, ingenuity, achievement, health, natural legacy,

Canadian quarters using the themes of celebration and wisdom to honor the country's future.

harmony, celebration, family, wisdom, creativity, freedom, and community. Among the most interesting was the March coin, for "achievement," which showed a rocket heading into a sky filled with stars. The July coin, for "celebration," showed six children with a Canadian flag and fireworks exploding in the sky. The September coin, for "wisdom," showed an old man handing a maple leaf—a symbol of Canadian heritage—to a young person.

The bond between a mother and child was the theme of the final $200 gold coin in Canada's "Native Cultures and Traditions" series. The design showed a mother looking lovingly into the eyes of her child. Another Canadian series featured sports, including steeplechasing, bowling, and curling, a popular winter sport in Canada.

The antelope-like pronghorn, the fastest land animal in North America, paused for a moment on platinum $30, $75, $150, and $300 coins from Canada. Canada also released a new $2 coin showing a mother polar bear and her two cubs. Gold and silver collector's versions were available. The coin's theme was the "path of knowledge," or the passing of wisdom from generation to generation.

Several countries used animal designs in coins marking the 2000 Summer Olympic Games. Why? Because Australia, which hosted

the games, is famous for its unique wildlife. For example, the Solomon Islands issued a four-coin set showing two Australian animals, the koala and the kangaroo, participating in Olympic events.

Australia also showed its wildlife on a series of 16 silver Olympic $5 coins. Each featured a different plant or animal with the Olympic logo. The silver coins were part of a huge Olympic issue that included eight gold $100 coins and 28 bronze $5 coins. The gold coins

Cook Islands' coin honoring *Garfield* the cartoon cat; and Niue's coin celebrating the 50th anniversary of the comic strip *Peanuts*.

focused on athletic themes, such as dedication and achievement. The bronze coins showed Olympic sports. This was the first coin series to feature all the sports at the Games.

Cartoon characters appeared on several new issues. The Cook Islands marked the 21st birthday of *Garfield* the cartoon cat with a 13-coin set. The 50th anniversary of the comic strip *Peanuts* was celebrated on silver and gold coins from the island of Niue.

In the Chinese lunar calendar, 2000 was the Year of the Dragon. China, Australia, the Isle of Man, Canada,

Sierra Leone's coin marking the Year of the Dragon.

Singapore, Sierra Leone, and a host of other nations tamed the mythical fire-breathing creature for an appearance on special collector coins.

ROBERT VAN RYZIN
Editor, *Coins* magazine

Canada's coins featuring steeplechasing and a mother polar bear and her two cubs.

SPORTS

An ecstatic Marion Jones raises her hands in victory as she wins the women's 100-meter sprint at the 2000 Summer Olympics, held in Sydney, Australia. The "world's fastest woman" went on to win gold medals in the 200-meter dash and the 1,600-meter relay, and bronze medals in the long jump and 400-meter relay. This made her the first woman to win five medals in track and field in the same Olympics.

THE 2000 SUMMER OLYMPIC GAMES

Australia was the host of the 27th Summer Olympic Games, which lasted from September 15 through October 1, 2000. The official site of the Games was Australia's largest city, Sydney, located on the nation's southeastern coast. Ceremonies marking the opening and closing of the Olympics were held in Sydney, as were most of the sports events. But other competitions took place in some of Sydney's suburbs and in other cities in the southeast.

More than seven million tickets were sold to the various Olympic events. Tens of millions of people around the world watched the Games on television. And almost 200,000 people—athletes, coaches, Olympic officials, volunteers, and journalists—were officially involved in the Games. The 11,000 athletes came from 200 countries. But the flavor of the

Performers gather to create a colorful map of Australia during the spectacular opening ceremonies of the 2000 Summer Olympic Games. Inset: Australian sprinter Cathy Freeman lights the Olympic flame.

Games was definitely "Aussie." And the word on everyone's lips was "G'Day,"— Aussie for "Hello."

The Opening Ceremonies. The opening ceremonies started with a spectacular Olympic pageant in Sydney's new Olympic Stadium. The pageant honored Australia and its Abo-

riginal people, whose ancestors lived in Australia long before the English settled there two centuries ago. The pageant included colorfully costumed dancers, marching bands, and fantastic fireworks.

Following the pageant was the Parade of Nations. Country by country, from Albania to Zimbabwe, the athletes made their way into the stadium. About 40 percent of them were women—a record number for an Olympics.

The athletes from North and South Korea got an especially warm welcome. The two Koreas have long been enemies. So it was an excellent sign that their governments allowed their athletes to march—although not compete—as one nation.

The final event of the ceremonies was the lighting of the Olympic flame. The Olympic torch had made its way from Greece to Australia. Once in Australia, it was carried for 100 days, to 1,000 cities and towns. It traveled by train, plane, and camel. A special torch was even carried underwater along Australia's Great Barrier Reef.

Then, at the Olympic Stadium, the torch was passed to Cathy Freeman, a world-champion sprinter who is an Aborigine and a great hero to her people. Her lighting of the Olympic flame was a dazzling conclusion to the opening ceremonies.

Australia, the host country, was fourth in the medal standings. It won 58, compared to 41 in the 1996 Games. And the Aussies' gold-medal take was 16, 7 more than in 1996. The performances of the Aussie athletes was amazing when you consider that Australia has a population of less than 20 million people. Usually, countries with large populations win the most medals because they have a greater pool of athletic talent.

Some other countries with small populations also did well. Barbados, Kuwait, Kyrgyzstan, Saudi Arabia, and Vietnam won their first-ever Olympic medals, although none were gold.

Russian gymnast Aleksei Nemov won two golds. One was for the men's individual all-around title—allowing him to be called the world's best men's gymnast.

THE CHAMPIONS

The Olympians of 2000 competed in some 300 different events and walked away with 927 medals. The United States won the most medals—97, including 40 gold. Russia was second, with 88 medals, 32 of them gold. And China was third, with 59 medals, including 28 gold.

Gymnastics. A disappointed American gymnastics team didn't win a single medal in Sydney. The Russians, however, were outstanding, winning 20 medals overall, including 9 of the 18 golds. The star of the Russian team was Aleksei Nemov, who won 6 medals, 2 of them gold. One of the golds was for the men's individual all-around title—and the right to be called the world's best men's gymnast.

Sixteen-year-old Andreea Raducan of Romania won the women's individual all-around title. But her gold medal was taken away by the International Olympic Committee (IOC). The IOC said she had taken a banned drug. A Romanian team doctor had given her medicine for a cold—and it contained the drug. The gold was then given to the silver medalist, Simona Amanar, also of Romania. Amanar also shared the gold medal for the women's team competition.

Raducan was allowed to keep her team gold medal, but the glory of being the world's best female gymnast was gone. The men's team gold medal was won by China. Chinese gymnasts also won gold medals in the men's parallel bars and the women's balance beam.

Track and Field. On the Olympic track, the man and the woman who win the 100-meter races are considered the world's fastest athletes. At Sydney, those honors went to Marion Jones and Maurice Greene. This was the first time since the 1988 Olympics that the honors went to two Americans.

Jones's Olympic victory in the 100-meter, in a time of 10.75 seconds, was her 35th consecutive win in that event. She also won gold medals in the 200-meters and the 1,600-meter relay. And she won bronze medals in the long jump and the 400-meter relay. This made her the first woman to win five medals in track and field in the same Olympics.

Maurice "Mo" Greene crossed the finish line in 9.87 seconds, breaking the 10-second mark for the 31st time in his career. Greene won another gold medal, too—as part of the 400-meter relay team.

Speed racers: American Maurice Greene (*left*) won the 100-meter dash—and the title of world's fastest man. American Michael Johnson (*center*) and Australian Cathy Freeman (*right*) took the golds in the men's and women's 400-meter sprints.

Swimming standouts: Australian Ian Thorpe (*above*), American Jenny Thompson (*top right*), and American Lenny Krayzelburg (*bottom right*) dominated the Olympic swimming events.

There's no one better at the 400-meter sprint than Michael Johnson. He holds the world record in the event. He won the 400 at the 1996 Olympics. He's won the last four World Championships in the 400. In the eleven years preceding the 2000 Olympics, he had run that race 82 times and won it 79! And at Sydney, Johnson made that "Win Number 80," becoming the first man to win back-to-back Olympic 400-meter titles. He also won a gold medal in the 400-meter relay.

In other men's events, Konstantinos Kenteris of Greece won the 200-meters, and Noah Ngeny of Kenya won the 1,500 meters. In distance running, the Ethiopians outdistanced almost everyone else, winning gold medals in the men's marathon, the men's 5,000-meters, and the men's and women's 10,000 meters.

In other women's events, Australian sprinter Cathy Freeman, who had lit the Olympic Flame during the opening ceremonies, won the gold medal in the 400 meters. "This has been a dream since I was a little girl," she said.

Other individual gold medalists in women's track and field included Naoko Takahashi of Japan, who set an Olympic record (2 hours, 23 minutes, 14 seconds) in the marathon and became the first Japanese woman to win a gold medal in track and field.

Swimming and Diving. A specially designed pool and high-tech swimsuits seemed to make swimmers swim faster. Eighteen world and Olympic records fell by the poolside at Sydney. U.S. swimmers raced to 14 golds and 33 medals overall in 32 events. Both the Australian and the Netherlands teams won 5 gold medals, but Australia had 18 medals overall, while the Netherlands had 8.

The top male performer in the pool was Australian Ian Thorpe, who stands 6 feet, 5 inches tall, weighs 210 pounds, has size 17 flipperlike feet, and is nicknamed "the

Thorpedo." On the first day of the swimming competition, he won two gold medals by smashing the record in the men's 400-meter freestyle and helping smash the record in the 400-meter freestyle relay. He went on to collect two more medals, a gold in the 800-meter freestyle relay and a silver in the 200-meter freestyle.

Lenny Krayzelburg, born in Ukraine and an American citizen since 1995, was another standout swimmer. He won three gold medals, in the men's 100-meter and 200-meter backstroke (both Olympic records) and in the 400-meter medley relay. Pieter van den Hoogenband of the Netherlands won two golds—in the 100- and 200-meter freestyle races; and two bronzes—in the 50-meter freestyle and the 800-meter freestyle relay. He set a world record in the 200-meters.

Also outstanding was Italian Domenico Fioravanti, who won two gold medals, in the 100- and 200-meter breaststroke. His teammate Massimiliano Rosolino gave Italy its third goal with a win in the 200-meter individual medley.

The top female performers were Inge de Bruijn of the Netherlands and Jenny Thompson of the United States. De Bruijn won three golds, in the 100-meter butterfly (a world record) and the 50- and 100-meter freestyle, as well as a silver in the 400-meter freestyle relay.

Thompson won her sixth, seventh, and eighth Olympic gold medals at Sydney. That made her the winningest woman swimmer in Olympic history. As with her previous five

Chinese divers Fu Mingxia and Gou Jingjing captured the gold medal in a new Olympic sport—synchronized platform diving.

golds (two in 1992 and three in 1996), she won them as part of U.S. relay teams—in the 400-meter freestyle relay, the 800-meter freestyle relay, and the 400-meter medley relay. She also won a bronze in an individual event—the 100-meter freestyle.

The Chinese again dominated diving, winning five of the eight events, which included men's and women's synchronized platform and synchronized springboard. Over all, the Chinese won 10 of the 24 diving medals. The only U.S. medal was Laura Wilkinson's gold in the women's platform. Anne Montminy of Canada won the bronze medal in that event, as well as a silver medal in the women's synchronized platform.

Team Sports. The U.S. women's softball team won the gold medal at the 1996 Olympics in Atlanta. And they were the odds-on favorite to win gold in 2000. They did just that, defeating Japan 2–1 in the championship game. But that outcome was seriously in doubt early in the tournament.

Coming into the Sydney Olympics, the Americans were on a 110-game winning streak. And in the first two games of the Olympics, they defeated Canada and Cuba to extend the streak to 112. Then, in quick order, the Americans were stunned by Japan (2–1), China (2–0), and Australia (2–1) in three exhausting overtime games. Could they recover from these defeats? Could they even make it into the medal round?

They did—and there waiting for them were the same three teams that had defeated them earlier. The results were different this time.

U.S. softball players rush to teammate Laura Berg (*right*), after Berg's fly ball scored the winning run against Japan for the gold medal.

The Americans downed the Chinese 3–0, the Australians 1–0, and, in the gold-medal game, the Japanese 2–1.

While the American women softballers were expected to win gold, the men's baseball team wasn't. The Cubans had dominated Olympic baseball since it became an Olympic sport in 1992. They won the gold medal that year and in 1996, and they were expected to win again in 2000. But in a stunning upset, the American team of young players and aging minor leaguers downed the Cubans 4–0 and took home the gold.

As expected, the United States hoopsters, with such National Basketball Association stars as Alonzo Mourning, Vince Carter, and Tim Hardaway, won the gold medal in basketball. But not before Lithua-

The Olympic Mascots

Meet Olly the kookaburra, Syd the platypus, and Millie the echidna. They were the mascots of the 2000 Olympic Games. Kookaburra, platypus, and echidna? What kinds of beasts are they? you may ask. They are three of Australia's unique species of animals.

The kookaburra is a pigeon-size snake-eating bird that's also known as the laughing jackass. That's because its song sounds like rowdy laughter. The kookaburra mascot was named Olly, which is short for "Olympic." Olly is a symbol of friendship among the peoples of the world.

The platypus is one of the strangest mammals in the world. Like other mammals, it produces milk for its young. But it lays reptile-like eggs and has a duck-like bill, a beaver-like tail, and large webbed feet. The platypus mascot was named Syd—short for Sydney. Syd is a symbol of the environment.

The echidna is another mammal that produces milk and lays eggs. And like the kangaroo, it's a marsupial and has a small pouch to carry its young. Its other features include a long sticky tongue and sharp spines. It uses its tongue to catch its favorite food—termites and ants. Because of its love of ants and its spines, the echidna is also called the spiny anteater. Millie (short for millennium) the echidna is a symbol of hope, happiness, and sportsmanship.

167

nia threw a scare into them in the semifinals by almost winning the game with a 3-point shot with seconds to go. The United States also had problems in the gold-medal game against France, but finally won 85–75.

The U.S. women's basketball team played better than the men, downing Australia 76–54 to take their second straight Olympic gold medal and their fourth since the sport became an Olympic event in 1976.

In men's soccer, the team from Cameroon won the gold medal. The U.S. team finished out of the medals, but the women's team, the defending Olympic champions, took silver

Other Sports. Cuban boxers continued to perform well at the Olympic Games, taking home four gold and two bronze medals. Also impressive were the boxers from Russia (two golds) and Kazakhstan (two golds). American boxers came away with two silver and two bronze medals.

One of the biggest upsets of the Sydney Olympics came in Greco-Roman wrestling, with Rulon Gardner of Afton, Wyoming, defeating Russia's Aleksander Karelin in the super heavyweight division (130 kg). Karelin had never before lost an international wrestling match.

Simon Whitfield of Canada won the gold medal in the Olympic's first-ever triathlon. This grueling event consists of swimming, running, and cycling.

in one of the most exciting women's games ever played. Norway, the only country with a winning record against the Americans, captured the gold by downing the Americans 3–2 in sudden-death overtime.

In volleyball, Yugoslavia took the gold medal in the men's competition, and Cuba repeated its 1996 victory in the women's competition. In beach volleyball, Americans Dain Blanton and Eric Fonoimoana defeated the Brazilian team in the gold-medal game. Australia walked off with the gold medal in women's beach volleyball.

In the women's single tennis final, American superstar Venus Williams defeated the up-and-coming Elena Dementieva of Russia in the gold-medal match. Venus then joined her younger sister Serena to capture the women's doubles title. Russia's champion Yevgeny Kafelnikov won the men's singles title, and Canada's Sebastien Lareau and Daniel Nestor netted gold in the men's doubles.

In the Olympics' first-ever triathlon, which consists of swimming, running, and cycling, Simon Whitfield of Canada won

New Events, New Gear

Five new events were added for the 2000 Olympic Games: the trampoline; tae kwon do (a martial arts sport); platform and springboard synchronized diving; and the triathlon (swimming, running, and cycling). And women competed in seven events that were once "for men only": weight lifting; water polo; the pole vault; the hammer throw; trap and skeet shooting; and the modern pentathlon (swimming, cross-country running, equestrian steeplechase, fencing, and target shooting).

But it wasn't just the sports events that were new. It was also the high-tech gear used by the athletes.

Kayakers, for example, made their way through the watery course in computer-designed kayaks made of carbon, fiberglass, and kevlar. These high-speed, lightweight boats had special hulls that could slice through the water. One type of kayak was even called the Krypton, after Superman's planet in a faraway galaxy.

In rowing, rowers used new oars that had built-in sensors, so coaches could tell which rowers were pulling their weight—and which weren't. On the track, sprinters wore special shoes and suits. The shoes were designed to help the sprinter get out of the block faster and grip the track better. And body suits, some of them head to ankle, protected the runners' muscles and helped them run faster.

The high-tech development that caused the biggest Olympic stir was the body suit for

swimmers (photo above). These tight-fitting suits cut down on drag and made the swimmer more buoyant. The suit has been compared to the skin of a shark—the fastest finned fish in the sea. But many people don't like the suits. They say that Olympic swimmers should stick with their regular swimsuits.

Whatever people think of all this high-tech gear, it's probably here to stay. The Olympic motto, after all, is *Citius, Altius, Fortius*— "Swifter, Higher, Stronger."

---

the men's gold medal, and Brigitte McMahon of Switzerland won the women's gold. In the trampoline, a new event in the gymnastics group, Irina Karavaeva and Aleksandr Moskalenko, both of Russia, bounced, somersaulted, and twisted their way to gold medals.

ONWARD TO ATHENS

The 27th Olympic Games were among the best ever. The friendly, sports-loving Aussies made everyone feel welcome. The late winter-early spring weather cooperated with lots of sunshine. And the level of competition was superb. But on October 1, after sixteen days of exciting competition, the Olympic flame was extinguished, and the Games came to an end. The next Summer Olympic Games will be held in 2004, in Athens, Greece, the country where the Olympics originated more than 2,700 years ago. Many people also looked forward to the 2002 Winter Olympics, which will take place in Salt Lake City, Utah.

2000 SUMMER OLYMPIC GAMES
Sydney, Australia

FINAL MEDAL STANDINGS

Country	Gold	Silver	Bronze	Total	Country	Gold	Silver	Bronze	Total
United States	40	24	33	97	Taiwan	0	1	4	5
Russia	32	28	28	88	Iran	3	0	1	4
China	28	16	15	59	Turkey	3	0	1	4
Australia	16	25	17	58	Finland	2	1	1	4
Germany	13	17	26	56	Uzbekistan	1	1	2	4
France	13	14	11	38	New Zealand	1	0	3	4
Italy	13	8	13	34	Argentina	0	2	2	4
Cuba	11	11	7	29	North Korea	0	1	3	4
Great Britain	11	10	7	28	Austria	2	1	0	3
South Korea	8	9	11	28	Azerbaijan	2	0	1	3
Romania	11	6	9	26	Latvia	1	1	1	3
Netherlands	12	9	4	25	Yugoslavia	1	1	1	3
Ukraine	3	10	10	23	Estonia	1	0	2	3
Japan	5	8	5	18	Thailand	1	0	2	3
Hungary	8	6	3	17	Nigeria	0	3	0	3
Belarus	3	3	11	17	Slovenia	2	0	0	2
Poland	6	5	3	14	Bahamas	1	1	0	2
Canada	3	3	8	14	Croatia	1	0	1	2
Bulgaria	5	6	2	13	Saudi Arabia	0	1	1	2
Greece	4	6	3	13	Moldova	0	1	1	2
Sweden	4	5	3	12	Trinidad & Tobago	0	1	1	2
Brazil	0	6	6	12	Costa Rica	0	0	2	2
Spain	3	3	5	11	Portugal	0	0	2	2
Norway	4	3	3	10	Cameroon	1	0	0	1
Switzerland	1	6	2	9	Colombia	1	0	0	1
Ethiopia	4	1	3	8	Mozambique	1	0	0	1
Czech Republic	2	3	3	8	Ireland	0	1	0	1
Kazakhstan	3	4	0	7	Uruguay	0	1	0	1
Kenya	2	3	2	7	Vietnam	0	1	0	1
Jamaica	0	4	3	7	Armenia	0	0	1	1
Denmark	2	3	1	6	Barbados	0	0	1	1
Indonesia	1	3	2	6	Chile	0	0	1	1
Mexico	1	2	3	6	India	0	0	1	1
Georgia	0	0	6	6	Iceland	0	0	1	1
Lithuania	2	0	3	5	Israel	0	0	1	1
Slovakia	1	3	1	5	Kyrgyzstan	0	0	1	1
Algeria	1	1	3	5	Kuwait	0	0	1	1
Belgium	0	2	3	5	Macedonia	0	0	1	1
South Africa	0	2	3	5	Qatar	0	0	1	1
Morocco	0	1	4	5	Sri Lanka	0	0	1	1

GOLD MEDAL WINNERS

ARCHERY

Men's Individual: Simon Fairweather, Australia
Women's Individual: Yun Mi Jin, South Korea
Men's Team: South Korea
Women's Team: South Korea

BADMINTON

Men's Singles: Ji Xinpeng, China
Women's Singles: Gong Zhichao, China
Men's Doubles: Indonesia
Women's Doubles: China
Mixed Doubles: China

BASEBALL

United States

BASKETBALL

Men: United States
Women: United States

BEACH VOLLEYBALL

Men: United States
Women: Australia

BOXING

Light Flyweight: Brahim Asloum, France
Flyweight: Wijan Ponlid, Thailand
Bantamweight: Guillermo Rigondeaux Ortiz, Cuba
Featherweight: Bekzat Sattarkhanov, Kazakhstan
Lightweight: Mario Kindelan, Cuba
Light Welterweight: Mahamadkadyz Abdullaev,
    Uzbekistan

Welterweight: Oleg Saitov, Russia
Light Middleweight: Yermakhan Ibraimov,
  Kazakhstan
Middleweight: Jorge Gutierrez, Cuba
Light Heavyweight: Aleksandr Lebziak, Russia
Heavyweight: Felix Savon, Cuba
Super Heavyweight: Audley Harrison, Britain

CANOEING
Men

500-m Kayak Singles: Knut Holmann, Norway
500-m Kayak Pairs: Hungary
1,000-m Kayak Singles: Knut Holmann, Norway
1,000-m Kayak Pairs: Italy
1,000-m Kayak Fours: Hungary
Kayak Slalom Singles: Thomas Schmidt, Germany
500-m Canoe Singles: Gyorgy Kolonics, Hungary
500-m Canoe Pairs: Hungary
1,000-m Canoe Singles: Andreas Dittmer, Germany
1,000-m Canoe Pairs: Romania
Canoe Slalom Singles: Tony Estanguet, France
Canoe Slalom Pairs: Slovakia

Women

500-m Kayak Singles: Josefa Idem Guerrini, Italy
500-m Kayak Pairs: Germany
500-m Kayak Fours: Germany
Kayak Slalom Singles : Stepanka Hilgertova, Czech
  Republic

CYCLING
Men

Pursuit: Robert Bartko, Germany
Team Pursuit: Germany
Keirin: Florian Rousseau, France
Madison: Australia
Points Race: Juan Llaneras, Spain
Individual Time Trial: Vyacheslav Yekimov, Russia
1-km Time Trial: Jason Queally, Britain
Sprint: Marty Nothstein, U.S.
Olympic Sprint: France
Road Race: Jan Ullrich, Germany
Mountain Bike: Miguel Martinez, France

Women

Pursuit: Leontien Zijlaard, Netherlands
Points Race: Antonella Belluti, Italy
Individual Time Trial: Leontien Zijlaard, Netherlands
500-m Time Trial: Felicia Ballanger, France
Sprint: Felicia Ballanger, France
Road Race: Leontien Zijlaard, Netherlands
Mountain Bike: Paola Pezzo, Italy

EQUESTRIAN
3-Day Event: David O'Connor, U.S.
Team 3-Day Event: Australia
Dressage: Anky van Grunsven, Netherlands
Team Dressage: Germany
Jumping: Jeroen Dubbeldam, Netherlands
Team Jumping: Germany

FENCING
Men's Epee: Pavel Kolobkov, Russia
Women's Epee: Timea Nagy, Hungary
Men's Team Epee: Italy
Women's Team Epee: Russia
Men's Saber: Mihai Claudiu Covaliu, Romania
Men's Team Saber: Russia
Men's Foil: Kim Young Ho, South Korea
Women's Foil: Valentina Vezzali, Italy
Men's Team Foil: France
Women's Team Foil: Italy

FIELD HOCKEY
Men: Netherlands
Women: Australia

GYMNASTICS
Men
All-Around: Aleksei Nemov, Russia
Floor Exercise: Igors Vihrovs, Latvia
Horizontal Bar: Aleksei Nemov, Russia
Parallel Bars: Li Xiaopeng, China
Pommel Horse: Marius Urzica, Romania
Rings: Szilveszter Csollany, Hungary
Vault: Gervasio Deferr, Spain
Team: China
Trampoline: Aleksandr Moskalenko, Russia

Women
All-Around: Simona Amanar, Romania
Balance Beam: Liu Xuan, China
Floor Exercise: Yelena Zamolodtchikova, Russia
Uneven Parallel Bars: Svetlana Khorkina,
  Russia
Vault: Yelena Zamolodtchikova, Russia
Team: Romania
Trampoline: Irina Karavaeva, Russia
Individual Rhythmic: Yulia Barsukova, Russia
Team Rhythmic: Russia

HANDBALL
Men: Russia
Women: Denmark

JUDO
Men
Extra Lightweight: Tadahiro Nomura, Japan
Half Lightweight: Huseyin Ozkan, Turkey
Lightweight: Giuseppe Maddaloni, Italy
Half Middleweight: Makoto Takimoto, Japan
Middleweight: Mark Huizinga, Netherlands
Half Heavyweight: Kosei Inoue, Japan
Heavyweight: David Douillet, France

Women
Extra Lightweight: Ryoko Tamura, Japan
Half Lightweight: Legna Verdecia, Cuba
Lightweight: Isabel Fernandez, Spain
Half Middleweight: Severine Vandenhende, France

Middleweight: Sibelis Veranes, Cuba
Half Heavyweight: Tang Lin, China
Heavyweight: Yuan Hua, China

MODERN PENTATHLON

Men: Dmitri Svatkovsky, Russia
Women: Stephanie Cook, Britain

ROWING
Men

Single Sculls: Rob Waddell, New Zealand
Double Sculls: Slovenia
Quadruple Sculls: Italy
Pairs Without Coxswain: France
Fours Without Coxswain: Britain
Lightweight Double Sculls: Poland
Lightweight Four Without Coxswain: France
Eights: Britain

Women

Single Sculls: Ekaterina Karsten, Belarus
Double Sculls: Germany
Quadruple Sculls: Germany
Pairs Without Coxswain: Romania
Lightweight Double Sculls: Romania
Eights: Romania

SHOOTING
Men

Air Pistol: Franck Dumoulin, France
Free Pistol: Tanyu Kiriakov, Bulgaria
Rapid-Fire Pistol: Sergei Alifirenko, Russia
Running Game Target: Yang Ling, China
Air Rifle: Yalin Cai, China
Rifle, 3 Positions: Rajmond Debevec, Slovenia
Rifle Prone: Jonas Edman, Sweden
Open Skeet: Mykola Milchev, Ukraine
Open Trap: Michael Diamond, Australia
Double Trap: Richard Faulds, Britain

Women

Air Pistol: Tao Luna, China
Sport Pistol: Maria Grozdeva, Bulgaria
Air Rifle: Nancy Johnson, U.S.
Rifle, 3 Positions: Renata Mauer-Rozanska, Poland
Skeet: Zemfira Meftakhetdinova, Azerbaijan
Trap: Daina Gudzineviciute, Lithuania
Double Trap: Pia Hansen, Sweden

SOCCER

Men: Cameroon
Women: Norway

SOFTBALL

United States

SWIMMING AND DIVING
Men

100-m Backstroke: Lenny Krayzelburg, U.S.
200-m Backstroke: Lenny Krayzelburg, U.S.
100-m Breaststroke: Domenico Fioravanti, Italy
200-m Breaststroke: Domenico Fioravanti, Italy

100-m Butterfly: Lars Froelander, Sweden
200-m Butterfly: Tom Malchow, U.S.
50-m Freestyle: Anthony Ervin/Gary Hall, Jr., U.S.
100-m Freestyle: Pieter van den Hoogenband,
   Netherlands
200-m Freestyle: Pieter van den Hoogenband,
   Netherlands
400-m Freestyle: Ian Thorpe, Australia
1,500-m Freestyle: Grant Hackett, Australia
400-m Freestyle Relay: Australia
800-m Freestyle Relay: Australia
200-m Individual Medley: Massimiliano Rosolino, Italy
400-m Individual Medley: Tom Dolan, U.S.
400-m Medley Relay: United States
Platform Diving: Tian Liang, China
Synchronized Platform Diving: Russia
Springboard Diving: Xiong Ni, China
Synchronized Springboard Diving: China

Women

100-m Backstroke: Diana Mocanu, Romania
200-m Backstroke: Diana Mocanu, Romania
100-m Breaststroke: Megan Quann, U.S.
200-m Breaststroke: Agnes Kovacs, Hungary
100-m Butterfly: Inge de Bruijn, Netherlands
200-m Butterfly: Misty Hyman, U.S.
50-m Freestyle: Inge de Bruijn, Netherlands
100-m Freestyle: Inge de Bruijn, Netherlands
200-m Freestyle: Susie O'Neill, Australia
400-m Freestyle: Brooke Bennett, U.S.
800-m Freestyle: Brooke Bennett, U.S.
400-m Freestyle Relay: United States
800-m Freestyle Relay: United States
200-m Individual Medley: Yana Klochkova, Ukraine
400-m Individual Medley: Yana Klochkova, Ukraine
400-m Medley Relay: United States
Platform Diving: Laura Wilkinson, U.S.
Synchronized Platform Diving: China
Springboard Diving: Fu Mingxia, China
Synchronized Springboard Diving: Russia

SYNCHRONIZED SWIMMING

Duet: Russia   Team: Russia

TABLE TENNIS

Men's Singles: Kong Linghui, China
Women's Singles: Wang Nan, China
Men's Doubles: China
Women's Doubles: China

TAE KWON DO
Men

58 kg: Michail Mouroutsos, Greece
68 kg: Steven Lopez, U.S.
80 kg: Angel Valodia Matos Fuentes, Cuba
Over 80 kg: Kim Kyong Hun, South Korea

Women

49 kg: Lauren Burns, Australia
57 kg: Jung Jae Eun, South Korea
67 kg: Lee Sun Hee, South Korea
Over 67 kg: Chen Zhong, China

TENNIS

Men's Singles: Yevgeny Kafelnikov, Russia
Women's Singles: Venus Williams, U.S.
Men's Doubles: Canada
Women's Doubles: United States

TRACK AND FIELD

Men

100-m: Maurice Greene, U.S.
200-m: Konstantinos Kenteris, Greece
400-m: Michael Johnson, U.S.
800-m: Nils Schumann, Germany
1,500-m: Noah Ngeny, Kenya
5,000-m: Millon Wolde, Ethiopia
10,000-m: Haile Gebrselassie, Ethiopia
400-m Relay: United States
1,600-m Relay: United States
20-km Walk: Robert Korzeniowski, Poland
50-km Walk: Robert Korzeniowski, Poland
110-m Hurdles: Anier Garcia, Cuba
400-m Hurdles: Angelo Taylor, U.S.
3,000-m Steeplechase: Reuben Kosgei, Kenya
Marathon: Gezahgne Abera, Ethiopia
Decathlon: Erki Nool, Estonia
Discus: Virgilijus Alekna, Lithuania
Hammer Throw: Szymon Ziolkowski, Poland
High Jump: Sergei Kliugin, Russia
Javelin: Jan Zelezny, Czech Republic
Long Jump: Ivan Pedroso, Cuba
Pole Vault: Nick Hysong, U.S.
Shot Put: Arsi Harju, Finland
Triple Jump: Jonathan Edwards, Britain

Women

100-m: Marion Jones, U.S.
200-m: Marion Jones, U.S.
400-m: Cathy Freeman, Australia
800-m: Maria Mutola, Mozambique
1,500-m: Nouria Merah-Benida, Algeria
5,000-m: Gabriela Szabo, Romania
10,000-m: Derartu Tulu, Ethiopia
400-m Relay: Bahamas
1,600-m Relay: United States
20-km Walk: Wang Liping, China
100-m Hurdles: Olga Shishigina, Kazakhstan
400-m Hurdles: Irina Privalova, Russia
Marathon: Naoko Takahashi, Japan
Hammer Throw: Kamila Skolimowska, Poland
Heptathlon: Denise Lewis, Britain
Discus: Ellina Zvereva, Belarus
High Jump: Yelena Yelesina, Russia
Javelin: Trine Hattestad, Norway
Long Jump: Heike Drechsler, Germany
Pole Vault: Stacy Dragila, U.S.
Shot Put: Yanina Korolchik, Belarus
Triple Jump: Tereza Marinova, Bulgaria

TRIATHLON

Men: Simon Whitfield, Canada
Women: Brigitte McMahon, Switzerland

VOLLEYBALL

Men: Yugoslavia
Women: Cuba

WATER POLO

Men: Hungary
Women: Australia

WEIGHT LIFTING

Men

56 kg: Halil Mutlu, Turkey
62 kg: Nikolay Pechalov, Croatia
69 kg: Galabin Boevski, Bulgaria
77 kg: Zhan Xugang, China
85 kg: Pyrros Dimas, Greece
94 kg: Akakios Kakiasvilis, Greece
105 kg: Hossein Tavakoli, Iran
Over 105 kg: Hossein Rezazadeh, Iran

Women

48 kg: Tara Nott, U.S.
53 kg: Yang Xia, China
58 kg: Soraya Jimenez Mendivil, Mexico
63 kg: Chen Xiaomin, China
69 kg: Lin Weining, China
75 kg: Maria Isabel Urrutia, Colombia
Over 75 kg: Ding Meiyuan, China

WRESTLING, FREESTYLE

54 kg: Namig Adbullayev, Azerbaijan
58 kg: Alireza Dabir, Iran
63 kg: Mourad Oumakhanov, Russia
69 kg: Daniel Igali, Canada
76 kg: Brandon Slay, U.S.
85 kg: Adam Saitiev, Russia
97 kg: Saghid Mourtasaliyev, Russia
130 kg: David Moussoulbes, Russia

WRESTLING, GRECO-ROMAN

54 kg: Sim Kwon Ho, South Korea
58 kg: Armen Nazarian, Russia
63 kg: Varteres Samourgachev, Russia
69 kg: Filiberto Azcuy, Cuba
76 kg: Mourat Kardanov, Russia
85 kg: Hamza Yerlikaya, Turkey
97 kg: Mikael Ljungberg, Sweden
130 kg: Rulon Gardner, U.S.

YACHTING

Finn: Iain Percy, Britain
49ers: Finland
Laser: Ben Ainslie, Britain
Soling: Denmark
Star: United States
Tornado: Austria
Mistral, Men: Christoph Sieber, Austria
Mistral, Women: Alessandra Sensini, Italy
Men's 470: Australia
Women's 470: Australia
Women's Europe: Shirley Robertson, Britain

Shortstop Derek Jeter's batting and fielding helped the New York Yankees defeat the New York Mets in the World Series. Jeter was named World Series MVP.

BASEBALL

Sports fans in New York City received a rare treat in 2000: The New York Yankees and the New York Mets won the titles of their respective leagues and faced each other in the World Series. For the Mets, it was their first appearance in the Fall Classic since 1986; for the Yankees, the story was more familiar—the "Bronx Bombers" won their third straight Series, dispatching their crosstown rivals in five games. The Yanks thus became the first team to capture three consecutive world championships since the Oakland A's of 1972–74.

In the regular season, manager Joe Torre's Yanks finished atop the Eastern Division of the American League (AL), but with only the fifth-best record in the AL. The other AL squads qualifying for post-season play were the Central Division champion Chicago White Sox, the Western Division champion Oakland A's, and the wild-card team, the Seattle Mariners, from the Western Division.

The Yanks defeated Oakland in the division series (the first round of the playoffs), 3 games to 2. Seattle, meanwhile, swept Chicago in three straight. New York then scuttled the Mariners, 4 games to 2, in the American League Championship Series (ALCS). Yankee right-handed hurler Roger Clemens threw a scalding one-hit shutout in Game 4, striking out 15 Mariners. But named the Most Valuable Player (MVP) of the ALCS was New York left fielder David Justice, whose clutch hitting kept sending his Bomber teammates across the plate.

In the National League (NL), the Mets posted the fourth-best regular-season mark; they earned the wild card, finishing behind the Atlanta Braves in the NL Eastern Division. The Central Division champs were the St. Louis Cardinals; and leading the Western Division were the San Francisco Giants, who compiled the best won-lost mark in either league.

Undaunted, the Mets cut down the Giants, 3 games to 1, in the division series; two of the contests, both won by New York, required extra innings. St. Louis, meanwhile, eliminated Atlanta in a three-game sweep. In the National League Championship Series (NLCS), the Mets knocked down the Cards in five games; New York left-handed pitcher Mike Hampton won the first and final contests and was named MVP of the NLCS.

In Game 1 of the World Series, played in Yankee Stadium, Justice doubled in Chuck Knoblauch and Derek Jeter in the sixth inning to give the Yanks a 2–0 lead; the Mets countered with 3 in the seventh and took a 3–2 margin into the last of the ninth. But Knoblauch tied the score with a sacrifice fly, and the contest went into extra innings. In the last of the twelfth inning, Yankee second baseman Jose Vizcaino singled in the winning run; it was his fourth hit of the game. Final score: 4–3. Yankee reliever Mike Stanton held the Mets scoreless in the last two frames to notch the victory.

Roger Clemens was masterful in Game 2, striking out nine Mets and allowing only two hits. Scott Brosius homered, and Derek

2000 WORLD SERIES RESULTS

		R	H	E	Winning/Losing Pitcher
1	Mets	3	10	0	Turk Wendell (L)
	Yankees	4	12	0	Mike Stanton (W)
2	Mets	5	7	3	Mike Hampton (L)
	Yankees	6	12	1	Roger Clemens (W)
3	Yankees	2	8	0	Orlando Hernandez (L)
	Mets	4	9	0	John Franco (W)
4	Yankees	3	8	0	Jeff Nelson (W)
	Mets	2	6	1	Bobby Jones (L)
5	Yankees	4	7	1	Mike Stanton (W)
	Mets	2	8	1	Al Leiter (L)

Visiting team listed first, home team second

Jeter, Paul O'Neill, and Tino Martinez each contributed three hits to the Yanks' cause. Clemens left the game after eight innings with a 6–0 lead; the Mets exploded in the top of the ninth—Mike Piazza and Jay Payton clubbed homers—but fell one run short. The Yankees won, 6–5, and carried a 2-games-to-none margin to Shea Stadium, the home of the Mets, where Games 3, 4, and 5 would be played.

Game 3 resulted in the Mets' only triumph of the Series, by a 4–2 score. Robin Ventura homered for the Mets, and relief pitcher John Franco picked up the victory. For the Yanks, O'Neill, with three hits, and Jeter, with two, continued their hot hitting.

The Yanks used five pitchers in Game 4, and the Mets used four. Yankee reliever Jeff Nelson got the victory, and Jeter—the Yanks' All-Star shortstop—contributed two hits, including a home run. His teammates O'Neill and Martinez also had two each. The final score was 3–2, and the Yankees led the Series, 3 games to 1.

Game 5, won by the Yankees by a 4–2 score, ended the 2000 Fall Classic. Yank center fielder Bernie Williams, who had been hitless through the first four games, collected two hits, including a home run. Derek Jeter also smacked another four-bagger; for his superb all-around play, not to mention his .409 batting average, Jeter was named MVP of the Series. He set a record for a five-game Series with 19 total bases; he had nine hits, as did Paul O'Neill.

The AL regular-season MVP was Oakland's Jason Giambi, who compiled 41 home runs, 133 runs batted in (RBIs), and a .330 batting average. Jeff Kent of the San Francisco Giants was NL MVP; no second baseman since Hall-of-Famer Rogers Hornsby had been such an offensive threat—in 2000, Kent batted .334, socked 33 homers, and amassed 125 RBIs.

Arizona Diamondback left-hander Randy Johnson won the NL Cy Young Award for the second consecutive year; he had 19 wins against 7 losses, a 2.64 earned run average (ERA), and 347 strikeouts in 248.2 innings pitched. The AL honoree, also for the second straight year, was Pedro Martinez of the Boston Red Sox; along with his 18–6 won-lost mark, he posted a minuscule 1.74 ERA and fanned 284 batters in 217 innings.

Rookie-of-the-Year Awards went, in the AL, to Seattle reliever Kazuhiro Sasaki, who saved 37 games; and in the NL, to Rafael Furcal, who hit .295 for Atlanta.

With a 19–7 record and a 2.64 earned run average, Arizona Diamondback southpaw Randy Johnson won the NL Cy Young Award for the second year in a row.

MAJOR LEAGUE BASEBALL FINAL STANDINGS

AMERICAN LEAGUE

Eastern Division

	W	L	Pct.	GB
*New York	87	74	.540	—
Boston	85	77	.525	2½
Toronto	83	79	.512	4½
Baltimore	74	88	.457	13½
Tampa Bay	69	92	.429	18

Central Division

	W	L	Pct.	GB
Chicago	95	67	.586	—
Cleveland	90	72	.556	5
Detroit	79	83	.488	16
Kansas City	77	85	.475	18
Minnesota	69	93	.426	26

Western Division

	W	L	Pct.	GB
Oakland	91	70	.565	—
Seattle	91	71	.562	½
Anaheim	82	80	.506	9½
Texas	71	91	.438	20½

*League Championship Series winners

NATIONAL LEAGUE

Eastern Division

	W	L	Pct.	GB
Atlanta	95	67	.586	—
*New York	94	68	.580	1
Florida	79	82	.491	15½
Montreal	67	95	.414	28
Philadelphia	65	97	.401	30

Central Division

	W	L	Pct.	GB
St. Louis	95	67	.586	—
Cincinnati	85	77	.525	10
Milwaukee	73	89	.451	22
Houston	72	90	.444	23
Pittsburgh	69	93	.426	26
Chicago	65	97	.401	30

Western Division

	W	L	Pct.	GB
San Francisco	97	65	.599	—
Los Angeles	86	76	.531	11
Arizona	85	77	.525	12
Colorado	82	80	.506	15
San Diego	76	86	.469	21

MAJOR LEAGUE LEADERS

AMERICAN LEAGUE

Batting
(top 10 qualifiers)

	AB	H	Avg.
N. Garciaparra, Boston	529	197	.372
D. Erstad, Anaheim	676	240	.355
M. Ramirez, Cleveland	439	154	.351
C. Delgado, Toronto	569	196	.344
D. Jeter, New York	593	201	.339
D. Segui, Cleveland	574	192	.334
M. Sweeney, Kansas City	618	206	.333
J. Giambi, Oakland	510	170	.333
F. Thomas, Chicago	582	191	.328
J. Damon, Kansas City	655	214	.327

Home Runs

	HR
T. Glaus, Anaheim	47
J. Giambi, Oakland	43
F. Thomas, Chicago	43
T. Batista, Toronto	41
A. Rodriguez, Seattle	41
D. Justice, New York	41
C. Delgado, Toronto	41

Pitching
(top qualifiers, based on number of wins)

	W	L	ERA
T. Hudson, Oakland	20	6	4.14
D. Wells, Toronto	20	8	4.11
A. Pettitte, New York	19	9	4.35
P. Martinez, Boston	18	6	1.74
A. Sele, Seattle	17	10	4.51

NATIONAL LEAGUE

Batting
(top 10 qualifiers)

	AB	H	Avg.
T. Helton, Colorado	580	216	.372
M. Alou, Houston	454	161	.355
V. Guerrero, Montreal	571	197	.345
J. Hammonds, Colorado	454	152	.335
J. Kent, San Francisco	587	196	.334
L. Castillo, Florida	539	180	.334
J. Vidro, Montreal	606	200	.330
J. Cirillo, Colorado	598	195	.326
G. Sheffield, Los Angeles	501	163	.325
E. Alfonzo, New York	544	176	.324

Home Runs

	HR
S. Sosa, Chicago	50
B. Bonds, San Francisco	49
J. Bagwell, Houston	47
V. Guerrero, Montreal	44
R. Hidalgo, Houston	44

Pitching
(top qualifiers, based on number of wins)

	W	L	ERA
T. Glavine, Atlanta	21	9	3.40
D. Kile, St. Louis	20	9	3.91
R. Johnson, Arizona	19	7	2.64
G. Maddux, Atlanta	19	9	3.00
C. H. Park, Los Angeles	18	10	3.27

LITTLE LEAGUE BASEBALL

Two young men with strong arms hooked up in a pitchers' duel in the final game of the Little League World Series on August 24, 2000. Ruben Mavarez, on the mound for Maracaibo, Venezuela, the Latin American champions, hurled a complete game—six innings—as did Alex Atherton for Bellaire, Texas, the United States champions. Mavarez yielded four hits and struck out six batters, while Atherton allowed only two hits and fanned twelve. But at the end of the game, the Venezuelan team had won, 3–2, and claimed the Little League world championship.

Venezuela picked up two runs in the top of the first inning, as Ali Castillo and Adrian Chourio both scored on wild pitches by Atherton. Texas responded with one run in the bottom of the first when Michael Johnson tripled and came home on Atherton's double.

In the third inning, Venezuela took a 3–1 lead when Mavarez doubled and scored on an error in the Texas outfield. Texas got its second run in the bottom of the same inning, as Mitchell Malone scored on a wild pitch by Mavarez. But there the scoring ended, and three innings later, Mavarez struck out Texas's Hunter Johnson for the final out of the contest.

The Venezuelan ballplayers were from the Sierra Maestra Little League in Maracaibo. They reached the title game of the World Series by defeating Tokyo, Japan, the Far East champs, 5–4 in the International championship game. The other teams in the International Division of the annual tournament were the Canadian titlists, from Toronto, Ontario; and, representing Europe, a squad from Dhahran, Saudi Arabia.

In the United States Division of the tournament, Bellaire, Texas, representing the U.S. South, qualified for the final by blanking Davenport, Iowa, the Central champs, 8–0 in the U.S. championship game. The

Venezuelan pitcher Ruben Mavarez falls to his knees after leading his team to victory in the 2000 Little League World Series. Maracaibo, Venezuela, defeated the U.S. team, 3–2, in the championship game.

other regional representatives were Vancouver, Washington, from the West; and Goffstown, New Hampshire, from the East.

The Little League World Series is held each year at Howard J. Lamade Stadium in Williamsport, Pennsylvania.

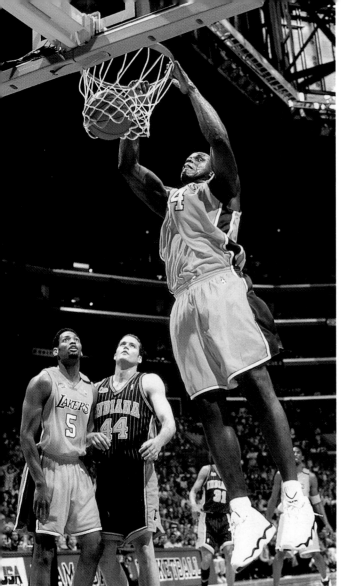

BASKETBALL

The Los Angeles Lakers have won many National Basketball Association (NBA) titles in their history—and all their championship teams have been led by great centers: George Mikan in the 1940's and 1950's, when the Lakers played in Minneapolis; Wilt Chamberlain in the 1970's; and Kareem Abdul-Jabbar in the 1980's. In the 1999–2000 season, the Lakers won their twelfth NBA championship as they defeated the Indiana Pacers, four games to two, in the playoff finals. And as before, the Lakers were powered by a dominating center: Shaquille O'Neal.

Standing 7 feet, 1 inch tall and weighing 330 pounds, "Shaq" was nearly unstoppable. But no player wins a championship alone. His teammates included Kobe Bryant, the young, talented guard who, like O'Neal, has achieved superstar status; forwards Glen Rice, A. C. Green, Robert Horry, and Rick Fox; and guards Ron Harper, Derek Fisher, and Brian Shaw. For Los Angeles coach Phil Jackson, it was his first year at the Laker helm; he had piloted the Chicago Bulls to six NBA titles in the 1990's.

Los Angeles compiled the best regular-season record in the NBA, leading the Pacific Division of the league's Western Conference. Four other teams from that division qualified for post-season play: the Portland Trail Blazers, the Phoenix Suns, the Seattle Supersonics, and the Sacramento Kings. The playoff teams from the Midwest Division of the Western Conference were the first-place Utah Jazz, the defending NBA champion San Antonio Spurs, and the Minnesota Timberwolves.

In the best-of-five first-round series of the playoffs, Los Angeles required all five games to eliminate Sacramento. The later playoff rounds were all best-of-seven: The Lakers eclipsed the Suns, four games to one, in round two, and then came from behind to defeat Portland in the seventh game of the Conference finals.

Indiana, coached by all-time great Larry Bird, finished first in the Central Division of the Eastern Conference. The other Central teams reaching the post-season were the Charlotte Hornets, the Toronto Raptors, the Detroit Pistons, and the Milwaukee Bucks. In the conference's Atlantic Division, the Miami Heat came in first and were joined in the playoffs by the New York Knicks and the Philadelphia 76ers.

The Pacers narrowly avoided elimination in round one of the playoffs, holding off Milwaukee by one point in Game 5. Indiana then outmatched Philadelphia, four games to two, in

NBA FINAL STANDINGS

EASTERN CONFERENCE

Atlantic Division

	W	L	Pct.
Miami	52	30	.634
New York	50	32	.610
Philadelphia	49	33	.598
Orlando	41	41	.500
Boston	35	47	.427
New Jersey	31	51	.378
Washington	29	53	.354

Central Division

	W	L	Pct.
Indiana	56	26	.683
Charlotte	49	33	.598
Toronto	45	37	.549
Detroit	42	40	.512
Milwaukee	42	40	.512
Cleveland	32	50	.390
Atlanta	28	54	.341
Chicago	17	65	.207

WESTERN CONFERENCE

Midwest Division

	W	L	Pct.
Utah	55	27	.671
San Antonio	53	29	.646
Minnesota	50	32	.610
Dallas	40	42	.488
Denver	35	47	.427
Houston	34	48	.415
Vancouver	22	60	.268

Pacific Division

	W	L	Pct.
L.A. Lakers	67	15	.817
Portland	59	23	.720
Phoenix	53	29	.646
Seattle	45	37	.549
Sacramento	44	38	.537
Golden State	19	63	.232
L.A. Clippers	15	67	.183

NBA Championship: L.A. Lakers

COLLEGE BASKETBALL

Conference	Winner
Atlantic Coast	Duke (regular season and tournament)
Atlantic Ten	Temple; Dayton (regular season) Temple (tournament)
Big East	Syracuse, Miami (tied, regular season) St. John's (tournament)
Big Ten	Ohio State, Michigan State (tied, regular season) Michigan State (tournment)
Big Twelve	Iowa State (regular season and tournament)
Big West	Utah State; Long Beach State (regular season) Utah State (tournament)
Ivy League	Pennsylvania
Missouri Valley	Indiana State (regular season) Creighton (tournament)
Pacific-10	Stanford, Arizona (tied)
Southeastern	Tennessee, Kentucky, Florida (tied, regular season); Louisana State Arkansas (tournament)
Southwestern Athletic	Alcorn State (regular season) Jackson State (tournament)
Western Athletic	Tulsa (regular season) Fresno State (tournament)

NCAA, men: Michigan State
women: Connecticut

NIT: Wake Forest

round two, and in the Eastern Conference finals, they needed another six games to defeat New York.

The opening two games of the playoff finals were contested at Staples Center, the Lakers' home court, in Los Angeles. Game 1, played June 7, was a rout. The Lakers won, 104–87, as O'Neal poured in 43 points and

snared 19 rebounds. Kobe Bryant chipped in with 14 points and Ron Harper added 12. Meanwhile, Indiana's star guard Reggie Miller endured one of the poorest games of his playoff career, connecting on just one of sixteen shots from the floor.

Game 2 resulted in another victory for Los Angeles; O'Neal again dominated, amassing 40 points and 24 rebounds. The Pacers' center Rik Smits, though 3 inches taller than Shaq, couldn't stop him, and Indiana tried the "Hack-a-Shaq" defense: Knowing that O'Neal isn't a good foul shooter, the Pacers tried fouling him frequently, hoping to regain possession of the ball when he missed from the free-throw line. O'Neal sank only 18 of 39 free throws. But ultimately, the Pacers' strategy failed, as the Lakers won, 111–104.

Conseco Fieldhouse in Indianapolis was the site of Games 3 through 5. The Pacers thrilled the home crowd in Game 3, winning 100–91. Reggie Miller registered 33 points, and team-

Shea Ralph (with arms outstretched) led the University of Connecticut Huskies to the NCAA championship and was named tournament MVP.

mate Jalen Rose had 21. For Los Angeles, O'Neal also had 33. Bryant, nursing an ankle injury he suffered in Game 2, didn't play.

Game 4 was close, an overtime struggle. His ankle still sore, Bryant played most of the game, coming up big when the chips were down. The teams were tied 104–104 as regulation time expired. O'Neal recorded 36 points and 21 rebounds, but he fouled out halfway through overtime. So Bryant took command, controlling the offense, and finishing with 28 points. Final score: 120–118. Miller scored 35 for Indiana, but Los Angeles now had a three-games-to-one margin.

Playing their last home game of the 1999–2000 season in Game 5, the Pacers trounced the Lakers by 33 points. Indiana's Rose had 32 points and Miller 25, while Shaq totaled 35 for Los Angeles.

Back in California for Game 6, the teams battled like two brave fighters. The Pacers led most of the way, but Bryant's four free throws in the closing seconds gave the Lakers a 116–111 victory and the NBA title. He had 26 for the game, and O'Neal, overpowering once again, had 41.

Shaq O'Neal was named Most Valuable Player (MVP) of the finals; he averaged 38 points and 16.7 rebounds per game. O'Neal thus achieved a rare "triple": He also won the MVP awards for the NBA All-Star game, played in February; and the 2000 regular season, during which he was the league's leading scorer, at 29.7 points per game.

Co-winners of the Rookie of the Year Award were forward Elton Brand of the Chicago Bulls and guard Steve Francis of the Houston Rockets. Miami Heat center Alonzo Mourning was named Defensive Player of the Year.

The WNBA. For every year of the four-year existence of the Women's National Basketball Association (WNBA), the Houston Comets have won the league championship. Also for the fourth time in as many years, Houston's Cynthia Cooper was named MVP of the playoffs; she and her teammates defeated the New York Liberty two games to none in the best-of-three playoff finals. For the regular season, Houston's Sheryl Swoopes was the WNBA's top scorer (with 20.7 points per game), league MVP, and Defensive Player of the Year.

College Play. The winners of the women's National Collegiate Athletic Association (NCAA) basketball championship for 2000 were the Huskies of the University of Connecticut, who dispatched the Lady Vols of the University of Tennessee by the score of 71–52 in the final game of the NCAA tournament. UConn's Shea Ralph was named tourney MVP; the Huskies are coached by Geno Auriemma.

Michigan State won the men's NCAA title. Coached by Tom Izzo, the Spartans outscored Florida, 89–76, in the final. Michigan State's star point guard, Mateen Cleaves, sparked his teammates; despite a second-half injury, he notched 18 points and dished off four assists. He was named tourney MVP.

FOOTBALL

The St. Louis Rams won their first Super Bowl ever in the year 2000; the Rams last won the National Football League (NFL) championship in 1951, when they represented Los Angeles. In the Canadian Football League, the B.C. Lions collected top honors. And among college teams, the Sooners of Oklahoma were ranked number one at the end of the regular season.

THE NFL PLAYOFFS AND SUPER BOWL XXXIV

In the 1999 regular season, St. Louis finished first in the Western Division of the NFL's National Conference (NFC). The other NFC division leaders were the Washington Redskins and the Tampa Bay Buccaneers, while the Minnesota Vikings, the Detroit Lions, and the Dallas Cowboys qualified for the playoffs as wild-card teams.

In the first round of the playoffs, the Redskins shot down the Lions, 27–13; meanwhile, Minnesota routed Dallas, 27–10. A week later, St. Louis overpowered Minnesota, 49–37, as Ram quarterback Kurt Warner completed 27 of 33 passes, five for touchdowns. Tampa Bay squeaked by Washington, 14–13; the Buccaneers' Shaun King became the first rookie signal-caller since 1976 to win a playoff game.

In the NFC title game, the Rams scored the only touchdown, late in the game, which gave them the victory: With less than five minutes left in the game, Kurt Warner connected on a 30-yard touchdown pass with wide receiver Ricky Proehl. St. Louis held on for an 11–6 win—and the Rams were the NFC champs.

The American Conference (AFC) division leaders were the Indianapolis Colts, the Jacksonville Jaguars, and the Seattle Seahawks. Wild-card spots went to the Tennessee Titans, the Buffalo Bills, and the Miami Dolphins.

In the first round of the playoffs, Miami upset Seattle, 20–17. Meanwhile, the Titans beat the Bills by 22–16. The following week, Tennessee upset Indianapolis, 19–16, as Eddie George rushed for 68 yards. Jacksonville, meanwhile, steamrolled Miami by 62–7. This would be the last game in the career of Miami quarterback Dan Marino; he officially retired in March 2000.

One of the finest receivers of all time, Cris Carter caught 96 passes in the 2000–2001 regular season for the NFC Central champion Minnesota Vikings.

In the AFC title game, Jacksonville tallied all its points in the first half, leading 14–10 at the intermission. But Tennessee exploded for 16 points in the third quarter and added another touchdown in the final period. Final score: Titans, 33–14. Tennessee quarterback Steve McNair completed 14 passes for 112 yards and rushed for another 91.

So the Titans, coached by Jeff Fisher, earned their first trip to the Super Bowl. For coach Dick Vermeil's Rams, it had been 20 years since their last Super Bowl; in 1980, as the Los Angeles Rams, they lost to the Pittsburgh Steelers.

One of the most exciting NFL championship games in recent history, Super Bowl XXXIV was played at the Georgia Dome in Atlanta on January 30, 2000, before more than 72,000 people. St. Louis scored first, on a 27-yard field goal by Jeff Wilkins in the first quarter; he added a 29-yarder and a 28-yarder in the second period. The Rams led 9–0 at halftime.

Midway through the third quarter, St. Louis scored again, raising its margin to 16–0. As the third period was about to end, the game really began. Culminating a 66-yard drive, Eddie George gave Tennessee its first points with a one-yard TD. A two-point conversion attempt failed, and the Rams led 16–6 as the fourth quarter started.

The Titans then executed another long drive, marching 79 yards in 13 plays. At almost the midpoint of the period, George found the end zone again, this time from two yards out; St. Louis now was up by only three points. And just over five minutes later, that three-point lead was gone, as Titan placekicker Al Del Greco split the uprights from 43 yards. Score 16–16. But barely 18 seconds later, Ram quarterback Warner teamed with wide receiver Isaac Bruce on a 73-yard touchdown pass, and St. Louis regained the lead, 23–16.

And Tennessee still wouldn't quit. Titan quarterback McNair and his teammates ran off ten plays and went 87 yards to the St. Louis 10-yard line. With five seconds remaining in the contest, McNair hit wide receiver Kevin Dyson with a pass; Dyson struggled toward the goal line but was tackled one yard short as the gun sounded. The Rams won—but the Titans didn't really "lose"; time just ran out for them. It was a great game.

Already honored as the Most Valuable Player (MVP) for the 1999–2000 regular season, Warner was named the game's MVP; he completed 24 of 45 passes for a Super Bowl record 414 yards.

THE 2000 REGULAR SEASON

St. Louis finished second in its division in the 2000 regular season, earning a wild-card berth in the playoffs. The NFC division leaders were the New Orleans Saints, the New York Giants, and Minnesota; the other wild-card teams were Tampa Bay and the Philadelphia Eagles.

In the AFC, Tennessee, Miami, and Oakland topped their respective divisions; wild cards went to Denver, Indianapolis, and Baltimore.

THE CANADIAN FOOTBALL LEAGUE

The B.C. (British Columbia) Lions won the Canadian Football League (CFL) title in 2000, outlasting the Montreal Alouettes by the score of 28–26 in the Grey Cup Game, played November 26, 2000, in Calgary, Alberta. The Lions had had a less-than-mediocre regular season, finishing with an 8–10 record; but they qualified for the playoffs, and never lost again.

COLLEGE FOOTBALL

Oklahoma (12–0) was ranked number one in college football at the end of the regular season. The "Sooners" defeated number-three Florida State (11–1) in the Orange Bowl.

Number-two Miami (10–1) topped Florida (10–2) in the Sugar Bowl; Washington (10–1) bested Purdue (8–3) in the Rose Bowl; Kansas State (10–3) dropped Tennessee (8–3) in the Cotton Bowl; Oregon State (10–1) trounced Notre Dame (9–2) in the Fiesta Bowl; and Virginia Tech (10–1) whipped Clemson (9–2) in the Gator Bowl.

Florida State quarterback Chris Weinke won the Heisman Trophy as the best college player. The 28-year-old threw 33 TD passes and led the nation with 4,167 yards passing.

Quarterback Rich Gannon led the Oakland Raiders' powerful offense in 2000–2001; the team finished first in the AFC West.

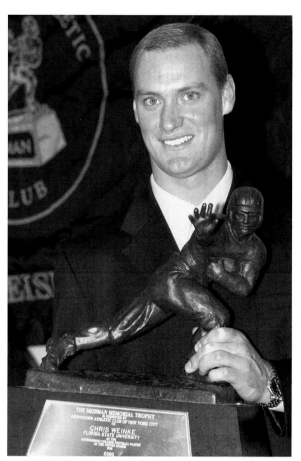
Florida State quarterback Chris Weinke won the 2000 Heisman Trophy as the best college player.

COLLEGE FOOTBALL

Conference	Winner
Atlantic Coast	Florida State
Big Ten	Michigan, Northwestern, Purdue (tied)
Big Twelve	Oklahoma
Big West	Boise State
Pacific-10	Washington, Oregon, Oregon State (tied)
Southeastern	Florida
Western Athletic	Texas Christian University, UTEP (tied)

Cotton Bowl: Kansas State 35, Tennessee 21
Fiesta Bowl: Oregon State 41, Notre Dame 9
Gator Bowl: Virginia Tech 41, Clemson 20
Orange Bowl: Oklahoma 13, Florida State 2
Rose Bowl: Washington 34, Purdue 24
Sugar Bowl: Miami 37, Florida 20

Heisman Trophy: Chris Weinke, Florida State

2000 NFL FINAL STANDINGS

AMERICAN CONFERENCE

Eastern Division

	W	L	T	Pct.	PF	PA
Miami	11	5	0	.688	323	226
Indianapolis	10	6	0	.625	429	326
N.Y. Jets	9	7	0	.563	321	321
Buffalo	8	8	0	.500	315	350
New England	5	11	0	.313	276	338

Central Division

	W	L	T	Pct.	PF	PA
Tennessee	13	3	0	.813	346	191
Baltimore	12	4	0	.750	333	165
Pittsburgh	9	7	0	.563	321	255
Jacksonville	7	9	0	.438	367	327
Cincinnati	4	12	0	.250	185	359
Cleveland	3	13	0	.188	161	419

Western Division

	W	L	T	Pct.	PF	PA
Oakland	12	4	0	.750	479	299
Denver	11	5	0	.688	485	369
Kansas City	7	9	0	.438	355	354
Seattle	6	10	0	.375	320	405
San Diego	1	15	0	.063	269	440

NATIONAL CONFERENCE

Eastern Division

	W	L	T	Pct.	PF	PA
N.Y. Giants	12	4	0	.750	328	246
Philadelphia	11	5	0	.688	351	245
Washington	8	8	0	.500	281	269
Dallas	5	11	0	.313	294	361
Arizona	3	13	0	.188	210	443

Central Division

	W	L	T	Pct.	PF	PA
Minnesota	11	5	0	.688	397	371
Tampa Bay	10	6	0	.625	388	269
Detroit	9	7	0	.563	307	307
Green Bay	9	7	0	.563	353	323
Chicago	5	11	0	.313	216	355

Western Division

	W	L	T	Pct.	PF	PA
New Orleans	10	6	0	.625	354	305
St. Louis	10	6	0	.625	540	471
Carolina	7	9	0	.438	310	310
San Francisco	6	10	0	.375	388	422
Atlanta	4	12	0	.250	252	413

In golf, the year 2000 was definitely the Year of the Tiger—Tiger Woods, that is. Woods had won the Masters Tournament in 1997 and the PGA Championship in 1999. In June 2000, the popular 24-year-old golfer won the U.S. Open. In July he won the British Open. He thus became the youngest person to win all four of golf's "Grand Slam" events. In August, Woods went on to win his second PGA Championship— becoming the first golfer in 47 years to win three Grand Slam tournaments in one year. And THEN he won the World Golf Championships and the Canadian Open!

GOLF

PROFESSIONAL		AMATEUR	
	Individual		Individual
Masters	Vijay Singh	U.S. Amateur	Jeff Quinney
U.S. Open	Tiger Woods	U.S. Women's Amateur	Marcy Newton
Canadian Open	Tiger Woods	British Amateur	Mikko Ilonen
British Open	Tiger Woods	British Ladies Amateur	Rebecca Hudson
PGA	Tiger Woods	Canadian Amateur	Han Lee
World Golf Championships	Tiger Woods	Canadian Ladies Amateur	Jan Dowling
U.S. Women's Open	Karrie Webb		
Ladies PGA	Juli Inkster		Team
		Curtis Cup	United States

New Jersey Devils defenseman and team captain Scott Stevens was named the Most Valuable Player of the NHL playoffs. Stevens led the Devils to a four-games-to-two victory over the Dallas Stars.

HOCKEY

The New Jersey Devils won the National Hockey League (NHL) championship in the year 2000. They captured the Stanley Cup by defeating the Dallas Stars in the playoff finals, four games to two. In a series matching the league's best defenses, every possession of the puck was challenged and few goals came easily; the last two contests required multiple overtimes to decide the winners. And in an unusual turn of events, New Jersey took three of its four victories as the visitors, on the home ice of Dallas, the defending Stanley Cup champs.

In fact, New Jersey had an unusual year. Robbie Ftorek, the Devils' coach for most of the season, was replaced by assistant coach Larry Robinson with eight games left in the regular schedule. Robinson, a member of the Hockey Hall of Fame, was one of the great defensemen on the Montreal Canadien teams that won six Stanley Cups in the 1970's and 1980's. New Jersey finished the 1999–2000 regular season with 103 points, second in the Atlantic Division to the Phil-adelphia Flyers' 105. Dallas, piloted by Ken Hitchcock, led the Pacific Division with 102 points.

Other division winners were the Toronto Maple Leafs in the Northeast (100 points), the Washington Capitals in the Southeast (102 points), the St. Louis Blues in the Central Division (leading the NHL with 114 points), and the Colorado Avalanche in the Northwest (96 points).

In the first round of the playoffs, New Jersey swept the Florida Panthers in four games. The Devils then eliminated Toronto in six games in round two. In the Eastern Conference finals, New Jersey came back from a three-games-to-one deficit to oust Philadelphia, four games to three.

Dallas advanced through the post-season competition by besting the Edmonton Oilers, four games to one, in round one, and the San Jose Sharks, four games to one, in round two. The Stars then triumphed in the Western Conference finals by wearing down the Avalanche, four games to three.

In Game 1 of the Stanley Cup finals—played May 30 on the Devils' home ice in East Rutherford, New Jersey—the Devils overwhelmed Dallas by the score of 7–3. Petr Sykora scored four points for the victors, on two goals and two assists. Sykora's linemate Jason Arnott also sent the puck twice into the Dallas net. New Jersey defenseman Ken Daneyko, a longtime veteran who has participated in every playoff game in the Devils' history, collected his first post-season goal since 1995, which was the first time New Jersey won the Stanley Cup. The Stars' fine goalie, Ed Belfour, had a cold, and his reactions were slow; he was replaced by Manny Fernandez in the third period.

Game 2 was a different story—the Stars won, 2–1. Belfour was back to his usual

Defenseman Chris Pronger of the St. Louis Blues was the NHL's Most Valuable Player of the regular season.

self, stopping 27 New Jersey shots, and Dallas's Brett Hull scored two goals, the second with only 4 minutes, 16 seconds left to play, as the Stars evened the series at one game apiece.

The Dallas arena was the site of Games 3 and 4, but the change of location had no ill effect on the Devils. New Jersey won Game 3 by a 2–1 tally. Though the Stars scored first, the Devils countered with goals by Arnott in period one and Sykora in period two, the latter on a power play. And New Jersey defenseman and team captain Scott Stevens held in check Dallas's two top scorers, Brett Hull and Mike Modano. The Devils now led the series, two games to one.

In Game 4, the Devils were behind 1–0 early in period three, but in rapid succession—within four minutes—New Jersey's Sergei Brylin and rookies John Madden and Brian Rafalski each netted the puck to put the game on ice. Madden's was a short-handed goal. The final score was 3–1, and the Devils were up, three games to one.

The last two contests—Games 5 and 6—will long be remembered. As New Jersey fought intensely to win the Stanley Cup, Dallas fought back with equal intensity, refusing to lose.

Game 5, played in New Jersey, was scoreless through three periods of regulation and two of sudden-death overtime. Finally, in the third overtime period, after more than 106 minutes of competition, Dallas's Modano deflected a shot by Hull for the winning score. Until then, New Jersey goalie Martin Brodeur had made 40 saves, while Dallas's Belfour had stopped 48 Devil shots. Final score: 1–0. The Stars were now down three games to two, and on their way home for Game 6.

Both teams tallied in period two of Game 6, New Jersey on a goal by Scott Niedermayer, and Dallas on a goal by Mike Keane. But the score remained 1–1 after regulation time, and another sudden-death overtime battle ensued. At last, at 8 minutes, 20 seconds of the second overtime, the Devils' Arnott took a pass from Patrik Elias and knocked the puck past Belfour with a wrist shot. The series was over, and the Stanley Cup belonged to New Jersey.

NHL FINAL STANDINGS

EASTERN CONFERENCE

Atlantic Division

	W	L	T	RT	Pts.
Philadelphia	45	25	12	3	105
New Jersey	45	29	8	5	103
Pittsburgh	37	37	8	6	88
N.Y. Rangers	29	41	12	3	73
N.Y. Islanders	24	49	9	1	58

Northeast Division

	W	L	T	RT	Pts.
Toronto	45	30	7	3	100
Ottawa	41	30	11	2	95
Buffalo	35	36	11	4	85
Montreal	35	38	9	4	83
Boston	24	39	19	6	73

Southeast Division

	W	L	T	RT	Pts.
Washington	44	26	12	2	102
Florida	43	33	6	6	98
Carolina	37	35	10	0	84
Tampa Bay	19	54	9	7	54
Atlanta	14	61	7	4	39

WESTERN CONFERENCE

Central Division

	W	L	T	RT	Pts.
St. Louis	51	20	11	1	114
Detroit	48	24	10	2	108
Chicago	33	39	10	2	78
Nashville	28	47	7	7	70

Northwest Division

	W	L	T	RT	Pts.
Colorado	42	29	11	1	96
Edmonton	32	34	16	8	88
Vancouver	30	37	15	8	83
Calgary	31	41	10	5	77

Pacific Division

	W	L	T	RT	Pts.
Dallas	43	29	10	6	102
Los Angeles	39	31	12	4	94
Phoenix	39	35	8	4	90
San Jose	35	37	10	7	87
Anaheim	34	36	12	3	83

Stanley Cup: New Jersey Devils

OUTSTANDING PLAYERS

Hart Trophy (most valuable player)	Chris Pronger, St. Louis
Ross Trophy (scorer)	Jaromir Jagr, Pittsburgh
Vezina Trophy (goalie)	Olaf Kolzig, Washington
Norris Trophy (defenseman)	Chris Pronger, St. Louis
Selke Trophy (defensive forward)	Steve Yzerman, Detroit
Calder Trophy (rookie)	Scott Gomez, New Jersey
Lady Byng Trophy (sportsmanship)	Pavol Demitra, St. Louis
Conn Smythe Trophy (Stanley Cup play)	Scott Stevens, New Jersey

For his stellar defensive play against the Stars, New Jersey's Scott Stevens was awarded the Conn Smythe Trophy as the Most Valuable Player (MVP) of the playoffs.

Another defenseman, Chris Pronger of the St. Louis Blues, was named MVP for the regular season. Jaromir Jagr of Pittsburgh was once again—for the third straight year and the fourth time overall—the league's leading scorer, compiling 96 points on 42 goals and 54 assists. And New Jersey's Scott Gomez was named rookie of the year.

Also of note during the 1999–2000 hockey year:

A change was introduced in determining league standings—a new category, "Regulation Ties" (RT), was added. Under this rule, a team earns one point for a tie in regulation time, even if it loses the game in overtime.

Hall-of-Famer Maurice Richard, the lengendary "Rocket," who played for the Montreal Canadiens from 1942 to 1960, died in 2000 at the age of 78. Richard was the first hockey player to tally 50 goals in one season (1944–45).

College Play. The University of North Dakota won the U.S. National Collegiate Athletic Association (NCAA) Division I hockey championship, defeating Boston College, 4–2, in the final game of the NCAA tournament.

North Dakota senior forward Lee Goren was named MVP of the "Frozen Four" tourney. Boston College defenseman Mike Mottau won the Hobey Baker Memorial Award as the U.S.'s top college player.

Michelle Kwan
Wins Again...And Again!

It was April Fool's Day, 2000. But Michelle Kwan wasn't fooling around! For the third time, she won the World Figure Skating Championships. Six weeks earlier, she had won her fourth U.S. championship.

At the world championships, held in Nice, France, Kwan finished a disappointing third in the short program. Ahead of her were two Russian skaters, Irina Slutskaya and Maria Butyrskaya, the defending world champion.

In the free program, however, Kwan put on a dazzling display of ice skating. She landed seven triple jumps, including a triple toe-triple toe combination. "Michelle," she told herself, "you skated the best program of your life."

For some time, many people had questioned whether 19-year-old Kwan still had it in her to skate such a program. They felt that younger skaters, such as 14-year-old Sarah Hughes (who finished fifth), would begin to outshine her. But Kwan proved them wrong.

What's next for Kwan? Right now, she's attending college at UCLA, in California. But she's thinking ahead to the 2002 Winter Olympics at Salt Lake City, Utah—and her first Olympic gold medal.

ICE SKATING

FIGURE SKATING

World Championships

Men	Alexei Yagudin, Russia
Women	Michelle Kwan, United States
Pairs	Maria Petrova/Alexei Tikhonov, Russia
Dance	Marina Anissina/Gwendal Peizerat, France

United States Championships

Men	Michael Weiss
Women	Michelle Kwan
Pairs	Kyoko Ina/John Zimmerman
Dance	Naomi Lang/Peter Tchernyshev

SPEED SKATING

World Championships

Men	Gianni Romme, Netherlands
Women	Claudia Pechstein, Germany

SKIING

WORLD CUP CHAMPIONSHIPS

Men	Hermann Maier, Austria
Women	Renate Goetschl, Austria

U.S. ALPINE CHAMPIONSHIPS

Men

Downhill	Chris Puckett
Slalom	Erik Schlopy
Giant Slalom	Casey Puckett
Super Giant Slalom	Daron Rahlves
Combined	Casey Puckett

Women

Downhill	Kirsten Clark
Slalom	Caroline Lalive
Giant Slalom	(canceled due to weather problems)
Super Giant Slalom	Kirsten Clark
Combined	Caroline Lalive

TRACK AND FIELD

Stacy Dragila Finds Gold at the End of a Vault

The year 2000 was a great one for 29-year-old pole-vaulter Stacy Dragila. In March she set a new world record—15 feet, 1¾ inches—in the women's indoor pole vault. In July she set a new world record—15 feet, 2¼ inches—in the women's outdoor pole vault. And at the 2000 Summer Olympic Games in Sydney, Australia, she walked away with that sport's first-ever Olympic gold medal with a vault of 15 feet, 1 inch.

"The gold medal is beyond any world record," she said. "I don't think there's anything better."

Stacy first took up pole vaulting in 1993, at Idaho State University. Her first jump was a mere 6 feet. But she improved rapidly.

In 1997, Dragila won the gold medal in the pole vault at the first-ever World Indoor Championships. Two years later she won the gold medal at the World Outdoor Championships. And by the end of 2000, Stacy Dragila had been the U.S. outdoor champion four times and the U.S. indoor champion five times.

Venus Williams is joyous after winning the U.S. Open—her second Grand Slam title of the year.

TENNIS

The tennis story in the year 2000 began with Andre Agassi and Lindsay Davenport. But it ended with the rise of Venus Williams, an improbable but impressive victory by a young Russian named Marat Safin, and what may have been the last hurrah of Pete Sampras.

In January, the 29-year-old Agassi won the **Australian Open,** defeating Yevgeny Kafelnikov, the 25-year-old Russian, in four sets: 3–6, 6–3, 6–2, 6–4. It was the sixth major title of Agassi's career, and his second Australian; he had won his first in 1995. But thereafter, he went into a decline, and he would reach no more Grand Slam singles finals in 2000.

Another American, 23-year-old Lindsay Davenport, captured the women's Australian crown, besting Martina Hingis of Switzerland, 6–1, 7–5. Hingis, 19, ranked number-one in the world at the time of the match, was overpowered by her opponent in the first set. In the second set, Davenport led 5–1 before Hingis mounted a fine comeback. But Davenport held on to win. As with Agassi, it would be Davenport's only Grand Slam title in 2000; but unlike Agassi, she would appear in two more finals.

In June, Mary Pierce became the first Frenchwoman to win the **French Open** since Françoise Durr in 1967. The victory for Pierce, 25, came at the expense of Conchita Martinez of Spain, by scores of 6–2, 7–5. Pierce also teamed with Hingis to win the women's doubles championship.

The men's French title went to Gustavo Kuerten. In a grueling 3-hour, 44-minute match, the 23-year-old Brazilian outlasted Magnus Norman of Sweden, 6–2, 6–3, 2–6,

TOURNAMENT TENNIS

	Australian Open	French Open	Wimbledon	U.S. Open
Men's Singles	Andre Agassi, U.S.	Gustavo Kuerten, Brazil	Pete Sampras, U.S.	Marat Safin, Russia
Women's Singles	Lindsay Davenport, U.S.	Mary Pierce, France	Venus Williams, U.S.	Venus Williams, U.S.
Men's Doubles	Ellis Ferreira, South Africa/ Rick Leach, U.S.	Mark Woodforde, Australia/ Todd Woodbridge, Australia	Mark Woodforde, Australia/ Todd Woodbridge, Australia	Lleyton Hewitt, Australia/ Max Mirnyi, Belarus
Women's Doubles	Lisa Raymond, U.S./ Rennae Stubbs, Australia	Mary Pierce, France/ Martina Hingis, Switzerland	Venus Williams, U.S./ Serena Williams, U.S.	Julie Halard-Decugis, France/ Ai Sugiyama, Japan

Davis Cup Winner: Spain

7–6 (6). Kuerten had also won the French Open in 1997. In the men's doubles, the "Woodies"—Mark Woodforde and Todd Woodbridge of Australia—set a record by winning their 58th doubles tournament; but it was their first triumph at the French Open.

Then came the All-England Tennis Championship, held in **Wimbledon** in July—and then came Venus Williams. The 20-year-old American burst into tennis superstardom by collecting her first Grand Slam title, taking the women's crown by defeating Davenport in the finals, 6–3, 7–6 (3). For good measure, Williams and her 18-year-old sister, Serena, also won the women's doubles.

American Pete Sampras, 28, already considered by many the greatest tennis player of all time, made more history at Wimbledon. In defeating Australia's Patrick Rafter by scores of 6–7 (10), 7–6 (5), 6–4, 6–2, Sampras won his record-tying seventh Wimbledon singles title. More important, it was the 13th Grand Slam singles crown of Sampras's career—the highest total ever, surpassing the 12 of Australian Roy Emerson, a mark that had stood since 1967.

But at the **U. S. Open** in September, spectators saw what may be the future of men's tennis: 20-year-old Marat Safin of Russia swept past 29-year-old Sampras in the final in straight sets: 6–4, 6–3, 6–3. Suddenly, tennis fans were wondering if Pete Sampras was contemplating retirement. For his part, Sampras wasn't saying.

Venus Williams continued her mastery, winning the U.S. Open, and the second Grand Slam title of her young career, by downing Davenport in the final, 6–4, 7–5. On a roll, Venus took off for the Olympic Games in Australia, where she trounced Russia's Elena Dementieva, 18 years old, in the gold-medal match by scores of 6–2, 6–4. And Venus won another Olympic gold in the women's doubles, teaming with her sister Serena for the victory.

Always subject to rapid change, the women's world tennis rankings following the U.S Open showed Hingis first, Davenport second, and Venus Williams third; the men's order was Kuerten, Safin, and Sampras.

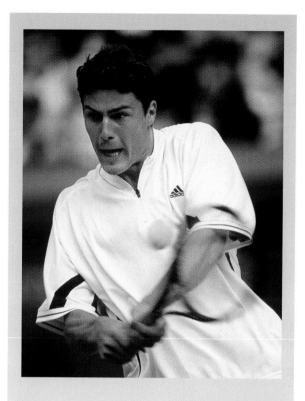

The New Kid: Marat Safin

It would be impossible not to notice the new tennis star Marat Safin. The young Russian is 6 feet, 4 inches tall, with the looks of a movie star, and a serve that seems shot from a cannon. And when he won the U.S. Open men's singles championship, he became the first Russian to win that crown.

Safin's victory over Pete Sampras was impressive. With more weapons than just his serve, he won numerous points on blistering passing shots with both forehand and backhand. Sampras, who has won the U.S. Open four times, said of his youthful opponent, "He reminded me of myself when I was 19 and came here and won the first time."

Born in January 1980, Safin moved with his parents to Valencia, Spain, when he was 16. The professional tennis tour has proven difficult for him at times. He has struggled with his hot temper, which has surfaced when his game isn't up to par, and he has even considered quitting the sport. But that may all have changed with the U.S. Open. How good can Marat Safin be? Let Pete Sampras answer that question: "He could be number-one—if he wants to do it."

LIVING HISTORY

The United States has grown and changed since the first census was taken in 1790. Its people trace their ancestry to many parts of the world. And in 2000, a new census took a snapshot of the nation as it is today. This was the country's 22nd nationwide head count. It set out to discover who Americans are, where they are from, and where and how they live. The main purpose of the count was to make sure that every American is equally represented in Congress. But the information gathered by census-takers will be used in many other ways.

The 2000 United States census provided a detailed portrait of the nation: who its people are, where they're from, and where and how they live.

THE COUNTING OF AMERICA

On April 1, 2000, the United States sat for a national family portrait. It was Census Day—the day on which the U.S. government attempts to count every man, woman, and child in the country.

The 2000 census was the 22nd nationwide head count undertaken in the United States. And it was the biggest ever—the government tried to reach some 275 million people! What did the government want to know? Beyond mere numbers, the census was designed to provide a detailed picture of the United States: who its people are, where they're from, and where and how they live.

WHY COUNT?

The U.S. Constitution requires the government to take a census every ten years, so that everyone will be properly represented in the House of Representatives. Every state is guaranteed at least one seat in the House. But the rest of the 435 seats are divided among the states on the basis of their population. Every ten years, seats are reapportioned, or divided up again, based on new census information.

Census information is also used by state and local governments, to redraw the boundaries of congressional, state, and local voting districts. The goal is to have roughly the same number of people in each district. This helps ensure that everyone is represented equally in Congress and in state and local legislatures.

Census information also helps determine how billions of dollars in federal funds will be used. Federal programs that provide aid for everything from highway construction to school lunches use census figures to find out which areas are most in need of funds. Towns, civic groups, and businesses also use the census figures. For example, census figures showing the number of preschool children in your town could help the town decide if it will need a new school.

After hurricanes and other disasters, census information helps relief workers by providing estimates of the number of people missing. Census figures help businesses locate new stores near potential shoppers and new manufacturing plants near potential workers. Individuals use census figures, too. You may use them to write a report, for example.

TAKING THE CENSUS

Although April 1, 2000, was officially Census Day, the count actually started months before and continued for months after that date. The director of the Census Bureau kicked off the count on a cold day in January, bundling up in a fur-lined parka and traveling to the remote little village of Unalakleet, Alaska. The census started early in Alaska because remote parts of that state are easier to reach in winter, when the ground is frozen. And people are likely to be at home.

While people in Unalakleet answered census questions in person, most Americans answered the questions by mail. Census questionnaires were mailed to 120 million households nationwide. Most people received a short questionnaire that asked seven basic questions about the number of people living at each address and their age, sex, and race. One household in six received a longer form, with 53 questions about the way people at that address lived, the languages they spoke, even their plumbing and kitchen equipment.

The Census Bureau ran ads on television to encourage people to fill out and return their questionnaires. And 67 percent of households did send in the forms. That was an improvement over the 1990 census, when 65 percent responded. Still, although people are required by law to complete census forms, many didn't. Some tossed out the form by mistake, thinking it was a piece of junk mail. Some found the form (especially the long form) too confusing or time-consuming to fill out.

Others felt that the questions on the form invaded their privacy. They worried that the information might be used against them in some way. But the Census Bureau promises that the census information is confidential. And census workers are sworn to secrecy.

Because the census should be as complete as possible, the Census Bureau tried to track down people who didn't return their questionnaires or sent in incomplete forms. It hired half a million extra workers who combed city streets to find missed households. Census workers knocked on 42 million doors, hoping to get people to answer in person the questions they had failed to answer by mail. Even so, it was clear that the count couldn't be really complete.

The director of the U.S. Census Bureau gets a dogsled ride to the village of Unalakleet, in Alaska, to kick off Census 2000.

In the past, minorities, the homeless, and illegal aliens (foreign citizens living in the United States without permission) have been the most difficult groups to count. More people in these groups responded in 2000 than in past years. But there were still concerns that the final results wouldn't reflect the U.S. population accurately.

To find out how many people were missed, census officials did a quality-check. Workers contacted 300,000 households across America, and the results of their interviews were compared to the census results. The Census Bureau then used statistical methods to estimate how many peo-

portion the seats in the U.S. House of Representatives. By April 1, 2001, the Census Bureau will provide more-detailed population counts, broken down into 7 million census blocks. This information will be used for redistricting and for decisions about where to build schools, roads, and fire stations.

Long before then, the Census Bureau was predicting some of the results. The U.S. population was expected to be about 275 million. And the census was expected to show states in the South and West growing faster than those in the North and East. New York and Pennsylvania stood to lose two seats in Congress. Connecticut, Illinois, Mississippi, Ohio, Oklahoma and Wisconsin could lose one seat each. Arizona, California, and Texas stood to gain two seats; and Colorado, Florida, Georgia, Montana, and Nevada could each gain one.

The Census Bureau set up outreach centers to help people fill out their questionnaires. Census workers also knocked on 42 million doors nationwide.

ple hadn't been counted nationwide. Only the actual count could be used for reapportioning seats in the House of Representatives. But estimated totals might be used for other purposes.

ADDING IT UP

As census workers knocked on doors, computers whirred around the clock to sort and add the information from the forms. As required by law, the Census Bureau was ready to deliver a state-by-state population report to President Bill Clinton by December 31. These counts will be used to reap-

A mural in Los Angeles, California, depicts ethnic diversity. The Census Bureau predicts that by 2100, Hispanics, African Americans, and Asians would make up the nation's fastest-growing minority groups.

Looking Ahead . . .

What will life in the United States be like in 100 years, when the census of 2100 is taken? No one knows. But you can be sure that there will be more people just about everywhere!

In January 2000, the U.S. Census Bureau came out with its first population predictions for the year 2100. The bureau said that today's population of about 275 million will more than double by then, to 571 million. That means more cars on the road and bigger crowds in stores, among other things. But Americans still won't be as tightly packed as people in Europe. Parts of Europe are already more crowded than the United States will be in 2100.

The U.S. population will increase as today's young people grow up and have families of their own and as new immigrants arrive in the country. The Census Bureau expects the fastest growth to be among minority groups. Here are some projections:

◆ The U.S. population will be older in 2100. The median age then is expected to be about 40. Right now, the median age is just under 36. (Median means half of all Americans are older and half are younger than that age.)

◆ The Hispanic population will triple by 2050. There were 31.4 million Hispanic Americans in 1999. The Census Bureau expects the number to be 98.2 million in 2050. That would make Hispanics the nation's largest minority group, accounting for almost 25 percent of the total population.

◆ The African-American population will grow from 34.9 million in 1999 to 59.2 million in 2050. African Americans would then make up 15 percent of the population.

◆ The number of Asians and Pacific Islanders will increase from 10.9 million in 1999 to 37.6 million in 2050, to make up 9 percent of the population.

◆ Thanks to better medical care, there will be more than 5 million people over the age of 100 in the year 2100. Today there are just 65,000 people over 100.

Will the predictions hold true? The answers will come in 2001, as thousands of pages of detailed census reports are released to the public. The reports will be available to everyone on CD-ROMs, on the Internet—and, of course, on paper. Together, they will provide a portrait of the United States.

FIREWORKS: SHOWERS OF LIGHT

On January 1, 2000, the world exploded—with fireworks. As midnight rolled around through each of the world's time zones, dazzling fireworks displays greeted the start of a new millennium. Rockets burst into showers of colored stars over cities from Moscow, Russia, to Toronto, Canada.

In the United States, fireworks glowed over New York City, where huge crowds packed Times Square on New Year's Eve. And Chicago put on the biggest fireworks extravaganza in the city's history.

The spectacular shows drew oohs and aahs from crowds and from millions of television viewers. Here are some highlights:

● In **Sydney, Australia,** a million people gathered for one of the biggest fireworks shows ever. Twenty tons of fireworks exploded over Harbour Bridge in the city's harbor. The show cost more than $3.5 million and lighted the night sky for 24 minutes.

● In **Paris, France,** the Eiffel Tower was packed with fireworks. As midnight neared, thousands of lights flickered on, forming a column up the tower. Then, as the New Year began, the fireworks exploded. Glowing streamers shot out from the structure, creating a brilliant tower of fire.

● In **London, England,** at least two million people lined the Thames River to watch a fireworks display that rivaled the one in Paris. The chimes of Big Ben, the famous clock in the tower of the Houses of Parliament, were the signal for the show to start. For fifteen minutes, fireworks turned the Thames into a "river of fire."

● In **Cairo, Egypt,** the pyramids were the site of a show that blended old and new. Fireworks combined with laser lights created a modern sky spectacular over these ancient monuments.

● In **Rio de Janeiro, Brazil,** some five million people danced on the famous Copacabana beach, while showers of yellow and green fireworks exploded overhead.

● In **Washington, D.C.,** the Washington Monument, covered with temporary scaffolding for repairs, was the centerpiece of the show. The scaffolding was packed with fireworks that turned the monument into a giant white sparkler.

Fireworks were the perfect way to celebrate the new millennium. They have been one of the most popular forms of entertainment for centuries—because they mix color, light, and sound in a very dramatic way.

EARLY FIREWORKS

No one knows for sure just when or how fireworks were invented. The credit usually goes to the Chinese, who were the inventors of gunpowder. (Black nation of a king, the signing of an important treaty, a religious festival.

Early fireworks displays were usually put on by the military, who were used to handling gunpowder. It was a dangerous business—spectators and fireworks handlers were sometimes killed when the explosions were set off. Later, kings and queens employed firemasters, specialists who were charged with coordinating fireworks displays.

Gradually fireworks developed into an art form. Often the displays included rockets exploding in the sky as well as elaborate "set pieces" on the ground. The set pieces were spe-

Cities around the world ushered in the new millennium with dazzling fireworks displays. Shown here (*left to right*) are Washington, D.C.; Sydney, Australia; Paris, France; and London, England.

powder, a form of gunpowder, is the explosive used to make fireworks.) Arab traders probably brought fireworks from China to Europe in the Middle Ages. By the 1300's, fireworks displays were becoming popular in Europe as a way of celebrating special events—the coro-

cially designed forms, such as a replica of a famous building or the portrait of a ruler, outlined with glowing fireworks. One of the most popular pieces was a fire-breathing dragon. To create such pieces, the firemaster employed a whole team of assistants. They would build a

199

frame of willow or whalebone, attach fireworks at strategic points, cover the whole form with papier-mâché, and then set it off. Their hours of work would go up in smoke, sound, and fire as the creation exploded, lasting just a few beautiful moments.

Fireworks displays were often set to music. Handel's *Music for the Royal Fireworks* was written in the mid-1700's for a British fireworks show. It is still performed by symphony orchestras. Water was another important element in early fireworks shows. Displays were often staged over lakes and rivers, for safety and so

Cascading Waterfall

Glowing Chrysanthemums

that the brilliance of the fireworks would be reflected in the water.

Fireworks were just as popular in North America as they were in Europe. In the United States, fireworks on the Fourth of July have been a tradition almost since the founding of the nation. At one time, people celebrated the Fourth by setting off fireworks in their own backyards. (Home fireworks are banned in most places today because they are extremely dangerous.)

Public displays drew throngs, too. In the late 1800's, elaborate set pieces were the biggest crowd pleasers at public fireworks shows. In one of the most spectacular shows of this time, a fireworks maker simulated Niagara Falls by pouring golden showers over the Brooklyn Bridge.

TODAY'S SPECTACULAR SKY SHOWS

Since the early days of fireworks, advances in chemistry have allowed fireworks masters—called pyrotechnicians—to create explosions in incredibly brilliant colors. The colors are produced by adding chemical salts to the explosive powder. Strontium salts make red; calcium, orange; copper, blue; and sodium, yellow. There have also been improvements in the original black-powder formula.

Today aerial displays are the most popular. People thrill to see rockets that burst into enormous, glowing chrysanthemums or waterfalls of golden fire and smoke, and fountains of fire that shoot up from the ground. Pyrotechnicians create these spectacular effects by packing dozens of explosive pellets, called stars, into a shell made of papier-mâché. Stars of different types and sizes produce different effects—blobs and streaks of light, showers of sparks, tiny comets that squiggle through the air. Sometimes several different types are packed together into the shell. A charge of black powder is also put in. All this is done by hand, very carefully. Fireworks can't be made by machine because a machine might produce a spark—and suddenly ignite the explosive materials.

An aerial display is unleashed with a double explosion. First the shell is launched from a mortar, a short metal tube. An explosive lift charge hurls the shell out of the mortar and

Fountains of Fire

Graceful Palm Tree

hundreds of feet into the air. The lift charge also ignites a time-delay fuse, which burns as the shell rockets upward. When this fuse burns down, it sets off the black powder. Then— BOOM! The shell explodes, igniting the stars. Suddenly, the sky fills with color, light, and sound. Some fireworks explode with a loud bang; others pop, crackle, or whistle in the sky.

And some shells burst in several phases, each exploding in a different color or pattern. For a really big effect, several shells may be set to go off at the same time.

Fireworks companies have some other tricks that make today's displays more spectacular than ever. A big fireworks show is a very carefully planned event. There may be thousands of rockets. Each is carefully placed and timed to go off at just the right moment. Sometimes fireworks are combined with laser lights that comb the sky. Setting up a show like this can take days.

Fireworks shows are still often accompanied by music. Now, however, the fireworks can be set off from a computerized control panel. The panel sends electrical signals to the fuses that light the fireworks, and they can be set to go off just milliseconds apart. In this way, the brilliant explosions of a set piece, for example, can be perfectly timed with the notes of a piece of music, whether it be rock or classical.

Fireworks have been around for hundreds of years, but people still thrill to see the night sky fill with exploding colored stars. It seems these dazzling displays will be as popular in the new millennium as they were in the last.

The fall of Saigon on April 30, 1975, marked the end of the Vietnam War. In 2000—25 years later—Vietnam and the United States were on their way to putting the war's bitter legacy behind them.

THE VIETNAM WAR: 25 YEARS LATER

The year 2000 marked the 25th anniversary of an important event: the end of the Vietnam War. On one level, that war was a struggle between Communists and non-Communists in Vietnam, a small country in Southeast Asia. But the war was also part of a larger struggle, in which the United States and other Western democracies hoped to halt the spread of Communism in Southeast Asia and other parts of the world. The war's end unified Vietnam under a Communist government, but not before more than a million Vietnamese were killed.

The end of the war also closed a troubled chapter in the history of the United States. Nearly 58,000 Americans were killed or reported missing while fighting to help the non-Communist side. People in the United States were bitterly divided over the war. Americans still hold different opinions about it. But, 25 years later, the bitterness is mostly gone.

Today, Vietnam and the United States are still struggling in some ways to overcome the effects of the war. However, the two nations are beginning to get along.

HOW THE WAR BEGAN

The Vietnam War is sometimes called the Second Indochina War. That's because it was the second part of a wider conflict in the former French colony of Indochina, which included present-day Cambodia and Laos as well as Vietnam. From 1946 to 1954, Vietnamese nationalists fought for independence from France. Their leader, Ho Chi Minh, was a Communist, but not all those who fought with him were.

In 1954, France agreed to give up control of Indochina. Vietnam was divided into two zones. North Vietnam, with its capital in Hanoi, was led by Ho Chi Minh. South Vietnam, with its capital in Saigon, was led by Ngo Dinh Diem. He was supported by the United States. The plan was to unify the two zones under an elected government. Elections, however, were never held. Instead, in 1957, fighting broke out.

In South Vietnam, Communist guerrillas known as the Vietcong began to attack, hoping to overthrow the government. At first, North Vietnam just trained and supported the Vietcong. North Vietnam, in turn, received aid from the Soviet Union. By 1964, North Vietnam was sending its own soldiers to fight in South Vietnam. Troops and supplies moved south by sea or followed a route called the Ho Chi Minh Trail, which cut through parts of Laos and Cambodia. Some slipped across the Demilitarized Zone (DMZ), a buffer zone between north and south at the 17th parallel.

The United States sent aid and military advisers to help the South Vietnamese. But the South Vietnamese army wasn't effective. And Diem, who ruled as a dictator, was unpopular. In 1963, he was overthrown in a military coup. South Vietnam then went through a series of different governments. And the United States began to play a greater role in the war. In 1965, the United States began to send combat troops. By mid-1968 there were about 550,000 U.S. troops in South Vietnam. The United States also carried out extensive bombing missions against North Vietnam.

DIVISION IN THE UNITED STATES

As the U.S. role in the war grew, so did the controversy surrounding it. On the one hand, U.S. leaders and many Americans believed that the country had to fight to stop Communism. "Hawks" who supported the war feared that all of Southeast Asia might fall to the Communists if they won in South Vietnam. And Communist forces elsewhere might be encouraged to fight, they said, if the United States didn't defend its ally, South Vietnam.

But many Americans were opposed to the war. "Doves" viewed the conflict as a civil war, between factions in a small country halfway around the world. They didn't think that American soldiers should fight and die in such a war. They opposed the military draft, which required young men to serve in the army. And they were against the bombing of North Vietnam. When American planes went after targets in North Vietnamese cities, they said, innocent civilians were killed.

The Vietnam War was the first in which U.S. forces fought abroad and didn't achieve victory. The war devastated Vietnam and deeply divided American society. Some scenes from the conflict: South Vietnamese soldiers stand guard in Saigon (*left*); U.S. troops disembark from a helicopter onto the battlefield (*center*); antiwar protestors demonstrate in Washington, D.C. (*right*).

The Vietnam War drained as well as divided the country. The United States was spending nearly $30 billion a year to keep up the fight, and there was no end in sight. Americans were alarmed by scenes of killing that appeared on the nightly news. And antiwar feeling grew stronger.

The war became an issue in the U.S. presidential election of 1968. President Lyndon Johnson decided not to seek re-election because his policies had helped deepen U.S. involvement in Vietnam. Richard Nixon won the election, and after he took office in 1969 the United States began to withdraw its troops. South Vietnamese troops took on more of the fighting. Peace talks also began.

THE END OF THE WAR

In 1973 a peace agreement was signed in Paris, and the last U.S. combat troops pulled out. But the peace agreement didn't end the fighting. And without U.S. help, the South couldn't fend off North Vietnamese attacks. The Soviet Union increased its aid to North Vietnam, and in December 1974 the North launched the war's final campaign. Thousands of South Vietnamese who didn't want to live under Communism scrambled to flee the country. In the process, many families became separated.

By April 29, 1975, North Vietnamese troops were poised to take Saigon, South Vietnam's capital. Panicked crowds tried to clamber aboard helicopters at the U.S. embassy and other places. Some made it and were carried to the safety of American warships waiting off the coast.

The fall of Saigon ended the war. On April 30, the government of South Vietnam surrendered. North and South were unified under

Missing in Action

Since the end of the Vietnam War, the United States has been searching for news of U.S. soldiers listed as "missing in action" (MIA). More than 2,000 names are on the list. Many of the missing were members of air crews shot down over North Vietnam, Cambodia, or Laos. Some were shot down over water or in other places where recovery is unlikely. Their remains may never be found. But the U.S. government has promised to get the fullest possible accounting of the Vietnam MIA's.

Several government agencies are involved in the job of accounting for the MIA's. The U.S. Army Central Identification Laboratory, Hawaii, is the leading agency in the search. Its job is to find and identify remains of missing service members from World War II, the Korean War, and other conflicts, as well as the Vietnam War. Several times a year, the agency sends research teams into the field in Vietnam, Laos, and Cambodia. The researchers follow up on leads, such as reported sightings of plane wreckage, soldiers' dog tags, or claims that an American was sighted. Since the fall of Saigon in 1975, the U.S. government has received more than 21,000 reports relating to Americans in Southeast Asia.

In recent years the government of Vietnam has become more cooperative, and the search has made progress. So far, the remains of more than 550 MIA's from Southeast Asia have been identified and returned to their families. Other remains have been recovered from crash sites and jungle graves. Scientists are using laboratory tests to try to identify these remains.

Every year thousands of people visit the Vietnam Veterans Memorial in Washington, D.C. Engraved on its walls are the names of nearly 58,000 Americans who were killed or classified as missing in action in the Vietnam War.

Communist rule. Saigon was renamed Ho Chi Minh City, after the Vietnamese Communist leader.

AFTER THE WAR

The war left hard feelings that are only now beginning to fade. After the war ended, South Vietnam struggled to adapt to the Communist system. Many of its citizens were packed off to "re-education" camps. Thousands of Vietnamese refugees left the country in the years after the war. And, besides taking a terrible death toll, the war had destroyed Vietnam's economy. Today many Vietnamese still struggle with poverty and other effects of the war. The neighboring nations of Cambodia and Laos were also affected.

In the United States, people struggled to make sense of the conflict that had torn the country apart. This was the first time that U.S. forces had fought abroad and not achieved victory. How was it that the United States, so much larger and stronger than North Vietnam, hadn't prevailed? One reason, many people came to believe, was that the North Vietnamese wanted the victory more. For them, the war was a fight for national liberation, and they were determined to win at all costs. The U.S.

military also drew many lessons from the war. One important lesson was the importance of having strong public support for any military action.

Today, Vietnam is one of the few remaining Communist countries in the world. But it has given up some of its Communist policies. It has begun to allow more economic freedom. And slowly, the United States and Vietnam have mended ties. In 1995, the two nations formally established full diplomatic relations. In 1999, a new U.S. consulate was dedicated in Ho Chi Minh City; U.S. Secretary of State Madeleine Albright traveled there for the ceremony.

In March 2000, as the 25th anniversary of the war's end neared, U.S. Defense Secretary William Cohen visited Vietnam. In July, the United States and Vietnam signed a trade agreement, which would allow more American companies to do business in Vietnam. And in November, President Bill Clinton traveled to Vietnam. He was the first president to visit since the war years. In his meetings with government and business leaders, Clinton focused on the future. "Vietnam is a country, not a war," he said. His visit was a sign that both nations were finally ready to put the war behind them and begin a new chapter of history.

THE HANOVER WORLD'S FAIR

Hike from the rain forests of Costa Rica to the Canadian glaciers. See the beaches of Australia and the deserts of Saudi Arabia. Hear mythological tales of jaguars, watch a volcano erupt, dance to tango music or a disco beat, cheer agile streetball players. All these things were possible in a single day at EXPO 2000, the first world's fair of the new millennium. Held in Hanover, Germany, from June 1 through October 31, the fair featured non-stop enjoyment for visitors.

Almost 200 nations and international organizations—more than ever before at a world's fair—participated in EXPO 2000. They used the fair's central theme, Humankind-Nature-Technology, to highlight the diversity of humans, and to demonstrate how people, nature, and technology can interact in positive ways.

Each national pavilion had attractions unique to its homeland. The Himalayan kingdom of Bhutan presented its pavilion in the form of a Buddhist temple. Mongolia erected a yurt—the dome-shaped tent made of felt that's home to nomads on their journeys. The focal point of Pakistan's pavilion was a color-fully painted bus, just like the thousands that travel that country. At the Ethiopian pavilion, the main attraction was Lucy, the 3-million-year-old skeleton of one of our oldest ancestors and one of many important archeological discoveries made in Ethiopia.

Ecology was another important theme. Japan's pavilion was made almost entirely of recycled paper; the arched framework consisted of thick paper tubes, which were covered with a layer of fire-resistant, waterproof paper that allowed light to pass through. The Spanish pavilion used cork as its main construction material because cork is economical and allows large areas of Spain's forests to be preserved. When EXPO 2000 ended, the cork was reused rather than thrown away. The Netherlands created the fair's highest pavilion, with modern wind turbines and other energy-efficient features. The Norwegian pavilion included a roaring waterfall plunging down from a height of 45 feet (13.7 meters)—a reproduction of a famous waterfall in Norway and a tribute to the fact that Norway's entire energy requirements are met by means of waterpower. Waterfalls also appeared in Venezuela's pavilion, falling

into ponds stocked with colorful tropical fish. The waters circulated through an irrigation system that maintained lush gardens on four terraces of the open-sided building.

Projects for the 21st century were everywhere: glass recycling in Colombia, butterfly farming in Papua New Guinea, reclamation of desert land in Egypt, an ecological truck wash in

and puppets from around the world. For kids, there was an obstacle course in a gigantic tepee, a swing with a wooden mesh basket, and a giant ferris wheel. One play area included a ship, raft, treasure island, and lookout tower.

In Tanzania's pavilion, people could step into the footprints of rhinos, lions, elephants, and buffaloes. In China, they could get on space scales to discover what they would weigh on Mars. In Indonesia, they could be pho-

EXPO 2000: The Japanese pavilion (*left*) was made almost entirely from recycled paper. Venezuela's open-sided pavilion (*below*) featured waterfalls and lush gardens. In the Planet of Visions (*right*), people could describe their visions of the world for the next 1,000 years.

Germany, a camel milk dairy in Israel, a radio program for homeless street children in Haiti, efforts to control malaria in Vietnam, combating erosion in Uruguay.

Many nations offered workshops in traditional crafts. In the South Pacific Forum, visitors could learn how to husk coconuts. In Senegal, glass painting was demonstrated in a traditional mud house. A renowned Singapore artist painted orchids. Pakistani craftspeople demonstrated carpet tufting and jewelry making. Homegrown coffee was available in Uganda, papayas in Central America, and freeze-dried astronaut food in Bulgaria.

There was continuous entertainment, including music, art, dance, plays, films, acrobats,

tographed wearing traditional Bali costumes. And at the IBM-sponsored Planet of Visions, people could describe their visions of the world for the next 1,000 years. The resulting "Library of Visions" became available online, to be added to and shared by people everywhere.

Every evening, a show combining fireworks, laser beams, computer-activated fountains, and "human torch" bungee jumpers exploded at sunset. As the show ended, many visitors called it a day. But some stayed on the fairgrounds long after darkness fell. Billed as the world's fair that never slept, EXPO 2000 invited visitors to dance the night away as disk jockeys kept the music going until 6 A.M. the following morning!

U.S. President Bill Clinton and First Lady Hillary Rodham Clinton open a prototype of the National Millennium Time Capsule in Washington, D.C. The actual time capsule, which will be opened in 2100, contains such items as the Bill of Rights, a computer chip, a cell phone, and a Twinkie snack cake.

CAPTURING TIME

It's the year 3000. Archeologists digging at the site of an ancient civilization come across a small sealed container. Cracking it open, they find a wealth of artifacts. Yellowed papers are covered with writing, all in an unfamiliar language. Faded photographs show people dressed in strange clothes. A shiny silver disk may hold some type of code. Small printed cards carry pictures of weird monsters—perhaps the "gods" of these ancient people.

The archeologists have stumbled on a time capsule from the year 2000. The people who made it wanted to tell future generations what life was like in their time. So they filled the container with lists, letters, newspapers, photographs, a CD, even

This youngster sealed his own message to the future inside a personal millennium time capsule.

Pokémon cards. Then they sealed it and buried it. They may have left instructions for the capsule to be opened on some specific date. But those instructions were lost, and the capsule remained sealed for 1,000 years.

A time capsule—a sealed container holding artifacts of a certain time—is a way to send a message to the future. It may be a chamber filled with thousands of objects, or a simple box holding a few personal items. Either way, the goal is the same: to tell those who will open it what life was like in the past. And in 2000, there was great interest in time capsules. Groups, individuals, schools, and governments filled containers with

208

items that reflected life at the start of the new millennium. Then they sealed and stored the containers for future generations to find.

MESSAGES FROM THE PAST

The idea for time capsules came from archeology. Archeologists have learned a great deal about ancient civilizations from artifacts left in tombs—the pyramids of Egypt, for example—and other sites. These objects weren't buried with the thought that other people might find them. But their discovery gave people an idea: Why not plant objects for future archeologists to find?

The first containers for these objects were probably the **cornerstones of buildings.** A cor- nerstone is a foundation block set at a corner. By the 1800's it was common to set corner- stones in special ceremonies. Often, people hol- lowed out the cornerstone and placed a few objects—coins, papers, and so on—inside. They figured that one day the building would be torn down (or fall down). Then future generations would find the objects and have a glimpse of what life was like when the building went up.

What may have been the first true time cap- sule was created in 1876 in Philadelphia. The United States celebrated its 100th birthday that year. As part of the celebration, a collec-

Right: A typewriter, sewing machine, and cash register are among the items stored in the Crypt of Civilization. Bottom left: The 1939 World's Fair time capsule is to remain sealed for 5,000 years. Bottom right: This time capsule buried on the grounds of a British estate will never get lost!

HAVE YOU SEEN THIS TIME CAPSULE?

Many, if not most, time capsules are sealed, stored, and never seen again. Their owners forget about them or forget where they are. The International Time Capsule Society (ITCS), based at Oglethorpe University in Georgia, is trying to help. The ITCS maintains a registry of time capsules. And according to the ITCS, these are three of the "most-wanted" missing time capsules.

U.S. Capitol Cornerstone—George Washington may have helped seal artifacts in the original cornerstone of the U.S. Capitol in 1793. Since then, the building has been expanded, remodeled, and rebuilt—and no one can find that cornerstone.

Bicentennial Wagon Train Time Capsule—This capsule was to hold the signatures of 22 million Americans. But on July 4, 1976, when President Gerald Ford arrived for the sealing ceremony in Valley Forge, Pennsylvania, the capsule was missing—stolen from an unattended van.

The *M*A*S*H* Time Capsule—In a secret ceremony in 1983, cast members of the hit TV show *M*A*S*H* buried a foot-locker time capsule holding props and costumes from the show (including Klinger's yellow dress). The time capsule is under a Hollywood studio parking lot. . .somewhere.

tion of important items—mainly autographs and photographs—was placed in a safe. **The Century Safe,** as it was called, remained sealed for 100 years. It was opened in 1976, as part of the celebration for the country's 200th birthday.

Old photos, coins, and papers are interesting, but they don't give a very full picture of how people live. In 1936, Thornwell Jacobs, president of Oglethorpe University in Georgia, had a grander idea: Why not preserve a full record of society? The result was the **Crypt of Civilization,** which was sealed in 1940. The Crypt is a chamber the size of a swimming pool, deep in the granite foundation of the university's administration building.

The chamber holds 640,000 microfilmed pages from books and other printed material, along with hundreds of newsreels and recordings. Also locked inside are thousands of items from daily life, including chewing gum, soft drinks, the contents of a woman's purse, a typewriter, and a cash register. There are even toys—a set of Lincoln Logs, model trains, Donald Duck and Lone Ranger dolls. And there's a device designed to teach the English language to the Crypt's finders. The chamber is to remained sealed until the year 8113, and chances are that English will be a forgotten language by then!

MESSAGES TO THE FUTURE

The Crypt of Civilization drew a lot of interest. Scientists at Westinghouse Electric Corporation were inspired to mount a similar project for the 1939 World's Fair, in New York City. The term "time capsule" was first used to describe the container they created—a cylinder 7 feet (2 meters) long, with tapered ends that made it look like a torpedo or an artillery shell. In fact, some people called it a "time bomb"!

The **1939 World's Fair time capsule** was waterproof, shockproof, and made of Cupaloy, a copper alloy that wouldn't break down even after thousands of years underground. That was important, because the capsule was to remain buried for 5,000 years. Before it was sealed and lowered into the ground at the fairgrounds, it was filled with all sorts of things. In went samples of seeds, fabrics, metals, and materials such as rubber and cement. So did dozens of common items—an alarm clock, a toothbrush, a pair of bifocals, a Bible, a safety pin, and more. A newsreel and a microfilmed essay were also placed inside. They detailed culture, science, industry, religion, and education in the world of 1939.

When the **1965 World's Fair** came to New York, Westinghouse scientists decided to bury a second time capsule next to the first. Into that capsule went a credit card, a bikini bathing suit, contact lenses, an electric toothbrush, and other objects that were undreamed of in 1939. Also placed inside were a piece of a U.S. spacecraft and some items that represented the nuclear age.

Since then, other time capsules have been buried at world's fairs in several cities. And many towns, cities, and states have marked anniversaries and other events by creating time capsules. One of the most elaborate projects is the **Washington State Centennial Capsule.** The first section of this capsule was filled in 1989, to mark the state's 100th birthday. Sixteen more sections are still empty. One section will be filled every 25 years. To make sure the job gets done, Washington appointed hundreds of "Keepers of the Capsule." The keepers are all volunteers who were 10 years old in 1989. In 2014, when they're 35, they'll fill the next section of the capsule. They'll also appoint new keepers, to keep the cycle going. The opening will take place in 2389.

MILLENNIUM TIME CAPSULES

When the year 2000 rolled around, time capsules became quite a fad. Lots of people wanted to mark the start of the new millennium by sending a message to the future. Individuals created personal time capsules, using everything from specially made containers to cereal boxes. Most of those time capsules were designed to be opened in five or ten years. But some major time-capsule projects were designed to last much longer.

The **National Millennium Time Capsule** is at the National Archives in Washington, D.C. Designed to look like the U.S. flag, it's made

of three metals. The flag's white stripes are stainless steel, representing America's industrial past. The red stripes are silicon bronze, representing communication. The blue field of stars is titanium, a space-age metal representing the future.

People from all over the country contributed items for the capsule. It holds essays from school students, photos of Earth from space, a computer chip, the Bill of Rights, the Cherokee alphabet, a cell phone, a World War II sol-

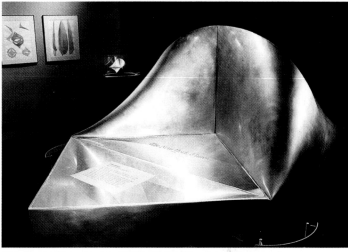

The Times Capsule, on display at the American Museum of Natural History in New York City, will be opened in 3000.

dier's helmet, and a Twinkie snack cake. This capsule won't be buried. It will be stored at the National Archives and opened in 2100.

A time capsule created by the newspaper *The New York Times* will be sealed much longer—until the year 3000. The **Times Capsule** is at the American Museum of Natural History in New York City. It's a 2-ton shell of stainless steel that looks something like a futuristic flower.

The newspaper asked readers what to put in the capsule, and suggestions poured in from all around the world. Readers nominated everything from barbed wire to Beanie Babies, penicillin to parking tickets, soccer jerseys to Spam. The capsule contains recordings of popular songs and daily sounds. Whoever opens the capsule in the year 3000 will have an instant snapshot of life at the start of the millennium.

Vikings from Scandinavia sailed uncharted seas in open boats powered only by oars and a single sail. They were probably the first Europeans to reach North America.

THE VIKINGS ARE HERE!

When did Native Americans and Europeans first meet? Not in 1492, when Christopher Columbus sailed to the New World. The first meeting probably took place almost 500 years earlier—in the year 1000. That's when the Vikings reached North America.

These bold seafarers from Scandinavia, in northern Europe, braved the Atlantic Ocean in slender boats called longships. They had no compasses or other navigational tools; they steered by the sun and stars. Their ships were powered by oars and a single sail. They set out to explore the lands to the west with no idea what they would find.

The year 2000 marked the thousand-year anniversary of the Vikings' arrival in North America. And in honor of the anniversary, the Smithsonian Institution's National Museum of Natural History put on a special exhibition.

A Viking chieftain's helmet has slanting eye holes that added to his fierce appearance. But Viking helmets didn't have horns, although pictures from later times sometimes show horned helmets.

Silver and bronze inlaid swords show the intricate designs that were favored by the Vikings. Swords such as these were marks of high status among the Vikings.

"Vikings: The North Atlantic Saga" opened at the museum in Washington, D.C., in April. It moved to the American Museum of Natural History in New York City in October. And it will tour North America until 2002, with stops in Chicago, Illinois; Houston, Texas; Los Angeles, California; and Ottawa, Ontario, Canada.

Other events were held to mark the anniversary, too. In the summer of 2000, for example, replicas of Viking ships sailed along the Newfoundland coast, where the Vikings landed. These events and the exhibit were designed to shed light on the mysterious Vikings. What made them leave their homelands? How did they cross the North Atlantic? Where in North America did they travel?

NOT JUST RAIDERS

The Vikings were adventurers and warriors. During their heyday—from the late 700's to about 1050—Viking chieftains and their followers raided Europe's coasts. People feared the sight of Viking ships, with their square sails and high, curved prows. Viking raiders struck quickly, overwhelming castles and monasteries. They killed the defenders, grabbed everything of value, and dragged women and children off to be sold into slavery.

But the Vikings were also traders and explorers. They traded with places as far away as Baghdad, in what is today Iraq. And they represented only one part of the Norse culture, which flourished in Scandinavia at that time.

Many more Norse people were farmers, herders, and artisans.

Unlike many Europeans of that time, the Vikings weren't afraid to sail into uncharted seas. As they prospered, they began to look for new lands to settle. Norse settlers put down roots in islands off the western coast of Scotland. The climate of the North Atlantic region was warmer than it is today, and that encouraged them to look even farther afield. In the 800's, Norse colonies grew up in the Faeroe Islands and in Iceland.

In these colonies, people lived much as they had in Scandinavia. They grew crops and raised animals such as sheep, pigs, cattle, and goats. They fished and hunted seals, walruses, and

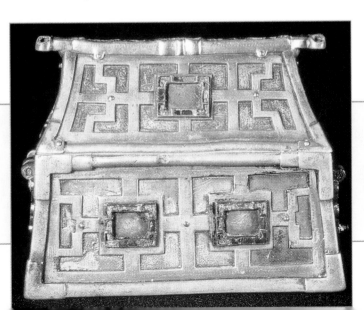

This beautiful chest, made of copper and enamel, was once Viking loot. Viking raiders stole it from a church in Scotland. It was given to a woman named Ranvaig in Norway. She carved her name on the bottom, and the chest is now known as Ranvaig's casket.

L'Anse aux Meadows, in northern Newfoundland, is the site of a Viking outpost that dates to around A.D. 1000—to the time when Leif Ericson journeyed to North America. Several of the sod buildings at the site have been reconstructed. Visitors can see reenactments of the old Viking way of life.

other sea mammals for their skins, ivory, and oil, which were important trade goods.

About the same time, a Viking named Eric the Red sailed west and founded a new colony in a land to the west of Iceland. He named it Greenland, supposedly so that people would want to settle there. His son, Leif Ericson, would be the first to reach North America.

THE VOYAGE TO VINLAND

Viking legends, or sagas, tell that around the year 1000 Ericson led a band of Vikings west from Greenland to a new land. They first reached a rocky coast they called Helluland (Flat Stone Land). It was probably present-day Baffin Island. Then they sailed south along the shore to a place they named Markland (Woodland). It was probably Labrador. Continuing south, they reached the northern tip of present-day Newfoundland. There, in a green meadow at the edge of the sea, they established a base camp. From this site, the Vikings explored the coasts around the Gulf of St. Lawrence, in Nova Scotia and New Brunswick. They found

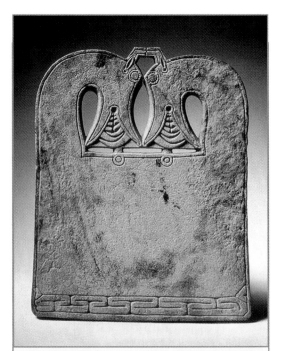

A Norse woman once used this whalebone ironing board to smooth linen, pressing the cloth against the flat surface with a glass weight. Everyday objects were often beautifully decorated in Norse homes.

wild grapes there, the sagas say, so they named the region Vinland (Wineland).

Were the sagas just stories? For years, many people thought so. But in the 1960's, archeologists found the remains of a Viking outpost called L'Anse aux Meadows, on the northern tip of Newfoundland. They think this site was the base camp from which the seafarers explored Vinland. Those ruins are the only confirmed Viking site found so far in North America. And they date to the time when Ericson would have made his voyage.

The site includes the ruins of eight sod buildings, several of which have been restored.

The camp at L'Anse aux Meadows was used only for about ten years. Conflict with American Indians was probably one reason that the Vikings decided not to stay. While the Vikings were safe at L'Anse aux Meadows, they skirmished with people they called "skraelings" as they explored the area. The Indians outnumbered the Vikings. And, unlike Europeans who reached America later, the Vikings didn't have guns.

The Vikings didn't continue their search for new lands partly because of changes in Europe. By the early 1100's, the Viking world was

Pieces from a 13th-century chess set show the range of the Norse world. The pieces were made of walrus ivory from the Norse settlements in Greenland. They were carved by craftsmen in Norway. And they were found on the Isle of Lewis, in the Hebrides, off Scotland.

Three of the buildings were longhouses where many people—perhaps more than 30—lived together. Smaller buildings seem to have been workshops. Many Viking items have been found at the site. They include a bronze pin probably used to fasten a cloak, soapstone oil lamps, a bone needle, and part of a spindle once used for making thread. The fact that spinning and weaving were done at L'Anse aux Meadows indicates that some of the people were women. But there were no barns or farming tools. That suggests that the Vikings didn't plan to stay.

changing in many ways. Through trade and raiding, the Vikings had come in contact with other European peoples—and they had become more like those peoples. They had adopted Christianity. They founded cities and kingdoms. Raiding ended, and Norse culture began to blend in with the culture of medieval Europe.

The Vikings' visits to North America are a little-known, mysterious chapter in the history of the continent. The anniversary was a chance to take an imaginary voyage of discovery—and learn about these ancient adventurers.

A BIRTHDAY FOR THE WHITE HOUSE

If buildings could talk, imagine what stories the White House could tell. The house at 1600 Pennsylvania Avenue in Washington, D.C., has been home to every U.S. president except George Washington. It has been at the center of many of the most important events in American history.

In 2000, Americans celebrated the 200th birthday of the White House. Exhibits and other special events marked the occasion. In its two centuries as the official residence of the president, the White House has undergone many changes. It has become much more than the president's home. It's also the president's office, a mansion where foreign leaders are entertained, and a historic monument visited by millions of tourists each year. And it has become an honored symbol of the presidency and the nation.

Right: Gardens and fountains adorn the south lawn of the White House. Below: Historical rooms include (*1*) State Dining Room; (*2*) Red Room; (*3*) Blue Room; (*4*) Green Room; (*5*) East Room; (*6*) Library; (*7*) Vermeil Room; (*8*) China Room; (*9*) Diplomatic Reception Room; and (*10*) Map Room.

THE PRESIDENT'S HOUSE

George Washington didn't live in the White House, but he helped build it. As the first president, he chose the site for the new

216

The Green Room and the Red Room are two of the three state parlors named for the colors of their walls.

U.S. capital—Washington, D.C. And along with the designer of the city, Pierre Charles L'Enfant, he selected a site for a presidential residence. Architects were invited to submit designs for the presidential residence. James Hoban, an Irish-born architect, came up with the winning plan.

Construction of the President's House, as it was then called, began in October 1792. Blocks of Virginia sandstone, set in place by stonemasons from Scotland, formed the exterior walls. Bricks and plaster for the interior walls were made on site. Lumber for paneling and woodwork was brought from North Carolina and Virginia.

On November 1, 1800, the first resident moved in—John Adams, the second U.S. president. He wrote to his wife, Abigail, "I pray heaven to bestow the best of blessings on this house and all that shall hereafter inhabit it. May none but the wise men ever rule under this roof." Abigail joined John in Washington two weeks later. For them, life in the President's House was almost like camping out. Only six rooms were fully completed. The family hung laundry to dry in the huge, unfinished East Room.

Adams lost the election of 1800 to Thomas Jefferson, who began to turn the President's House into an elegant mansion. He directed both interior furnishing and exterior landscaping, and he opened the house for public tours. However, during the War of 1812, while James Madison was president, British soldiers attacked Washington and set fire to the mansion. The stone walls stayed up, but most of the interior was burned.

It took three years to repair the damage. Then the President's House once again welcomed visitors—sometimes in overwhelming numbers. In 1829, President Andrew Jackson was forced to flee his own inaugural reception when 20,000 people tried to press their way into the mansion. They tracked mud across the floors, stood on chairs, and broke dishes. The White House was the biggest house in the United States at the time, but it wasn't big enough for that crowd.

MAKING A MARK

Every First Family has made its mark on the official presidential residence. After the Civil War, the mansion's rooms were decorated in the Victorian style. The state rooms were filled with carved sofas and chairs, while potted palms lined the halls and stairways. During the administration of Chester Arthur (1881–85), newspapers reported that "twenty-four wagon loads of furniture and other household articles were sold at public auction," to make room for the latest Victorian pieces.

When Theodore Roosevelt and his family moved in, in 1901, the mansion's second floor contained both the private family quarters and the presidential offices. But the Roosevelts had six children, and that made the building very crowded. There were wrestling matches in the East Room, and young Roosevelts roller-skated down the halls. To solve the crowding problem, the mansion was given a makeover and an addition. An executive wing—the West Wing—was built to house the president's offices. The main building was redecorated in a simpler style. Roosevelt also gave the mansion a new official name—the White House.

From 1948–1952, while Harry S. Truman was president, the White House was extensively rebuilt. The interior was gutted, and the original wall paneling was carefully numbered and stored. A new basement and foundation were built under the original outside walls, and a new steel framework was put in. Then the original paneling was replaced. During the renovation, President Truman and his family lived across the street from the White House, in Blair House, ordinarily used to house important foreign visitors.

In the early 1960's, First Lady Jacqueline Kennedy led an effort to redecorate the rooms with historical paintings and furnishings. These efforts have continued, with each president making his own changes and additions to the public and private rooms.

The president's private office, the Oval Office, is named for its elliptical shape.

INSIDE THE WHITE HOUSE

Keeping the White House white is no small task. It takes 570 gallons of paint to cover the outside. Altogether, the White House has six floors—two basements, two public floors, and two floors for the First Family. There are 132 rooms, 32 bathrooms, 7 staircases, and 3 elevators for all the people who live, work, and visit there. There are also 412 doors, 147 windows, and 28 fireplaces. The presidential residence has its own tennis court, jogging track, swimming pool, movie theater, billiard room, and bowling lane. The kitchen, staffed with five full-time chefs, can turn out dinner for 140 guests and hors d'oeuvres for more than 1,000.

The White House is the only private residence of a head of state that's open to the public, free of charge. On an average day, 6,000 people visit the mansion. Tourists see only part of the building, mainly a group of historic rooms. These include three state parlors named for the colors of their walls. The oval Blue Room is used as a reception room for foreign dignitaries. During the holiday season, the White House Christmas tree is set up in this room. The Green Room looks as it might have in Jefferson's day, with furnishings from the Federal period (1780–1820). The Red Room has furnishings from the Empire period (1810–1830). Also on the tour are the State Dining Room, used for formal dinners, and the East Room, the largest room in the White House. The East Room has been used for everything from press conferences to dances, concerts, weddings, and funerals.

Visitors don't get to tour the private areas on the upper floors, where the president and his family live. Also off-limits are the many "working" areas of the White House—including the

The White House On Fire!

In 1812, while James and Dolley Madison lived in the White House, the United States and England went to war. For the Americans, the war reached a low point on August 24, 1814, when British troops overran American forces at Bladensburg, Maryland, and marched into Washington. The British set fire to a number of important buildings—including the White House. Paul Jennings, a servant at the White House at the time, recalled the events this way:

"Even that very morning General Armstrong assured Mrs. Madison there was no danger. The President. . .rode out on horseback to Bladensburg to see how things looked. Mrs. Madison ordered dinner to be ready at 3, as usual; I set the table myself, and brought up the ale, cider, and wine and placed them in coolers, as all the Cabinet and several military gentlemen and strangers were expected. While waiting, at just about 3. . .James Smith, a free colored man who had accompanied Mr. Madison to Bladensburg, gallopped up to the house, waving his hat, and cried out, 'Clear out, clear out! General Armstrong has ordered a retreat!' All then was confusion. Mrs. Madison ordered her carriage, and passing through the dining-room, caught up what silver she could crowd into her old-fashioned reticule [a drawstring bag], and then jumped into the chariot. . . .When the British did arrive, they ate up the very dinner, and drank the wines. . .that I had prepared for the President's party."

Many historians recount that Dolley Madison saved a famous portrait of George Washington by Gilbert Stuart as she fled. Jennings's account is different. The First Lady, he says, "had no time for doing it. It would have required a ladder to get it down. All she carried off was the silver in her reticule, as the British were thought to be but a few squares off, and were expected every moment." Instead, the president's doorkeeper and gardener took down the painting and loaded it onto a wagon with other valuables.

After they ate the presidential dinner, the British soldiers set fire to the house. Luckily, a summer thunderstorm put out the fire before the White House burned to the ground.

kitchen, the library, the offices of the White House physician and the curator, and the offices of the first lady and her staff. The offices of the president and his staff are in the West Wing. The president does most of the business of the country—signing bills, meeting with staff and officials, and so on—in the Oval Office.

A trip to the White House is awe-inspiring. Visitors walk where Jefferson, Lincoln, and other great presidents walked. They know that just down the hall, top leaders are at work on the nation's most important business. And they have a chance to experience a place that, after 200 years, is an honored symbol of the United States.

SPOTLIGHT ON YOUTH

Some people think the high-school years are the best years of life. Others think those years are the hardest. Who's right? On television, at least, the answer is clear: The high-school years are the funniest! *Freaks and Geeks* was one of several TV sitcoms that had audiences chuckling over student troubles in 2000. The show revolved around the adventures of three nerdy freshmen (the group standing to the right in this picture) as they tried to get along in high school. The show won wide praise for its wit and its realistic portrayal of school and family life.

WWW.COOLSITES

Do you know the story behind "The Star-Spangled Banner"? Want to find a neat new game to play every day? Learn how to make a thermometer? Listen to the calls of various frogs? Find the answers on the Internet's World Wide Web—one of the coolest places to be these days. The Web is a huge community in cyberspace filled with thousands of sites that contain information on every subject imaginable. If your computer is connected to an on-line service, just type in the address exactly as shown here. In seconds you'll be at the site.

The Star-Spangled Banner
http://americanhistory.si.edu/ssb

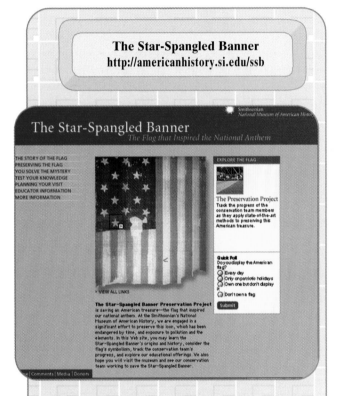

During the War of 1812, Francis Scott Key watched as British warships attacked Fort McHenry, in Baltimore Harbor. As he peered through the clearing smoke, he saw that the American flag was still flying proudly over the fort! Inspired, he wrote a poem that began, "Oh, say can you see, by the dawn's early light." That poem became America's national anthem. And the flag itself became one of the nation's most cherished treasures. But with the passage of time, the flag's condition seriously deteriorated. This Web site from the Smithsonian Institution describes the flag's history and tells what measures are being taken to repair and preserve it.

Bonus.com
http://www.bonus.com

There's a mind-boggling selection of activities at this "SuperSite for Kids." Click on Color, and you'll laugh at other kids' jokes (and submit your own). In Imagine, read all about the latest pop crazes. In Explore, you can choose among topics such as dinosaurs, heroes, natural disasters, and the Earth—each with a dozen or more things to look at, read, or do. The New Fun section offers a great variety of non-stop games and new activities every day. It also lets you give your opinions, by voting on celebrities, reviewing your favorite movies, and even offering advice to other kids.

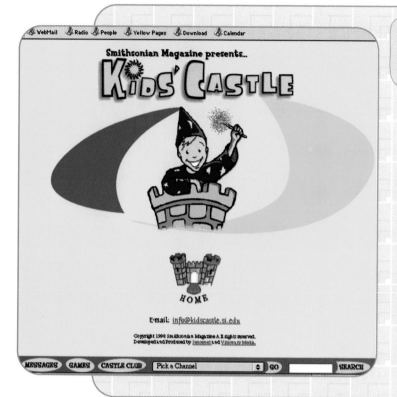

Smithsonian Magazine presents...

KIDS' CASTLE

HOME

E-mail: info@kidscastle.si.edu

Copyright 1998 Smithsonian Magazine. All rights reserved.
Developed and Produced by Sonnet and Voices in Media.

MESSAGES · GAMES · CASTLE CLUB · Pick a Channel ⬍ GO · SEARCH

Kids' Castle
http://www.kidscastle.si.edu

This Web site from *Smithsonian* magazine is filled with fascinating information and activities. There are sections on science, animals, sports, the arts, history, personalities, air and space, and the world. Each section includes news, articles, photos, and message boards. Let other kids know who's your sports hero, what's your favorite food, and where you'd like to travel. Discover what an astrarium is, and make a thermometer like the very first one, invented by Galileo. Join the Castle Club and you'll receive a free newsletter by e-mail, containing stories and poems from other kids—and announcements of new contests and games at Kids' Castle!

Frogs
http://www.exploratorium.edu/frogs

Hop onto the Web and learn about the amazing, adaptable frog and its predecessor, *Ichthyostega,* otherwise known as "the first four-legged fish." Listen to the calls of various frogs and the nighttime sounds of a rain forest. Simple directions explain how you can make a rainstick so that you can re-create rain-forest sounds in your own home. At this site you'll also discover how different cultures viewed frogs and toads, from people who saw them as gods to others who considered them evil creatures. And you'll travel to Frog City USA, where the first Frog Derby was held.

frogs

expl○rato

EXHIBITION NEWS
Extended through February 6, 2000!
Frogs are here! See amazing frogs from all over the planet. To find out more, read About the Exhibition.

Find out what's going on--see this month's events.

Coming to visit? We've got directions and hours pages.

To celebrate the exhibition, a selection of frog books and gifts are available at the online Exploratorium Store.

Features
The Amazing, Adaptable Frog
Inside the Lab & Out in the Field
Cold-Blooded Solutions to Warm-Blooded Problems

Tales and Tours
Rayne, Louisiana: Frog City USA
Frog Myths Across Cultures

Online Exhibits
Frog Tracker
Disappearing Act

Activities and Sounds
Make Your Own Rainstick
The Sounds of the Rain Forest

If you enjoy working with numbers and can make quick decisions, you might consider a career in finance.

CAREERS IN FINANCE

Do you love math and thrive on pressure? Can you think on your feet and make quick decisions? Do you want to make lots of money, even if that means putting in long hours? Then you may want to consider a career in finance.

People who work in financial services deal with money. They raise it, manage it, lend it, and invest it. In recent years, finance has been an exciting field to work in—especially those areas of finance that focus on investments. Money has poured into investment markets in the United States and elsewhere. Stock prices have shot up to undreamed of heights. Meanwhile, computers and the Internet have linked financial markets and investors around the world.

The people who work in the financial industry have been in the middle of it all. Many have had an opportunity to earn high salaries and big bonuses. Of course, financial markets have their ups and downs. And when the down times come along, people who work in these markets earn less. But if you choose to work in finance, the training and knowledge you gain will prove valuable in just about any business career.

Financial services include many lines of work. Commercial banking, accounting, securities trading, asset management, financial planning, and investment banking are some of the most important fields.

COMMERCIAL BANKING

When you think of businesses that handle money, you probably think first of commercial banks. Commercial banks make loans and offer checking and savings accounts to businesses and individuals. In recent years they have begun to branch out into other areas of financial services, such as investment banking and financial planning.

Commercial banks employ people in many different roles. **Tellers** deal directly with customers who come to the bank to deposit money, cash checks, or obtain other services. Patience and a pleasant manner are very important in this job. So are good math skills and an eye for detail. Most tellers have at least a high-school diploma, with courses in accounting and bookkeeping. Tellers can advance to higher positions—to head tellers or customer service representatives, for example.

Loan officers work in commercial banks. They decide whether to lend money to individuals or businesses who apply for credit.

Bank managers, or officers, are in charge of various aspects of the bank's work. For example, **branch managers** make sure the bank's branches run smoothly. **Loan officers** decide whether to lend money to individuals and businesses who apply for credit. **Trust officers** manage estates and trusts. They may invest funds on behalf of their clients and provide financial advice.

Management positions in banking call for at least a four-year college degree, and a master's in business administration (MBA) is often required. So is experience in the banking industry.

ACCOUNTING

Accountants keep track of money for businesses, government, and private individuals. Many accountants specialize in certain areas of their field, such as taxes or corporate finance.

Public accountants work on their own or for large accounting firms. Their clients may include businesses and individuals. Helping to prepare tax returns and providing tax advice is an important part of the work. Some public accountants act as consultants, helping businesses set up record-keeping and other systems. Some are auditors. They check business financial statements for accuracy and issue reports on their findings.

Corporate or management accountants work for businesses. They keep records and prepare financial reports that show where income comes from, how money is spent, whether a company is profitable, and other important information. They're also involved in planning and budgeting. Some work as internal auditors, making sure that the company's records are accurate.

Government accountants may work in local, state, or federal government agencies. Some government accountants keep financial records and make sure that agencies comply with any laws controlling their income and spending. Others work for agencies that regulate financial services, such as banking and securities trading. Those who work for the Internal Revenue Service may audit the financial records of businesses or individuals, to see if their tax returns are accurate.

Good math, computer, and analytical skills are important for accountants. So is a bachelor's degree in accounting or a related field. Most accountants have a master's degree as well. Professional certification is an advantage in getting ahead in this field. To become a Certified Public Accountant (CPA),

Accountants keep track of money for businesses, government, and individuals. Some specialize in preparing tax returns.

you need to take certain courses and pass a tough, two-day exam. Accountants generally start out in assistant, trainee, or "junior" positions. They advance to management positions. Some become corporation vice presidents or chief financial officers (CFO's).

DEALING IN SECURITIES

Securities dealers sell securities—mainly stocks and bonds. Dealing in securities is an exciting, high-pressure field that offers several different lines of work. Those who succeed in this field have a chance to make a lot of money.

When investors want to buy or sell stocks or bonds, they place an order with a **securities sales representative, or broker.** Brokers bring buyers and sellers together and collect a commission or fee for seeing the sale through. They also give advice to their clients. Brokers usually must be licensed by state governments

Investing 101

Like most fields, investing has a vocabulary that's all its own. Here are some terms you're likely to hear when people talk about investments.

Asset—Anything of value. Stocks, bonds, cash, houses, and jewelry are all assets.

Bond— A certificate of debt. Bonds are like IOU's. When companies and government agencies sell bonds to investors, they promise to back the bonds' value, plus interest, within a set time.

Bear Market—A period in which stock prices fall.

Bull Market— A period in which stock prices rise.

Dow Jones Industrial Average—An average that tracks the prices of 30 important stocks on the New York Stock Exchange. It's one of several averages that are used to measure performance in the stock market.

Exchange—A place where securities such as stocks and bonds are bought and sold. The largest securities exchange is the New York Stock Exchange.

IPO (Initial Public Offering)—A company's first public stock issue. Many companies are privately held. Only certain individuals own their shares. When one of these companies decides to raise money by issuing stock that anyone can buy, it makes an IPO and "goes public."

Mutual Fund—A fund that pools the money of many investors, or shareholders, and invests it for them. The fund may put the money in stocks, bonds, currencies, or other investments.

NASDAQ (National Association of Securities Dealers Automated Quotations)—A computerized trading system that acts like a virtual stock exchange. Stocks listed on NASDAQ are traded by phone and computer, not on a trading floor. They are called "over the counter" stocks.

Securities—Stocks, bonds, and similar investment products.

Stock—Ownership shares. Investors who buy shares of stock become part owners in the company. They stand to gain if the company does well—and lose if it does poorly.

Stock Market—The buying and selling of stocks. The term refers to the activity, not a specific place.

Above: Floor traders on the New York Stock Exchange buy and sell stocks for their clients. Right: The Internet is changing the way people trade on the stock market. It allows investors to use online accounts to send orders directly to a trader, skipping the broker.

and register as agents of the firm where they work. They often specialize in particular types of securities, such as stocks or bonds.

Brokers spend a lot of time on the phone, drumming up clients or selling particular stock or bond issues. A successful broker builds a large "book" of clients. More clients bring more trades—and more commissions. Successful brokers sometimes move up to become **branch managers at brokerage firms.** They are responsible for seeing that their office meets the company's sales targets.

Brokers arrange securities trades, but they don't actually carry out the deals. They pass the orders they receive to **traders** who are registered with the exchanges, or markets, where securities are sold. Like sales representatives, traders collect a commission or fee when the sale goes through. Traders also "take positions" in stocks or bonds. This means that they buy and sell large quantities of securities on their own or their employer's behalf. They may make huge profits—or lose money.

Floor traders are on the scene at the New York Stock Exchange and other major exchanges. They rush around the trading floor, trying to find someone to buy or sell at the price specified in the client's order, or ticket. One leading stock exchange doesn't have a trading floor. On the NASDAQ exchange, sales are made by **desk traders** at the brokerage firm. They work on phones and computers to follow fluctuating stock prices and bring buyers and sellers together.

Wall Street, in New York City, is the heart of the securities industry. It's the site of the New York Stock Exchange. But computers and the Internet are changing the securities industry, making it possible for dealers to carry out trades all over the world. The Internet is also

227

Warren Buffett: Top Investor

Warren Buffett doesn't look rich. He wears plain suits and drives his own car. He lives in a simple house in Omaha, Nebraska. He drinks Cherry Coke and eats at Dairy Queen. But don't let appearances fool you. Buffett is one of the most successful investors of all time. He has amassed a fortune worth more than $30 billion. And he started his career as a kid!

Buffett was born in 1930 in Omaha, where his father was a stockbroker. Growing up, he earned money by selling soda door to door and working at his grandfather's grocery store. He also hung out at his father's office, charting stock prices for fun. When he was 11, he made his first investment, buying three shares of oil company stock.

Later, when the Buffetts moved to Washington, D.C., Warren ran five paper routes. He and a friend also earned money by leasing pinball machines to barber shops. All along, through high school and college, he invested his earnings. By 1950 he had $9,800. Then, as a graduate student at Columbia Business School in New York City, he studied securities analysis and other subjects. And he put his learning to work in his own investment strategy. In just six years, his holdings increased to $140,000.

Buffett then began to take on investment partners—first family and friends, and later other investors. The partners benefited from Buffett's expertise in exchange for a share of profits. From 1957 to 1969, the partnership investments grew more than 29 percent a year—far more than the stock market as a whole.

Buffett had similar success with Berkshire Hathaway, a Massachusetts textile company. The New England textile industry was in decline when he acquired control of the company in 1965. He invested Berkshire Hathaway's funds into a wide range of other businesses. Berkshire Hathaway soon became one of the hottest holdings in the stock market.

If there's a secret to Buffett's success, it may be his ability to take a long view. He buys stocks in companies he believes in and holds those stocks for years. That steadiness is reflected in his lifestyle. He's a multi-billionaire. But he lives simply and enjoys every minute of his work. "I get to do what I like to do every single day of the year," he says.

changing the way people buy and sell stocks. With an online account, an investor can send orders directly to a trader, skipping the broker.

Brokers and traders need nerves of steel, the ability to think and act quickly, and a good aptitude for numbers. Brokers also need good customer relations and sales skills. There are no specific educational requirements, but brokers and traders generally have a four-year degree that includes business and accounting courses.

ASSET MANAGEMENT

Asset managers invest money for others and try to make a profit for them. They research and evaluate investments and decide where the money should go. Many asset managers work for mutual funds, investing the money contributed by the funds' shareholders. Others work for banks, corporations, or wealthy individuals.

At a mutual fund company, asset management includes several different jobs. **Researchers** collect information about possible investments. If a fund is considering buying a certain stock, for example, researchers obtain earnings reports and other information that shows whether that corporation is making money and has a good outlook for the future.

holders make money. The fund manager also ensures that the fund lives up to its investment philosophy. Many funds focus on certain types of stocks or other investments, limiting the choices.

This is a high-paying and competitive field. People often start out in sales or some other position with a mutual-fund company, and then switch into asset management. To succeed, it helps to love working with numbers. A four-year degree with plenty of courses in statistics

Financial planners provide investment advice. They help people manage their money and reach financial goals, such as saving for retirement or for a child's college education.

Many researchers move up to become analysts. **Analysts** study the information provided by researchers and use it to create financial models and projections. Then they come up with a recommendation to buy or sell. They may also meet with managers of the corporation in question. And they confer with brokers to keep track of market trends.

An analyst who's successful at picking good investments can become a **fund manager**. Fund managers are the ones who make the final decisions about what becomes part of the fund's portfolio, or basket of investments. They are responsible for the performance of the fund—that is, for making sure that share-

and accounting is required for a researcher's job, and an MBA helps. Most fund managers have an MBA or CFA (Certified Financial Analyst) certification. To get a CFA, they must pass a series of three exams.

FINANCIAL PLANNING

Financial planners provide investment advice and a wide range of services. They help people manage their money and reach financial goals, such as saving for retirement or for a child's college education. Some planners specialize in certain areas, such as helping people manage debts. Most work with individuals, but some provide services to businesses.

Financial planners meet with clients and review their income, expenses, debts, and long-term goals. Then they recommend a plan of savings and investment that will help reach the goals. For example, the planner might recommend that a client put a percentage of income into a retirement savings account, and another percentage into mutual funds or some other investment. Planners also advise their clients about other financial matters, including budgets, insurance, taxes, and preparing wills. Besides drawing up plans for their clients, they may help put the plans into action. For example, they may arrange stock purchases or other investments.

Most financial planners are self-employed or work for financial planning firms. They earn fees from their clients. Some work for brokerage firms or insurance companies, and they may collect commissions for the investments they recommend.

Besides knowledge and expertise in the world of finance, financial planners need to enjoy working with people. Many financial planners are former accountants, brokers, analysts, or corporate financial executives. They have bachelor's and, often, master's degrees. Many also earn a Certified Financial Planner (CFP) designation or similar professional certification. To get a CFP, they must complete

Getting Started

If you're interested in finance, discuss these careers with your school guidance counselor, and read books about the field. Get hands-on experience by managing your own money. Develop a budget, and set goals for your savings. People must generally be 18 or 21 to buy investments such as stocks or mutual funds, but some kids invest with their parents help.

You can also learn about investing by building a "phantom" portfolio. Read about companies that interest you. Decide which ones you think would make good investments. Then follow the prices of their stocks, in the newspaper or online, over a period of time.

For more information about careers in finance, contact these organizations:

American Institute of Certified Public Accountants—1211 Avenue of the Americas, New York, NY 10036

Canadian Institute of Financial Accountants—2380 Holly Lane, Ottawa, Ontario K1V 7P2

Securities Industry Association—120 Broadway, New York, NY 10271

The Canadian Securities Institute—121 King Street West, P.O. Box 113, Toronto, Ontario M5H 3T9

American Financial Services Association—919 18th Street NW, Washington, DC 20006

The Canadian Association of Financial Planners—439 University Avenue, Toronto, Ontario M5G 1Y8

Institute of Certified Financial Planners—3810 East Florida Avenue, Denver, CO 80210

Association for Investment & Management Research—P.O. Box 3668, Charlottesville, VA 22903

approved college courses and pass a two-day exam.

INVESTMENT BANKING

Investment bankers, or i-bankers, help businesses merge, buy other businesses, and issue stocks and bonds. I-bankers are expert at calculating what a business is worth. That helps them set the value of a merger or a stock offering. Businesses pay substantial fees for this valuation service and for other services that i-banks provide. Some large investment banks also offer brokerage and asset management services to the public.

Most investment banks divide their services into several professional areas. The **corporate finance division** helps businesses raise money through stock and bond sales. For example, an investment bank may underwrite a company's stock or bond offering. This means that the i-bank agrees to purchase the offering at a set price, and then resell the securities to the public. The corporate finance division also helps businesses with financial planning.

The bank's **sales and trading department** is in charge of reselling securities that the bank underwrites. This often involves getting major investors, such as mutual funds, to agree in advance to buy the stocks or bonds when they come on the market. The investment bank makes money by reselling the offering at a higher price than the price it pays the company issuing the securities.

The **public finance division** provides much the same services as the corporate finance division. But its clients are city and state governments and public agencies. The investment bank helps these clients raise money by issuing bonds and similar securities.

The **mergers and acquisitions division** advises companies that are buying other com-

Investment bankers help local governments raise money by issuing bonds. This high school was built with money funded by a bond issue.

panies or are about to be bought. In this role, the investment bank helps determine the value of a company and negotiate the price and terms of the deal.

All these divisions depend on the work of the investment bank's **research department.** Researchers help price securities and acquisitions. They investigate individual companies. They monitor trends in the securities markets, in various industries, and in the economy as a whole. And they provide forecasts and recommendations to clients and to the investment bank's other divisions. This work involves analyzing financial statements and other information, meeting with company managers, and making presentations.

Careers in investment banking require a four-year college degree and, often, an MBA. It isn't easy to break into this high-paying field, and competition for jobs is intense.

OTHER CAREERS

The field of finance offers many other careers. Do you like to take chances? You might enjoy working for a venture capital firm. These firms invest in new businesses, or start-ups, in exchange for a share of ownership. They hope to make huge profits when the start-up "goes public" (sells stock) or is bought by another company. Of course, sometimes the start-up isn't successful, and the venture capital firm loses money.

There are plenty of less risky careers. For example, corporations employ people in many financial management positions. They include financial analysts, budget managers, credit managers, and others.

High risk or low risk, any career in finance will keep you "in the money."

KID STUFF

Young British actor **Daniel Radcliffe** (center) landed the role of a lifetime in 2000. Daniel, 11, was picked to play Harry Potter, the wizard hero of the most popular children's books ever, in the upcoming movie version of *Harry Potter and the Sorcerer's Stone.* Emma Watson, 10 (left), and Rupert Grint, 11 (right), were chosen to play Harry's best friends, brainy Hermione Granger and good-natured Ron Weasley. The movie is due out in November 2001.

Harry Potter and the Sorcerer's Stone is the first book in J. K. Rowling's series. At the start of the story, Harry doesn't know that he has magical talents. He lives with his dreadful aunt and uncle, the Dursleys, and their spoiled, bullying son. Then he gets an invitation to Hogwarts School of Witchcraft and Wizardry. Before long, Harry meets Hermione and Ron and learns to fly a broom and cast spells. He also tangles with Lord Voldemort, a truly terrifying villain.

Daniel is an experienced actor. He played the title role in a 1999 British television production of Charles Dickens's *David Copperfield,* and he's appeared in a film called *The Tailor of Panama.* Emma and Rupert are newcomers to movies. Their only acting experience has been in school plays. But the film's producers are sure that all three young actors will bring magic to their roles.

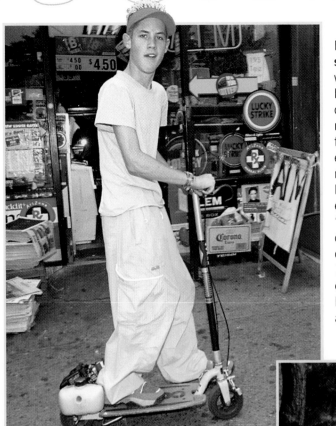

Need to go someplace in a hurry? Try a **scooter**! A fad in the 1950's, scooters were back in 2000. And they were the hottest way to get around. Scooter fans could choose from a wide range of models—from toy kick scooters designed for little kids to electric- and gas-powered models, some of which could travel more than 15 miles (24 kilometers) an hour. Some of the most popular models, however, were fold-up aluminum "racing" scooters that whizzed along on old-fashioned leg power. But scooters can also be dangerous—more than 10,000 scooter injuries were reported during the year. So make sure to wear helmets, knee pads, and elbow pads to avoid getting hurt.

Police work is dangerous—for police dogs as well as police officers. The dogs can be hurt or even killed. But **Stephanie Taylor** of Oceanside, California, did something to protect them. In 1998, 10-year-old Stephanie read about a police dog that was shot and killed in the line of duty. She decided to raise money to buy bulletproof vests, or body armor, for the six police dogs in her town. She placed collection boxes for her Vest-a-Dog program in pet stores and veterinary clinics. In just a month she had raised enough money to get vests for all six dogs. The vests cost about $475 each. And now people from other areas who heard about her campaign have started similar fund-raising efforts in their towns.

Denmark's three largest sections are a peninsula and two big islands. Can you name two of the three? **Felix Peng,** 13, of Guilford, Connecticut, could and did. His answer won the 2000 National Geographic Bee—and a $25,000 college scholarship. The geography contest's national finals were held in May in Washington, D.C. Alex Trebek, host of the quiz show *Jeopardy!,* moderated the two-hour final round. One by one, the contestants stumbled. Finally just two were left—Felix and George Abraham Thampy, 12, of Maryland Heights, Missouri. Felix won. But two weeks later. . .

. . .**George Abraham Thampy** won the finals of the 2000 Scripps Howard National Spelling Bee, also held in Washington, D.C. George clinched the title by spelling the word "demarche," a term for a diplomatic initiative. (He is shown here with his parents.)

A tornado carries a girl named Dorothy and her little dog Toto from Kansas to the magical land of Oz. There they set off down a yellow brick road to the Emerald City. Dorothy, of course, is the heroine of **The Wonderful Wizard of Oz,** by L. Frank Baum. This children's fantasy was published in 1900. Dorothy and her friends the Scarecrow, the Tin Woodman, and the Cowardly Lion have delighted readers of all ages ever since.

The year 2000 marked the 100th anniversary of the book, and several events marked the occasion. Among them was a special exhibit at the Library of Congress, in Washington, D.C.—"The Wizard of Oz: An American Fairy Tale." With flying monkeys, magic shoes, and good and evil witches, Baum's book really *is* like a fairy tale. It's been translated into many languages, including Latin. There have been stage versions of the story (poster, above) and several movies. The most famous was *The Wizard of Oz,* a musical version released in 1939. It starred Judy Garland as Dorothy (top), and it has become a film classic.

Roll it into a ball and bounce it. Stretch it like a piece of taffy. Use it to pick up lint and clean your computer keyboards. Astronauts have even used it to keep tools from floating away in the weightlessness of space. What is it? It's **Silly Putty!** And 2000 marked the 50th anniversary of this screwy, gooey, pink-colored toy. Silly Putty was invented by accident during World War II, by scientists who were trying to make an inexpensive substitute for rubber. The goo they came up with didn't work the way they hoped. And no one could figure out what to do with it—until Peter Hodgson came along in 1950. He bought $147 worth of the goo, packed one-ounce (28-gram) balls of it in colored plastic eggs, and sold it under the name Silly Putty. Everyone bought it!

Viviana Risca, 17, from Port Washington, New York, won first place and a $100,000 scholarship in the Intel Science Talent Search (STS) in March. The STS is America's most important pre-college science contest. Viviana's project involved a type of secret code called steganography.

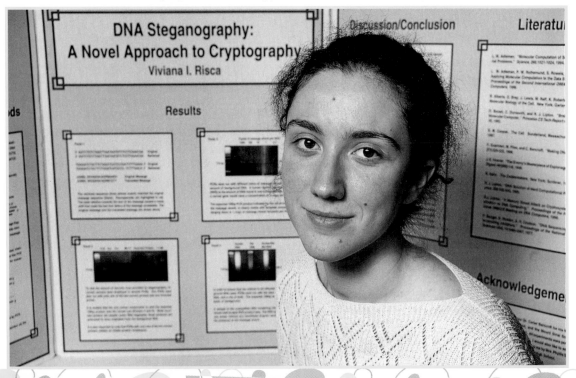

Malcolm in the Middle was 2000's craziest new television comedy. And as the title character, 14-year-old actor **Frankie Muniz** was in the middle of a hit. On the show, Frankie plays a boy genius whose family life is non-stop comic mayhem. Malcolm's brothers are troublemakers. His mother is frantic and disorganized. And his cheerful father just tunes it all out.

Frankie's own life is much less wild. He was just 8 when he started acting in plays around his hometown of Wood-Ridge, New Jersey. Pretty soon he was winning parts on television sitcoms and dramas. When he auditioned for the lead role in *Malcolm in the Middle*, Frankie didn't think he did well enough to get the part. But the show's producers knew right away that they had found the Malcolm they wanted. Frankie also landed the lead role in the film *My Dog Skip*. With his career taking off, he and his family moved to Los Angeles, the center of the entertainment industry.

JASON: THE ULTIMATE FIELD TRIP

How would you like a personal tour of a rain forest in Peru? A chance to see the strange animals of the Galápagos Islands? A view of the ocean floor from an underwater laboratory? Hundreds of thousands of kids have had those opportunities and more, thanks to the JASON Project. Each year this special program takes kids on a different "virtual field trip," letting them participate in exciting scientific projects.

The JASON Project was started by Robert Ballard, an explorer and oceanographer. In 1985, Ballard led the expedition that found the wreck of the ocean liner *Titanic* on the bottom of the Atlantic Ocean. After that, he received thousands of letters from students who wanted to know about his work. Many even asked if they could go with him on his next expedition.

Ballard couldn't take students along. But he decided to do the next-best thing: Give them a chance to see how scientists live and work in the field. The JASON Project uses the Internet and other tools to do that. The program is geared to students in grades 4 through 9. Hundreds of thousands of kids in the United States, Canada, and several other countries take part.

A VIRTUAL ADVENTURE

Each school year, the JASON Project mounts a major scientific expedition, focusing on a different place and theme. Following JASON guidelines, students conduct their own classroom projects and experiments during the year. These projects are designed to mirror the work of the scientists involved in the main expedition. Through the JASON Web site, teachers and students link to the expedition and with other JASON classes worldwide. They can catch live broadcasts and take part in live chats with other participants. They can share ideas and information and get feedback from expedition scientists. They can also access prerecorded videos and various background materials.

The high point of each year's program is a two-week "field trip." In many years a few lucky students and teachers get to work side-by-side with scientists in the field, at the sites they've been studying all year. Thousands more have the feeling of being there through what the JASON Project calls "telepresence." They tune into special direct satellite broad-

Each year the JASON Project lets a few lucky students participate in actual scientific expeditions. The 1999–2000 program took young explorers to the final frontiers of sea and space. Far left: At the Johnson Space Center in Texas, Student Argonauts suit up before handling fragile Antarctic meteorites. Left: Students watch scientists at work at the U.S. Aquarius Underwater Laboratory, in the Florida Keys. Below: Thousands of other kids took part in the field trip through "telepresence" broadcasts.

casts at one of more than three dozen large-screen interactive viewing sites. These "primary interactive network" (PIN) sites are multimedia auditoriums, mostly operated by science museums and universities. During the broadcasts, students can exchange information with scientists and students who are working at the field site.

The JASON Project is run by a foundation based in Needham Heights, Massachusetts, and funded by donations from major corporations. It's named for a hero of Greek mythology, Jason, who sailed a ship called the *Argo* in search of a valuable prize—the Golden Fleece. The members of his crew were called Argonauts. Today, the students and teachers who actually work with JASON scientists in the field are called Student Argonauts and Teacher Argonauts. *Jason* is also the name of an ROV—a remotely operated vehicle—that Ballard has used on many undersea expeditions.

EXPLORING THE WORLD

The JASON Project developed its first program in 1989. That year students took a virtual trip to the bottom of the Mediterranean Sea. They used a two-way satellite audio system to question scientists who were exploring the seafloor. The expedition discovered the first hydrothermal vents in the Mediterranean, examined an ancient Roman shipwreck, and collected artifacts from the seafloor.

The next year's project took students to the bottom of Lake Ontario. There, scientists examined two perfectly preserved shipwrecks dating from the War of 1812. A satellite link allowed students to "drive" the JASON ROV. In 1991, the program visited the Galápagos Islands, off the west coast of South America. The virtual field trip included live broadcasts from an undersea diver. Since then, JASON Project expeditions have visited Mexico's Baja California and the coral reefs and rain forests of Belize. They have studied the Florida wetlands and the hot springs of Yellowstone National Park and Iceland. They have also visited the ocean environments of California's Monterey Bay and Bermuda, as well as the rain forests of the Pacific Northwest and Peru.

The 1999–2000 program was called "Going to Extremes." It looked at sea and space through the eyes of modern-day explorers, asking why scientists risk life and limb to explore the unknown and how they develop ways to survive in hostile environments. Students had a chance to learn how scientists live

Robert Ballard: Ocean Explorer

Robert Ballard has probably seen more of the seafloor than anyone. He has been exploring the ocean depths for most of his life and has led or taken part in more than 65 underwater expeditions.

Ballard was fascinated by the sea even as a child. Born in 1942, he grew up in southern California, where he spent hours exploring the beaches. His favorite book was Jules Verne's *20,000 Leagues Under the Sea*. He took up scuba diving as a teen. Later, he studied geology and chemistry in college and did postgraduate work in marine geology at the University of Hawaii. While in school, he worked at a marine park, training dolphins.

In 1967, Ballard joined the U.S. Navy. He was assigned to the Deep Submergence Laboratory at the Woods Hole Oceanographic Research Institute in Massachusetts. When his Navy service was up, he became a marine scientist on the Woods Hole staff. In the years that followed, he and his team undertook a series of underwater expeditions to chart the ocean floor. He made many dives in a small three-person submarine called the *Alvin*.

In 1973 and 1974, Ballard and his crew explored the Mid-Atlantic Ridge, a huge underwater mountain range in the middle of the Atlantic Ocean. In 1977, they discovered giant tubeworms living around hot springs on the ocean floor near the Galápagos Islands. In 1979, he found "black smokers" off the coast of Baja California. These underwater volcanoes shoot hot fluids from the seafloor, through chimneys formed by mineral deposits.

Ballard's most famous expedition came in 1985. That's when he and his crew found the wreck of the ocean liner *Titanic,* which sank in 1912. They designed a robot, the *Jason Jr.,* to go inside the wreck and send back pictures. The success of that expedition led Ballard to start the JASON Project, so that young people could share the excitement of exploration.

Since 1997, Ballard has been president of the Institute for Exploration in Mystic, Connecticut. He has written many books and articles about his work, and his explorations have been featured in a number of television programs.

Yum! Students munch on cricket-filled chocolates during the JASON Project's 1998–99 mission to the tropical rain forests of Peru. Experiencing different cultures is an important part of the program.

and work in extreme conditions at the National Oceanic and Atmospheric Administration (NOAA) Aquarius Underwater Laboratory, in the Florida Keys. And they learned how the National Aeronautics and Space Administration (NASA) *International Space Station* will allow scientists to live and work in space. In classroom work, they studied the history of exploration and the development of navigation and mapping technologies. Site trips visited the underwater lab and the Johnson Space Center in Texas, where work on the space station is being done. About 400,000 students across the United States and in Bermuda, Mexico, Britain, and Australia took field trips to PIN sites to catch "telepresence" broadcasts.

OFF TO HAWAII

The JASON Project's expedition for 2000–2001 is "Hawaii—A Living Laboratory." It's an in-depth look at the unique landscape and life of the Hawaiian Islands, led by Robert Ballard and a team of researchers. There's a little of everything—geology, biology, oceanography, chemistry, physics, astronomy, technology, mathematics, geography, art, literature, history,

and culture. But the expedition's special focus is Hawaii's awe-inspiring volcanoes.

The expedition is exploring how volcanoes have shaped the islands over millions of years. Scientists are giving students a close look at the active volcano Kilauea, on the island of Hawaii, as well as an active underwater volcano. Students are also learning about volcanoes elsewhere on Earth and throughout the solar system. They are examining the role volcanoes and undersea thermal vents may have played in the origin and distribution of life on Earth.

Another aspect of the expedition is giving students a chance to learn how Hawaii's geology and climate provide homes for plants and animals found nowhere else. About 90 percent of the plants and animals are unique to the islands. Students are also learning how people settled in Hawaii and how human activity has affected these special islands.

The isolation of the Hawaiian Islands has made them a "living laboratory" where natural processes can be studied as they happen. Thanks to the JASON Project, thousands of young people are sharing the excitement of exploration firsthand.

CREATIVITY

Cows went to town in "Moo" York City in the summer of 2000. More than 500 life-size cow statues were placed all over New York. There were cows in parks, cows on traffic islands, cows in the subway. . .wherever a cow could fit. Each fiberglass statue was dressed and decorated by a different artist. And New York was just one of several cities that staged similar, and very popular, outdoor art exhibits during the year.

comic strip, retired. Schulz, 77, was ill. The last new daily *Peanuts* strip ran in newspapers on January 3. And in a sad coincidence, Schulz died on February 12, the day before the last new Sunday strip appeared.

Old installments of *Peanuts* have continued to run in newspapers. For fans of the strip, these "re-runs" have brought memories. And they have given new fans a chance to chuckle over the doings of Charlie Brown and his grade-school friends.

THE *PEANUTS* GANG

The *Peanuts* characters are all kids and animals who live in a nameless American suburb. Schulz drew them simply, with balloon-shaped heads and dots for eyes. But their personalities are anything but simple. They have traits you may recognize in people you know. Here are a few of the best-known characters from the strip:

Charlie Brown is a good-natured "loser." He worries about everything. And no wonder—no matter what he sets out to do, something is sure to go wrong. He'll never win a baseball game or the heart of the little red-haired girl he loves. But that doesn't stop him from trying. And he's always friendly and polite—"Good Ol' Charlie Brown." Even when he's disappointed (and he's most *always* disappointed), his strongest exclamation is "Good grief!"

Lucy Van Pelt is Charlie Brown's opposite in every way. She's loud, she's bossy, and she's always sure she's right. She's self-

GOOD-BYE, CHARLIE BROWN

His baseball team always lost. His kite always got caught in a tree. Every time he tried to kick a football, it was snatched away at the last minute. And his dog outsmarted him all the time.

That's Charlie Brown, the hero of the comic strip *Peanuts*. Charlie and his friends delighted fans for almost 50 years. But in 2000, the *Peanuts* gang took their final bow. Charles Schulz, who created and drew the

ish and grouchy, too. And she's not above playing tricks on people—for example, snatching a football away just as Charlie Brown is about to kick it. When Lucy smiles, it usually means she's planning something *really* rotten.

Linus Van Pelt is Lucy's little brother. He's constantly cuddling up with his security blanket. In fact, Linus inspired the term "security blanket"! Even though he's one of the youngest *Peanuts* characters, he's the comic strip's main brain. When it's time for show-and-tell at school, Charlie Brown brings a toy. Linus brings a homemade copy of the Dead Sea Scrolls.

Schroeder is Lucy's heart-throb. But he's more interested in Beethoven than in Lucy! Schroeder can usually be found bent over his piano, playing the music of the composer he idolizes. Only Lucy's unwanted attentions can break his concentration.

Peppermint Patty is a "tomboy." She's bold and brash, but she's always friendly and good-hearted. And Patty's a star at baseball. But she's definitely not a star at school, where she spends most of the day asleep at her desk. Patty has a secret crush on Charlie Brown. She's the only

character who calls him "Chuck"—much to his embarrassment.

Sally is Charlie Brown's little sister, and she usually has him wrapped around her little finger. In letters and speech, she doesn't hesitate to say exactly what she thinks—but she often mixes up her words, with comical results. Sally has a rather serious crush on Linus, whom she calls her "Sweet Babboo."

Pig Pen lives up to his name. He's always dirty, and he's surrounded by a cloud of dust wherever he goes. The dirt doesn't bother him, and he's given up trying to stay clean.

Snoopy is Charlie Brown's dog, and he may be the most famous *Peanuts* character of all. Schulz based Snoopy on a childhood pet who was, he said, "the smartest and most uncontrollable dog that I have ever seen." In the strip, Snoopy has a vivid imagination and multiple personalities. Lying on the roof of his doghouse, he dreams that he's a World War I flying ace, a great author, a vulture, "Joe Cool" in sunglasses, and more.

Woodstock is Snoopy's buddy and personal secretary. Being a bird, he expresses himself in "birdspeak"—that is, bird scratches enclosed in cartoon balloons.

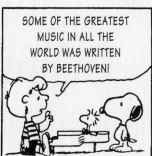

TOMORROW IS BEETHOVEN'S BIRTHDAY

SOME OF THE GREATEST MUSIC IN ALL THE WORLD WAS WRITTEN BY BEETHOVEN!

© 1980 United Feature Syndicate, Inc.   12-15

┌ ¹⁄₁? ⌐

NO, HE WASN'T A BIRD!

PEANUTS AT THE TOP

The first *Peanuts* comic strip appeared on October 2, 1950. It took a few years for the new comic to really catch on. But by the mid-1950's, millions of people were following the doings of Charlie Brown and the other characters. *Peanuts* eventually became the most popular comic strip in the world. It ran in the Red Baron," recorded by the Royal Guardsmen, helped make the dog-turned-flying-ace the strip's most popular character. There was even a Broadway show, *You're a Good Man, Charlie Brown,* based on the strip. And there was plenty of *Peanuts* merchandise—calendars, toys, games, stickers, greeting cards, and everything in between.

2,600 newspapers in 75 countries and 21 languages. Millions of people grew up with *Peanuts* and its characters.

The *Peanuts* characters have popped up in all kinds of unexpected places. Paperback *Peanuts* books became best-sellers. There were *Peanuts* television specials, including *A Charlie Brown Christmas,* which won an Emmy in 1965. In 1966 the song "Snoopy vs.

The comic strip became big business, and it made Charles Schulz wealthy. But the strip always kept its warmth and quiet, understated humor. That's why *Peanuts* never lost its appeal or its ability to make people laugh. It was a sad day for the "funny pages" when the strip ended. But in the hearts of the millions of *Peanuts* fans, Charlie Brown and his friends will live forever.

Charles Schulz: Born to Draw Comic Strips

Some comic strips are taken on by new artists when their creators retire or die. But everyone agreed that *Peanuts* could never be the same without Schulz. He devoted his life to the comic strip and made it one of the best-loved cartoons of all time.

Schulz was involved with cartoons even as a boy in St. Paul, Minnesota. He was nick-named "Sparky" for a character in the comic strip "Barney Google." He loved to draw, and he especially loved to draw cartoons. He even took a correspondence course in cartooning. "It seems beyond comprehension of people that someone can be born to draw comic strips," Schulz once said. "But I think I was. My ambition from earliest memory was to produce a daily comic strip."

After serving in the military in World War II, Schulz began to draw comics for a living.

The character Charlie Brown first appeared in a weekly single-panel comic called "L'il Folks," which Schulz drew for *The St. Paul Pioneer Press.* In 1950, that comic was expanded to a strip and renamed *Peanuts.* Schulz never liked the name, but it stuck.

Schulz drew on his own childhood experiences to create installments of *Peanuts.* And he drew every one of the daily and Sunday strips—more than 18,000 in all. He took time off only for his 70th birthday. Even then, he worked ahead, so the strip would still appear while he was off.

When he could no longer continue, Schulz made the decision to end the strip. *Peanuts* reflected his sense of humor, and he knew it wouldn't be the same if someone else drew it. "I feel very blessed to have been able to do what I love for almost 50 years," he said.

Dear Friends,
    I have been fortunate to draw Charlie Brown and his friends for almost 50 years. It has been the fulfillment of my childhood ambition.
    Unfortunately, I am no longer able to maintain the schedule demanded by a daily comic strip, therefore I am announcing my retirement.

    I have been grateful over the years for the loyalty of our editors and the wonderful support and love expressed to me by fans of the comic strip.
    Charlie Brown, Snoopy, Linus, Lucy...how can I ever forget them...

Charles M. Schulz

1-3-00

Kevin Spacey (best actor) in *American Beauty* (best motion picture).

ACADEMY

Awards

CATEGORY	WINNER
Motion Picture	*American Beauty*
Actor	Kevin Spacey (*American Beauty*)
Actress	Hilary Swank (*Boys Don't Cry*)
Supporting Actor	Michael Caine (*The Cider House Rules*)
Supporting Actress	Angelina Jolie (*Girl, Interrupted*)
Director	Sam Mendes (*American Beauty*)
Cinematography	*American Beauty*
Visual Effects	*The Matrix*
Song	"You'll Be in My Heart" (*Tarzan*)
Foreign–Language Film	*All About My Mother* (Spain)
Documentary Feature	*One Day in September*
Documentary Short	*King Gimp*

2000

Left: Hilary Swank (best actress) in *Boys Don't Cry.* Above: Angelina Jolie (best supporting actress) and Clea Duvall in *Girl, Interrupted.* Below: Michael Caine (best supporting actor) and Tobey Maguire in *The Cider House Rules.*

Pearls, with their warm and glowing beauty, are one of nature's most wonderful creations.

GLOWING GEMS OF THE SEA

The pearl is the hidden soul of the oyster.
Ancient Chinese scribe

In terms of beauty, the average oyster wouldn't win any prize: It's a spineless (even slimy) animal encased in a dull, bumpy shell. Imagine, then, the surprise of prying open an oyster and finding inside it a pearl—pale, perfect, and glowing with a mysterious inner beauty.

Pearls are one of nature's most wonderful creations, and people have long been fascinated by them. Most gems are minerals that are mined from beneath the earth. But pearls are one of the very few organic gems—that is, gems made by a living creature.

Pearls can develop inside any shellfish that lines its shell with nacre (mother-of-pearl), an iridescent substance that's made up mostly of calcium carbonate. But only a few kinds of shellfish produce nacre fine enough to create a gem-quality pearl. They include several species of oysters, which create saltwater pearls, and freshwater mussels, which create freshwater pearls.

A natural pearl begins when a foreign object—a grain of sand, a chip of shell, or even a tiny fish or worm—accidentally finds its way inside the shell. The foreign body is irritating, so the shellfish begins to coat it with thin layers of smooth nacre. As time goes by, more and more layers of nacre surround the foreign body, and a pearl is formed.

It generally takes about seven years for a shellfish to produce a pearl large enough to be valuable, and these are usually small to moderate in size. After twenty years, a pearl might measure an inch (2.54 centimeters) or more across. Giant pearls like these are extremely rare—in fact, natural pearls of any kind are rare. You would have to collect thousands of oysters to find just a handful of pearls. And of that handful, only a few pearls would be of high quality.

This is why, since earliest times, pearls have been prized as rare gems. People have paid small fortunes to possess them and have them made into spectacular pieces of jewelry. And over the years, pearls have been seen as symbols of beauty, elegance, and luxury.

But today people seldom go hunting for natural pearls. Instead, they give nature a helping hand by inserting an irritant—a shell bead—into the shellfish, thus tricking the animals into producing pearls. These pearls are called cultured pearls, and they are produced in great quantity at pearl farms. As a result, pearls are more popular today than ever.

PEARL LORE

Until the late 1800's pearls were the most sought after of all gems, valued more highly than diamonds. The ancient Romans, for example, were famous for their love of pearls. No wealthy Roman woman could be without her pearls—some even wore them to bed. The Roman emperors favored pearls as marks of their rank and wealth. Nero's scepter, Constantine's helmet, and Caligula's slippers were all encrusted with pearls. Caligula even had a pearl necklace for his horse.

Prices of pearls reached such heights in ancient Rome that one general was said to have paid for an entire campaign by selling a single pearl earring. Costly pearls also figured in the famous romance between the Roman leader Marc Antony and Cleopatra, queen of Egypt. According to one story, Cleopatra bet the Roman that she could serve him the most expensive dinner in history. When he accepted the wager, she took off one of her huge pearl earrings, crushed the gem into a goblet of wine, and drank it. She then did the same with the other earring, offering the wine to her guest—and winning the bet. The value of the two pearls was said to have been nearly two million ounces of silver.

The love of pearls began long before the days of ancient Rome, however. Pearls are mentioned in the Bible as symbols of worth. There is evidence that early civilizations in the Middle East and Asia valued these gems as long ago as 3500 B.C. The oldest pearl necklace in existence dates from about 350 B.C. and was found in Susa, in western Iran.

Nor were pearls valued only in the Old World. Pearl jewelry dating from about

Pearls were the height of fashion in Europe during the 1580's, when England's Queen Elizabeth I posed for this famous portrait. The queen often wore gowns encrusted with pearls and other precious gems.

251

500 B.C. has been found in Mexico and Peru. The Hopewell Indians used freshwater pearls in jewelry and placed them in tombs, to accompany the dead on their journey to the next life. In fact, early Spanish explorers sometimes referred to America as the Land of Pearls. Later, in the 1800's, there were "pearl rushes" along the Mississippi River, as fortune-seekers hunted for freshwater pearls.

But for centuries, the pearl trade centered in Asia and the Middle East. The greatest numbers of pearls were gathered in the Persian Gulf. There, long before the days of scuba equipment, divers would brave sharks and other hazards in search of the gems. A diver might bring up hundreds of oysters each day—and obtain perhaps fewer than a dozen pearls. These were often bought by dealers in Bombay, India, who resold the gems to kings, princes, nobles, and wealthy people throughout Europe and Asia.

Because of their great rarity and value, some of the most fabulous pearls wound up among the crown jewels of various countries, adorning royal crowns, scepters, and collars. Pearls thus became associated with royalty. Some rulers even issued special laws to keep their subjects from wearing pearls.

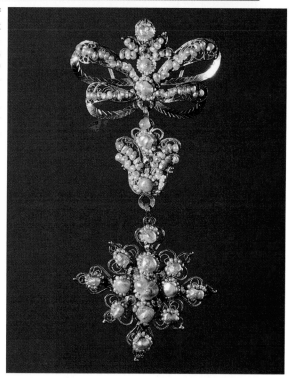

Since earliest times, pearls have been prized as symbols of elegance and luxury. Opposite page, top: This gold peacock brooch is set with pearls, diamonds, rubies, and emeralds. Opposite page, bottom: Kokichi Mikimoto designed this model of the Liberty Bell, which is studded with 12,250 cultured pearls. Center: Strings of dyed cultured freshwater pearls display a gorgeous range of hues. Above: An archbishop's crown, made in the 18th or 19th century, is decorated with pearls and uncut gems. Right: Irregularly shaped pearls, such as those in this pendant, are known as baroques, and their oddity is part of their beauty.

Some large and rare natural pearls have become famous. One, an enormous teardrop-shaped pearl named La Peregrina ("the wanderer" in Italian), was discovered in the Gulf of Panama in the 1500's. Over the years, it belonged to various royal families. In 1969, the actor Richard Burton bought this pearl as a Valentine's Day gift for the actress Elizabeth Taylor. Unfortunately, her dog got hold of the pearl and gnawed on it, leaving toothmarks on the priceless gem.

In the United States, "pearl fever" reached a peak in the 1800's, when pearls changed hands for astronomical sums. One pearl fancier in New York City even turned over a Fifth Avenue mansion to the jeweler Cartier in exchange for a double strand of pearls. (Today, the mansion is worth millions of dollars—while the pearls would bring only a fraction of that.)

Meanwhile, several Japanese experimenters were working on techniques for producing cultured pearls. Kokichi Mikimoto was the first to be granted a patent for his method, in the early 1900's. He promoted his cultured pearls with fantastic creations, such as a model of the Liberty Bell studded with 12,250 pearls and 366 diamonds. But the real reason cultured pearls caught on was that their prices were far below those of natural pearls. Suddenly, many people could afford to own these beautiful gems.

Today nearly all the pearls used in jewelry are cultured. Some natural pearls are still sold, and they still bring very high prices—a natural pearl may sell for perhaps forty times as much as a comparable cultured pearl. A natural pearl is nearly solid nacre, while a cultured pearl has just a coating of nacre around a shell-bead nucleus, or center. Nevertheless, it's difficult even for experts to tell good-quality cultured pearls from natural ones—only an X ray will reveal the shell bead.

Along with cultured pearls, artificial pearls have also appeared. Most of these consist of a plastic bead covered with a thin, nacrelike film obtained from fish scales. Some are good enough to fool the eye, at least at first glance. One way to tell a real pearl from a fake is to run the pearl over your teeth: The genuine one will feel slightly rough.

PEARLY PERFECTION

Natural or cultured, relatively few pearls are of good enough quality to be marketable. Their value is based on a number of characteristics. Shape is one of the most important. The ideal pearl is round, or nearly round, and these fetch the highest prices. Irregularly shaped pearls are known as baroques, and some people value them for their oddity. Half pearls are rounded on one side and flat on the other. They are most often used in earrings.

Besides shape, experts look for other qualities when they judge pearls: luster (the surface shine), orient (the reflective, inner glow), and cleanliness (a surface free of cracks, dents, and flaws). Another term, wink, refers to imperfections in the layers of nacre that show up as bright spots on the pearl.

Color is also important. Most pearls are white or nearly so, but they carry a great range of tints—cream, pink, gold, green, blue, and dark gray (the color of a black pearl). The most desirable are cream, pink, and black. No one is sure what creates the tint of a pearl; the same oyster can produce several pearls of different tints at the same time. And although the practice is frowned on among producers of quality gems, some pearls are dyed to enhance their color. This is done after a hole has been drilled in the pearl, so that the dye seeps under the nacre and a hint of color shines through.

The best pearls are used to make fine jewelry—earrings, necklaces, bracelets, rings, and brooches. Pearl jewelry has a classic look that is never entirely out of fashion, although its popularity may fluctuate from time to time. In the 1960's, for instance, people preferred off-beat fashions and seldom wore pearls. But in the

As these X rays show, a natural pearl (*left*) is nearly solid nacre, while a cultured pearl (*right*) has a comparatively thin coating of nacre around a large shell-bead nucleus. Even experts, however, find it difficult to tell good-quality cultured pearls from natural ones.

The Cultured Look

Most cultured saltwater pearls are produced in Japan and other Asian countries. Cultured freshwater pearls, which are often small and irregularly shaped, are produced in Japan, China, and the United States. Especially valued for their size and thick nacre are South Sea pearls, produced by giant oysters in the South Pacific. And among the most valued of all are black pearls, which have a bluish-black or gray cast. They are produced by black-lipped oysters in the South Pacific.

A shell bead is carefully inserted into the mantle of the oyster.

Some saltwater farms begin by collecting oysters from the ocean. But many pearl farms raise their own oysters, suspending them in the water in wire baskets. When the oysters are large enough, they are taken out of the water. A technician carefully makes a tiny slit in the oyster's mantle. (The mantle is the fleshy part of the oyster that produces nacre.) A round bead made from a mussel shell is inserted into the slit; this becomes the pearl's nucleus. Then a small bit of tissue from the mantle of another living oyster is placed over the shell bead, so that the nucleus is completely surrounded by mantle tissue.

The oysters are then returned to the water. The mantle tissue begins to secrete nacre around the irritating shell bead, and a pearl begins to form. Usually one to three years later, the oysters are taken out of the water again, and the pearls are gently removed. In general, the longer the pearl stays in the oyster, the more nacre there will be—and thick nacre is what produces a radiant, high quality pearl. A finished pearl may have a thousand layers of nacre around the nucleus.

Depending on the size of the oyster and the size of the pearl desired, a single oyster may produce five or more pearls at a time. But the system isn't foolproof: Some of the oysters die, and many of the pearls are misshapen or flawed in some other way.

After they are harvested, the pearls are sorted for size, shape, and quality.

1980's, classic styles returned to favor, and the demand for pearls became bigger than ever.

Today a strand of pearls is considered a basic by many women. Pearl necklaces come in various lengths: choker, which rings the base of the neck; princess, which falls halfway to the breastbone; matinee, about 2 feet (60 centimeters) long; opera, up to 3 feet (1 meter) long; and rope, the longest of all. Pearls are also combined with other gems, such as diamonds, in necklaces, earrings, and other pieces of jewelry. Their warm glow provides a lovely contrast to the glitter of the other jewels.

While pearls are less costly than some other gems, they are also shorter-lived. Pearls can be scratched, and they can be damaged by perfume and makeup. And even with care, a pearl can eventually lose its luster. But for warmth and simple elegance, no other gem can match the pearl.

PEOPLE, PLACES, EVENTS

Pigs parked in Cincinnati, Ohio. Mr. Potato Head popping up all over the state of Rhode Island. Summer 2000 saw outdoor art exhibits featuring **whimsical fiberglass statues** in many places—and people loved them. The events were inspired by "Cows on Parade," a 1999 exhibit in Chicago. New York City and several smaller cities staged their own cow parades in 2000. But some cities were more inventive.

Cincinnati drew on its history for the "Big Pig Gig" (right). This city was once known as Porkopolis, for its meat-packing industry. Some 360 decorated pigs celebrated that past. A herd of fiberglass moose turned Toronto, Canada, into an outdoor "moose-eum." St. Paul, Minnesota, featured an animal that never was: Snoopy, the canine character from the comic-strip *Peanuts*. And Rhode Island chose a toy—Mr. Potato Head (top), which was created in the state in 1952.

What's the best-known ZIP code in the United States? From 1990 to 2000, there was only one answer: 90210, as in the hit TV show **Beverly Hills, 90210.** The Fox Network show began as a series about a group of high-school sophomores in Beverly Hills, California. In the ten years that the show ran, the characters grew up, graduated, fell in and out of love, and generally endured all the trials expected in a soap opera. Fans loved it. The final episode, aired May 17, featured the wedding of Donna (Tori Spelling) and David (Brian Austin Green), high-school sweethearts in the early days. (Shown here is one of the later casts.)

Wings of Witness, an enormous sculpture commemorating victims of the Holocaust, started at a junior high school in Mahomet, Illinois. To demonstrate the huge numbers of people murdered by German Nazis in the Holocaust, during World War II, students there collected 11 million pull tabs from soda cans—one for each victim. Jeffrey Schrier, a New York artist, fashioned the tabs into this dramatic sculpture.

In April 1800, President John Adams authorized $5,000 to purchase books for use by Congress. That was the beginning of the **Library of Congress,** which celebrated its 200th birthday in 2000. Today the Library of Congress is the largest library in the world. It has an awe-inspiring main reading room (above) and 530 miles (852 kilometers) of bookshelves. But it got off to a rocky start. During the War of 1812, the British attacked Washington and burned the Capitol and its library. To replace the lost books, Thomas Jefferson (right) sold his own books to Congress. The library marked its birthday by looking back to that act, with a special exhibition on Jefferson. It also looked ahead, by launching a Web site for kids: **www.americaslibrary.gov**

A young prince from a distant planet travels to Earth, searching for wisdom. Among the things he learns is this: "It is only with the heart that one can see rightly. What is essential is invisible to the eye."

This story is told in *The Little Prince*, a fantasy tale that's become a children's classic. *The Little Prince* was written by **Antoine de Saint-Exupéry,** a French author and pilot whose life story reads like an adventure tale. June 29, 2000, marked the 100th anniversary of his birth.

Saint-Exupéry (below, right) was a pilot in the early days of aviation. He flew airmail routes in France, North Africa, and South America. It was risky work, and he had many close calls. He told about his experiences and the thoughts they inspired in several books, including *Night Flight* and *Wind, Sand and Stars.* During World War II, he flew dangerous missions for the Allied forces in North Africa. On July 31, 1944, he and his plane were lost.

Saint-Exupéry left behind a great legacy in his books. *The Little Prince,* published in 1943, is the best known. It's more than a children's fantasy. It has lots to say about what's really important in life.

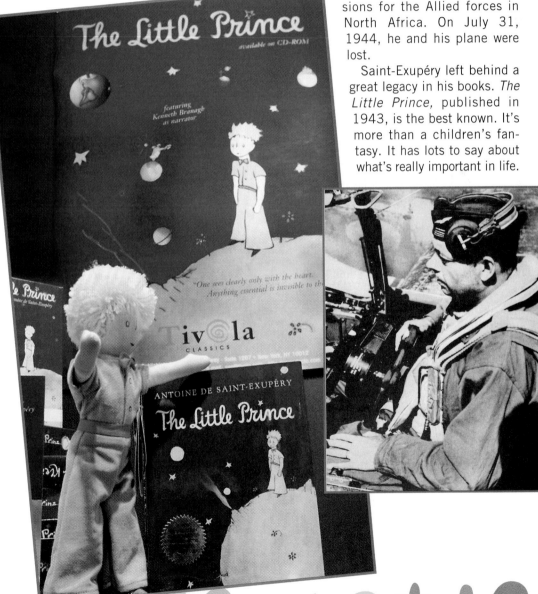

The Plant—about a bloodthirsty vine that terrorizes a publishing company—was posted one chapter at a time. Downloaders were asked to pay $1 a chapter on the honor system, with the understanding that future chapters wouldn't be posted unless at least 75 percent of them paid. At first, most did. But after five installments (and a price increase to $2 per chapter), the number of downloaders had fallen from 120,000 to 40,000. Many weren't paying, so King stopped posting chapters.

Despite the mixed results of King's experiments, electronic publishing may have a future. Most people still prefer curling up with an old-fashioned book to an e-book. But as more titles become available electronically, this reading revolution may catch on.

Best-selling author **Stephen King** helped start a reading revolution in 2000. King, who is famous for his terrifying tales of the supernatural, gave electronic publishing a double boost during the year. In March, King's 66-page novella *Riding the Bullet* was published in electronic form. For $2.50, readers could download the chilling ghost story onto their computers or read it on a portable hand-held monitor designed just for e-books. The text was specially coded, so it couldn't be copied or printed out. Fees were shared by booksellers, King, and his publisher.

Riding the Bullet was a big hit: Simon & Schuster, the publisher, reported 400,000 orders the first day the book went on sale. And in July, King went a step further. He cut out his publisher and released a new e-book himself, on his own Web site.

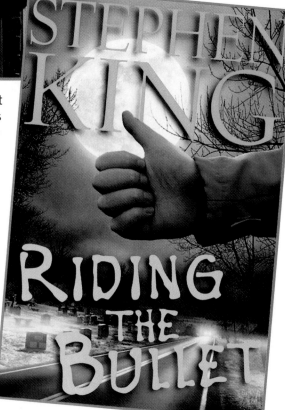

Art critics once dismissed the artworks of **Norman Rockwell.** They said paintings such as *The Babysitter* (right), were just sentimental illustrations. But Rockwell (below, with some of his works) has become one of the best-loved American artists of all time. And in 2000, his work was hanging in top museums—in a show called "Norman Rockwell: Paintings for the People."

Rockwell specialized in painting scenes of small-town American life. From the 1920's until his death in 1978, he was America's top illustrator. His works are filled with humor and images that touch people's hearts. The show includes 70 oil paintings and all 300 covers the artist did for *The Saturday Evening Post,* a popular magazine during Rockwell's day. The show will tour a number of cities in the United States through 2001.

Tobey Maguire has been acting for more than a dozen years. But 2000 turned out to be the year in which he achieved star status. Maguire, who turned 25 during the year, took up acting in junior high school. His mother, a former actress, offered him $100 to take a drama course instead of a cooking course. He was hooked, and he landed his first professional work in TV commercials. Appearances on several television shows led to his first film role, in the 1993 movie *This Boy's Life.* That film starred Leonardo De Caprio, who became a good friend of Maguire's. In recent years Maguire has starred in a string of highly praised films, including *Ride With the Devil* and *The Cider House Rules* in 1999 and *Wonder Boys* in 2000.

Puppy, a work of art covered with colorful blooms, towered over tourists at New York City's famous Rockefeller Center in June 2000. The sculpture was created by Jeff Koons. Koons is an artist who is well known for taking subjects familiar in popular culture—such as puppies and flowers—and working them into avant-garde artworks. *Puppy* stood 43 feet (13 meters) tall and was covered with some 70,000 fresh flowers. It stood in the same spot that, in winter, is occupied by Rockefeller Center's famous Christmas tree. Before coming to New York, the flower-filled sculpture had previously been displayed in Germany and Australia. Another version of *Puppy* is part of the permanent collection of the Guggenheim Museum in Bilbao, Spain.

Which U.S. president appeared on the television show *Laugh-In*? John Carpenter (below, left) knew the answer to that question: Richard Nixon. And his correct response made Carpenter, a 31-year-old Internal Revenue Service employee, the first person to win $1 million on the hit television quiz show ***Who Wants to Be a Millionaire.***

Quiz shows were a TV craze in 2000. Millions of people tuned in to see if contestants—average people, just like those in the audience—could answer questions and win huge cash prizes. The craze started in 1999, when ABC aired *Who Wants to Be a Millionaire* to spice up its summer schedule. The show was a huge hit and soon joined the network's regular program line-up.

Who Wants to Be a Millionaire is emceed by daytime TV star Regis Philbin (above, on the right). He asks multiple-choice questions, and as long as a contestant answers correctly, the prize money grows—up to $1 million! Contestants can get help from people in the studio audience, who vote for answers they think are right. They can try to narrow their choices by eliminating two of the four answers. They can also make a phone call to anyone in the country for advice. And contestants can choose to walk away with their winnings at any time.

With the success of *Who Wants to Be a Millionaire,* other networks rushed to air quiz shows of their own. This wasn't the first time television audiences were caught up in a quiz-show craze. Quiz shows such as *Twenty One* and *The $64,000 Question* were hits in the 1950's. But those shows died a sudden death in 1958, when it was revealed that the games were faked. Contestants had been given the answers! Television executives promised that wouldn't happen with the new crop of shows.

Denzel Washington (right) starred as the coach of a newly integrated football team in *Remember the Titans.*

MOVIE TIME!

Thrills, chills, and laughs brought audiences to movie theaters in 2000. The year's top films included action-packed dramas, science-fiction thrillers, romantic comedies, and live-action versions of classic cartoons.

HEROES OF ALL KINDS

Racial conflicts on and off the football field were the underlying theme of *Remember the Titans.* Denzel Washington starred as the new coach of a newly integrated football squad in Alexandria, Virginia, in 1971. Based on actual events, the film follows the team through the season as players, their classmates, and their families learn to get along.

Race was also the central issue in *Men of Honor,* about the first African American to become a Navy SEAL. The film featured Cuba Gooding, Jr., in the starring role and Robert De Niro as a racist senior officer.

Pay It Forward began with an off-beat idea. In this film, a social-studies teacher, Eugene Simonet (Kevin Spacey), tells his class to figure out ways to make the world a better place. One student, Trevor (Haley Joel Osment),

comes up with this plan: Do a favor for a stranger and, instead of asking to be paid back, ask the stranger to "pay it forward" by doing three favors for three other strangers. The film traces the results of Trevor's idea as a romance develops between the teacher and Trevor's alcoholic mother (Helen Hunt).

Filmmakers turned to history for *The Patriot,* a film set during the Revolutionary War. Mel Gibson portrayed a South Carolina planter who at first wants nothing to do with the rebellion of the colonists against the British. After a British soldier kills one of his children, though, he takes up his musket. Critics questioned the historical accuracy of the movie, but it presented a great dramatic spectacle all the same.

Julia Roberts brought star power to *Erin Brockovich,* a movie based on a true story. Roberts played the title character, a divorced mom who lands a job doing clerical work for a law firm. She turns up evidence of a major crime: A power company has been covering up the fact that pollution from its plants is causing illness and death. Brockovich investigates and helps take the case to court.

In *Pay It Forward*, Haley Joel Osment (with Helen Hunt) played a student who comes up with a plan to make the world a better place.

ACTION AND ADVENTURE

A true story was also the basis for one of the year's most suspenseful action films, *The Perfect Storm*, based on the book of that title by Sebastian Junger. The story follows a group of New England fishermen caught in "the storm of the century"—a terrific gale that raged along the coast on Halloween in 1991. George Clooney starred as captain of the *Andrea Gail*, a ship struggling to stay afloat in the storm. Special effects brought the storm's howling winds and huge waves to the screen.

Four of Hollywood's top leading men—Clint Eastwood, James Garner, Tommy Lee Jones, and Donald Sutherland—joined forces to make *Space Cowboys*. The four play former Air Force pilots who, back in the early days of the U.S. space program, missed their chance to become astronauts. They've long since gone on to other careers. But they're called out of retirement when an important satellite malfunctions, because they're the only ones who

Chicken Run

Chickens plot a daring egg-scape in *Chicken Run*, the most unusual and humorous animated feature of 2000. Instead of drawn animation, this was "claymation." The filmmakers used flexible model figures that were repositioned for each frame of film. As a result, *Chicken Run* seemed much more realistic than most animated films.

The hens in *Chicken Run* are miserable—trapped in the hen house at Tweedy Farm, laying eggs all day. Led by a spunky hen named Ginger (the voice of Julia Sawalha), they're always trying to escape. The hens' hopes soar when Rocky the Flying Rooster (Mel Gibson) crashes into their yard. He promises to teach them to fly, so they can finally get away.

Chicken Run was created by British directors Nick Park and Peter Lord. They have used the same technique in award-winning short animated films featuring the characters Wallace, a bumbling inventor, and Gromit, his dog.

George Clooney was the captain of a ship struggling to keep afloat in *The Perfect Storm*, based on a true story.

Top stars James Garner, Tommy Lee Jones, Clint Eastwood, and Donald Sutherland joined forces to make *Space Cowboys*.

can fix it. There's plenty of suspense as the four rocket into space on their mission—and plenty of humor, too.

History and spectacle also combined in *Gladiator*. This film starred Russell Crowe as a Roman soldier who is sold into slavery. To win his freedom, he must fight as a gladiator in the public battles that were staged for entertainment in the ancient Roman Empire. The film's elaborate production and sets harked back to the epic historical films of the past.

Actor Tom Cruise played the action hero in *Mission: Impossible 2,* a sequel to the 1996 film *Mission: Impossible.* His task: track down a bad guy who has stolen the only antidote to a deadly new virus. Special effects and stunts were this action film's real stars. The *M:I* films were based on a 1970's television series, and another 1970's action series, *Charlie's Angels,* was also transformed into a movie in 2000. It starred Drew Barrymore, Cameron Diaz, and Lucy Liu as a trio of undercover agents who are as tough as they are beautiful.

JUST FOR LAUGHS

Meet the Parents was a classic comedy about a situation that most families reach at some time. When a young couple (Ben Stiller and Teri Polo) decide to marry, they spend a weekend with her family so the would-be groom can meet his future in-laws. The bride's father (Robert De Niro) is an ex-CIA agent who rarely cracks a smile, and the young man's attempts to please him have hilarious results.

Frankie Muniz shared leading-role honors with a Jack Russell terrier in *My Dog Skip.* A comedy with a bittersweet edge, the movie was set in the 1940's and told the story of a boy and his dog. *Billy Elliott* was another low-key comedy with serious notes. The title character is an 11-year-old boy (played by Jamie Bell) who just doesn't fit in his hometown—a coal-mining city in northern England. Billy's dream is to be a ballet dancer, something his coal-miner father just can't understand.

Galaxy Quest spoofed science-fiction epics. The main characters in this film are a group of actors who once starred in a television series

Almost Famous

In 1973, when he was just 15, Cameron Crowe landed a dream job: The magazine *Rolling Stone* sent him on the road to report firsthand on a rock band. Today, Crowe is a screenwriter and film director whose credits include movies such as *Jerry Maguire* and *Say Anything*. And in 2000, he drew on his own early experiences to create a new, critically acclaimed film, *Almost Famous*.

Almost Famous is the story of William Miller (Patrick Fugit), a fictional 15-year-old who, like Crowe, gets an assignment from *Rolling Stone*. He goes on the road with Stillwater, a Midwestern rock band that's just on the verge of making the big

time. Miller dives head first into the wild music scene of the early 1970's, and the audience goes along for the ride.

The film's portrayal of this fast-paced life, which was known for wild parties and drug use, earned it an R rating (no one under 17 was allowed in without a parent or guardian). Jason Lee played the band's lead singer, and Billy Crudup was the lead guitarist. Kate Hudson (shown with Fugit, above) played Penny Lane, leader of the "groupies" who follow Stillwater on the road. Frances McDormand portrayed Miller's very worried mother.

something like *Star Trek*. Aliens pick up the broadcast signal and travel to Earth to recruit them for an intergalactic war—unaware that the brave *Galaxy Quest* crew did all their fighting with make-believe weapons and special effects.

Beautiful, starring Minnie Driver and Hallie Kate Eisenberg, lampooned the world of beauty pageants with cutting satire. *Best in Show* was a "mockumentary"—a fake documentary—poking fun at the world of dog shows. Dog owners and handlers gather in Philadelphia for a show, and they turn out to be even weirder and funnier than their pampered pets.

FANTASY COMES TO LIFE

Moviemakers have turned to classic cartoons as inspiration for live-action films in recent years, and that trend continued in 2000. *The Adventures of Rocky and Bullwinkle* brought characters from a popular 1960's television cartoon show to the big screen. The Flintstones were back in *Viva Rock Vegas,* a sequel to the 1994 live-action movie *The Flintstones.* Also returning to the screen were the adorable puppies of *101 Dalmatians.* In their sequel, *102 Dalmatians,* the puppies once again escape the plotting of the evil Cruella De Vil (Glenn Close).

Several favorite children's books also made it to movie theaters. Among them was E. B. White's *Stuart Little,* a fantasy about a mouse who is a member of a human family. Dr. Seuss's *How the Grinch Stole Christmas* featured comedian Jim Carrey mugging his way through lots of green fur and makeup.

Dinosaur was the year's biggest animated spectacular. With amazing realism, the filmmakers at Walt Disney placed computer-animated dinosaurs in real-world landscapes. The result brought the prehistoric world to life on the screen. The Disney animated classic *Fantasia* returned to movie theaters, too. This film, made up of short animated segments set to classical music, first appeared in 1940. For 2000, animators added seven new segments, including one that featured animals (including Donald Duck) boarding Noah's Ark.

Sean Hayes (best supporting actor, comedy series), Eric McCormack, Debra Messing, and Megan Mullally (best supporting actress, comedy series) in *Will & Grace* (best comedy series).

EMMY

CATEGORY	WINNER
Comedy Series	*Will & Grace*
Actor—comedy series	Michael J. Fox (*Spin City*)
Actress—comedy series	Patricia Heaton (*Everybody Loves Raymond*)
Supporting actor—comedy series	Sean Hayes (*Will & Grace*)
Supporting actress—comedy series	Megan Mullally (*Will & Grace*)
Drama Series	*The West Wing*
Actor—drama series	James Gandolfini (*The Sopranos*)
Actress—drama series	Sela Ward (*Once and Again*)
Supporting actor—drama series	Richard Schiff (*The West Wing*)
Supporting actress—drama series	Allison Janney (*The West Wing*)
Miniseries	*The Corner*
Variety, Music, or Comedy Series	*Late Show With David Letterman*

Left: Michael J. Fox (best actor, comedy series) in *Spin City*. Above: Ray Romano and Patricia Heaton (best actress, comedy series) in *Everybody Loves Raymond*. Below: Richard Schiff (best supporting actor, drama series), Allison Janney (best supporting actress, drama series), Bradley Whitford, Martin Sheen, Rob Lowe, Moira Kelly, and John Spencer in *The West Wing* (best drama series).

'N Sync was riding the crest of the boy-band pop-music wave in 2000. The group's album *No Strings Attached* sold an amazing 2.41 million copies in its first week!

THE MUSIC SCENE

New faces and new releases from established artists made 2000 an exciting year in the music world. "Boy bands" and other polished pop performers were big with young teens. Many performers crossed traditional lines, blending rock, hip-hop, R&B, and other musical styles to come up with unique styles.

WHAT'S NEW

Teen pop singers continued their great popularity with new releases. Britney Spears followed up her 1999 smash debut album with *Ooops!. . .I Did It Again* and scored another hit. The album sold 1.3 million copies and topped the pop charts in its first week. The boy band 'N Sync did even better in first-week sales with their second album, *No Strings Attached.* And the Backstreet Boys saw first-week sales of 1.6 million copies of their latest album, *Black & Blue,* released in November.

Teen sensation Christina Aguilera released *Mi Reflejo,* her second album and her first in Spanish. It featured Spanish-language versions of several of her earlier hits, including "Genie in a Bottle" and "I Turn to You." New voices joined the teen pop chorus in 2000, too. Twelve-year-old Aaron Carter, younger brother of Backstreet Boy Nick Carter, released an album of his own, *Aaron's Party (Come Get It).* The Norwegian duo M2M—Marion Raven, 15, and Marit Larsen, 16—won fans with their first U.S. album, *M2M.* It showcased tuneful harmonies in songs such as "Pretty Boy" and "The Day You Went Away."

Teen stars weren't the only artists to top the charts. Boyz II Men, who started out as a teen group in 1991, was going strong in 2000. The group showcased classy vocal harmonies and soulful ballads in their fifth album, *Nathan Michael Shawn Wanya.* Creed had a number-one single in "With Arms Wide Open," from the group's hot-selling album *Human Clay.* Toronto pop group Barenaked Ladies was back with *Maroon,* a new album that included

Australian duo Savage Garden topped the charts with "I Knew I Loved You," from their second album, *Affirmation*.

the hit single "Pinch Me." Vitamin C had a hit with "Graduation (Friends Forever)." The song became an anthem for graduating high-school seniors and got heavy radio play, with many stations editing it on the air to include messages from local graduates.

Australian pop duo Savage Garden released their second studio album, *Affirmation*. A sweet ballad from that album, "I Knew I Loved You," topped the charts as a single. Mariah Carey paired with Joe and 98° for "Thank God I Found You." Sting picked up two Grammy Awards in the pop category, for his *Brand New Day* and the title track from that album. Pop star Madonna was back with *Music,* an album with strong techno and disco overtones. And Latin pop star Ricky Martin released his second English-language album, *Sound Loaded,* late in the year.

SPOTLIGHT ON ... Christina Aguilera

"Omigod, you guys. I seriously do not have a speech prepared whatsoever." That was how Christina Aguilera reacted when her name was announced at the 2000 Grammy Awards in February. Christina, 19, won the award for best new artist.

Christina may have been surprised by the award, but most others weren't. Her 1999 debut album, *Christina Aguilera,* had sold more than five million copies. And she'd had two hit singles—"Genie in a Bottle," which topped the pop charts for five straight weeks, and "What a Girl Wants." Music critics raved about her voice, saying that it had exceptional power and range.

After picking up her Grammy, Christina didn't slow down. She had another number-one single, "Come on Over Baby (All I Want Is You)." She released her first Spanish-language album, *Mi Reflejo.* And she kept up a busy concert schedule that took her all over the country.

Pop's newest star started performing as a toddler, belting out songs to her stuffed animals. Eventually she won a spot on *The New Mickey Mouse Club* television show at age 12. As a *Mickey Mouse* cast member, she met other future pop stars—including Britney Spears and members of 'N Sync.

Next, Christina performed in Japan and Europe. Back in the United States in 1998, she recorded the song "Reflection" for the Disney film *Mulan.* And she began work on her first album.

Christina stands just 5 feet 2 inches tall, but everyone thinks she'll accomplish big things.

The Red Hot Chili Peppers and Limp Bizkit were among the groups that kept rock fans happy during 2000. The alternative rock group Vertical Horizon had a major hit with "Everything You Want," from their album of the same title. British alternative rockers Radiohead released *Kid A*, the group's first new album since 1997. No Doubt came out with *Return of Saturn*, with fourteen songs written or co-written by lead singer

TOP TREND: BOY BANDS

Before 1998, only one recording artist had ever sold more than a million copies of an album in the first week. That record-holder was country superstar Garth Brooks. Then came the Backstreet Boys (photo, right), whose 1999 album *Millennium* sold 1.1 million copies in its first week out. And that record was smashed in 2000 by 'N Sync, whose *No Strings Attached* sold 1.1 million copies in its first day, and an amazing 2.41 million copies in its first week!

The sales highlighted the huge popularity of "boy bands"—teen pop acts that saturated the airwaves during 2000. Light, bouncy songs, close harmonies, and carefully choreographed dance moves were features shared by these groups.

The trio Hanson is generally credited with helping to start the boy-band wave. Brothers Isaac, Zac, and Taylor Hanson, who write their own music, stormed the pop charts in 1997 with their first commercial album, *Middle of Nowhere.* Hanson released a second major album, *This Time Around,* in 2000. But by that time, Hanson faced stiff competition.

Nick Carter, Howie Dorough, and A. J. McLean formed the core of the Backstreet Boys in Orlando, Florida, in 1993. They soon added Kevin Richardson and his cousin Brian Littrell. Now in their 20's, the five singers blend their voices in tight harmonies. Rhythm-and-blues and hip-hop influence their music. Their U.S. debut album, *Backstreet Boys,* had five hit singles, including "I'll Never Break Your Heart" and "All I Have to Give."

'N Sync—Justin Timberlake, Joey Fatone, James Lance Bass, Chris Kirkpatrick, and JC Chasez—formed in 1996, also in Orlando, Florida. Like Britney Spears and Christina Aguilera, Justin Timberlake and JC Chasez were cast members on *The New Mickey Mouse Club* television show. In 1998, 'N Sync's self-titled debut album sold more than ten million copies and included four number-one singles, including "I Want You Back" and "Tearing Up My Heart." "Bye Bye Bye," off *No Strings Attached,* was also a huge hit.

Another popular boy band, 98°, released its fourth album in 2000. *Revelation* featured the rich four-part harmonies for which this group—Justin Jeffre, Jeff Timmons, and brothers Nick and Drew Lachey—is known.

With their good looks and well-rehearsed stage moves, most of the boy bands have been criticized for being slick and shallow. By choosing the title *No Strings Attached* for its second album, 'N Sync hoped to answer critics who say that boy bands are just puppets created by record companies. The bands were riding a pop-music wave in 2000—and with millions of fans packing their concerts and buying their records, it was a big wave.

Gwen Stefani. The Icelandic rock singer Björk made her movie debut in the off-beat independent film *Dancer in the Dark.* Her album *Selmasongs,* based on the movie soundtrack, was released in September.

Matchbox Twenty released *Mad Season,* its first new album since 1996. "Bent" was a top-selling single from the album. And at the 2000 Grammy Awards, in February, Matchbox Twenty lead singer Rob Thomas teamed with veteran rocker Carlos Santana to perform "Smooth," a song Thomas co-wrote for Santana's 1999 album *Supernatural.* The album

R&B singer and hot new star Macy Gray won an MTV Video Music Award as best new artist.

and the single brought Santana eight Grammy Awards, tying the record set by Michael Jackson in 1983 for the most awards won in a single year.

Santana first gained fame in 1969, when his fiery guitar playing wowed the crowd at the original Woodstock music festival. And he wasn't the only old-timer who was still on the scene in 2000. Eric Clapton paired with blues legend B. B. King for *Riding With the King;* the title track from that album got plenty of airtime during the year. Neil Young, another Sixties legend, released *Silver & Gold,* an album featuring acoustic guitar and folk-rock tunes.

Grunge rockers Pearl Jam featured extended guitar jams on "Nothing as It Seems," from the album *Binaural.* Another grunge group, Smashing Pumpkins, disbanded in 2000, after its last album, *Machina/The Machines of God,* saw weak sales.

The Irish rock group U2 dropped the techno style featured in the group's last release, *Pop,* and came out with *All That You Can't Leave Behind.* Tracks such as "Beautiful Day" (also released as a single) featured arrangements more like those that boosted this group to stardom in the 1980's.

HIP-HOP AND R&B

Macy Gray was among the new stars of the R&B scene. In her debut album, *On How Life Is,* Gray blended funk and soul with rock and hip-hop to produce a one-of-a-kind style that didn't fit easily into any category. Her "I Try," from that album, brought her an MTV Video Music Award as best new artist in 2000.

The trio Destiny's Child had hits with "Jumpin', Jumpin'" and "Say My Name," from their debut album, *The Writing's on the Wall.* Wyclef Jean of Fugees fame came out with his second solo album, *The Ecleftic—Two Sides of*

The trio Destiny's Child had major hits with "Jumpin', Jumpin'" and "Say My Name."

a Book, with guest artists that included Mary J. Blige. Blige's own album, *Mary,* confirmed her position as one of today's top female singers.

TLC picked up a Grammy in the R&B category for "No Scrubs." Controversial rapper Eminem walked away with two MTV awards and two Grammy Awards for "The Real Slim Shady" and *The Slim Shady LP.* He followed up with a new album under his own name: *The Marshall Mathers LP.* Dr. Dre, who produced the Eminem recording, had a success of his own with the album *Dr. Dre—2001.*

The year saw a flood of other new hip-hop albums. Nelly (short for Cornell Haynes, Jr.) topped the charts in September with his *Country Grammar* album. Joe (Joe Thomas) had a top-ten hit with "I Wanna Know," a single from his platinum album *My Name Is Joe.* Erykah Badu, acclaimed as a hip-hop star when her first album appeared in 1997, released a new album, *Mama's Gun,* late in 2000.

Busta Rhymes, who has been recording hip-hop hits since the early 1990's, featured his reggae-flavored rap in *Anarchy.* Rhymes also co-starred with Samuel L. Jackson in a remake of the 1970's film *Shaft.* The soundtrack featured rap and R&B from Outkast and others. And LL Cool J, who started it all with his 1985 single "I Can't Live Without My Radio," was back in 2000 with an album filled with hardcore raps, *G.O.A.T. Featuring James T. Smith: The Greatest of All Time.*

COUNTRY

New releases from established stars made 2000 a banner year for country music. Emmy-

Twelve-year-old Billy Gilman became the youngest artist ever to land on the country singles chart.

lou Harris came out with *Red Dirt Girl,* a collection of songs she both wrote and performed. It was her first solo album since 1995. Willie Nelson enlisted B. B. King and other guest artists for *Milk Cow Blues.* Johnny Cash, Merle Haggard, Lyle Lovett, Loretta Lynn, Travis Tritt, and Trisha Yearwood also released new albums during the year. The Dixie Chicks' 1999 *Fly* continued to sell well and picked up two Grammy Awards, including the prize for best country album. And Faith Hill made the pop charts with "Breathe," from her album of the same title.

While teens dominated the pop scene, they also made their mark in the world of country music. Alecia Elliott, a 17-year-old from Alabama who began performing at age 9, put together a group of eleven bluesy songs for her album *I'm Diggin' It.* Tennessee teen Jessica Andrews, 16, had a hit with "Unbreakable Heart," from her debut album, *Heart Shaped World.* And Billy Gilman set a record with his single "One Voice," from an album with the same title. Just 12, he become the youngest solo artist ever to make the country singles chart.

MUSIC NOTES

Artists who hit the road for major tours in 2000 included 'N Sync, Santana (with Macy Gray), Red Hot Chili Peppers, Phish, Wyclef Jean, Blink 182, and the Dave Matthews Band.

Three solo performers and three groups were inducted into the Rock and Roll Hall of Fame. They were Eric Clapton; Bonnie Raitt; James Taylor; the Moonglows, a 1950's doo-wop group; the 1960's band Lovin' Spoonful;

and the 1970's soul group Earth, Wind & Fire. For the first time, the R&R Hall of Fame also recognized backup musicians. Among the first of these "sidemen" to be inducted were Scotty Moore, who backed up Elvis Presley on guitar, and Hal Blaine, drummer on many 1960's hits.

Thirty years after their breakup, the Beatles remained one of rock's most influential groups. During 2000, a dozen new books about the Fab Four were published. The book that made the biggest splash was *The Beatles Anthology*, a complete history of the band that included personal photos, and interviews with band members and their friends.

Singer-guitarist Carlos Santana swept the Grammy Awards, walking off with top honors in eight categories.

2000 Grammy Awards

Record of the Year	"Smooth"	Santana, artists
Album of the Year	*Supernatural*	Santana, artists
Song of the Year	"Smooth"	Itaal Shur, Rob Thomas, songwriters
New Artist of the Year		Christina Aguilera
Pop Song, Female	"I Will Remember You"	Sarah McLachlan, artist
Pop Song, Male	"Brand New Day"	Sting, artist
Pop Song, Group	"Maria Maria"	Santana, artists
Rock Song, Female	"Sweet Child O' Mine"	Sheryl Crow, artist
Rock Song, Male	"American Woman"	Lenny Kravitz, artist
Rock Song, Group	"Put Your Lights On"	Santana, artists
Rhythm and Blues Song, Female	"It's Not Right But It's Okay"	Whitney Houston, artist
Rhythm and Blues Song, Male	"Staying Power"	Barry White, artist
Rhythm and Blues Song, Group	"No Scrubs"	TLC, artists
Rap Album	*The Slim Shady LP*	Eminem, artist
Rap Song	"My Name Is"	Eminem, artist
Rap Song, Group	"You Got Me"	The Roots, featuring Erykah Badu, artists
Music Video Performance	"Freak on a Leash"	Korn, artists
Alternative Music Performance	*Mutations*	Beck, artist
Score for a Motion Picture	*A Bug's Life*	Randy Newman, composer
Musical Show Album	*Annie Get Your Gun*	Stephen Ferrera & John McDaniel, producers
Classical Album	*Stravinsky: Firebird; The Rite of Spring; Persephone*	Michael Tilson Thomas conducting the San Francisco Symphony Orchestra

People at a computer convention in Las Vegas, Nevada, listen to music downloaded from the Internet in MP3 format.

THE INTERNET MUSIC MALL

Do you listen to music on CD's? Someday those shiny discs may be nothing more than curiosities. Now you can get music on your home computer, over the Internet. And this new trend may send the CD the way of vinyl records and other recording formats that have come and gone over the years.

In fact, the Internet is fast becoming a worldwide music mall. And computer-savvy music fans are thrilled. But everyone isn't so excited about the trend. Musicians and record companies are worried about it.

LOG ON AND LISTEN

Several different audio formats are being used to send music over the Internet. They rely on the same kind of digital code used for CD's and for information stored in your computer. One of the most talked-about formats is MP3. MP3 files are highly compressed. A song in MP3 format takes up only one-tenth the space of a song in CD format.

Because they're compressed, MP3 files can easily be sent over the Internet. The system works best if you have a high-speed cable modem. With a standard modem, it can take ten minutes or more to download a single song.

To hear the songs on your computer, you need a special computer program called a "player" to decode the files. Many such programs are available for free on the Internet. There are also portable MP3 players, so you can take your songs on the road.

The new formats offer lots of options. You can download music from commercial Internet sites such as Liquid Audio and MP3.com. Many of these sites charge for each song downloaded. But there are also free songs, produced by musicians who want to promote their work. Thousands of titles are available, and you can listen to samples before you decide to download a song.

With the right equipment, it's possible to make, or "burn," a CD of songs that you download. The system works in the opposite way, too. People can record music from a CD onto a computer. From there, it can be compressed into MP3 format. Some people have used this method to post pirated copies of songs on the Internet.

An Internet service called Napster has become popular, especially on college campuses. Napster doesn't store music. It just lists all the songs that other Napster users have stored on computer hard drives in the MP3 format. Napster users can find and download these files. The service was started by Shawn Fanning, a 18-year-old college student, as a way to trade music files with friends. Now students at some schools have used Napster so much that college computer networks have been clogged. Some schools have banned Napster as a result.

FREE FOR ALL?

People in the record industry have been worried about Napster and similar services for another reason. Musical artists and recording companies make money by selling recordings. They depend on that money to earn a living and keep working. If people start copying music and posting it on the Internet, musical artists and recording companies won't earn anything. Pirating music in this way violates copyright laws.

Many artists have spoken out against this practice. They include little-known musi-

didn't know what files its users were sharing. Sharing music files is perfectly legal—if a user just downloads an MP3 version of a song he or she already owns on CD. But some people went further. They said that home computer users should be able to download all the songs they want for free. They argued that CD's are overpriced—and outdated.

So far the courts haven't agreed. In 2000, a judge ruled against a service set up by MP3.com. MP3.com had created a huge database of songs and allowed customers to access it anytime via the Internet. Record companies said this violated copyright laws, and the judge agreed.

Late in the year, Napster agreed to start charging for its file-sharing service. Part of the fee charged would go to pay royalties to record companies and artists. For their part, record companies seemed to be realizing that Internet music is here to stay.

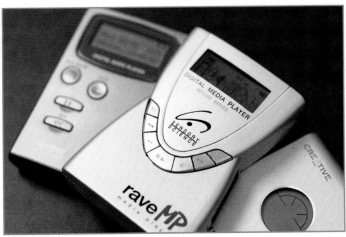

These portable MP3 players let you take your favorite music on the road. There are even players that you can wear like a wristwatch!

cians, who don't make much money from their music, and famous artists. The rapper Dr. Dre and the rock band Metallica both filed lawsuits against Napster for copyright infringement. The Recording Industry Association of America (RIAA) and several major record companies also sued Napster.

Defenders of Napster argued that the service wasn't violating any laws because it

Record companies are figuring out ways to jump on the bandwagon. They are releasing new singles on line, and developing formats that provide copyright protection by limiting the number of copies that can be made of a recording. They are also producing fewer CD's, figuring that music fans of the future will be doing more shopping at the Internet music mall.

FUN TO READ

Joseph is a clever tailor. When his overcoat wears out, he resews it into a jacket. Then, when the jacket is full of holes, Joseph turns it into a vest. Then the frayed jacket becomes a scarf. Finally there's nothing left—but the story isn't over. Joseph Had a Little Overcoat, written and illustrated by Simms Taback, is based on a Yiddish folk song. It won the 2000 Caldecott Medal as the best American picture book for children.

The world that the English writer Rudyard Kipling created for children is a magical one. It's a world where animals speak and have spine-tingling adventures in far-off, exotic lands. Although Kipling's stories were written a hundred years ago, they remain favorites with young people today.

Kipling was a product of the British Empire. He was born in India in 1865 and learned the language and culture of that country as a young boy. (India was a British colony at that time.) At 5, he was sent to live in England, where he attended school. There, he first began to write, and he later recalled his school days in the book Stalky and Co. (1899). He returned to India in 1882 and began a career as a newspaper reporter. He also wrote short stories and poems. By 1889, he was already a well-known author. He published a novel, The Light That Failed, two years later.

Kipling traveled widely, visiting America, South Africa, New Zealand, and Australia as well as India. In 1892 he married Carrie (Caroline Starr) Balestier and moved with her to Vermont. There, after their first child was born, he wrote The Jungle Books (1894–95). These stories tell mostly of Mowgli, an Indian boy raised by animals. During his Vermont years he also wrote Captains Courageous (which was published in 1897). Kipling continued to write for children as well as for adults after returning to England in 1896, producing Kim (1901), the Just So Stories (1902), and other works. And he continued to travel, often to South Africa.

In 1907, Kipling was awarded the Nobel Prize for Literature. He also received many other awards, and at his death in 1936 he was one of Britain's most honored writers. Today some of his works seem out of date. They reflect the British colonial view that whites had an obligation to bring "civilization" to the other peoples of the world. But many of the tales he wrote are just as wonderful today as they were when they first appeared. Here is one of them—the story of the Indian mongoose Rikki-tikki-tavi, adapted from the first Jungle Book.

 # Rikki-tikki-tavi

This is the story of the great war that Rikki-tikki-tavi fought single-handed. Darzee, the tailorbird, helped him, and Chuchundra, the muskrat, who never comes out into the middle of the floor, but always creeps by the wall, gave him advice. But Rikki-tikki did the real fighting.

He was a mongoose, rather like a little cat in his fur and his tail, but quite like a weasel in his head and his habits. His eyes and the end of his restless nose were pink. He could scratch himself anywhere he pleased, with any leg, front or back, that he chose to use. He could fluff up his tail till it looked like a bottle-brush, and his war cry as he scuttled through the long grass was *Rikk-tikk-tikki-tikki-tchk!*

One day, a high summer flood washed him out of the burrow where he lived with his father and mother, and carried him, kicking and clucking, down a roadside ditch. He found a little wisp of grass floating there and clung to it till he lost his senses. When he revived, he was lying in the hot sun in the middle of a garden path, very draggled indeed, and a small boy was saying: "Here's a dead mongoose. Let's have a funeral."

"No," said his mother. "Let's take him in and dry him. Perhaps he isn't really dead."

They took him into the house, and a big man picked him up between his finger and thumb and said he was not dead but half choked. So they wrapped him in cotton-wool and warmed him, and he opened his eyes and sneezed.

"Now," said the big man (he was an Englishman who had just moved into the bungalow), "don't frighten him, and we'll see what he'll do."

It is the hardest thing in the world to frighten a mongoose because he is eaten up from nose to tail with curiosity. The motto of all the mongoose family is "Run and find out"; and Rikki-tikki was a true mongoose. He looked up, ran around the table, sat up and put his fur in order, scratched himself, and jumped on the small boy's shoulder.

"Don't be frightened, Teddy," said his father. "That's his way of making friends."

"Ouch! He's tickling under my chin," said Teddy.

Rikki-tikki looked down between the boy's collar and neck, snuffed at his ear, and climbed down to the floor.

"Good gracious," said Teddy's mother, "and that's a wild creature! I suppose he's so tame because we've been kind to him."

"All mongooses are like that," said her husband. "If Teddy doesn't pick him up by the tail or try to put him in a cage, he'll run in and out of the house all day long. Let's give him something to eat."

They gave him a little piece of raw meat. Rikki-tikki liked it immensely, and when it was finished he went out onto the veranda and sat in the sunshine and fluffed up his fur to make it dry to the roots. Then he felt better.

"There are more things to find out about in this house," he said to himself, "than all my family could find out in all their lives. I shall certainly stay and find out."

He spent all that day roaming over the house. He nearly drowned himself in the bathtub, put his nose into the ink on a writing table, and burned it on the end of the big man's cigar, for he climbed up in the big man's lap to see how writing was done. At nightfall he ran into Teddy's nursery to watch how kerosene lamps were lighted, and when Teddy went to bed Rikki-tikki climbed up too. But he was a restless companion because he had to get up and attend to every noise all through the night and find out what made it. Teddy's mother and father came in, the last thing, to look at their boy, and Rikki-tikki was awake on the pillow. "I don't like that," said Teddy's mother. "He may bite the child." "He'll do no such thing," said the father. "Teddy's safer with that little beast than if he had a bloodhound to watch him. If a snake came into the nursery now. . ."

But Teddy's mother wouldn't think of anything so awful.

Early in the morning Rikki-tikki came to breakfast on the veranda riding on Teddy's shoulder, and they gave him a banana and some boiled egg.

Then Rikki-tikki went out into the garden to see what was to be seen. It was a large garden, only half cultivated, with rose bushes as big as summer houses, lime and orange trees, clumps of bamboo, and thickets of high grass. Rikki-tikki licked his lips. "This is a splendid hunting ground," he said, and he scuttled up and down the garden, snuffing here and there till he heard very sorrowful voices in a thornbush.

It was Darzee, the tailorbird, and his wife. They had made a beautiful nest by pulling two big leaves together and stitching them up the edges with fibers, and had filled the hollow with cotton and downy fluff. The nest swayed to and fro, as they sat on the rim and cried.

"What is the matter?" asked Rikki-tikki.

"We are very miserable," said Darzee. "One of our babies fell out of the nest yesterday and Nag ate him."

"H'm!" said Rikki-tikki, "that is very sad—but I am a stranger here. Who is Nag?"

Darzee and his wife only cowered down in the nest without answering, for from the thick grass at the foot of the bush there came a low hiss—a horrid cold sound that made Rikki-tikki jump back two feet. Then inch by inch out of the grass rose up the head and spread hood of Nag, the big black cobra, and he was five feet long from tongue to tail. When he had lifted one-third of himself clear of the ground, he stayed balancing to and fro exactly as a dandelion tuft balances in the wind, and he looked at Rikki-tikki with the wicked snake's eyes that never change their expression, whatever the snake may be thinking of.

"Who is Nag?" he said. "*I* am Nag. The great god Brahm put his mark upon all our people when the first cobra spread his hood to keep the sun off Brahm as he slept. Look, and be afraid!"

He spread out his hood even more, and Rikki-tikki saw the spectacle-mark on the back of it that looks exactly like the eye part of a hook-and-eye fastening. He was afraid for a minute. But it is impossible for a mongoose to stay frightened for long, and though Rikki-tikki had never met a cobra before, he knew that a mongoose's purpose in life was to fight and eat snakes. Nag knew that too, and at the bottom of his cold heart he was afraid.

"Well," said Rikki-tikki, and his tail began to fluff up again, "marks or no marks, do you think it is right for you to eat fledglings out of a nest?"

Nag was thinking to himself and watching a little movement in the grass behind Rikki-tikki. He knew that mongooses in the garden meant death sooner or later for him and his family. But he wanted to get Rikki-tikki off his guard. So he dropped his head a little and put it on one side.

"Let us talk," he said. "You eat eggs. Why should I not eat birds?"

"Behind you! Look behind you!" sang Darzee.

Rikki-tikki jumped up in the air as high as he could go, and just under him whizzed by the head of Nagaina, Nag's wicked wife. She had crept up behind him as he was talking, to make an end of him, and he heard her savage hiss as the stroke missed. He came down almost across her back, and if he had been an older mongoose he would have known that then was the time to break her back with one bite. But he was afraid of the terrible lashing return-stroke of the cobra. He bit, indeed, but did not bite long enough, and he jumped clear of the whisking tail, leaving Nagaina torn and angry.

"Wicked Darzee!" said Nag, lashing up as high as he could reach toward the nest in the thornbush. But Darzee had built it out of reach of snakes, and it only swayed to and fro.

Rikki-tikki felt his eyes growing red and hot (when a mongoose's eyes grow red, he is angry), and he sat back on his tail and hind legs like a little kangaroo and looked all around him, and chattered with rage. But Nag and Nagaina had disappeared into the grass. So he trotted off to the gravel path near the house and sat down to think. Just then, Teddy came running down the path, and Rikki-tikki was ready to be petted.

But just as Teddy was stooping, something flinched a little in the dust, and in a tiny voice said: "Be careful. I am death!"

It was Karait, the dusty brown snakeling whose bite is as dangerous as the cobra's. But he is so small that nobody thinks of him, and so he does more harm to people.

Rikki-tikki's eyes grew red again, and he danced up to Karait with the peculiar rocking, swaying motion that he had inherited from his family. It looks very funny, but it is so perfectly balanced a gait that you can fly off from it at any angle you please, and in dealing with snakes this is an advantage. If Rikki-tikki had only known, he was doing a much more dangerous thing than fighting Nag, for Karait is so small, and can turn so quickly, that unless Rikki bit him close to the back of the head, he would get the return-stroke in his eye or lip. But Rikki did not know. His eyes were all red and he rocked back and forth, looking for a good place to hold. Karait struck out. Rikki jumped sideways and tried to run in, but the wicked little dusty gray head lashed within a fraction of his shoulder, and he had to jump over the body, and the head followed his heels close.

Teddy shouted to the house: "Oh, look here! Our mongoose is killing a snake." And Rikki-tikki heard a scream from Teddy's mother. His father ran out with a stick, but by the time he came up, Karait had lunged out once too far, and Rikki-tikki had sprung, jumped on the snake's back, bitten as high up the back as he could get hold, and rolled away. That bite paralyzed Karait, and Rikki-tikki was just going to eat him when he remembered that a full meal makes a slow mongoose. If he wanted all his strength and quickness, he must keep himself thin.

Then Teddy's mother picked him up and hugged him, and Teddy's father said that he had saved Teddy from death, and Teddy looked on with big scared eyes. Rikki-tikki was amused at the fuss.

That night, at dinner, he could have stuffed himself with nice things. But he remembered Nag and Nagaina, and though it was pleasant to be petted by Teddy's mother, and to sit on Teddy's shoulder, his eyes would get red from time to time, and he would chant his long war cry of *"Rikk-tikk-tikki-tikki-tchk!"*

Teddy carried him off to bed and insisted on Rikki-tikki sleeping under his chin. Rikki-tikki was too well bred to bite or scratch, but as soon as Teddy was asleep he went off for his nightly walk around the house. In the dark he ran up against Chuchundra, the muskrat, creeping round by the wall. Chuchundra is a broken-hearted little beast. He whimpers and cheeps all night, trying to make up his mind to run into the middle of the room, but he never gets there.

"Don't kill me," said Chuchundra, almost weeping. "Rikki-tikki, don't kill me."

"Do you think a snake-killer kills muskrats?" said Rikki-tikki scornfully.

"Those who kill snakes get killed by snakes," said Chuchundra, more sorrowfully than ever. "And how am I to be sure that Nag won't mistake me for you some dark night?"

"There's not the least danger," said Rikki-tikki. "But Nag is in the garden, and I know you don't go there."

"My cousin Chua, the rat, told me. . ." said Chuchundra, and then he stopped.

"Told you what?"

"Hush! Nag is everywhere, Rikki-tikki. You should have talked to Chua in the garden."

"I didn't—so you must tell me. Quick, Chuchundra, or I'll bite you!"

Chuchundra cried till the tears rolled off his whiskers. "I never had spirit enough to run out into the middle of the room! I mustn't tell you anything! Can't you *hear*, Rikki-tikki?"

Rikki-tikki listened. The house was as still as still, but he thought he could just catch the faintest scratch-scratch—a noise as faint as that of a wasp walking on a windowpane—the dry scratch of a snake's scales on brickwork.

"That's Nag or Nagaina," he said to himself. "And he is crawling into the bathroom sluice."

Rikki stole off to the bathroom. At the bottom of the smooth plaster wall there was a brick pulled out to make a sluice for the bathwater. And as Rikki-tikki crept in, he heard Nag and Nagaina whispering together outside in the moonlight.

"When the house is emptied of people," said Nagaina to her husband, *"he* will have to go away, and then the garden will be our own again. Now, go in quietly."

"But are you sure that there is anything to be gained by killing the people?" said Nag.

"Everything. When there were no people in the bungalow, did we have any mongoose in the garden? So long as the bungalow is empty, we are king and queen of the garden. And remember that as soon as our eggs in the melon patch hatch (which may be tomorrow), our children will need room and quiet."

"I had not thought of that," said Nag. "I will go and kill the big man and his wife, and the child if I can, and come away."

Rikki-tikki tingled all over with rage and hatred at this, and then Nag's head came through the sluice, and his five feet of cold body followed it. Angry as he was, Rikki-tikki was very frightened as he saw the size of the big cobra. Nag coiled himself up, raised his head, and looked into the bathroom in the dark, and Rikki could see his eyes glitter.

"Now, if I kill him here, Nagaina will know. And if I fight him on the open floor, the odds are in his favor. What am I to do?" said Rikki-tikki-tavi.

Nag waved to and fro, and then Rikki-tikki heard him drinking from the big water jar that was used to fill the bath. "That is good," said the snake. "Now, I shall wait here until the big man comes in to bathe in the morning."

Nag coiled himself down, coil by coil, round the bulge at the bottom of the water jar, and Rikki-tikki stayed as still as death. After an hour he began to move, muscle by muscle, toward the jar. Nag was asleep, and Rikki-tikki looked at his big back, wondering which would be the best place for a good hold. "If I don't break his back at the first jump," said Rikki, "he can still fight. And if he fights—Oh, Rikki!" He looked at the thickness of the neck below the hood, but that was too much for him. And a bite near the tail would only make Nag savage.

"It must be the head," he said at last. "The head above the hood, and, when I am once there, I must not let go."

Rikki-tikki jumped. He had just one second's time, and he made the most of it. Then he was battered to and fro as a rat is shaken by a dog—

to and fro on the floor, up and down, and round in great circles. But his eyes were red, and he held on as the body cartwhipped over the floor, upsetting the tin dipper and the soap dish, and banged against the tin side of the bath. As he held he closed his jaws tighter and tighter. He was dizzy, aching, and felt shaken to pieces when something went off like a thunderclap just behind him. A hot wind knocked him senseless and red fire singed his fur. The big man had been wakened by the noise, and had fired both barrels of a shotgun into Nag.

Rikki-tikki held on with his eyes shut, but the head did not move. The big man picked him up and said: "It's the mongoose again, Alice. The little chap has saved *our* lives now." Then Teddy's mother came in and saw what was left of Nag, and Rikki-tikki dragged himself to Teddy's bedroom and spent half the rest of the night shaking himself tenderly to find out whether he really was broken into forty pieces, as he fancied.

When morning came he was very stiff, but well pleased with his doings. "Now I have Nagaina to settle with, and she will be worse than five Nags. And there's no knowing when her eggs will hatch. Goodness! I must go and see Darzee," he said.

Rikki-tikki ran to the thornbush where Darzee was singing a song of triumph at the top of his voice. The news of Nag's death was all over the garden, for the sweeper had thrown the body on the rubbish heap.

"Oh, you stupid tuft of feathers!" said Rikki-tikki angrily. "Is this the time to sing? Where is Nagaina?"

"Nag is dead—is dead—is dead!" sang Darzee. "The valiant Rikki-tikki caught him by the head and held fast. The big man brought the bang-stick and Nag fell in two pieces! He will never eat my babies again."

"All that's true enough. But where's Nagaina?" said Rikki-tikki, looking carefully around him. "You don't know when

to do the right thing at the right time, Darzee. You're safe enough in your nest there, but it's war for me down here. Stop singing a minute!"

"For the great, the beautiful Rikki-tikki's sake I will stop," said Darzee. "What is it, Oh killer of the terrible Nag?"

"Where is Nagaina, for the third time?"

"On the rubbish heap, mourning for Nag. Great is Rikki-tikki with the white teeth."

"Bother my white teeth! Have you ever heard where she keeps her eggs?"

"In the melon patch, on the end nearest the wall, where the sun strikes nearly all day. She had them three weeks ago."

"And you never thought it worthwhile to tell me?"

"Rikki-tikki, you are not going to eat her eggs?"

"Not eat exactly, no. Darzee, if you have a grain of sense, you will fly off to the rubbish heap and pretend that your wing is broken and let Nagaina chase you away. I must get to the melon patch, and if I went there now, she'd see me."

Darzee was a feather-brained little fellow who could never hold more than one idea at a time in his head. And just because he knew that Nagaina's children were born in eggs like his own, he didn't think at first that it was fair to kill them. But his wife was a sensible bird, and she knew that cobras' eggs meant young cobras later on. So she flew off from her nest and left Darzee to keep the babies warm and continue his song about the death of Nag. Darzee was very like a man in some ways.

She fluttered in front of Nagaina by the rubbish heap and cried out, "Oh, my wing is broken!"

Nagaina lifted up her head and hissed, "You warned Rikki-tikki when I would have killed him. Indeed and truly, you've chosen a bad place to be lame in. What is the use of running away? I am sure to catch you. Little fool, look at me!"

Darzee's wife knew better than to do *that,* for a bird who looks at a snake's eyes gets so frightened that she cannot move. Darzee's wife fluttered on, piping sorrowfully, and never leaving the ground, and Nagaina quickened her pace.

Rikki-tikki heard them going up the path, and he raced for the melon patch. There, in the warm litter about the melons, he found twenty-five eggs, each with a whitish skin instead of a shell.

"I was not a day too soon," he said, for he could see the baby cobras curled up inside the skin, and he knew that the minute they were hatched they could each kill a man or a mongoose. He bit off the tops of the eggs as fast as he could, until there was only one left. But as he started to destroy it, he heard Darzee's wife screaming: "Rikki-tikki, I led Nagaina toward the house, and she has gone onto the veranda, and she means killing!"

Rikki-tikki tumbled backward down the melon bed with the last egg in his mouth, and scuttled to the veranda as hard as he could put foot to ground. Teddy and his mother and father were there at breakfast, but Rikki-tikki saw that they were not eating. They sat stone-still, and their faces were white. Nagaina was coiled up on the matting by Teddy's chair, within easy striking distance of Teddy's bare leg, and she was swaying to and fro.

Teddy's eyes were fixed on his father, and all his father could do was whisper, "Sit still, Teddy. You mustn't move." Then Rikki-tikki came up and cried: "Turn around, Nagaina. Turn and fight!"

"All in good time," said she, without moving her eyes. "I will settle my account with *you* presently. Look at your friends, Rikki-tikki. They are still and white. They are afraid. They dare not move, and if you come a step nearer I strike."

"Look at your eggs," said Rikki-tikki, "in the melon patch near the wall. Go and look, Nagaina."

The big snake turned half around and saw the egg on the veranda. "Ah-h! Give it to me," she said.

Rikki-tikki put his paws one on each side of the egg, and his eyes were blood-red. "What price for a snake's egg? For a young cobra? For the last—the very last—of the brood?"

Nagaina spun clear around, forgetting everything for the sake of the one egg. And Rikki-tikki saw Teddy's father shoot out a big hand, catch Teddy by the shoulder, and drag him acoss the little table, safe and out of reach of Nagaina.

"Tricked! Tricked! Tricked! *Rikk-tck-tck!*" chuckled Rikki-tikki. "The boy is safe." Then he began to jump up and down, all four feet together, his head close to the floor. "Come then, Nagaina. Come and fight with me."

Nagaina saw that she had lost her chance of killing Teddy, and the egg lay between Rikki-tikki's paws. "Give me the egg, Rikki-tikki. Give me the last of my eggs, and I will go away and never come back," she said, lowering her hood.

"Yes, you will go away and never come back, for you will go to join Nag. Fight, widow!"

Rikki-tikki was bounding all around Nagaina, keeping just out of reach of her stroke, his little eyes like hot coals. Nagaina gathered herself together and flung out at him. Rikki-tikki jumped up and backward. Again and again she struck, and each time her head came with a whack on the matting of the veranda, and she gathered herself together like a watch spring.

He had forgotten the egg. It still lay on the veranda, and Nagaina came nearer and nearer to it till at last, while Rikki-tikki was drawing breath, she caught it in her mouth, turned to the veranda steps, and flew like an arrow down the path.

Rikki-tikki knew that he must catch her or all the trouble would begin again. She headed straight for the long grass, and as he was running, Rikki-tikki heard Darzee still singing his foolish little song of triumph. But Darzee's wife was wiser. She flew off her nest as Nagaina came along and flapped her wings about Nagaina's head. That instant's delay brought Rikki-tikki up to her, and as she plunged into the rat hole where she and Nag used to live, his little teeth were clenched on her tail, and he went down with her—and very few mongooses, however wise and old they may be, care to follow a cobra into its hole. It was dark in the hole, and Rikki-tikki never knew when it might open out and give Nagaina room to turn and strike at him. He held on savagely, and struck out his feet to act as brakes on the dark slope of the hot, moist earth.

Then the grass by the mouth of the hole began to quiver, and Rikki-tikki, covered with dirt, dragged himself out of the hole leg by leg, licked his whiskers, shook some of the dust out of his fur, and sneezed. "It is all over," he said. "The widow will never come out again."

Rikki-tikki curled himself up in the grass and slept till it was late in the afternoon. "Now," he said, when he awoke, "I will go back to the house. Tell the coppersmith, Darzee, and he will tell the garden that Nagaina's dead."

The coppersmith is a bird who makes a noise exactly like the beating of a little hammer on a copper pot. And the reason he is always making it is because he is the town crier to every Indian garden, and tells all the news to everybody who cares to listen. As Rikki-tikki went up the path, he heard his "attention" notes like a tiny dinner gong, and then the steady *Ding-dong-tock! Nagaina is dead—dong!"* That set all the birds in the garden singing, and the frogs croaking, for Nag and Nagaina used to eat frogs as well as little birds.

When Rikki got to the house, Teddy and his mother and father came out and almost cried over him. That night he ate all that was given to him till he could eat no more, and he went to bed on Teddy's shoulder, where Teddy's mother saw him when she came to look late at night.

"He saved our lives," she said to her husband.

Rikki-tikki woke with a jump, for all the mongooses are light sleepers. "Oh it's you," said he. "What are you bothering for? All the cobras are dead. And if they weren't, I'm here."

Rikki-tikki had a right to be proud of himself, but he did not grow too proud. And he kept that garden as a mongoose should keep it, with tooth and jump and spring and bite, till never a cobra dared show its head inside the walls.

POETRY

JACK FROST

When it's cold in winter-time,
  On the window-panes I see
Fairy pictures that Jack Frost
  Draws upon the glass for me.

Sometimes they are lovely flowers,
  Glittering like a rose of snow,
Sometimes they are palaces,
  Where frost princes come and go.

Sometimes they are magic things,
  Curlycues and scrolls and stars,
I have found a banner with
  Half-a-dozen silver bars.

Once I saw Jack Frost himself,
  Sketching pictures just for me,
And his hair and beard and clothes
  Were as icy as could be.

His long fingers on the glass
  Traced a hundred stars aflame;
But he disappeared before
  I could catch him at his game!

Rupert Sargent Holland (1878–1952)

CHAIN-MAIL

A chestnut dropped in. A goldfish rose to drink.
Their widening rings of water interlink.

Kijirô (dates unknown)

CATERPILLAR

Brown and furry
Caterpillar in a hurry,
Take your walk
To the shady leaf, or stalk,
Or what not,
Which may be the chosen spot.
No toad spy you,
Hovering bird of prey pass by you;
Spin and die,
To live again a butterfly.

Christina Rossetti (1830–1894)

THE OWL AND THE PUSSY-CAT

The Owl and the Pussy-cat went to sea
   In a beautiful pea-green boat,
They took some honey, and plenty of money,
   Wrapped up in a five-pound note.
The Owl looked up to the stars above,
   And sang to a small guitar,
"O lovely Pussy! O Pussy, my love,
   What a beautiful Pussy you are,
      You are,
      You are!
What a beautiful Pussy you are!"

Pussy said to the Owl, "You elegant fowl!
   How charmingly sweet you sing!
O let us be married! too long we have tarried:
   But what shall we do for a ring?"
They sailed away, for a year and a day,
   To the land where the Bong-tree grows,
And there in a wood a Piggy-wig stood
   With a ring at the end of his nose,
      His nose,
      His nose,
With a ring at the end of his nose.

"Dear Pig, are you willing to sell for one shilling
   Your ring?" Said the Piggy, "I will."
So they took it away, and were married next day
   By the Turkey who lives on the hill.
They dined on mince, and slices of quince,
   Which they ate with a runcible spoon;
And hand in hand, on the edge of the sand,
   They danced by the light of the moon,
      The moon,
      The moon,
They danced by the light of the moon.

EDWARD LEAR (1812–1888)

FROLIC

The children were shouting together
And racing along the sands,
A glimmer of dancing shadows,
A dovelike flutter of hands.

The stars were shouting in heaven,
The sun was chasing the moon:
The game was the same as the children's,
They danced to the self-same tune.
The whole of the world was merry,
One joy from the vale to the height,
Where the blue woods of twilight encircled
The lovely lawns of the light.

A.E. (G.W. RUSSELL) (1867–1935)

Bud, Not Buddy

AWARD-WINNING BOOKS

Life isn't easy for 10-year-old Bud Caldwell, the hero of *Bud, Not Buddy* by Christopher Paul Curtis. The story is set in Michigan in the 1930's—the time of the Great Depression. Bud's mother has died, and he doesn't know who or where his father is. His only clue is an old flyer left behind by his mother. It's an ad for a show by a legendary musician—Herman E. Calloway. Could Calloway be his dad?

Bud is determined to solve the mystery of his past. He runs away from his abusive foster home and begins to search for his father, and the search becomes an unforgettable adventure. Before it's over, Bud has plenty to add to his personal list of survival tactics: "Rules and Things for Having a Funner Life and Making a Better Liar of Yourself." This book won the 2000 Newbery Medal, considered the top award in American children's literature. It also won the Coretta Scott King Author Award, given for excellence by an African-American writer for children and young adults.

Joseph Had a Little Overcoat, a colorful picture book written and illustrated by

LOOKING AT BOOKS

The amazing Harry Potter once again kept readers under his spell in 2000. The fourth book in J. K. Rowling's series about the young wizard-in-training was a best-seller even before its release in July.

But young readers had lots of other choices during the year. The shelves of bookstores and libraries were crammed with everything from new versions of old folktales to novels about the trials of preteen life.

Katie and the Mona Lisa

Simms Taback, won the 2000 Caldecott Medal, awarded to the best American picture book for children. Based on a Yiddish folk song, it tells the story of Joseph, a clever tailor who re-sews his worn-out overcoat into smaller and smaller garments. The tale is set in Poland in the days before World War II, and the illustrations capture life in a Jewish village at that time. They are filled with details that reflect the bouncy merriment of the story. Holes in the worn coat are matched

The Governor General's Literary Award for English-language children's literature (text) went to *A Screaming Kind of Day,* by Rachna Gilmore. The young heroine of this book is filled with life and a sense of mischief. In the course of a day, she finds ways to express those traits—and exasperate her parents.

PICTURE BOOKS

Have you ever stared at a picture so long that it seems to come to life? In *Katie and the*

The Great Poochini

by cutouts in the pages, letting readers peek ahead to see what the next garment will be. (See also pages 278-79.)

To the humans in his life, Jack is just a dog. But in the dog world, he's Signor Poochini, star of the Muttropolitan Opera. *The Great Poochini,* written and illustrated by Gary Clement, follows this celebrated canine on an important night. Signor Poochini is scheduled to sing the title role in the premiere performance of Dog Giovanni—but his owner has left him locked in his apartment. Will the star escape and get to the opera house in time? This book won the Canadian Governor General's Literary Award for best illustration in an English-language children's book.

Mona Lisa, by James Mayhew, a young girl visits an art museum and does more than that. She climbs right into Leonardo da Vinci's famous painting the *Mona Lisa.* She soon discovers that the painting's subject is lonely. So, hand in hand, Katie and Mona Lisa tour the museum, jumping into one painting after another—and causing a lot of confusion.

There's plenty of confusion in *The Prog Frince,* too. As you might guess from its title, this is a mixed-up tale. Written by C. Drew Lamm and illustrated by Barbara McClintock, it's based on the famous fairy tale "The Frog Prince." As in that tale, a magic spell turns a prince into a frog. But in this version, it isn't a kiss from a princess that restores him.

293

Ouch!, written by Natalie Babbitt and illustrated by Fred Marcellino, retells a less well-known fairy tale, "The Devil and His Three Golden Hairs." To win the hand of a princess, young Marco must complete a dangerous mission: He must pluck three hairs from the head of the Devil himself. He succeeds with the help of the Devil's grandmother—and even gets revenge on the greedy king who sent him on the mission.

Author and illustrator Aliki combines history, biography, literature, and more in

The Prog Frince

William Shakespeare & the Globe. The text and illustrations present the world of the theater in Elizabethan England, during the 1500's, when Shakespeare wrote his famous plays. Shakespeare's life and the story of the Globe Theatre, where many of his plays were first presented, are woven together. The book also tells how a modern replica of the Globe Theater was recently built in London. Quotations from Shakespeare are sprinkled throughout the text.

Ouch!

William Shakespeare & the Globe

MIDDLE AND OLDER READERS

Hundreds of thousands of loyal "Muggles" (non-wizards) ordered copies of the fourth Harry Potter book before its publication date—without even knowing its title. *Harry Potter and the Goblet of Fire* took Harry back for another term at Hogwarts School of Witchcraft and Wizardry, and fans of the series weren't disappointed. With three more books and a movie in the works, they have plenty to look forward to.

Harry Potter wasn't the only popular fictional character to return to children's literature in 2000. Ramona Quimby, the heroine of books by Beverly Cleary, also reappeared. *Ramona's World* was the first book in Cleary's series since 1984. In this installment, Ramona is in fourth grade and adjusting to lots of new experiences—including a new baby sister.

Family history and personal experience inspired books by several authors. Tomie

dePaola has illustrated more than 200 picture books. But he broke new ground with *26 Fairmount Avenue,* a book for middle readers about his own childhood. Set in the 1930's, his humorous account tells how his family built a house, how he "quit kindergarten," and lots more.

Jennifer L. Holm was inspired by a diary left by her great-aunt when she wrote *Our Only May Amelia.* The story opens in 1899. Amelia is the only girl in a large Finnish-American farming family in Washington. Not surprisingly, she has little interest in becoming a "proper young lady." And as events unfold, she needs every bit of her natural spunk.

Author Louise Erdrich also drew on family history in *The Birchbark House.* This book is set in 1847—roughly the same era as Laura Ingalls Wilder's *Little House* books. It's the story of an Ojibwa Indian girl whose life is disrupted as white settlers move west into Indian territory.

In 1960, 6-year-old Ruby Bridges was the first African-American student in a formerly all-white grade school in New Orleans. In *Through My Eyes,* she tells what it was like. News reports of the time fill in the background. The result is a powerful story—and a living history lesson.

Harry Potter and the Goblet of Fire

A world's fair brings together people from all over the world. At these great expositions, held from time to time in cities around the globe, people share ideas and glimpse what the future may—or may not—be like. The first world's fair was held in 1851, at the Crystal Palace in London, England. In 2000, the city of Hanover, Germany, was the site of Expo 2000, a world's fair with the theme "Humankind, Nature, Technology."

Perhaps no world's fair has captured the imagination of Americans more than the New York World's Fair of 1939–40, the setting for the story that follows. The year 1939 was one of great hope and deep uncertainty for the American people. After a decade of bank closings and bread lines, the Great Depression seemed to be ending. The nation's economy showed signs of reviving—and so did the confidence of the people. Yet at the same time, events in Europe were casting a dark shadow on the future. German dictator Adolf Hitler was a growing menace to peace. War seemed just over the horizon.

In those fragile, unsettled times, the New York World's Fair reflected the yearning for material well-being and world harmony. The fair opened on April 30, 1939—the 150th anniversary of George Washington's inauguration as the first president of the United States. Except for that one glance backward, however, the fair looked only to the future. Its slogan was "Building the World of Tomorrow With the Tools of Today." Its theme song was "Dawn of a New Day." And at the heart of the fairgrounds stood two massive structures that symbolized the fair's central themes: the round Perisphere, representing world unity, and the tall, tapering Trylon, representing human aspiration.

Located in Flushing, Queens, the fairgrounds covered 1,216 acres (492 hectares) of what had been marshlands and dumping grounds. After three-and-a-half years of preparation, the "World of Tomorrow" brought together hundreds of exhibitors, including dozens of corporations, 33 U.S. states and territories, the U.S. government, and more than 50 foreign countries.

The fair was divided into three general areas. The Main Exhibit Area featured futuristic displays on communications, transportation, science, and education by such corporations as Bell Telephone, General Motors, and General Electric. The Government Area was the site of the national and state pavilions. The lakeside Amusement Zone had carnival rides, game booths, and sideshow attractions. All in all, said one newspaper, the World of Tomorrow offered "the largest and most varied assortment of wonders and entertainments ever assembled under one sky."

The fair was a showcase for amazing new technology. Its opening marked the introduction of television to the American public. The first broadcast featured the fair's opening ceremonies, with a speech by President Franklin Roosevelt. Other modern "miracles" at the fair included everything from fluorescent lights to nylon stockings to electric milking machines. Visitors were also treated to a dazzling glimpse of the future. Exhibits showed a world of towering cities, bustling superhighways, and elec-

tronic homes. At a time of uncertainty, the vision of a peaceful, prosperous, well-ordered future made a powerful impression.

More than 26 million people visited the fair in its first season. But by the time that season ended, on October 31, 1939, much had changed on the world scene. Hitler had invaded Poland in September, starting World War II in Europe. No war news was broadcast at the fairgrounds, but an air of crisis crept in. Several nations closed their pavilions. When the 1940 season opened the following May 11, the fair had a new slogan; "For Peace and Freedom." The world of tomorrow would have to wait for the end of the war.

The story that follows is based on a real incident that took place at the fair during the summer of 1939. The two main characters and the details of their visit are fictionalized. But the description of the fair and the drama that unfolded there are true to life.

WORLD OF TOMORROW

"Welcome to the World of Tomorrow," crackled a voice from somewhere above. "Please use the entrance to your left."

Doreen Tuttle clutched the back of her husband's shirt as they made their way toward the ticket booth.

"Always this crowded on a weekday?" Harry asked the girl behind the counter, slipping two dollars under the glass.

"Pretty normal," said the girl, sliding two tickets and two quarters back through the slot. "Enjoy the fair!"

Inside the gate, the young couple stood to one side and scanned the grounds. Structures of curious shapes and styles, all of them modern and streamlined, sprang up like props in a science-fiction movie. Banners flew from buildings and lampposts. Wide, tree-lined streets were painted red, yellow, and blue. Tulip beds were radiant in the noontime sun. And everywhere there were people—people walking, people in line, people taking pictures.

"I sure hope the future is this clean and organized," said Harry. "It better be, with so many people!"

"Well, where to first?" asked Doreen, unfolding a guide map.

"How about those giant white things?" Harry suggested, pointing straight ahead.

"You mean the Trylon and the Perisphere?"

"Whatever," said Harry. "Is there anything inside?"

"Let's see," said Doreen, reading the guide. "You ride a long escalator part way up the Trylon. Then you cross a footbridge to the Perisphere. The interior is twice the size of Radio City Music Hall, they say, and there's a big exhibit called Democracity. When you come out, you walk down a long ramp called the Helicline."

"Perisphere? Trylon? Helicline?" Harry repeated. "Gee, I hope everything in the future isn't in Greek!"

"Come on, Harry," said Doreen, shaking her head. "Let's go."

Inside the Perisphere, the Tuttles looked down from a wide balcony that rotated slowly around the hollow globe. Below, twinkling in the darkness, a vast model of a planned urban paradise—called Democracity—filled the room. Citizens of this miniature metropolis lived in garden apartments outside the downtown area. Factories were built far away to reduce smog. As the sun came up, workers traveled to central office towers on wide highways and electric-powered trains that always ran on time. "In this brave new world," boomed the narrator, "brain and brawn, faith and courage, are linked in high endeavor as men march on toward unity and peace."

By now, the revolving balcony had come full circle. Night had fallen on Democracity, and the lights were twinkling once again. Harry let out a soft whistle. "Wow," he whispered.

Outside, atop the Helicline, Harry and Doreen had a bird's-eye view of the entire fair.

"I never imagined it would be like this," he marveled.

"Who could have?" answered Doreen. "We'll never be able to see it all in one day."

"What's that huge contraption over there?" asked Harry, pointing far in the distance.

Doreen consulted her map again. "Must be in the Amusement Zone," she concluded. "Maybe that's the Life Savers Parachute Jump."

"Parachute Jump! Fantastic! We've *got* to try it honey."

"Sure, Harry, sure. Maybe tonight. But you're going on it alone!"

"O.K., we'll see about that later. What now?"

"How about General Motors Futurama? Everyone says it's a *must.*"

"Then General Motors it is," agreed Harry.

At the bottom of the ramp, a tractor pulling six brightly colored canopied cars came to a stop and took on passengers. The driver blew his horn, which surprised everyone by playing the popular song "The Sidewalks of New York": *East side, west side, all around the town*. . .Laughing, the Tuttles climbed aboard.

The buggy took a roundabout way to the General Motors exhibit—behind the Theme Center and down Constitution Mall, a left on Rainbow Avenue past France and Brazil, up Petticoat Lane through the Communications Zone, then across the Bridge of Wheels. Doreen and Harry didn't mind the detour at all. It was a good way to see the fair.

As they were standing in line at General Motors, Harry kept looking at his watch. "Maybe I'd better call the office," he finally muttered. "Just to. . .ah. . .sort of check in, you know."

"Harold Tuttle! Can't you forget the office for one day? Just relax and have a good time. If you want to use the phone, call home and check with the sitter. Make sure the baby is O.K."

"You're right, honey. A day off is a day off. I'll call home; you hold our place."

As Doreen said afterward, Futurama was well worth the wait. A long line of moving chairs with built-in loudspeakers carried them over a sprawling scale model of America twenty-one years in the future—in the year 1960. They passed hundreds of miles of cities and towns, rivers and lakes, mountains, forests, and prairies, with smoking factories, working farms, and moving traffic. Skyscrapers were 150 stories high. Fourteen-lane superhighways unrolled across the landscape, carrying remote-controlled cars that sped along at 100 miles per hour. It would be a world on wheels, a nation of problem-free cities and cozy small towns woven together by a vast network of expressways, suspension bridges, tunnels, and cloverleaf interchanges.

Leaving the pavilion, each visitor was handed a souvenir button with the words, I HAVE SEEN THE FUTURE. Doreen wore it on the collar of her dress. Harry clipped it to the lapel of his sports jacket.

From General Motors, the young couple walked back across the Bridge of Wheels and made their way to the RCA pavilion. The building was shaped like a radio tube, with a giant antenna tower rising from the courtyard. Inside, the Tuttles pushed through the crowd for a glimpse of the new "picture radio," as Harry called it.

"It's called *television*," said Doreen, "and they say you can buy one for six hundred dollars."

"Six hundred bucks!" exclaimed Harry. "For that much we could buy a Pontiac. And a brand new one, at that."

Then it was on to General Electric, which Harry later described as a "shocking experience." The main attraction was an artificial lightning generator. A bolt of lightning arced thirty feet in the air, causing a tremendous crash. Doreen screamed, and Harry jumped. A puff of smoke and a strange burning smell hung in the room. At ten million volts, the announcer said, the electrical charge was strong enough to smash a boulder or split a tree trunk.

Doreen was impressed by the automatic dishwasher at the Westinghouse Pavilion and the nylon stockings at Du Pont. Harry especially liked the Heinz Tomato Man, a six-foot robot in top hat and tails that did a song and dance at the command of radio controls. But the highlight of the afternoon was a demonstration of a long-distance phone call—which was the prize of a drawing held by American Telephone & Telegraph.

When Harry's lucky number was surprisingly announced, he bounded to the front of the hall and entered a glass booth. Behind the booth, a map of the United States covered the wall. As the operator put through his telephone call, the connection was mapped in lights—New York to Chicago. The audience listened in on earphones.

"Hello?"

"Hello, Dad? This is Harry."

"Harry. . .Where are you?"

"The World of Tomorrow, Dad."

"What?. . .Where?. . .Is this some kind of joke?"

The audience exploded in laughter.

"No, Dad. It's really me. We're at the World's Fair, and I just won a free call. Anywhere in the United States."

"Well, I'll be darned. . .So what's it like, the World of Tomorrow?"

"Well, it's pretty amazing. Everything's neat and organized, and you can drive a hundred miles an hour. The buildings are a little strange, but you kind of get used to them. There's really only one problem."

"What's that, son?"

"Everything's in Greek!"

A bewildered silence came over the line. The audience looked puzzled, too. Only Doreen was laughing.

"Never mind, Dad. Everyone's fine here. Doreen sends her love. Everything okay with you?"

"Just fine," said Harry's father with a chuckle. "Love to Doreen and the baby. And be sure to write me about the fair."

"Sure will, Dad. Gotta go now, so take care."

"You too, Harry. Good-bye."

By six o'clock, Harry and Doreen were getting hungry. Harry wanted Nedick's hot dogs. Doreen craved Belgian waffles. They settled on both—hot dogs for dinner, waffles for dessert.

"That Parachute Jump looks like something out of *The War of the Worlds*," said Harry, wiping whipped cream from the corner of his mouth. "How about it?"

"I don't know," Doreen answered uneasily. "Let's see what else they've got."

A colorful tractor train came by a few minutes later, and the Tuttles hopped on. As the train pulled away, the driver blew his horn. *East side, west side, all around the town. . .*Harry and Doreen sang along, finishing the entire verse.

Strolling through the Amusement Zone, they noticed a giant red cash register revolving on the roof of a building. "National Cash Register," said Doreen, consulting the guide. "Seven stories tall, and the numbers at the top are today's attendance at the fair. Look. . .204,641. . .204,642. . . 204,643."

At Billy Rose's Aquacade they saw an underwater ballet, acrobatic divers, and Johnny Weissmuller of the *Tarzan* movies. At Frank Buck's Jungleland, they petted the monkeys and rode a camel. Then, after playing Skee Ball, they tried the Bumper Cars. Doreen caught Harry from behind, jolting him out of his seat.

The fireworks display started at ten-fifteen. Harry munched on a candy apple as tiny dots of light whistled through the air and exploded in brilliant colors. Pinwheels of blue and green. Showers of red and gold. The spectators oohed and aahed with each thundering burst. Powerful beams of light criss-crossed the night sky, and great jets of water shot high in the air from Fountain Lake.

When the display was over, everyone clapped and cheered. Doreen was flushed with excitement.

"O.K.," said Harry with a note of finality. "One last thrill before we leave." He was looking at the Parachute Jump.

"I don't know," murmured Doreen. "Maybe I'll just watch."

"Oh, come on," said Harry. "It'll be fun! Look, it's got double seats. We can go together."

After a moment's silence, Doreen was surprised to hear herself say, "Well, O.K. But just once, and then we go home."

As they waited their turn at the bottom of the tower, she wondered what had possessed her to go along. Lit up against the night, the steel-framed monstrosity *did* look like something out of *The War of the Worlds*. Higher and higher it rose, deep into

the blackness. A spoked wheel sat atop the tower like a mushroom cap, with several threadlike strands hanging from each spoke. From below, the billowing orange parachutes attached to the guide wires looked like tiny umbrellas floating to earth.

Doreen felt dizzy. Harry had sweaty palms.

"Don't look so scared," laughed a young boy in knickers behind them. "This is my seventh time. It's really fun!"

"How high is it, anyway?" asked Harry, trying to sound calm and relaxed.

"Only about 250 feet," he answered with a sly grin.

"Yeah, and you'll love every one of them," piped the boy's friend.

Harry paid eighty cents for two tickets and handed them to the attendant. Doreen stood to the side.

"C'mon, lady," said the attendant, chomping on a cigar stub. "We ain't got all night."

In a daze, Doreen shuffled forward and positioned herself in the seat next to Harry. She grabbed his arm and held it tight. The attendant strapped them in. "Number 3 ready!" he shouted.

Up they went.

The cranks and pulleys squeaked like worn car brakes. The parachute hung over them like a round orange canopy. The girders of the steel tower glided past as they climbed higher.

"W-w-wow! What a view!" quavered Harry. "Look! There's the Aquacade. . . and Frank Buck's Jungleland. . .And over there! The Trylon and Perisphere! Look, Doreen!"

Doreen wasn't looking. Somewhere below, a horn played "The Sidewalks of New York." Harry sang along. Doreen opened her eyes for a moment, catching a glimpse of Fountain Lake. Then she heard the horn again, slightly fainter this time. She squeezed her eyes shut and felt the ground fall farther and farther away.

Suddenly there was a loud wrenching sound. Halfway up the tower, they jolted to a stop. The chair rocked gently in the night. Seconds later came the same wrenching sound and another jolt.

"Oh no, oh no! What's happening?" shrieked Doreen, looking up and down frantically.

"Take it easy," said Harry nervously. "We must be stuck. I'm sure they'll have us moving any minute. Just don't rock."

Then he noticed the parachute. No longer a neatly draped canopy, it hung to one side at a steep slant, one end tangled in the guide wires. Harry could see a pulley jammed against the rigid supports, with the chute caught in between. He took a deep breath and held Doreen's hand. "It doesn't look good," he said as calmly as he could, "but it does look secure. Just stay calm, and don't move around."

He looked at his watch. Eleven-thirty. He looked at the tangle of guide wires and canvas. It *did* look secure, thank goodness. Meanwhile, to Harry's amazement, the ride continued to operate. All around them, parachutes climbed to the top of the tower and dropped smoothly back to earth. Across the way, the two boys in knickers whooped and hollered as their chute billowed with air and floated down. As Harry watched, he noticed a crowd of onlookers swarming around the base of the tower. Faces gazed up at them. Fingers were pointing.

Doreen looked white. "Are you okay, honey?" asked Harry.

"I was just thinking about the baby," she said mournfully. "Who will take care of her?"

"Don't worry," answered Harry, "Susie is fine. She's fast asleep by now, and we'll be home in less than an hour."

Just before midnight, a police emergency squad arrived, sirens wailing and lights flashing. Then came a hook and ladder. Quickly, the truck was positioned beneath Chute Number 3, and a team of firemen set the ladder upright. The top rung crept slowly toward the stranded couple, foot by foot. It didn't reach. The crowd moaned.

"We must be 220 feet in the air!" exclaimed Harry.

"Now what?" moaned Doreen.

As the ladder was being retracted, two members of the emergency squad were being lifted on Chute Number 4. Their chair came to a stop just parallel to the Tuttles, about twenty feet away.

"Good evening, folks," said one of them, matter-of-factly. "I'm Officer Williams. This is Officer Peterson. How are you doing?"

"Things are a little up in the air right now," said Harry with a forced smile. "But we're holding up."

"How can you joke at a time like this?" snapped Doreen.

"Everything's okay, ma'am," Officer Peterson said softly. "You're in no danger at all. Just stay calm and try to be patient while we find a way to get you down. You're perfectly safe."

"Hang in there pal," said Officer Williams, winking at Harry.

"Oh, please, please, can you do us a favor?" begged Doreen.

"Call our babysitter and tell her we've been delayed. Harry and Doreen Tuttle, 555-3967. Don't tell her about this, but please call."

"Of course, ma'am," said Officer Williams. "Meanwhile, you try to relax and. . .um. . .enjoy the view."

Shortly after one in the morning, firemen placed a large safety net directly below the jammed parachute. Loudspeakers were set up nearby.

"Just stay calm," came a staticky voice. "You're in no danger. We'll have you down soon."

"Stay calm," Doreen mimicked. "We'll have you down soon. . .They've been saying that for two hours. . .Get us down from here!" she yelled. "I want to get down!"

At two o'clock, the lights in the Amusement Zone began to go out, and the crowd began to disperse. Except for the bright floodlights and scurry of activity at the base of the Parachute Jump, the fair was dark and deserted.

Peering into the darkness, Harry thought about Democracity and Futurama, about towering skyscrapers and fourteen-lane highways. He thought about television and automatic dishwashers and long-distance phone calls and the Heinz Tomato Man.

"Strange," he said finally. "This afternoon it all seemed so fantastic— the future, I mean. Automated this, high-speed that, a brave new world marching toward unity and peace. But now I wonder. In all those bustling cities with remote-controlled cars and electronic living rooms, did you see any kids playing baseball? Flying a kite? Reading a book?"

"I think I know what you mean," said Doreen, nodding. "All afternoon I was thinking 'What will it be like for our children?' Everything just seemed so. . .well, perfect. . .and kind of cold. I mean, will *they* have real families? What will *their* kids do for fun? Sit around watching television all day?"

"There's a funny feeling hanging over this place," Harry mused. "It's like they forgot something. All this talk about unity and peace is great.

And the City of the Future would be great, too, if only they added some more flowers and a few baseball diamonds. But it's just not reality right now. A lot of people are still out of jobs. We could be at war any day, and guys like me have the army to think about. Heck, here we are stranded on an amusement park ride, and they can't even get us down!"

A thin smile came to Doreen's face. Harry looked puzzled. "I'm thinking about Dorothy from that new movie," she said.

"Who?"

"Dorothy from *The Wizard of Oz*. She gets carried off from Kansas by a tornado. When she wakes up, she's in this magical place over the rainbow—the land of Oz. All she wants to do is get back to Kansas, and the only one who can help her is the great and powerful wizard. But the wizard turns out to be a phony, a little old man who hides behind a curtain and talks on loudspeakers."

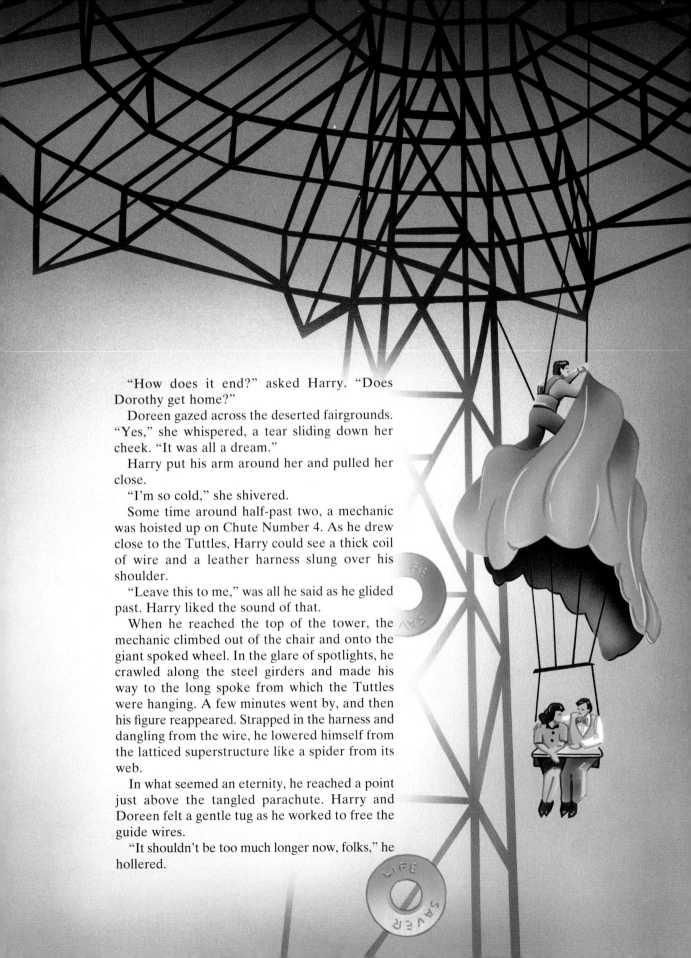

"How does it end?" asked Harry. "Does Dorothy get home?"

Doreen gazed across the deserted fairgrounds. "Yes," she whispered, a tear sliding down her cheek. "It was all a dream."

Harry put his arm around her and pulled her close.

"I'm so cold," she shivered.

Some time around half-past two, a mechanic was hoisted up on Chute Number 4. As he drew close to the Tuttles, Harry could see a thick coil of wire and a leather harness slung over his shoulder.

"Leave this to me," was all he said as he glided past. Harry liked the sound of that.

When he reached the top of the tower, the mechanic climbed out of the chair and onto the giant spoked wheel. In the glare of spotlights, he crawled along the steel girders and made his way to the long spoke from which the Tuttles were hanging. A few minutes went by, and then his figure reappeared. Strapped in the harness and dangling from the wire, he lowered himself from the latticed superstructure like a spider from its web.

In what seemed an eternity, he reached a point just above the tangled parachute. Harry and Doreen felt a gentle tug as he worked to free the guide wires.

"It shouldn't be too much longer now, folks," he hollered.

An hour later, the determined mechanic finally managed to dislodge the pulley, release the wires, and straighten the chute. He signaled to the crew below, and Harry and Doreen felt themselves being lowered. They touched ground at four-thirty, five hours after their ordeal had begun. They were greeted with blankets, hot coffee, and the popping of flashbulbs. Reporters shouted questions, but the couple were too numb to talk to anybody.

At five-thirty, Harry and Doreen Tuttle walked in the front door of their house. The babysitter was asleep on the chair. The baby was in her cradle, the blanket pulled to her chin.

The next morning was a blur of telephone calls and newspaper interviews. The phone started ringing at nine-thirty, and already a mob of reporters had gathered in front of the house. Harry took the calls and spoke briefly with the press. Doreen fed Susie and tried to keep her from crying, but there was just too much going on.

One of the phone calls was from Grover A. Whalen, president of the World's Fair. He called to apologize for the incident and to invite the Tuttles back for a special ceremony that evening. Harry thanked Whalen for the efforts of the police in rescuing them and said he would talk to his wife about the ceremony.

"We've got to put an end to this," said Doreen. "Besides, we've got some unfinished business to attend to. As I recall, we never did make that jump!" Harry's mouth fell open.

Late that afternoon, the Tuttles drove back to the fair. Pushing a baby carriage, they were greeted at the South Gate by a group of officials, including Mr. Whalen and New York City Mayor Fiorello La Guardia. The crowd at the base of the Parachute Jump was

almost as large as the one the night before. The news had gotten around. Standing beside Chute Number 3, Whalen introduced the Tuttles and publicly apologized for the mishap. Mayor La Guardia praised the couple's courage. Harry thanked the police, firemen, and emergency squad for helping them. Some of the men who helped in the rescue came up to shake hands.

"Will you ever try it again?" shouted a reporter.

When the laughter subsided, Doreen stepped forward and surprised everybody by saying, "Sure. How about right now?"

The crowd followed Harry and Doreen to Chute Number 9, on the opposite side of the tower from Number 3. Mayor La Guardia rocked the baby carriage as the couple settled into the familiar double seat. Up they went.

It was a clear, cool summer evening. The fairgrounds were buzzing with activity. A horn played "The Sidewalks of New York," and the Tuttles sang along. Halfway to the top, Doreen looked out on the World of Tomorrow and pointed toward the Trylon tower.

"That's what *we* forgot last night," she said.

"That Greek thing?" said Harry.

"Yes," Doreen smiled, "the Trylon. They say it's a symbol of hope. And last night in bed I got to thinking about Dorothy. I realized that whatever went wrong, she never stopped hoping. Then it occurred to me. Isn't that what it's all about? The future, I mean, and this fair. Aim high, keep at it, and hope for the best. There are no wizards, so what else can we do?"

Harry nodded. "I guess you're right," he said seriously. "But there's something else we can do."

"What's that, Harry?" asked Doreen.

"Brace ourselves, because we're about to drop 250 feet!"

For a moment they hung in the air like daredevils hanging from a plane. And then they were falling. Doreen grabbed Harry's arm and held on. The sky fell away, and objects flew by in a dizzying kaleidoscope. Whirling past like Dorothy's windswept house came the Trylon and Perisphere, towering skyscrapers, bridges and tunnels, televisions, telephones, and dishwashers, dancing robots, a giant spark, and exploding fireworks. Then came a loud whooshing sound as the parachute gathered air and bulged to fullness. Harry and Doreen floated slowly now, and objects on the ground came into focus—the base of the tower, a crowd of people, a baby carriage.

The jump had taken only ten seconds from top to bottom, but to Harry and Doreen Tuttle it seemed like five hours. Before they had a chance to clear their heads and fix their hair, flashbulbs were popping. Finally composing themselves, they held hands and faced the cameras. On their collars, they each wore a small clip-on button. I HAVE SEEN THE FUTURE, it said.

JEFFREY H. HACKER
Author, *Franklin D. Roosevelt*

307

Little Wildrose

There once lived an old man and an old woman. They had been very happy all their years together, but they would have been happier still if they had had children. Often they would sit beside the fire and talk of how they would have brought up their children if only some had come to bless their house.

One day the old man seemed more thoughtful than usual, and at last he said to his wife, "Listen to me, old woman! I am going on a long journey—all around the world—to see if I can find a child. For my heart aches to think that when we die, our house will fall into the hands of a stranger." Then he filled a bag with food and money and bade his wife farewell.

The old man wandered and wandered and wandered, but no child did he see. One morning his wanderings led him to a forest that was so thick with trees that no light could pass through the branches. The old man stopped when he saw this dreadful place, but summoning up all his courage he plunged boldly in.

After walking a long distance, he at last came to the mouth of a cave where the darkness seemed a hundred times darker than even the woods. And with a pounding heart he entered the cave.

For some minutes the silence and darkness so overwhelmed him that he stood where he was, not daring to move even one step. Then he made a great effort and went on a few paces, and suddenly, far before him, he saw a glimmer of light. He walked straight toward the faint rays until he could just barely see an old hermit with a long white beard. He cautiously approached him and said, "Good morning, wise father!"

"My son," whispered the hermit, in a voice that echoed through the cavern, "what brings you to this dark and dismal place? Hundreds of years have passed since my eyes have looked on the face of a man, and I did not think to ever look on one again."

"My misery has brought me here," replied the old man. "I have no child, and all our lives my wife and I have longed for one. So I left my home and went out into the world, hoping that somewhere I might find what I am seeking."

Then the hermit picked up an apple from the ground and gave it to him, saying, "Eat half of this apple and give the rest to your wife, and cease wandering throughout the world."

The old man joyously thanked the hermit and left the cave. He made his way through the forest as fast as he could and finally arrived in fields filled with flowers, which dazzled him with their brightness. Suddenly he was seized with a desperate thirst. He looked for a stream, but none was to be seen, and his tongue grew more parched every moment.

At last his eyes fell on the apple, which all this while he had been holding in his hand, and in his thirst he forgot what the hermit had told him. So instead of eating merely his own half, he also ate the half that was to have been for his wife. And after that he fell asleep.

When he awoke, he saw something strange lying on a bank a little way off, in the middle of long trails of pink roses, and he went to see what it was. To his surprise and joy, it proved to be a little girl about two years old, with skin as pink and white as the roses above her. He took her gently in his arms, but she did not seem at all frightened and cooed with delight. The old man wrapped his cloak around her and set off for home as fast as his legs would carry him.

When they were close to the cottage where he lived, he placed the child in a basket that was sitting near the door and ran into the house crying, "Come quickly, wife, for I have brought you a daughter, with hair of gold and eyes like stars!"

At this wonderful news the old woman flew downstairs, almost tumbling down in her eagerness to see the treasure. But when her husband led her to the basket, it was completely empty! The old man was nearly beside himself with horror, while his wife sat down and sobbed with grief and disappointment.

They searched everywhere, thinking that somehow the child might have gotten out of the basket and was hiding. But the little girl was nowhere to be found.

"Oh, where can she be?" moaned the old man in despair. "Why did I ever leave her, even for a moment? Have the fairies taken her or has some wild beast carried her off?"

And they began their search all over again, but neither fairies nor wild beasts did they meet. So with sore hearts they gave up and turned sadly into their cottage.

And what had become of the baby? Well, finding herself left alone in a strange place she began to cry with fright, and an eagle hovering above heard her and went to see what the sound was. When he beheld the fat pink and white creature he thought of his hungry little ones at home. Swooping down he caught the baby up in his claws and was soon flying with her over the tops of the trees. In a few minutes he reached the one in which he had built his nest, and laying little Wildrose (for so the old man had named her) among his downy young eaglets, he flew away.

The eaglets naturally were rather surprised at this strange animal, so unexpectedly dropped down in their midst. But instead of eating her, as their father had thought, they nestled up close to her and spread out their tiny wings to shield her from the sun.

Now, in the depths of the forest where the eagle had built his nest, there ran a stream whose waters were poisonous. And on the banks of this stream there lived a horrible serpent with two heads. The serpent had often watched the eagle flying overhead, carrying food to his young ones. And he carefully awaited the moment when the eaglets would begin to try their wings and fly away from the nest.

Of course, if the eagle himself were there to protect them, even the serpent, big and strong as he was, knew he could do nothing. But when the eagle was absent, any little eaglets that ventured too near the ground would be sure to disappear down the monster's throat.

That very day, the serpent was so hungry that he couldn't wait any longer for his supper, and he came out of the stream with a rushing noise and made straight for the tree. Four eyes of flame came creeping nearer and nearer, and two fiery tongues were stretching out closer and closer to the little birds who were trembling in the farthest corner of the nest. But just as the tongues almost reached them, the serpent gave a fearful cry and turned and fell backward.

Then came the sound of battle from the ground below, and there were such roars and snarls that the eaglets were more frightened than ever and thought their last hour had come. Only Wildrose was undisturbed and slept sweetly through it all.

When the eagle returned, he saw traces of the fight below the tree. He hastened to his nest and asked happily, "Who has slain the serpent?" The eaglets answered that they did not know, only that they had been in danger of their lives and at the last moment had been saved. Then a sunbeam struggled through the thick branches of the tree and caught Wildrose's golden hair as she lay curled up in the corner. And as the eagle looked, he wondered whether the little girl had brought him luck and if it was her magic that had killed his enemy.

From that day, Wildrose lived like a little princess. The eagle flew about the wood and collected the softest, greenest moss he could find to make her a bed. And he picked all the brightest and prettiest flowers in the fields to decorate it. And when the eaglets were able to fly from their nest, he taught them where to look for the fruits and berries that she loved.

So the time passed by. With each year Wildrose grew taller and lovelier, and she lived happily in her nest and never wanted to leave. She was content to just stand at the edge of the treetops in the sunset, looking upon the beautiful world. For company she had all the birds in the forest, who came and talked to her. For playthings she had all the strange flowers that the birds brought her from afar, and the butterflies that danced with her. And so the days slipped away and she was sixteen years old.

One morning the king's son went out to hunt, and he hadn't ridden far before a deer darted out from under a grove of trees and ran before him. The prince instantly gave chase, and where the swift stag led he followed until at length he found himself in the depths of the great forest.

The trees were so thick and the woods so dark that he paused for a moment and listened, straining to catch some sound to break the silence. But there was nothing. He stood still, wondering if he should go on, when he noticed a beam of light flowing through the top of a tall tree. In its rays he could see the nest, again filled with young eaglets, who were watching him over the side.

The prince fitted an arrow into his bow and took aim, but before he could let fly, another ray of light dazzled him. So brilliant was it that his bow dropped and he covered his face with his hands. When at last he ventured to peek, Wildrose, with her golden hair flowing around her, was looking at him. This was the first time that she had ever seen a man.

"Tell me how I can reach you," he cried. But Wildrose smiled and shook her head, and sat down quietly.

The prince saw that it was no use, and he turned and made his way out of the forest. But so strong was his longing for Wildrose that he twice returned to the forest in the hope of finding her. Fortune, however, failed him and he went home as sad as ever.

After a few days, the king sent for his son and asked him what was causing his unhappiness. The prince confessed that the image of Wildrose had filled his soul and that he would never be happy without her. At first the king felt rather distressed. He doubted whether a girl from a treetop would make a good queen. But he loved his son so much that he promised to do all he could to find her.

So the next morning heralds were sent forth throughout the whole kingdom to inquire if anyone knew where a maiden could be found who lived in a forest on top of a tree. Great riches were promised to anyone who should find her. But nobody knew.

All the girls in the kingdom had their homes on the ground and laughed at the notion of being brought up in a tree. "A nice kind of queen she would make," they said, as the king had done.

The heralds were almost in despair, when an old woman stepped out of the crowd and spoke to them. "I can show you the maiden who lives in the treetops," she said. But the heralds only laughed and said, "Go away, old witch! You will bring us bad luck." The old woman stood firm and declared that she alone knew where to find the maiden.

Finally, the eldest of the heralds said, "The king's orders are clear: Whoever knows anything of the maiden is to come at once to court. Put her in the coach and take her with us."

And in this fashion the old woman was brought to the court.

"You have declared that you can bring the maiden from the wood?" asked the king, who was seated on his throne.

"Yes, Your Majesty, and I will keep my word," said she.

"Then bring her at once," said the king.

"Give me first a kettle and a tripod," said the old woman, and the king ordered them brought instantly. The old woman tucked them under her arm and went on her way. A little distance behind followed the prince and the royal huntsmen. But when they reached the forest, the old woman bade them all wait outside and entered the dark woods by herself.

She stopped underneath the tree where the maiden dwelt, and, gathering some dry sticks, started a fire. Next, she placed the tripod over it and the kettle on top. But something was the matter with the kettle. As fast as the old woman put it where it was to stand, that kettle was sure to roll off. It really seemed bewitched, and no one knows what might have happened if Wildrose, who had been all the time peeking out of her nest, hadn't lost patience and cried out:

"The tripod won't stand on that hill; you must move it!"

"But where am I to move it to, my child?" asked the old woman, looking up to the nest, and at the same time trying to steady the kettle with one hand and the tripod with the other.

"Didn't I tell you that it was no good doing that? said Wildrose more impatiently than before. "Make a fire near a tree and hang the kettle from one of the branches."

The old woman took the kettle and hung it on a little twig, which immediately broke, and the kettle fell to the ground.

"If you would only show me how to do it, perhaps I should understand," she said.

Quick as a wink, the maiden slid down the smooth trunk of the tree and stood beside the old woman, to teach her how things ought to be done. But in an instant the old woman caught the girl up and swung her over her shoulder. And she ran as fast as she could to the edge of the forest where she had left the prince, who rushed eagerly to meet them.

When Wildrose saw the handsome prince, and came to know how kind and tender he was, she was overjoyed at her new life. She missed her friends in the forest very much, but she visited them often. And one day, not too long after, a wondrous wedding was celebrated in the kingdom. Dressed all in gold, with pearls and diamonds twined in her hair, Wildrose became the wife of the gentle prince. And everyone who saw the bride declared that a perfect queen could only be found on top of a tree!

The End

THE NEW BOOK OF KNOWLEDGE
2001

The following articles are from the 2001 edition of *The New Book of Knowledge*. They are included here to help you keep your encyclopedia up to date.

The fast-paced games in today's video arcades offer players exciting, realistic challenges. Here, a young expert engages in "hand-to-hand" combat.

VIDEO GAMES

Battle enemy starships in deep space, lead a team to the Super Bowl, drive a stock car at the Daytona 500, or run, jump, and shoot your way through a mazelike world. These are just a few of the adventures you can experience in video games.

Video games first appeared in the early 1970's, from companies such as Atari and Magnavox. In one of the earliest games, Pong, an electronic blip bounced back and forth across a television screen between two vertical bars. The bars served as crude ping-pong paddles, which players moved up and down on the screen using handheld devices.

Since that time, video games have grown much more challenging and colorful. They have also become more popular. The Japanese company Nintendo released its first video game console and games in 1988. Because of Nintendo's success, other companies, such as Sega and Sony, soon released their own game systems. The competition led to a race for the best game system. By 1999, the video game industry was selling $7 billion worth of games and game consoles a year.

▶ HOW VIDEO GAME SYSTEMS WORK

All video game machines have one thing in common—they all contain computers. The earliest game systems introduced the basic components still used today. The computer's "brain" is an electronic chip called a processor. It can be found inside a console (an electronic device built to play video games), a handheld unit, or a home computer. The games are displayed on a television, a built-in screen, or a computer monitor. Games are played with controllers plugged into the video game system. The controller might be a game pad with buttons, a joystick, a keyboard and mouse, or other devices such as a steering wheel.

Modern video games benefited from the development of personal computers in the 1980's and 1990's. More powerful processors allow more complex graphics and action. A processor's power is measured, in part, by the number of bits of data it can handle at a time. (Computer data contains bits, or binary digits, made up of strings of 1's and 0's.) More bits mean more data can be processed more quickly. The original Nintendo game system had an 8-bit processor. In the late 1990's and early 2000's, video game systems had 128-bit processors. Today's systems also have special graphics processors to generate and display the detailed images.

While newer game consoles began using more advanced technology, older technology became smaller and cheaper. Nintendo introduced the first handheld game system, Game Boy, in 1989. During the 1990's, other companies began producing handheld systems, but Game Boy remained the most popular.

Each game is a computer program. The program tells the processors to display graphics, move objects, play sounds, and receive signals from the controllers. In older systems, the game programs were built into the console or stored on memory chips in removable cartridges. Many games now come in formats similar to the compact discs, or CD's, that are used to store music. The CD-ROM and newer DVD-ROM formats can hold much more information than game cartridges can. The popular Sony PlayStation is an example of a video game system that uses CD-ROM's.

Game controllers and joysticks translate the push of buttons and the movement of handles or direction keys into signals that are sent to the game program. The signals tell the program how to change the action on screen.

▶ KINDS OF VIDEO GAMES

There are thousands of different video games. However, most games can be grouped into a handful of categories according to their basic strategies.

In **arcade-style games**, animated characters run through mazes, shoot at targets, dodge obstacles, and capture treasures. These fast-paced games appeared early in video game history and remain popular today.

In **combat games**, remote-controlled tanks, planes, and spaceships hunt and destroy enemy vehicles.

Handheld video game systems allow users to play their favorite games anyplace and anytime. A growing assortment of software is available, including the enormously popular Pokémon, shown above.

In **racing games**, the player races a car, motorcycle, or boat against opponents controlled by other players or by the game itself. Modern racing games have realistic vehicles, engine sounds, and collisions.

Sports games include baseball, football, tennis, golf, fishing, and other sports.

In **role-playing games**, the player explores a world, talks with other characters, collects items, and solves puzzles. In action-adventure role-playing games, the player must also defeat other characters through battles.

Fighting games began with the first boxing games. Modern fighting games have complex punches and kicks, realistic body movements, and, in some cases, bloody violence.

Simulations imitate parts of the real world. A player might pilot a plane through realistic storms, or design and control cities, amusement parks, even entire civilizations.

Board and card games, such as chess and solitaire, are also popular. Players can compete against one another or the computer.

Educational games use games from these categories and teach basic skills in mathematics, language, or other subjects.

In all the game categories, images and sounds have become very realistic and sometimes violent. Because of concerns about violence, the Entertainment Software Rating Board developed a rating system for video games in 1994. The ratings let parents decide if a game is appropriate for their children.

▶ THE FUTURE OF VIDEO GAMES

New computer technology will continue to guide video game advances. Computer networking, for example, allows players on personal computers or the newest game consoles to compete against opponents who may be in different parts of the country.

Another advance may be virtual reality. Some games create a virtual-reality environment through the use of special goggles a player wears. The goggles typically contain two screens, one for each eye, that trick the brain into seeing a three-dimensional world. Improvements in technology should make even more realistic virtual-reality games possible in the near future.

Other game advances include artificial intelligence, in which a game "learns" a player's behavior and reacts in new and unexpected ways. Force-feedback controllers allow the game to send signals back to the player. For example, a character on screen might push against the player, and the player then feels the push through the controller.

The future of video games is unclear. Parents wonder how they affect children. Are the games addictive? Do they promote violence or anti-social behavior? Can they help improve learning? The answers to these and other questions may affect the trends in video games in the coming years.

DAVID L. HART
External Relations Manager
San Diego Supercomputer Center

The *nalukatak*, or "blanket toss," is a ceremonial custom of the Inupiat of Alaska (*top left*), an Inuit group that is closely related to the Inuit of Siberia, Russia (*top right*). A father and son kayak in the Canadian territory of Nunavut (*above*). Two Inuit women in Canada's Northwest Territories leave church on a snowmobile (*right*).

INUIT

The Arctic is a region of vast, treeless plains, icy seas, and barren, rocky islands. This harsh, cold land is the home of the Inuit (formerly known as Eskimos), a people who live in scattered settlements in Greenland, Canada, Alaska, and Siberia. For thousands of years, they were isolated from other peoples. They developed a way of life well suited to their particular environment.

Today the Inuit are no longer cut off from the outside world, and their way of life has changed. If you were to visit an Inuit community, you would find most people living in modern houses, going to work or to school,

and taking part in activities not too different from your own. But the Inuit are still a distinct ethnic group of people who share the same ancestry and culture. Today most Inuit blend the old ways with the new.

▶ THE PEOPLE

The word "Inuit" means "the people" or "the real people." The Inuit first entered North America about 5,500 years ago, crossing the Bering Strait from Asia. They moved rapidly across northern Canada to Greenland. Some Inuit groups then moved westward again, back to the Bering Sea area. Today the Inuit population is not large, but it is growing. About 2,000 Inuit live in Siberia, 30,000 in Alaska, 22,500 in Canada, and 43,000 in Greenland.

As a racial and cultural group, the Inuit are quite distinct from North American Indians. They are descended from an ancient Mongoloid people of Siberia in northern Asia. The Aleuts, who live in the Aleutian Islands and other islands in the North Pacific Ocean off the coasts of Alaska and Siberia, are closely related.

Language. Inuit languages have been spoken for thousands of years, but they were not written down until modern times. They form the Inuit-Inupiaq language family, which has no known connections with other language groups. Differences among the Inuit-Inupiaq dialects are small. The Inuit from northern Alaska can be understood by those in Canada and Greenland. Dialects of the Yupik language are spoken in southwestern Alaska and Siberia.

▶ **TRADITIONAL WAY OF LIFE**

The Inuit's traditional way of life developed to meet the challenges of the far north. This section describes that way of life, which they followed until modern technology and other advancements became available.

Group Life. The Inuit lived in fairly small groups. There were villages of more than 500 people on the northern Alaska coast, but in the eastern regions (Greenland, Baffin Island, and Labrador), typical groups had only 25 to 45 people. Eastern groups moved from place

to place through the year, following a fairly fixed order of seasonal activities. They would spend winter near the coast, hunting seals and fishing. In summer, they would move inland to hunt caribou and gather berries. They crossed snow and ice in sleds pulled by dogs, and they traveled on water in open boats called umiaks.

Close cooperation was important if the members of a group were to survive. For example, in eastern groups ten to twelve hunters would be needed to harpoon seals at their breathing holes in the winter sea ice.

For thousands of years, the Inuit have survived by hunting and fishing in their frozen habitats (*above*). Fish (*left*) is a mainstay of the Inuit diet. It is cleaned, then dried on racks to preserve freshness.

Much larger groups—more than 100 people—would work together to hunt caribou and large sea mammals such as whales. A few activities could be carried on by individuals and small family groups—tracking bears, fishing with nets, and gathering berries.

Food Preparation. Meat, fat, and fish made up a large part of the Inuit diet. Vegetables were scarce. Very little food was wasted. But because the Inuit depended on hunting and fishing, hunger and even starvation were common when fish and game were not plentiful. Meat and fish caught in summer were stored in shallow pits that were dug down to permafrost and covered with piles of stones to keep out hungry animals.

Wood to make fires for roasting or baking was scarce in most areas. Meat and fish were often eaten raw. Raw meat or fish was frozen and cut into thin strips, which were dipped in whale or seal oil. Some meat, especially meat from large sea mammals, was eaten in a partly decayed state. The decay made tough meat more tender and easier to digest. If food was cooked, it was almost always boiled, using the heat from oil lamps.

Shelter. The Inuit word "igloo" means "shelter." It can refer to any kind of house, not only the dome-shaped snow houses that many people associate with the word.

In summer, most Inuit lived in tents made of animal skins. In western Alaska, very large winter tents were made by placing heavy walrus skins over wood frames. On the northern coast of Alaska, dome-shaped houses were built of logs and whale ribs. The dome was raised over a depression in the ground and was covered with frozen turf. In Greenland, houses were built of stone slabs.

Snow houses were used only in the eastern and central regions. They were made from blocks of packed snow (not ice), built into a dome. Small snow houses with short tunnel entrances were used while traveling. Larger snow houses were used as winter residences. Long tunnel entrances provided storage

See For Yourself

How to Build a Snow House

Snow houses were once built in parts of Canada and Greenland as winter homes. Today they are sometimes built for temporary shelter.

The house begins with a circle of blocks of snow (not ice). The blocks are set on edge, slanting inward, and shaped as shown in the illustration.

More blocks are added, spiraling upward and inward to form a dome.

A small air hole is left at the top of the dome. The original entrance is closed, and an entrance tunnel is dug below floor level, as shown in the photograph below.

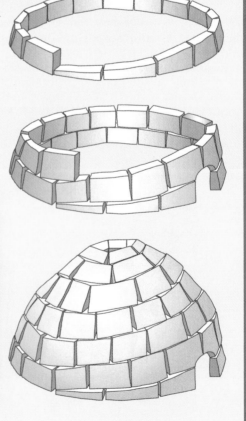

space; the entrance tunnel opened into the house below floor level.

Clothing and Crafts. The Inuit wore trousers, boots called mukluks, and hooded jackets called parkas—all made of animal skins. In winter, they wore two layers of clothing. Caribou fawn skin was preferred in winter because it was soft and warm. Coastal groups preferred sealskin in late spring and summer because it was waterproof. Clothing was often embroidered and had decorative fringes.

The Inuit decorated tools and objects for everyday use. Bone, ivory, wood, and a soft stone called soapstone were used to make small figures of people and animals, as well as weapons and tools. Tools were carefully carved to fit the hand of the user. In the Pacific and far western areas, masks were carved of wood, painted, and decorated with feathers and animal skins.

Religious Beliefs. The Inuit religion showed a deep concern with life, health, sickness, starvation, and death. All Inuit groups believed in a supernatural power called Sila. They shared belief in a small number of spirits (such as Sedna, the goddess of life, health, and food), and they believed that people and animals had souls that lived on after death. But each group had certain beliefs, rituals, and taboos of its own. Shamans (religious leaders), using trances, drama, and magic tricks, were believed to help establish and keep contacts with the spirit world.

Games of skill, such as wrestling, racing, and harpoon-throwing, were sometimes essential parts of religious rituals, as were storytelling, singing, drumming, and dancing. These activities were major sources of entertainment as well.

▶ **CONTACTS WITH THE OUTSIDE WORLD**

The first Europeans to encounter the Inuit were Vikings from Iceland, who established a settlement in Greenland. Contact between them began about A.D. 1200 and continued until about 1400. But some Inuit groups in the northern Arctic islands did not have much contact with outsiders until the late 1800's.

The Inuit are known for sculptures carved from soapstone (*above*) and other natural materials, such as ivory, wood, and bone.

After 1850, the arrival of European and American whalers and fur traders brought many changes. The Inuit worked for the whalers and sold furs to the traders. The outsiders, in turn, provided a steady source of metal tools and rifles. Because of the new tools and weapons and the new demand for furs, animals were hunted and killed in greater numbers. In some areas, animals such as caribou and seals were hunted almost to extinction.

The outsiders also brought new diseases to which the Inuit had no natural resistance. Smallpox, tuberculosis, influenza, whooping cough, pneumonia, mumps, scarlet fever, and diphtheria were the most dangerous of these diseases. After the late 1800's, when larger numbers of Europeans began to live year-round in the Arctic, these diseases became more widespread, and many Inuit died.

▶ **THE INUIT TODAY**

Today none of the Inuit live as their ancestors did. The once-isolated northlands have been opened up by air travel, highways, powerful modern ships, and satellite communications. Few—perhaps 10 percent—still live off the land, following a way of life based on hunting, fishing, and trapping. Another 10 to 15 percent have full-time, year-round jobs. Most, however, work and live in settlements for part of the year and hunt, trap, and fish the rest of the time.

In the settlements, most houses are simple wood-frame buildings. But they have heat, electricity, radios, telephones, color television sets, and other modern conveniences. In Greenland, many Inuit live in modern high-rise apartment buildings. Most settlements have schools providing instruction up to the eighth grade. Many have adopted Christianity, and most settlements have a church. Other public buildings include general stores, health care facilities, and a post office. Only a few communities do not have an airstrip.

Apart from traditional-style parkas and mukluks—now made of factory-produced materials—the people have adopted European and American dress. Flour, sugar, canned foods, dried milk, tea, coffee, and tobacco are supplied by trading centers and supermarkets. The Inuit buy some meat from stores. But caribou, seals, whales, and fish are still widely hunted. Many people who live and work in towns hunt and fish on weekends and vacations. Vegetables are expensive and not widely used. Wild blueberries, cranberries, and young Arctic willow roots are

Although modern technology and conveniences are increasingly available, many Inuit continue to depend on traditional ways of life. Dogsleds, for example, remain a popular and practical mode of transportation.

still collected and enjoyed. Fats—especially lard, butter, and margarine—are still important to the Inuit diet, especially in winter.

Economic and Political Issues. As more and more Inuit have changed their way of life, they have been drawn into mostly low-level, low-paying jobs. Many are unemployed or do not earn enough money to buy what they need. About half the population is considered poor by Western standards of society.

Many Inuit believe that the routines of employment are an invasion of their dignity, independence, and self-reliance, which may account for relatively high rates of violence, crime, alcoholism, and mental stress in Inuit communities. In addition, disease and malnutrition contribute to their difficulties. Infant deaths are more than ten times higher among the Inuit than among other North Americans.

Since the 1960's, the Inuit have fought to reclaim their rights to Arctic lands and to preserve their culture. In the eastern Canadian Arctic, the Inuit have formed several cooperative economic associations. These associations provide them with a way to market valuable soapstone carvings and other arts and crafts, which are in great demand. The Inuit have also worked to preserve their language. In Greenland, the Inuit language has been declared an official language equal in status to Danish. The Inuit language is taught in schools in Alaska and Canada.

The Inuit also have formed a number of political groups. The Alaska Federation of Natives is one of these. In Canada, several groups have been active. These include the Inuit Tapirisat (or Brotherhood), the Committee for Original Peoples Entitlement, and the Northern Quebec Inuit Association. Each of these associations has been successful in reaching agreements on land issues with the governments concerned. The first agreement, the Alaska Native Claims Settlement Act (1971), awarded land and cash settlements to 200 Inuit, Aleut, and Indian villages. There were similar agreements in Canada. The Northern Quebec Inuit Association signed the James Bay Agreement in 1975, and the Committee for Original Peoples Entitlement signed an agreement regarding the Mackenzie River Delta.

However, the most significant political achievement for the Inuit community came in 1992, when a plebiscite in the Canadian Northwest Territories authorized the creation of a new territory called Nunavut, meaning "our land." Nunavut, which was created out of the eastern half of the Northwest Territories (and covers one-fifth of Canada's total area), came under the administration of the Inuit people within the Canadian confederation on April 1, 1999.

DEREK G. SMITH
Carleton University

EMOTIONS

Everyone has feelings. Sometimes we feel happy and sometimes we feel sad. If you made a list of all the feelings you have experienced, it might include anger, surprise, embarrassment, guilt, confusion, and even indifference. It could be a very long list. Taken together, the many feelings that people experience are called emotions.

It is often possible to know when someone is feeling an emotion by the look

For most of us, young or old, a smile is an outward sign of a happy feeling.

on his or her face. For example, when people are happy, they usually smile or even laugh. When people are sad, they may show that feeling by crying. Babies, who are too young to talk, can still communicate their feelings with their facial expressions. This look on someone's face that communicates an emotion is called **affect**.

Emotion and affect are related to **mood**, which describes a person's overall emotional state. This relationship is similar to that between climate and weather. For example, it is much more likely to snow in colder climates, but that does not mean it could never snow in Florida. In the same way, it is much more likely for someone with a depressed mood to be sad and tearful, but that does not mean a person with a depressed mood could not smile or laugh on occasion. Compared with emotions, our moods last for longer periods of time. They also may influence how we experience the world.

▶ **WHY DO WE HAVE EMOTIONS?**

Our emotions help us organize our experiences. That is, the way we feel about something determines how much attention we give it, whether we will remember it, and how we will decide to deal with similar situations in the future.

For example, suppose you accidentally touched a hot stove. The feeling of pain in your finger would get you to take your finger away from the heat. You would then survey the situation, and perhaps feel angry at the stove, or at yourself for touching it, or at whoever left the stove on and did not tell you about it. Your brain would pay close attention to the circumstances surrounding this painful event, and the chances of accidentally touching that stove again would be reduced.

Emotions, attention, and memory are closely connected. The area of the brain mainly responsible for processing feelings and emotions is a structure called the **amygdala**. It is tightly linked to structures in the brain vital to memory processing, such as the **hippocampus**.

When we feel emotions, particularly intense feelings such as fear or anger, our brains prepare our bodies to respond. The best known of the responses to strong emotion is the "fight or flight" response. When we are frightened, the brain signals the adrenal glands (which sit on top of the kidneys) to release a hormone called adrenaline into the bloodstream. Adrenaline makes the pupils of the eye enlarge so that we can take in more light. It makes the heart beat faster so that we can run if necessary. And it even releases sugar from

A roller coaster ride allows us to experience intense emotions without putting ourselves in real danger.

fat stores in the body so that we will have energy. All these effects instantly prepare our body to pay attention and to be fully able to respond to whatever challenge has made us fearful. The "fight or flight" response is important for survival and is seen throughout the animal kingdom.

▸ HOW ARE EMOTIONS DETECTED?

There are differences among people in the way emotions are experienced and expressed. In part, we inherit a certain predisposition to experiencing emotions. This predisposition is sometimes referred to as **temperament**. One can detect differences in temperament even in babies. For example, some infants like to be held and some do not; some startle easily and others not.

In addition to genetic factors, our emotional response to situations or objects around us is influenced by our culture. For example, in a culture where snakes are worshiped, the emotional response to finding one in your house would probably be different than in a culture where snakes are not given divine qualities. Regardless of family background or culture, the human body's basic response to emotions is the same. People throughout the world smile when they are happy, and they cry when they are very sad.

Some medical conditions can alter a person's ability to experience or express emotions. In Parkinson's disease, facial expression can be quite limited due to reduced amounts of a brain chemical called dopamine. Although people with this disorder still feel emotions, it can be hard for others to tell just by looking.

Another neurological disorder that affects the perception of feelings is autism. Because of the way their brains process other people's facial expressions, people with autism have trouble reading others' emotions. As a result, they may anger or embarrass someone without meaning to. Imagine how hard it would be to figure out how to behave properly if you could not understand the emotional signals of people around you.

▸ EMOTIONS IN ILLNESS

Occasionally the term "emotional disorder" is used to describe a mental illness. This is not completely accurate, because the affected person still experiences emotions. However, some disorders of mood or anxiety do influence how we feel. For example, the mood disorder called **major depression** refers to a condition characterized by a prolonged period of deep sadness, loss of interest in activities, loss of energy, trouble sleeping, and many other problems, including thoughts of suicide. In this condition, a person's feelings of sadness are not always related to what is happening in his or her life. Instead they may reflect abnormal brain function, which establishes an internal mood of generalized sadness. Similarly, a person with an **anxiety disorder** may worry about things that most people would be able to overlook.

People exposed to a life-threatening event, such as a severe earthquake or tornado, may be traumatized. The intensity of their emotions may so activate the brain that they later have unwanted memories of the event. They may go out of their way to avoid experiences that might remind them of the trauma. When such feelings are persistent for more than six months, the diagnosis of **post-traumatic stress disorder** is sometimes considered.

Whatever their cause, emotional problems are treatable. This is fortunate, because emotions are an important and constant part of our daily lives, and they strongly influence our behavior.

BRYAN H. KING, M.D.
Professor of Psychiatry and Pediatrics
Dartmouth Medical School

Did you know that...

a lie detector tries to take advantage of the body's response to feelings?

If you are nervous, it is likely that you will perspire and that your heart will start beating faster. These responses may occur even if you can keep your face from showing that you are scared. A lie detector is a machine that records a person's heart rate and skin conductance (a sensitive measure of perspiration) as he or she is being questioned. If an experienced liar did not worry about being caught, it is less likely that the machine would detect anything significant. But if someone was quite frightened about being caught in a lie, a lie detector might capture the response. A lie detector cannot tell what is true, but it can pick up indicators of emotional responses that might be associated with the act of telling a lie.

MIDDLE AGES

The medieval period, known as the Middle Ages, covers nearly 1,000 years of European history. According to some historians, the era began in A.D. 476 when a German chieftain overthrew the last emperor of the Western Roman Empire. It lasted until about 1500, when the Renaissance, a period of tremendous innovation, became firmly established throughout western Europe.

The Middle Ages were once viewed as a time of ignorance—a "dark age" between the glories of the ancient world and the flowering of learning and culture that occurred during the Renaissance. But a great many things happened in Europe during these years.

Sir Lancelot, a legendary knight, does battle in this medieval scene. During the Middle Ages, knights went into battle in the service of feudal lords. In exchange, the knights received grants of land.

▶ THE EARLY MIDDLE AGES

At its height, the Roman Empire controlled most of western Europe. Roman rule provided a sort of glue that unified the region. Roman armies kept the peace. Roman roads linked various parts of Europe, and Roman aqueducts brought water to towns and cities. But by A.D. 400, the Roman Empire had been split into eastern and western halves. Germanic tribes had begun to move into the Western Empire, and Roman armies could no longer control them. In 410, the Visigoths (or West Goths) invaded Italy and plundered the city of Rome itself. It was hard for people of those times to believe that Roman power had grown so weak. "Who would believe," Saint Jerome, a Christian writer, asked, "that Rome, which had spread over the whole earth by means of its victories, could now fall so low?" The Eastern Empire (or Byzantine Empire), with its capital at Constantinople (now Istanbul, Turkey), continued to flourish. But the Western Empire fell apart.

Various Germanic tribes settled in what are today the countries of western Europe—the Visigoths in Spain, the Lombards in Italy, the Anglo-Saxons in England, and the Franks in France and western Germany. They lived alongside the inhabitants of the old empire. They did not wish to destroy all signs of Roman civilization. They adopted many of their neighbors' ways, including the Christian religion. But they lived under their own laws and under the rule of their own chiefs or kings.

Without a central government, life changed greatly. Roads and water-supply systems fell into disrepair. There was little trade, with the result that cities and towns became less important. The people in each region produced almost everything they used, which was often little more than the bare necessities. Learning also declined. Few Germanic people could read Latin, so they learned little about the civilization they had conquered.

During most of the early Middle Ages, Europe was carved up into small regions ruled by local lords. Each lord made his own laws, and this often led to conflict and disorder. Lords fought among themselves, and they tried to defend their lands from outside threats. One of the most serious threats came from Muslims from North Africa, who invaded Europe through Spain in 711.

Historians used to call the early Middle Ages the Dark Ages because this time was marked by confusion, disorder, and the breakdown of civilization in western Europe. But scholars today see this period as a time of change, rather than darkness, in Europe. As Rome's power crumbled, religion became the one thing shared by people throughout the former Roman realm. Today Christianity has many branches, but in western Europe during the Middle Ages there was only one. The Catholic Church, headed by the pope, played a central role in medieval life.

Charlemagne's Empire

During the early Middle Ages, several rulers tried to establish larger kingdoms. The most successful was the great Frankish king Charlemagne (742?–814), whose empire included much of western and central Europe. Charlemagne wanted to rule as the emperors of Rome had in ancient times. He was even crowned emperor of the Romans by Pope Leo III in 800. Charlemagne maintained order throughout his realm and kept close check on the great nobles and landlords, who were in the habit of doing as they wished. Into every district he sent special agents who saw that the nobles obeyed his commands.

Charlemagne also rewarded nobles for their military support. In exchange for providing knights, who were mounted warriors, he gave nobles grants of land called **fiefs**, or fiefdoms. This practice laid the foundation of **feudalism**, a system of government in which land was exchanged for military service by knights.

Charlemagne also encouraged interest in the Christian religion and ancient Latin learning. He established a palace school for the sons of nobles, gave support to scholars, and set scribes to work copying various ancient books to preserve their contents for future generations.

Charlemagne accomplished much, but his empire did not last long after his death. Later Frankish rulers could neither govern nor protect a large empire. Vikings from the Scandinavian lands found that there was no one to keep them from raiding the coast and sailing up the rivers to plunder the countryside. Muslim Arabs threatened in the south, as they had before Charlemagne became king.

With the breakup of Charlemagne's empire, local lords and their knights offered people the best protection. Europe became a patchwork of feudal realms. Feudal lords did give people some protection, but they also disturbed the peace with their private wars.

▶ THE HIGH MIDDLE AGES

After the year 1000, feudal realms began to grow into stable states. European kingdoms expanded their territory and their influence. Beginning in 1096, they united to fight in the **Crusades**, or "wars for the cross." This series of wars was aimed at gaining control of Christian holy places in Palestine, which was ruled by Muslims.

Kings and Nobles

Strong kings in several states succeeded in bringing their feudal lords under control and reducing the number of private wars.

France. In 987, the feudal lords of what is today France elected a king, Hugh Capet, the count of Paris (938?–96).

Musicians and scribes surround the Spanish ruler Alfonso the Wise (1221–84). Medieval kings and nobles enjoyed comforts, but everyday life was hard for most people.

Hugh had little power, but he founded a dynasty that eventually controlled all of France. Among the Capetian kings was Louis VI (1081–1137), who personally led campaigns to bring feudal lords under his control. His grandson, Philip II (1165–1223), or Philip Augustus, appointed special officials, called bailiffs, who traveled within their districts to keep watch on the nobles, somewhat as Charlemagne's agents had done.

Louis IX (1214–70), famous for his piety and sense of justice, did his best to see that no man was treated unfairly in his realm. He would sit under a tree and invite anyone who had been unable to get justice from his lord or the regular courts to come and state his case. After his death, the Roman Catholic Church declared him a saint. His grandson Philip IV (1268–1314) did even more to enhance the power and prestige of the king. By the end of his reign, France was the leading state of Europe.

England. William the Conqueror (1028?–87), duke of Normandy, invaded England in 1066 and won its crown by conquest. As William I of England, he withheld power and independence from his nobles so none could rise against him. The kings of England thus had greater power over their feudal lords than did the French monarchs.

William's son Henry I (1068–1135) and his great-grandson Henry II (1133–89) further strengthened the king's powers. Henry II encouraged people to look to the royal courts for justice rather than to their local courts or those of the lords. He did so partly by having the royal courts offer better service and fairer judgments.

By limiting the powers of feudal lords, English kings built a well-governed state. But the English discovered that royal powers needed limits as well. King John (1167?–1216), a reckless and unjust ruler, was reviled by both nobles and common people. In 1215 he faced a revolt of the lords. To keep his throne, John agreed to issue a charter called **Magna Carta.**

The wife of the lord of the manor oversaw many tasks. Among them were spinning and weaving.

In it he stated certain limits on his power. Among other things John promised that he would have no freeman arrested or punished except "by the law of the land." This was the first known document to decree that the head of the government was not above the law. Constitutional governments today are based on this idea.

In time the power of English kings became increasingly limited by Parliament, an assembly made up of the chief nobles, bishops of the church, and representatives of knights and townspeople. A king would assemble his Parliament before attempting to collect special taxes. Parliament could often obtain privileges and concessions from the king in exchange for voting to give him the money he wanted. Thus Parliament gradually increased its power over the king. The Parliament of the Middle Ages was very different from the modern British Parliament, but the modern representative body grew out of the older one.

Germany, Italy, and Spain. The German kings, like those of France and England, tried to reduce the independence of their feudal lords. In the 900's, the Saxon king Otto I (the Great) (912–73) extended his control over much of Germany and even revived the name Holy Roman Empire. But Otto and his successors never matched Charlemagne's empire, which had extended south almost to Rome.

Through the mid-1200's, various German kings tried to rule northern Italy, but they all failed. Germany remained a collection of small principalities until the 1800's. So did much of Italy. Among the strongest Italian city-states was Venice, which built a trading empire. In 1130 southern Italy and Sicily united as the Kingdom of Sicily.

The history of Spain in the Middle Ages is largely a story of struggle between Muslims and Christians. Christians gradually gained the upper hand, and as they did, several strong feudal states appeared, including Aragon, Castile, Navarre, and Portugal. When they were not fighting the Muslims, these states fought each other. But in the late 1400's, Aragon and Castile united to form the kingdom of Spain.

▶ MEDIEVAL LIFE

Although Europe was politically divided in the Middle Ages, daily life did not vary greatly from one realm to the next. Medieval society was tightly structured. Many people lived their entire lives in one village or manor. They were born to a certain social position and stayed in that position. Those who wanted something more had few choices. For all but the wealthiest, life was extremely hard.

The Manorial System

Medieval land holdings ranged from small estates called manors to huge fiefs as big as small countries. The lord of a large fief, such as a baron, might give individual manors to his knights, in exchange for their service. Those knights thus became lords of their own small manors. But they still owed allegiance to the baron.

A lord's word was law on his manor. But knights and barons were often away, fighting battles. Much of the daily management of the manor fell to the lord's wife. She oversaw planting, spinning, weaving, and other activities. She made sure servants did their jobs and ran the household smoothly. Often she also

handled the household financial accounts. But despite these responsibilities, women in medieval times had few rights. They were expected to obey their husbands and fathers in all things. Upper-class girls were married off early, as a way for powerful families to form alliances and build their wealth.

Most of the people on a feudal manor were peasants who spent their lives working in the fields. A great many of the peasants were **serfs**—that is, they were not free. Serfs could not leave their manor to try and find a better place. They belonged to the manor at which they were born and could move or change jobs only if their lord gave permission. The lords did not freely give away their serfs any more than they gave away their land or livestock. When a lord agreed to let one of his serfs marry a serf from another manor, he usually demanded a payment to make up for the loss.

Serfs led difficult lives. They had to till the land of the lord, as well as the strips in the manor fields in which they grew their own food. They knew little about the world and rarely met anyone from outside their village. They did not travel, nor could they read.

Town Life

There were few towns, particularly in northwestern Europe, during the early Mid-

Towns became increasingly important as centers of trade during the late Middle Ages. Here, merchants in Paris, France, display their wares.

dle Ages. The rule of the feudal lords discouraged trade, and towns lived by trade. Each lord collected a toll, for "protection," from all merchants who came into his neighborhood. A merchant paid many such tolls in traveling from one land to another. For example, a merchant taking a boatload of goods down the Loire River from Orléans had to pay 74 different tolls. Needless to say, the many tolls made goods expensive and trade difficult even in times of peace. During the frequent private wars trade became still more risky.

As private wars became less frequent, trade became easier. Towns grew in both number and size. Townspeople were better off than the serfs, for they were free. But their position was beneath that of the lords. Thus the townspeople became known as the middle class.

Most townspeople were merchants and artisans. Some merchants were little more than peddlers carrying their packs from village to village. Others brought goods by ship, riverboat, or pack train from distant lands to sell in town markets and fairs.

As towns grew larger, some people opened shops stocked with goods bought from the traveling merchants. One shopkeeper might sell drugs and spices brought from distant lands. Another shop might have furs or fine cloth and carpets from the East. Towns also

had butchers, bakers, and barbers. Artisans manufactured shoes, hats, cloth, ironware, and other goods in their workshops.

The right to do business in a town was a guarded privilege. The merchants and artisans banded together in special organizations for each trade or craft, called **guilds**. Only

The church played an important role in medieval life. Priests conducted services in Latin, and beautiful cathedrals were built in major towns.

Peter Abelard (1079–1142), born near Nantes, France, was a scholar and poet. The son of a knight, he gave up his inheritance to study philosophy. His brilliant writings explored the relation of language to truth, among other things. Abelard taught and studied in several cities, but primarily in Paris. There he became involved in a romance with one of his private students, Héloïse, the niece of a leading clergyman. They married secretly, but scandal and the wrath of Héloïse's uncle forced them apart. He became a monk, and she became a nun.

Charles Martel ("the Hammer") (688?–741), grandfather of Charlemagne, was a Frankish leader who stopped a Muslim invasion of Europe. As "mayor of the palace" of the territory of Austrasia (the eastern part of the divided Frankish realm), Charles exercised more power than the weak king of the ruling Merovingian dynasty. Able and ambitious, he reunited the Frankish kingdom by 719, and then extended his rule over neighbor-ing regions. In 732 a Muslim force advanced from Spain as far as Poitiers, in central France. Charles defeated the invaders at the Battle of Tours. Afterward, there were no major Muslim invasions north of Spain.

Eleanor of Aquitaine (1122?–1204) was perhaps the most powerful woman in medieval Europe. She inherited the vast domain of her father, William X, duke of Aquitaine, and in 1137 she married the heir to the French throne. He soon became King Louis II, and she became queen. A renowned beauty, she wielded strong influence over her husband and accompanied him on the Second Crusade in 1147. But they grew apart, and in 1152 their marriage was annulled. Eleanor promptly married the future king Henry II of England. Together, they ruled a realm that stretched from Scotland to the south of France. In 1173, Eleanor supported her sons in a rebellion against their father. When the rebellion failed, Henry held Eleanor prisoner until his death in 1189. In her final years, Eleanor helped manage the realm for her surviving sons, King Richard I and, after his death, King John.

Eleanor of Aquitaine

Geoffrey of Monmouth (1100?–54), bishop of Saint Asaph in Wales, was an English chronicler whose works are one of the main sources of legends about King Arthur. His most famous work, *Historia Regum Britanniae* (*History of the Kings of Britain*), was completed about 1136. A fictional history, it begins with the conquest of giants and ends with the prophecies of a sorcerer named Merlin. His work inspired future authors of Arthurian legends, including Chrétien de Troyes and Sir Thomas Malory.

---

members of the guilds could sell goods or practice a trade within the town walls. Guild members all charged the same prices for the same quality work, and they limited the number of people permitted to follow a particular occupation. The shoemakers' guild, for example, wanted to make sure that there were never more shoemakers in a particular town than could make a good living there.

Towns became increasingly important during the later Middle Ages. The middle class grew richer, and the kings began to choose middle-class lawyers to advise them on matters of government. Many merchants and craftsmen had their sons study law because it provided an opportunity for a young man to get ahead in the world.

The Role of the Church

Every town and almost every village in the Middle Ages had a church, where a priest conducted worship services, baptized babies, married young people, and buried the dead in the churchyard. In addition the priests taught the children at least the most important Christian prayers and beliefs.

The church grew great and powerful during the Middle Ages. It had its own laws and courts in which to try any person who broke church law. Church leaders also claimed that accused priests could only be tried by a church court. The church also collected tax payments for its support.

The church was governed by bishops and archbishops under the authority of the pope at Rome. Church leaders were involved in politics as well as spiritual matters. Some popes were very powerful. They rallied kings and lords to fight in the Crusades and to oppose heretics, those whose beliefs did not agree with church teachings. But sometimes kings opposed the popes in bitter struggles.

The church was also served by monks and nuns. Monks were men who lived together in a house called a monastery. They were under the rule of an abbot, and they devoted their lives mainly to prayer and religious service. The nuns were women who followed a similar life in houses usually called convents. Monks and nuns gave all of their property to the monastery or convent. They vowed never to marry and agreed to live under strict rules.

Godfrey of Bouillon (1060?–1100), born in Baisy, Brabant, was a French crusader and the first Christian ruler of Jerusalem after that city's capture in 1099. The duke of Lower Lorraine, Godfrey signed on for the First Crusade in 1096. He sold most of his possessions to raise an army, and his men were the first to storm the walls of Jerusalem. Elected to rule the city, Godfrey declined the title of king and called himself Defender of the Holy Sepulchre. He proved to be a weak ruler but was later portrayed in stories as "the perfect Christian knight."

Godfrey of Bouillon

Saladin

John Wycliffe

Innocent III (Lothar of Segni) (1161?–1216) was born in Anagni, Italy. He became pope in 1198, and his reign is thought to mark the height of the medieval church's power. Pope Innocent III increased the prestige of his office and required kings to accept the authority of the church. He launched the Fourth Crusade (1202–04), which set out for Palestine but changed course and attacked Constantinople. He also launched the brutal Albigensian Crusade to repress French heretics.

Saladin (1138?–93), born in Tikrit, Mesopotamia, was a Muslim ruler who battled the Crusaders. He began his career as a military commander and rose to power quickly, becoming ruler of Egypt in 1171. By 1186 he had extended his rule over Syria and northern Mesopotamia. Next he turned to Palestine, much of which had been captured by Christians in the First Crusade. In 1187, Saladin regained control of Jerusalem. He then blocked the Third Crusade, which was launched to retake the city.

John Wycliffe (1330?–84), born in Yorkshire, England, was a philosopher and church reformer. He studied and taught at Oxford University for most of his life. Wycliffe began the first English-language translation of the Bible. He urged the clergy to give up property and serve the poor, and he said that the church should be subject to the law of the land in all non-religious matters. He also criticized many traditional church doctrines. His views foreshadowed the Protestant Reformation of the 1500's.

Some monks worked in the monastery's fields, fed the poor who came to the monastery gate, or took care of travelers who asked for shelter. Others copied books in the monastery scriptorium, or writing room. Since there were no printing presses, all books had to be copied by hand. A few monks conducted schools where they taught boys to read and write Latin. It was necessary to learn Latin because both the Bible and the church services were in that language. Poetry and history were also written in Latin.

Bishops, too, established schools, called cathedral schools. Some cathedral schools became great centers of learning called universities. A number of the greatest thinkers of the Middle Ages, including Peter Abelard (1079–1142), Saint Albertus Magnus (1193?–80), and Saint Thomas Aquinas (1225?–74), studied and taught at Paris. University students began their studies with the seven liberal arts. These were Latin grammar, rhetoric (how to write and speak), logic (how to reason), arithmetic, geometry, astronomy, and music. Students could also go on to study law, medicine, arts (philosophy), or theology. The church also encouraged artists to erect magnificent cathedrals in stone and glass.

▶ **THE LATE MIDDLE AGES**

The years between 1300 and 1500 brought many changes to Europe. France and England fought the costly Hundred Years' War (1337–1453). This was really a series of wars, in which English rulers tried to win back lands they had once held in France.

From about 1347 to 1350, a terrible plague called the Black Death killed as many as one-third of Europe's total population. Farmland stood idle, with few laborers to work it. Discontented peasants rebelled, and many serfs were able to gain their freedom. At the same time, the church's power began to decline. But in the cities, the influence of the middle class increased, and there was a growing spirit of freedom. This change came first in the cities of Italy, in the 1300's. Historians consider this to be the beginning of a new age called the Renaissance, meaning "rebirth."

KENNETH S. COOPER
George Peabody College

The violent movement of snow can be seen in this photo of an avalanche on Mt. McKinley, Alaska. Avalanches can occur wherever snow accumulates on steep slopes.

AVALANCHES AND LANDSLIDES

On a sunny winter day, snow on a steep slope fractures and tumbles down a mountainside. The avalanche, a violent movement of snow that can also contain ice, soil, and rock, buries everything in its path.

On a rainy spring day, a huge water-soaked mass of land suddenly breaks away and falls down a steep hill, taking entire houses and roads along with it. Such a large movement of rock and soil is called a landslide.

Avalanches and landslides start for different reasons. However, they can both have a devastating impact on nearby settlements and recreation areas.

Snow builds up on a mountainside in layers. If a weak layer is buried under a strong one, the weight of a skier could trigger an avalanche.

▶ AVALANCHES AND THEIR CAUSES

In order for avalanches to occur, there must be an accumulation, or buildup, of snow on a steep mountainside over time. During the winter, storms continually deposit fresh layers of snow on existing snow, creating a snowpack. Because each layer is built up under different weather conditions, the tiny ice crystals making up the snow may form strong bonds between some layers but weak bonds between others. If the bonds between layers are too weak, the top layers of snow can't resist the downward pull of gravity.

At this stage, all that is needed for an avalanche to start is a "trigger event." This could be anything from the weight of new snow or a passing skier or animal to the impact of small chunks of snow and ice falling from above. Even a loud noise can set off an avalanche.

There are two main types of avalanches. A loose snow avalanche occurs when snow on or near the surface does not bond with the snow beneath it and begins to slide down a slope, gathering more and more snow as it continues down. The more common and deadly slab avalanche occurs when a weak layer of snow buried under a strong layer makes an entire snowpack unstable. A trigger event can then cause a single large plate, or slab, of snow to break off and fracture as it falls down the slope.

Avalanches are a danger wherever snow accumulates on steep slopes. The deadliest avalanche ever occurred in 1970, when an earthquake off the coast of Peru triggered an ice avalanche near the summit of Mount Huascarán. The descending mass of ice and rocks accelerated to a speed of more than 170 miles (280 kilometers) an hour, destroying villages below. More than 18,000 people were killed.

▶ LANDSLIDES AND THEIR CAUSES

A landslide occurs when part of a hillside becomes too weak to support its own weight. This weakening can be caused by earthquakes or when the ground becomes soaked with rain or melting snow. Some types of landslides move seasonally, during rainy periods of the year. Others may lie dormant (inactive) for long periods of time, moving only once every number of years.

Landslides are more frequent in areas where there is a lot of erosion—the gradual wearing down and carrying away of land. Erosion is especially noticeable along some streams, rivers, and seacoasts. But landslides also occur far from areas of active erosion.

Human activities can also contribute to landslides. For example, the construction of buildings on hillsides may involve excavating material from the bottom of a slope and adding material higher up to create a more level lot. As a result, the slope can become overloaded, meaning that it cannot safely support the weight of the added material.

There are three main types of landslides: slides, falls, and flows. Slides are large bodies of land that move together along a sloping surface. Slides that rotate backward along a curved surface are called slumps. Translational slides are slides along a straight sloping surface. Slumps and translational slides can move up to 100 feet (30 meters) a day, although some move much more slowly. Debris slides and rockslides can move slowly or rapidly.

Falls of rock and soil occur on cliffs and steep slopes. Large rockfalls can be catastrophic events. Even small falls can be hazardous. Every year, small amounts of falling rock kill motorists, hikers, and campers in mountainous areas.

Flows are landslides in which materials move more like a fluid. Debris flows are rapid movements of wet mud and debris, while earthflows are movements of wet, clay-rich material. Debris flows triggered by storms have caused many deaths and much property damage in the United States. There are also dry flows, in which dry materials flow rapidly over long distances. In 1920, an earthquake in China's Gansu Province triggered a large, rapid flow of dry loess (silt deposited by wind) that killed some 100,000 people.

▶ PREVENTION AND DAMAGE CONTROL

In ski areas and along highways and railways, explosives are used to intentionally trigger small avalanches rather than allowing the slabs to build up to large and destructive avalanches. Heavy-duty fencing can hold snow in place, and specially designed deflecting walls can turn snow away from an area to be pro-

A landslide on this California hillside caused these houses to collapse. Soaking rains of the season had weakened the ground.

tected. Avoiding avalanche-prone slopes when skiing or hiking is the best way to prevent triggering an avalanche .

A number of methods are used to prevent landslides as well. One way is to capture and drain excess water before it reaches a potential landslide area. Walls and buttresses are used to prevent deep-seated landslide movements. Special fences and nets can keep falling rocks from reaching highways. And maps of landslide-prone areas help builders and planners avoid dangerous areas.

Reviewed by DALE ATKINS
Colorado Avalanche Information Center
REX L. BAUM
U.S. Geological Survey

ELK AND MOOSE

In the Rocky Mountain foothills, a male elk tilts back his large, pointed antlers and makes a loud, squealing sound called a bugle. At the edge of a pond in Maine, two male moose lock antlers and begin to shove each other. During mating season, displays like these help the males attract a female.

Elk live in North America, mostly in the western states and provinces. Moose live across the northern United States and in Alaska and Canada. But moose also live in parts of Europe, where they are called elk. One way to avoid confusion is to call North American elk **wapiti**. It means "white rump" in the Shawnee language.

A male, or bull, elk in Yellowstone National Park. Elk inhabit mainly western North America, while moose live across the northern reaches of the continent.

Characteristics of Elk and Moose. Moose are the largest members of the deer family. Elk are the second largest. Males, or bulls, are bigger than females, or cows. A full-grown male moose may stand 7 feet (2 meters) tall at the shoulder and weigh 900 to 1,400 pounds (400 to 630 kilograms). An adult male elk weighs about 800 pounds (360 kilograms).

Adult moose have dark-brown coats; their young, called calves, are the color of a golden retriever. The shade of an elk's brown coat depends on where it lives, but all elk have a distinctive white rump. Males of both species grow a new set of antlers each spring.

Elk and moose eat mainly leaves, grasses, and twigs. In summer a male moose may gulp down 50 pounds (23 kilograms) of plant food a day. Moose often wade into ponds and duck underwater to eat water plants.

Elk and Moose and Their Young. Male elk are famous for their mating-season bugle calls in fall. Male moose give a similar call. The males of both species also dig wallows: They urinate in the dirt, then stomp around to splash the mixture on their legs. The odor attracts females. A male elk defends a harem, or group of cows; a male moose takes a single mate.

Females give birth in May to one or two calves. Mothers rear their young without help from the males. Newborn elk have white spots for camouflage. Their mothers hide them in tall grass and stay at a distance, visiting just to nurse. In a few weeks the calves are strong enough to join the herd. Newborn moose have no camouflage spots. They stay close to their mothers for a full year. In winter, mothers guide their calves to food.

The Life of Elk and Moose. Elk live in herds and take turns watching for predators. Moose usually live alone. Elk that spend summers in the mountains avoid deep snows by migrating to lower elevations in winter.

Wolves, bears, and mountain lions prey on young moose and elk and sometimes attack feeble adults. Moose sometimes suffer from deadly parasites.

Elk were once widespread in North America, but they were wiped out in the eastern states by the mid-1800's. Settlers killed them not just for meat, but also because they felt that their cattle had to compete with elk for grazing land.

In the late 1800's many more elk were killed for their canine teeth, which were made into good-luck charms. Elk numbers increased in the 1900's, but much of the land that was once elk habitat is now occupied by humans. Setting aside sufficient habitat is a conservation challenge.

Settlers also wiped out moose populations in some eastern states. But in recent years moose have expanded their range back into New Hampshire, Vermont, and the Adirondack Mountains of New York. However, new dangers exist for moose, such as being hit by cars or trains, now that they often live fairly close to humans.

CYNTHIA BERGER
Science Writer

REINDEER AND CARIBOU

It is spring on the Alaskan tundra, and a newborn caribou calf is just one hour old. Yet already it is strong enough to stand and follow its mother. Not far away, a wolf watches.

In northern Sweden, a man tends his reindeer herd. His shoes are made of reindeer leather, and his children drink reindeer milk. When they travel, reindeer pull their sled.

Reindeer and caribou are now classified as a single species. Caribou live in Alaska and Canada; reindeer live in Russia, Norway, Finland, and Sweden. Reindeer once lived in other parts of Europe, but those populations have been hunted to extinction.

Arctic peoples have hunted reindeer and caribou since prehistoric times. Nomadic groups followed the herds to get meat, skins for clothing, and bones for tools. About 200 years ago, reindeer were domesticated in parts of Scandinavia and Russia. Today some people still follow a traditional way of life based on reindeer herding.

Characteristics of Reindeer and Caribou. Caribou and reindeer are the only deer in which both males and females grow antlers. Scientists think having antlers helps females compete with males to find food.

Most reindeer and caribou are brown with white bellies and a white tail patch. But some in Greenland and eastern Canada are nearly white. Males are bigger than females. A typical male weighs about 300 pounds (135 kilograms), although the largest animals may weigh 700 pounds (315 kilograms) and stand almost 5 feet (1.5 meters) tall at the shoulder.

Reindeer and caribou have short legs and wide, flat hooves that help them walk in deep snow and across the spongy treeless plains known as the tundra. And they click when they walk! The sound is caused by a tendon that snaps against a bone in the foot.

Almost every plant that grows on the tundra is food for reindeer and caribou: new leaves, evergreen needles, even small twigs. They also have the unusual ability to digest lichens—these tiny organisms provide food for reindeer during the harsh winter months.

Reindeer and Caribou and Their Young. For most of the year, males and females stay in separate herds. But in the fall, when mating season begins, males and females come together, locating each other by means of a

A reindeer pulls a sleigh in Lapland. Reindeer are native to Europe's far north, where they have been domesticated by Lapps and other native peoples.

scent secreted from glands between the toes and around the anus. Males also call out, making a coughing sound. A single male defends a group of females, called a harem.

Pregnancy lasts for 228 days. Usually, all the calves are born within a five-day period. Their ability to stand and follow their mothers soon after birth helps protect the tiny calves from wolves and other predators.

The Life of Reindeer and Caribou. Reindeer and caribou live in herds of 10 to 1,000 animals. A few large herds on migration have 200,000 animals. Most herds migrate between the Arctic tundra in summer and woodland edges in the winter, traveling up to 600 miles (966 kilometers) each way.

In the summer, caribou and reindeer are tormented by mosquitoes and other biting insects. To get relief, they may stand in the middle of a snowfield, where insects are scarce.

Reindeer and caribou today are threatened because exploration for oil sometimes blocks their migration routes or destroys habitat. Some populations in Canada and the United States have been declared endangered.

CYNTHIA BERGER
Science Writer

Clockwise from right: A German artist captured the alien image of soldiers masked against the threat of poison warfare in his *Soldats Masques.* A heavy shell explodes during the five-month Battle of the Somme, 1916. Trench warfare began in France at the First Battle of the Aisne (Sept. 14–28, 1914), just one month after World War I began. British Royal Navy recruits line up for service, South London, 1914.

WORLD WAR I

On Sunday, June 28, 1914, an 18-year-old Serbian student, Gavrilo Princip, shot and killed Archduke Franz (Francis) Ferdinand, heir to the throne of Austria-Hungary and nephew of the emperor Franz (Francis) Joseph I. Slain with the archduke was his wife, Duchess Sophie. The double slaying took place in Sarajevo, the ancient capital of Bosnia. Princip, the assassin, belonged to a secret terrorist organization whose members were pledged to free Bosnia from Austrian rule and unite it with Serbia.

The deed that Princip saw as a blow for liberty instead touched off World War I. This terrible conflict lasted more than four years, involved more than 30 nations, and claimed more than 14 million lives, both military and civilian; it cost untold billions of dollars, ravaged Europe, toppled kings and emperors, and sowed the seeds of World War II.

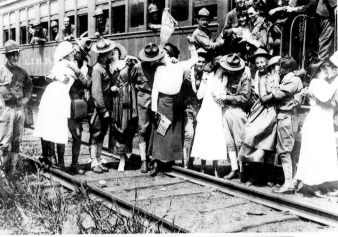

▶ BACKGROUND TO THE CONFLICT

Europe was ripe for World War I long before Princip fired the fatal shots. The origins of the war can be traced at least as far back as 1871. In that year Germany, guided by Chancellor Otto von Bismarck, crushed France in the brief Franco-Prussian War. Bismarck imposed harsh peace terms on France. The French were stripped of two rich provinces, Alsace and Lorraine, and in addition had to pay Germany billions of francs in reparations.

Beat back the HUN with LIBERTY BONDS

Clockwise from top left: German generals von Hindenburg (left) and Ludendorff (right) discuss war plans with Kaiser William II (center). American "doughboys" leave home to fight the "war to end all wars." French Algerian colonial troops are mobilized to the Western Front, 1914. A war propaganda poster urges American citizens to buy Liberty Bonds to "Beat back the Hun," meaning the Germans. British recruits train for service, 1914.

The Franco-Prussian War unified Germany and made it the most powerful nation in Europe. But Bismarck believed that someday the French would strike back to avenge the humiliation of 1871 and regain their lost provinces. To block this, Bismarck in 1882 forged the Triple Alliance, which bound Germany, Austria-Hungary, and Italy to mutual assistance in case of war.

France, fearing Germany, sought allies, too. In 1893–94 the French negotiated a military alliance with Russia called the Dual Alliance.

In 1904 France and England formed the Entente Cordiale; this became the Triple Entente when Russia joined the pact in 1907. Thus Europe was divided into two hostile camps by a complicated system of political alliances.

The Ambitious German Kaiser. Meanwhile, in 1888 a new kaiser (emperor), Wilhelm (William) II, had come to the German throne. In 1890, William took a step that helped open the door to war. He dismissed the old chancellor, Bismarck, and took Germany's future into his own hands.

William was an arrogant, impulsive man with great national ambitions for Germany. He wanted a colonial empire that would equal Great Britain's and foresaw a day when all middle Africa would be German. He envisioned a Berlin-to-Baghdad railway that would give Germany access to the oilfields of the Middle East and domination of the Balkan countries. William also began to build a large navy, boasting that soon Germany, not Great Britain, would rule the seas. This antagonized the British, who considered the Royal Navy the main defense of their island and their empire.

The kaiser was no diplomat, and he made enemies easily. In the early 1900's he tried to exert German influence in Morocco, which France claimed. This provoked two incidents that almost led to war and served to draw France and Great Britain closer together against him.

Austria-Hungary. In 1914, Austrians, Hungarians, and Balkan Slavs, plus a smaller number of Italians and Romanians, lived within the Dual Monarchy of Austria-Hungary. The many Slavs in the empire resented their domination by the ruling Austrians and Hungarians. The South Slavs (or "Yugo" slavs) sought to break away from Austria and join Serbia. The Serbs supported the aspirations of their fellow South Slavs—sometimes, as in the case of Princip, with violence.

Russia's Czar Nicholas II (left) and Britain's future King George V (right), pictured in 1904, were first cousins through their royal Danish mothers.

▶ **THE OUTBREAK OF WAR**

When the news of the archduke's death reached Vienna, Austria blamed the Serbian government for the assassination. The Austrians sent a list of harsh demands to Belgrade, the capital of Serbia. Unless their terms were met, they warned, they would attack Serbia. Actually, the Austrians had purposely made their demands so severe as to be unacceptable. Assured of German support, they were determined to crush Serbia.

Meanwhile, Russia had declared that it would defend Serbia in the event of attack by Austria-Hungary. To the Austrians' surprise, King Peter I of Serbia agreed to almost all their demands. Nevertheless, on July 28, 1914, urged on by Germany, Austria-Hungary declared war on Serbia. The next day Austrian gunboats bombarded Belgrade.

Events now moved very rapidly. Czar Nicholas II began to mobilize (prepare for war) the huge Russian army. Germany warned Russia to cease mobilizing or face war. The kaiser also called on France to give assurances of its neutrality in case of a conflict between Germany and Russia. France, which had promised Russia its support, began to ready its own army for war. The Russians continued to mobilize their forces. Last minute diplomatic efforts failed, and on August 1, Germany declared war on Russia. Two days later Germany announced that it was at war with France.

Germany Invades Belgium. Germany demanded that Belgium allow its troops to cross Belgian territory. The Germans were sure that tiny Belgium would not dare refuse, but they underestimated the courage of Al-

Near right: Germany's heavy artillery included Big Bertha, a 42-cm howitzer used to level fortifications.
Far right: In the absence of able-bodied men, women throughout Europe entered the labor force to produce weapons for the soldiers.

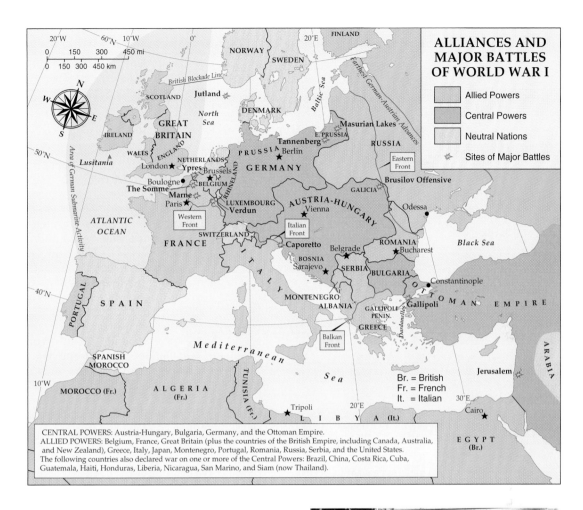

ALLIANCES AND MAJOR BATTLES OF WORLD WAR I

Allied Powers
Central Powers
Neutral Nations
★ Sites of Major Battles

Br. = British
Fr. = French
It. = Italian

CENTRAL POWERS: Austria-Hungary, Bulgaria, Germany, and the Ottoman Empire.
ALLIED POWERS: Belgium, France, Great Britain (plus the countries of the British Empire, including Canada, Australia, and New Zealand), Greece, Italy, Japan, Montenegro, Portugal, Romania, Russia, Serbia, and the United States.
The following countries also declared war on one or more of the Central Powers: Brazil, China, Costa Rica, Cuba, Guatemala, Haiti, Honduras, Liberia, Nicaragua, San Marino, and Siam (now Thailand).

bert I, king of the Belgians. Citing his nation's neutrality, which had been guaranteed in a treaty signed by all the great powers, Albert ordered his small army to resist any invader. On August 4, 1914, German cavalry crossed the Belgian border near Liège, and Belgian soldiers opened fire on them.

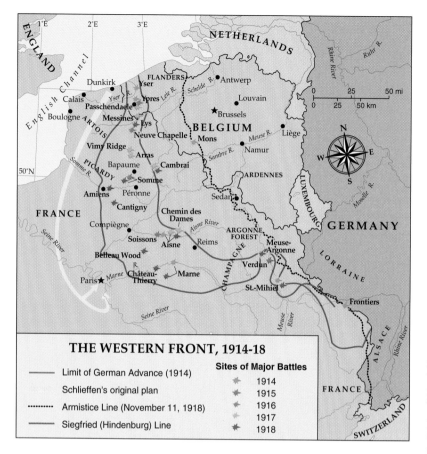

THE WESTERN FRONT, 1914-18

Sites of Major Battles
—— Limit of German Advance (1914)
—— Schlieffen's original plan
······ Armistice Line (November 11, 1918)
—— Siegfried (Hindenburg) Line
✳ 1914
✳ 1915
✳ 1916
✳ 1917
✳ 1918

The bright uniforms of the French offered easy targets for enemy marksmen.

French army officers employed military tactics as old-fashioned as their uniforms. Even the capable French commander in chief, General Joseph Joffre, whose men called him Papa, did not understand that a few men in trenches behind machine guns could wipe out an infantry charge. Joffre and his countrymen had to learn 20th-century methods of warfare through bitter and costly lessons on the battlefield.

The Schlieffen Plan. In 1905, General Alfred von Schlieffen, chief of the German general staff, had drawn up a master plan to be used in case of war with France. The Schlieffen Plan called for powerful German armies to attack France through Belgium, swing wide toward the English Channel and then south toward Paris, trapping the French armies in a huge semicircle. Von Schlieffen predicted that, if his plan was followed exactly, France would be defeated in six weeks. A quick victory was absolutely necessary, for what Germany dreaded most was a long, two-front war, with France in the west and Russia in the east.

Von Schlieffen died before his theories could be tested. His successor as chief of the general staff was General Helmuth von Moltke. General von Moltke altered the Schlieffen Plan slightly. He sent three divisions to guard Germany's eastern frontier against the Russians, thus weakening the force sent against France. This, plus the heroic stand of the Belgians and the stubborn resistance of the French and British, fatally delayed the German advance.

▶ **THE WESTERN FRONT, 1914**

From the beginning, the plans of the French army, known as Plan 17, called for an offensive to recapture the lost provinces of Alsace and Lorraine. As the Germans

The British government informed Germany that unless all German troops were withdrawn from Belgium by midnight, August 4, England would go to war in defense of Belgian neutrality. When the German government ignored this ultimatum, King George V signed the order declaring war. British foreign minister Sir Edward Grey sadly noted: "The lamps are going out all over Europe; we shall not see them lit again in our lifetime."

Grey's somber prediction did not dampen the patriotic enthusiasm that swept Europe. Before the month ended, Japan had entered the war on the side of the Allies (France, Great Britain, and Russia).

But in spite of all the cheering and enthusiasm, only Germany was prepared to fight a modern war. The Germans had the best-trained and best-equipped, as well as the strongest, army in Europe. German divisions were adequately supplied with machine guns and heavy artillery. German soldiers wore inconspicuous gray field uniforms, in sharp contrast to the French, who in 1914 still wore their 1871-style red trousers and blue jackets.

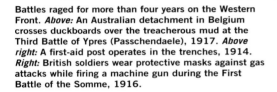

Battles raged for more than four years on the Western Front. *Above:* An Australian detachment in Belgium crosses duckboards over the treacherous mud at the Third Battle of Ypres (Passchendaele), 1917. *Above right:* A first-aid post operates in the trenches, 1914. *Right:* British soldiers wear protective masks against gas attacks while firing a machine gun during the First Battle of the Somme, 1916.

struck at Liège and Namur in Belgium, two vital strongholds blocking the road south, General Joffre began an attack on Alsace-Lorraine.

The Belgians fought so stubbornly that the Germans were held up at Liège until August 16 and outside Namur for another week. This ended German hopes for conquering France in six weeks. Meanwhile, French and German troops were engaged in a series of bloody clashes known as the Battle of the Frontiers. The French suffered more than 300,000 casualties as they hurled themselves against German machine guns to win small and short-lived gains in Alsace.

Meanwhile, the Germans had broken through the Belgian defenses at Liège. On August 20 they entered Brussels, the Belgian capital, and swept on toward France's northern border. Not until August 21, however, did General Joffre start rushing troops to check the oncoming enemy. Until then he had failed to see the seriousness of the German drive through Belgium.

Mons. Also marching to meet the Germans was the British Expeditionary Force (B.E.F.) of about 150,000 men, under Field Marshal Sir John French. These men included most of England's small regular (nonvolunteer) army. On August 23, near Mons, Belgium, 30,000 men of the B.E.F. ran head on into some 90,000 troops of the German First Army. Although greatly outnumbered, the British troops inflicted heavy losses on the Germans. But the British finally were driven back by sheer weight of numbers, and the Germans swept on irresistibly to the Marne River, outside Paris. As the French government fled to the city of Bordeaux, General Joffre ordered a last-ditch stand at the Marne.

The Miracle at the Marne. On September 5 the crucial Battle of the Marne began. It lasted a week, and at one point the situation grew so critical for the French that reinforce-

Consult the Index to find more information in *The New Book of Knowledge* about the following people associated with the Allied Powers of World War I: generals FERDINAND FOCH, JOHN J. PERSHING, and HENRI PHILIPPE PÉTAIN; Sergeant ALVIN YORK; prime ministers HERBERT HENRY ASQUITH, GEORGES CLEMENCEAU, and DAVID LLOYD GEORGE; kings and emperors ALBERT I, GEORGE V, and NICHOLAS II; U.S. president WOODROW WILSON; and Soviet revolutionary leader VLADIMIR ILICH LENIN.

Aleksei Brusilov

Aleksei Alekseyevich Brusilov (1853–1926), born in Tiflis, in the Russian province of Georgia, served as commander (1915–16) of the Russian Southwestern Front during World War I. Brusilov achieved a spectacular breakthrough against Austro-German forces. The Brusilov Offensive (June-September 1916) shattered the Austrian army, but the enormous number of Russian casualties also weakened the government of Czar Nicholas II. Later, as Supreme Russian commander, Brusilov sustained wounds in the Bolshevik Revolution of 1917, but in 1920 he helped Soviet forces against Poland and continued to work with the Red Army until his retirement in 1924. His memoirs, *A Soldier's Notebook, 1914–1918*, were published in English in 1930.

Edith Cavell

Edith Louisa Cavell (1865–1915), born in Norfolk, England, was the head nurse stationed at a Red Cross hospital in Brussels, Belgium, during World War I. From November 1914 through July 1915, she sheltered fugitive British, French, and Belgian soldiers and helped approximately 200 of them escape to the Dutch border. Discovered by the Germans, Cavell was condemned to death by a court-martial and executed by a firing squad. She quickly became a martyr of the Allied cause.

Douglas Haig, 1st Earl Haig (1861–1928), born in Edinburgh, Scotland, gained early military experience as a cavalry officer in the Sudan (1898), South Africa (1899–1902), and India (1903–06). At the start of World War I, he served as a corps com-

mander, then was promoted to commander of the First Army. In December 1915 he succeeded Sir John French as commander in chief of the British Expeditionary Forces on the Western Front, a position he held until the end of the war. Haig's attrition strategy— of conducting massive assaults on the German lines— resulted in few tangible gains, and at the cost of hundreds of thousands of lives. Although criticized by Prime Minister David Lloyd George for wasting manpower, Haig retained the confidence of most of his fellow generals. After the war, as president of the British Legion, he instituted Poppy Day to raise funds for disabled soldiers.

Joseph Jacques Césaire ("Papa") Joffre (1852–1931), born in Rivesaltes, France, was a veteran of the Franco-

Left to right: Allied generals Petain, Joffre, Foch, Haig, and Pershing.

ments were sped to the front in taxicabs. German scouts could see the spire of the Eiffel Tower, only 14 miles (22.5 kilometers) away, but they came no closer to the French capital. The Germans were beaten back and retreated to the Aisne River. On September 14, General von Moltke was replaced by General Erich von Falkenhayn as chief of the German general staff.

Although their hopes for a swift victory in France were shattered, the Germans captured the Belgian port of Antwerp on October 9, after a long siege. When the city fell, the Belgian army escaped and fought on in the region of Flanders until the end of the war.

Ypres. In October and November, British and German troops fought a series of brutal battles around the Belgian town of Ypres (pronounced EEP-re). Ypres was vital to the Allies, for if the Germans succeeded in breaking through, they would be able to capture the French channel ports—Dunkirk, Calais, and Boulogne. But the British held firm, and the ports remained in Allied hands.

As 1914 drew to a close, the fighting in the West had reached a stalemate, with neither side able to dislodge the other. The Western Front was a maze of deep trenches and barbed wire that stretched 1,000 miles (1,600 kilometers). Casualties were staggering. The French had suffered approximately 854,000

Lord Kitchener

Horatio Herbert Kitchener, 1st Earl Kitchener of Khartoum (1850–1916), born in County Kerry, Ireland, was appointed Britain's Secretary for War at the outset of World War I. A veteran military commander and a former Viceroy of Egypt and the Sudan (1911–14), Kitchener was renowned for his organizational and administrative skills. Through his remarkable recruitment of army volunteers, "Kitchener's Army" was expanded from 20 to 70 divisions by 1916. But as head of industrial mobilization, Kitchener was blamed for the munitions shortage on the Western Front. While on a secret mission to Russia, he was killed when his cruiser struck a German mine in the North Sea.

T(homas) E(dward) Lawrence ("Lawrence of Arabia") (1888–1935), born in Wales, was working as an archaeologist in the Middle East when World War I broke out. In 1916, having served as a British intelligence officer in Cairo, he was sent to the Arabian Peninsula to support the local Arab leaders in their revolt against the Ottoman Turks and became an advisor to Emir Faisal (later King Faisal I of Iraq). Using guerrilla tactics, they pushed back the Turks by raiding the Damascus-Medina railroad and other Ottoman strongpoints. The Arabs succeeded in taking Damascus in October 1918. After the

T. E. Lawrence

war, Lawrence attended the Paris Peace Conference, then returned to Britain to advise the government on Arab affairs. His best-known publication, *The Seven Pillars of Wisdom* (1926), described his legendary wartime experiences.

Wilfred Owen (1893–1918), born in Shropshire, England, was among the most admired of the World War I poets. Owen's finest work was produced in the space of a year, during which he experienced battle almost daily. His last collection included the haunting *Dulce et Decorum Est* and *Anthem for Doomed Youth*. He was killed in action in France on November 4, 1918, just one week before the armistice.

Edward Vernon (Eddie) Rickenbacker (1890–1973), born in Columbus, Ohio, was the most successful American flying ace of World War I. Accepted as a fighter pilot in the U.S. Army Air Corps in March 1918, Rickenbacker served as commander of the 94th Aero Pursuit Squadron. He became a national hero after shooting down 22 enemy planes and 4 enemy balloons, for which he received the Medal of Honor. After the war, he served as president (1938–53) and chairman of the board (1954–63) of Eastern Airlines. His publications include *Fighting the Flying Circus* (1919), *Seven Came Through* (1943), and an autobiography, *Rickenbacker* (1967).

Prussian War (1870–71) and various colonial military campaigns. In 1911 he was named commander in chief of the French army. In September 1914, at the beginning of World War I, Joffre was hailed as the savior of France for halting the German advance on Paris at the First Battle of the Marne. But subsequent failures at Champagne and Artois in 1915, followed by the disastrous losses at Verdun and the Somme in 1916, forced his retirement from active command. Joffre was instead named Marshal of France and served in an advisory position until his retirement after the war.

men killed, wounded, and missing; the Germans about 677,000. Of the 150,000 men of the B.E.F., only half remained in action.

▶ THE EASTERN FRONT, 1914–15

On August 17, 1914, while the Germans were advancing through Belgium, 200,000 Russian troops invaded East Prussia. At the Battle of Tannenberg, a German force under generals Erich Ludendorff and Paul von Hindenburg completely routed the Russians. At the Battle of the Masurian Lakes, in early September, the Germans won a second stunning victory against the Russians. In little more than a month, more than 150,000 of the original Russian soldiers who had invaded East Prussia had been killed, wounded, or captured.

But the Russians had greater success against the Austro-Hungarian army. Many of the soldiers fighting for Emperor Francis Joseph were Slavs, and they deserted to join the Russians by the thousands. The Serbs also inflicted heavy losses on the Austrians in the early days of the war.

▶ THE OTTOMAN EMPIRE

In October 1914, the Ottoman (Turkish) Empire entered the war on the side of the Central Powers, headed by Germany and Austria-Hungary. This shut the Dardanelles–Black Sea shipping route to the Allies and

Consult the Index to find more information in *The New Book of Knowledge* about the following people associated with the Central Powers: emperors FRANCIS JOSEPH and WILLIAM II; general HELMUTH JOHANNES VON MOLTKE; and the accused spy MATA HARI.

Kemal Atatürk

Erich von Falkenhayn

Manfred von Richthofen

Kemal Atatürk (Mustafa Kemal) (1881–1938), born in Thessaloniki, Greece, was the most notable Ottoman general of World War I. He defeated the British at Gallipoli (1915) and later kept the Turkish army of Syria together during the British-assisted Arab Revolt. After the war, he organized a national army that eventually drove the Allied occupying forces from Turkey. In 1923 he secured the signing of the Treaty of Lausanne (1923), which established an independent Republic of Turkey. In appreciation, his people bestowed on him the name Atatürk, meaning Father of the Turks. As the founder and first president of Turkey (1923–38), Atatürk instituted many democratic reforms, including an elected parliament.

Erich Georg Anton Sebastian von Falkenhayn (1861–1922), born in Burg Belchau, Prussia, succeeded Helmuth Johannes Ludwig von Moltke as chief of the German general staff following the Germans' defeat at the Battle of the Marne (1914). Von Falkenhayn adopted the attrition strategy of ceaseless bombardment and focused his armies on the Western Front. He opposed the plans of Generals Paul von Hindenburg and Erich Ludendorff for an offensive against Russia but was overruled by Emperor William II. In 1916, to break the stalemate in the west, von Falkenhayn planned a major assault on Verdun. But after six months he failed to achieve a victory and was dismissed from the general staff. He later commanded forces in Romania, Palestine, and Lithuania.

Paul Ludwig Hans Anton von Beneckendorff und von Hindenburg (1847–1934), born in Posen, Prussia, was a veteran officer and member of the general staff from 1877. Called out of retirement when World War I began, he won spectacular victories over the Russians at the battles of Tannenberg and the Masurian Lakes (1914) and was promoted to field marshal. Further victories in 1915 drove the Russians from Lithuania, Poland, and Galicia. In 1916, von Hindenburg succeeded von Falkenhayn as chief of the general staff, serving for the remainder of the war. In 1925 he won election as president of the fledgling Weimar Republic. In 1933, under pressure from the Nazi Party, he appointed Adolf Hitler chancellor. Hitler assumed all power when von Hindenburg died the following year.

Erich Friedrich Wilhelm Ludendorff (1865–1937), born in Kruszewina, Prussia, distinguished himself in the opening days of World War I by capturing the Belgian fortress-city of Liège. He was thereupon called to assist von Hindenburg on the Eastern Front, where they were hailed as heroes for their victories over the Russians. In 1916, Emperor William II appointed Ludendorff deputy chief of staff but to share equal responsibility with von Hindenburg for operations. In 1917, Ludendorff planned the successful offensive against the Italians at Caporetto and also approved the policy of unrestricted submarine warfare, which brought the United States into the war against Ger-

many. After the war, he became associated with Hitler's Nazi Party.

Manfred Freiherr von Richthofen (1892–1918), born in Breslau, Prussia, was an aviator and Germany's leading World War I fighter pilot. Early in the war, he served in the cavalry and then in the infantry. But in 1916 he signed on as a combat pilot. Eventually he became squadron leader of a group called Richthofen's Flying Circus. Nicknamed the Red Baron because of his red Fokker triplane, Richthofen was credited with shooting down 80 Allied planes, making him the most accomplished flying ace of the war. He was killed when his plane crashed near Amiens, France, in April 1918.

Alfred Peter Friedrich von Tirpitz (1849–1930) was born in Brandenburg, Prussia. He entered the Prussian Navy in 1865 and became a torpedo expert. In 1892, as chief of staff to the chief of the naval high command, he convinced his superiors, including Emperor William II, of the need for German naval expansion, which touched off an Anglo-German naval armaments race. As head of the Imperial Naval Office (from 1897) and grand admiral (from 1911), he skillfully built a battleship fleet second only to that of Great Britain. Disagreements with other German officials during World War I caused him to resign his office in 1916. From 1924 to 1928 he represented an extreme right-wing party in the Reichstag (legislature).

virtually cut off Russia from important sources of supplies. To aid the Russians and at the same time to bring pressure against Turkey, Britain's First Lord of the Admiralty Winston Churchill conceived a daring plan: a combined French and British naval attack to force a passage through the Turkish-held Dardanelles Strait. This would enable the Allies to capture Constantinople (now Istanbul), the capital of Turkey, and open the way to the Russian Black Sea port of Odessa. The first plan failed, however, when a number of Allied warships were sunk by mines and the attack was halted.

British war artist James McBey paid tribute to the 1917 Allied desert campaigns in Palestine in his *The Camel Corps: A Night March to Beersheba.*

Gallipoli. A second attempt by the Allies to win control of the vital strait was made in the spring of 1915. Hundreds of thousands of troops made up mostly of British and ANZAC (Australian and New Zealand Army Corps) were landed on the Gallipoli Peninsula of Turkey. But because of Allied mismanagement and strong Turkish resistance, the campaign proved a total failure and cost the British alone more than 200,000 casualties.

Elsewhere in the Middle East. In 1914, the Turks ruled a large area of the Middle East, including Palestine, Mesopotamia (modern Iraq), and Syria. The British, aided by Arabs seeking independence from the Ottoman Turks, launched a number of campaigns in the Middle East between 1914 and 1917, especially in Mesopotamia and Palestine. In 1917, British troops captured Baghdad and Jerusalem.

▶ THE BALKANS AND ITALY

In 1915, Bulgaria and Italy entered the war. The Bulgarians joined the Central Powers, while Italy, in spite of its earlier treaty with Germany and Austria-Hungary, sided with the Allies. The Italians engaged the Austrians in many bloody, indecisive battles that ranged back and forth between northern Italy and Austria. The Bulgarian army, reinforced by German and Austrian troops, finally defeated Serbia.

View from a German U-boat as it hits its target. Germany declared unrestricted submarine warfare on February 1, 1917. The United States entered the war two months later.

In 1916, Romania entered the war on the side of the Allies. But the Romanian army was quickly demolished by the Germans, who occupied Bucharest in December 1916. Greece also joined the Allies in 1916.

▶ THE WAR IN THE COLONIES

As soon as the fighting began in Europe, the Allies launched attacks against Germany's overseas possessions. In Africa, Allied troops took over the German colonies of Togoland (now part of Ghana and Togo), Cameroons (now part of Nigeria and Cameroon), German South West Africa (now Namibia), and German East Africa (now part of Tanzania). In China, Japanese and British soldiers captured the German colony of Kiaochow. And in the Pacific, Japanese, Australian, and New Zealand forces occupied the German-held islands of Western Samoa and the Marshalls, Carolines, and Marianas.

▶ THE WAR AT SEA

From the outset of the war the British Royal Navy played a key role in the Allied strategy. The powerful British fleet blockaded the ports of the Central Powers and swept Germany's merchant shipping from the seas. But the Germans set up a counterblockade of the British Isles. German U-boats (submarines) prowled beneath the seas, inflicting heavy losses on Allied shipping. Besides submarines, the Germans relied on raiders—fast,

heavily armed cruisers that roved the seas and preyed on merchant ships. Since Great Britain depended on its merchant marine to transport much of its food, the Germans hoped to thus starve the British into submission.

In May 1915, a German U-boat torpedoed the British passenger liner *Lusitania* off the coast of Ireland. Among the 1,198 passengers killed were 124 Americans. The sinking of the *Lusitania* caused an outcry in the United States. President Woodrow Wilson, who had denounced both the British and German blockades as violations of international law, sent strong notes of protest to the German government. The Germans argued that the British ship had been carrying arms and ammunition. But, anxious to keep the United States neutral, they agreed not to sink passenger ships without warning.

Since the beginning of the war, the entire world had waited for the inevitable clash between the German and British navies. Near the end of 1914 two sea battles were fought off the coast of South America. Near Coronel, Chile, a German squadron of five cruisers defeated a British squadron of four ships, sinking two of them. A second British squadron avenged this defeat by destroying most of the German force in a battle at the Falkland Islands, off Argentina.

But it was not until 1916 that the expected clash between the main German and British fleets finally took place.

The Battle of Jutland. On May 31, 1916, the British Grand Fleet and the German High Seas Fleet met in battle off Jutland, Denmark. A total of 252 warships, including 64 battleships and battle cruisers, took part in this greatest naval battle in history. The fight raged for hours, until the following morning. The result, however, was indecisive with both sides claiming victory. The larger British fleet had lost

The Imperial German Embassy warns passengers of the *Lusitania* of the perils of traveling on a British enemy ship during wartime.

more men and heavier ships. But the German fleet fled to its North Sea bases and never again came out to challenge Great Britain's mastery of the oceans. Instead, Germany later resumed a policy of unrestricted submarine warfare.

▶ THE WAR IN THE AIR

While battles were raging on land and sea, a new kind of war was being waged in the air. The airplane played an increasingly important role in World War I. From the crude and flimsy aircraft of 1914 they developed into the fast, well-built pursuit planes and bombers of 1918, which were forerunners of modern airpower. With the fighting on land bogged down in mud and the war at sea more often than not confined to submarines, what was left of the glamour of war was reserved for the aviators. Such fliers as Baron Manfred von Richthofen and Max Immelman of Germany, Georges Guynemer and René Fonck of France, William A. (Billy) Bishop of Canada, Albert Ball of England, and Eddie Rickenbacker of the United States became legends.

Meanwhile, far from the front lines, civilians felt the horror of air warfare as giant German zeppelins (airships) bombed both Paris and London.

▶ THE WESTERN FRONT, 1915–16

The fighting in the West during 1915 was marked by futile offensives by both sides and by the first use of poison gas. On April 22, 1915, during the Second Battle of Ypres, observers reported clouds of yellowish-green

The Sopwith FI Camel, introduced to the British Royal Air Force (R.A.F.) in 1917, was the most successful fighter plane of the war.

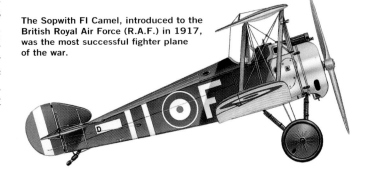

The German Albatross D-III, a single-engine biplane, was popular before the superior Fokker D-VII was introduced in 1918.

fog drifting toward the French and British lines. The Germans had released thousands of cylinders of deadly chlorine gas. The gas attack left gaping holes in the Allied defenses as soldiers fled choking and gasping from the fumes. But the Germans themselves were so wary of the deadly gas that they hesitated to occupy the undefended Allied positions. Meanwhile, British troops quickly plugged the gap, and a few days later gas masks were issued to the frontline troops.

Through the spring and summer of 1915 the Allies launched one attack after another against the German positions at a terrible cost of life. But despite all the fighting, the front lines did not move as much as 3 miles (5 kilometers) in any direction.

Verdun. On February 21, 1916, the Germans opened a devastating attack against the French fortress city of Verdun. Verdun's defenders, commanded by General Henri-Philippe Pétain, fought stubbornly for every piece of ground. The German attacks continued without letup until mid-July. When the German troops had spent their strength, the French counterattacked, and the enemy was driven back. The defense of Verdun became a symbol of French resistance. But it had cost France approximately 500,000 casualties to hold the city. The Germans lost almost as many men.

British soldiers, blinded by poison gas during the Lys Offensive, shuffle forward to receive medical attention, 1918.

After Verdun the top leadership in the French and German armies was shaken up. General Joffre was removed from command and replaced by General Robert Nivelle. General von Falkenhayn was succeeded by General Paul von Hindenburg.

The Somme. During the fighting at Verdun, the British, hoping to draw German pressure away from the French, opened a drive along the Somme River. General Sir Douglas Haig, who had replaced Field Marshal French as commander of the B.E.F., directed the attack, which lasted from July 1 until November 1916. The Somme Offensive cost the British hundreds of thousands of casualties (in one day alone they lost 60,000 men) but accomplished little.

At the height of the battle, the British uncovered a weapon that revolutionized ground warfare—the armored tank. On September 15, 1916, 49 of the crude, clumsy machines lumbered toward the German trenches, tearing through barbed wire, climbing obstacles, and crushing trenches. The Germans fled in terror, opening a wide gap in their lines. But there were too few tanks and not enough reserves to achieve a breakthrough.

By mid-October, rains made further fighting on the Somme impossible, as both armies were bogged down in mud. In the words of an English journalist, "The terrain was . . . a wasteland pockmarked with ditches and holes . . . a desolate stretch of truncated trees and wrecked villages where no dog barked, no bird sang, and the breeze was tainted by death . . . ."

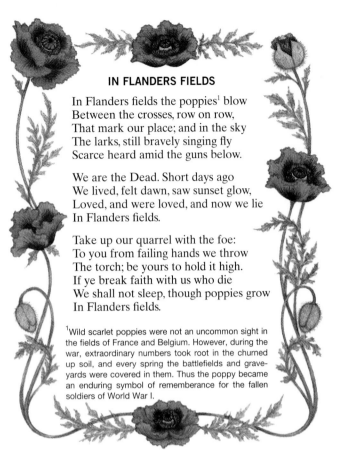

IN FLANDERS FIELDS

In Flanders fields the poppies[1] blow
Between the crosses, row on row,
That mark our place; and in the sky
The larks, still bravely singing fly
Scarce heard amid the guns below.

We are the Dead. Short days ago
We lived, felt dawn, saw sunset glow,
Loved, and were loved, and now we lie
In Flanders fields.

Take up our quarrel with the foe:
To you from failing hands we throw
The torch; be yours to hold it high.
If ye break faith with us who die
We shall not sleep, though poppies grow
In Flanders fields.

[1]Wild scarlet poppies were not an uncommon sight in the fields of France and Belgium. However, during the war, extraordinary numbers took root in the churned up soil, and every spring the battlefields and graveyards were covered in them. Thus the poppy became an enduring symbol of remembrance for the fallen soldiers of World War I.

Many profoundly moving poems were written during World War I. The most notable of the so-called War Poets were Rupert Brooke, Wilfred Owen, Isaac Rosenberg, Edward Thomas, and Siegfried Sassoon. However, one poem that particularly caught the public's attention, "In Flanders Fields" (1915), was written by a Canadian physician and poet Major John McCrae while he was stationed at a hospital in Boulogne, France. A collection of McCrae's poems was published after his death in 1918.

▶ THE EASTERN FRONT, 1916

In June 1916, the Russians, under General Aleksei Brusilov, unleashed a grand offensive against the Austrian province of Galicia. The Austrians, taken by surprise, fell back. As the Russians rolled on toward the heart of Austria, German reinforcements were quickly rushed east. The Brusilov Offensive finally was stopped, as much by lack of supplies as by the enemy. By September 1916, the Russians had suffered more than 1 million casualties. The failure of this last great offensive left the Russian army and people completely demoralized.

▶ THE WESTERN FRONT, 1917

The year 1917 was a dark one for the Allies. Repeated attempts to break through the German positions in northern France failed. The only success was the capture of the strategically important peak at Vimy Ridge by Canadian troops under the command of General J. H. G. Byng. At the Second Battle of the Aisne, parts of the French army, unable to bear the slaughter, mutinied. General Pétain, the hero of Verdun, replaced General Nivelle. The French soldiers trusted and respected Pétain, and he was able to end the mutiny.

The British, meanwhile, had unsuccessfully attempted a breakthrough at Arras. Then, in July, they attacked through knee-deep mud in the Third Battle of Ypres (also known as the Battle of Passchendaele). The fighting, which raged for months, proved completely futile and cost the British approximately 300,000 casualties.

The British were more successful at the Battle of Cambrai, in which they used some 400 tanks to push the Germans back several miles. But the exhausted troops could not follow up their advantage.

▶ THE RUSSIAN REVOLUTION

In March 1917, the Russians overthrew Czar Nicholas II and set up a democratic government under Alexander Kerensky. But

A Canadian infantryman thumbs his nose at his German adversaries while going "over the top" at Vimy Ridge, April 1917.

the Kerensky government itself was overthrown in November 1917, by the Bolshevik Communists, led by Vladimir Ilich Lenin. The Czar and his entire family later were executed by the Bolsheviks. In December 1917, Lenin took Russia out of the war, and the Soviets signed the peace treaty of Brest-Litovsk the following March.

▶ THE UNITED STATES ENTERS THE WAR

On April 2, 1917, after months of unavailing protest against Germany's unrestricted U-boat warfare, President Wilson called upon Congress for a declaration of war against the Central Powers. War was declared against Germany on April 6 and against Austria-Hungary eight months later on December 7.

In June 1917, units of the United States 1st Division, plus Marine brigades, landed in France. This was the vanguard of the American Expeditionary Force (A.E.F.), led by General John J. Pershing. The A.E.F. eventually numbered more than 2 million men.

Wilson's Fourteen Points. In January 1918, President Wilson set forth his famous Fourteen Points peace program. These included self-determination for the multiethnic peoples ruled by Austria-Hungary and Turkey, and independence for Poland—then divided between Russia, Austria-Hungary, and Germany. Wilson also called for the formation of an association, or league, of nations to prevent future wars.

▶ THE WAR REACHES A CLIMAX, 1918

By 1918 both the Allies and the Central Powers were in a critical situation. The French and British armies had been drained by more than three years of bitter fighting. In addition, several Allied divisions had to be sent to bolster the faltering Italian army, which had suffered a disastrous defeat in the Battle of Caporetto late in 1917. The position of the Central Powers was equally serious. Germany no longer could expect aid from its allies. Bulgaria and Turkey were almost defeated, and Austria was weakening rapidly. If the Central Powers were to win, Germany would have to do it alone.

With Russia out of the war, the Germans were able to transfer more than 1 million seasoned troops from the Eastern Front for a great spring offensive in the West. General Erich Ludendorff was chosen to lead the of-

In 1917, a Bolshevik Communist revolution in Russia forced the Russians to abandon World War I as civil war raged at home.

fensive. Ludendorff had to act quickly, before the arrival of more American troops increased the odds against Germany.

The Last German Offensive. On March 21, 1918, Ludendorff began the Second Battle of the Somme. The larger German forces overwhelmed the British and drove them back 14 miles (22.5 kilometers) in four days—the largest single gain of the war since 1914. The brutal fighting lasted until April 5, when the Germans were stopped just short of their goal, the city of Amiens.

Ludendorff did not pause long. On April 9 he launched an attack on the French channel ports. The action—known as the Lys Offensive—raged furiously for several weeks. Once again the Germans were halted within sight of their goal, but at a terrible price. The British suffered more than 350,000 casualties, and the Germans almost as many.

For a time, all was quiet. But on May 27, Ludendorff opened another attack, against the French on the Aisne River. Within a week, the Germans had reached the Marne at Château-Thierry—only 50 miles (80 kilometers) from Paris. Marshal Ferdinand Foch, newly appointed commander in chief of the Allied armies, searched desperately for reinforcements. The only troops available were inexperienced Americans. Foch had no choice. With Pershing's cooperation, Foch ordered the Americans up to the front. The Americans not only checked the Germans but also chased them back across the Marne in desperate fighting around Château-Thierry and Belleau Wood.

In 1919 the victorious Allied leaders met at Versailles, outside Paris. *From left to right:* British prime minister David Lloyd George, French premier Georges Clemenceau, Italian premier Vittorio Orlando, and U.S. president Woodrow Wilson.

Ludendorff tried once again. On July 15 he opened the Second Battle of the Marne. But heavy losses had taken their toll of the once-invincible German army, and the drive was quickly smothered. Soon the Germans were in full retreat.

Still, the fighting remained desperate. In some places, such as the Argonne Forest and the Ardennes, it matched the fiercest of the war. But German strength was waning. Every day the number of captured German soldiers grew larger.

The Collapse of the Central Powers. The battered Central Powers could not expect to hold out much longer. On September 30, 1918, Bulgaria surrendered. Turkey signed an armistice on October 30, 1918, after Allied forces captured Damascus and Beirut. Following uprisings by Czechs, Hungarians, and Yugoslavs within the empire, Austria signed an armistice on November 3. Germany was now alone.

But within a week of the Austrian surrender, the iron German discipline finally broke.

A mutiny broke out in the navy. Mobs rioted against the kaiser in Berlin and other cities. In Munich a Communist revolution flared. The kaiser held out stubbornly until November 9, when he abdicated. The following day he fled to Holland. Germany was declared a republic, with socialist Friedrich Ebert as president. Representatives of the new German government met with Allied leaders in a railroad car at Compiègne. There, on November 11, 1918, an armistice was signed. The war was over.

▶ THE PARIS PEACE CONFERENCE

In January 1919, the Allied Powers held a conference in Paris to arrange peace terms. Part of President Wilson's peace program already had been accomplished. Czechoslovakia and Yugoslavia had declared their independence, and a new state of Poland had been created. Finland, Estonia, Latvia, and Lithuania—once part of the Russian Empire—also became independent.

The Treaty of Versailles. On June 28, 1919, the Allies signed a peace treaty—the Treaty of Versailles—with Germany. Separate peace treaties later were signed with Austria, Hungary, Bulgaria, and Turkey. All the treaties together are known as the Peace of Paris.

THE HUMAN COST OF WORLD WAR I

	Total Force Mobilized	Military Battle Deaths (approx. % of total troops)	Military Wounded	Civilian Deaths
Allies				
France	8,410,000	1,357,800 (16%)	4,266,000	40,000
British Empire	8,904,467	908,371 (10%)	2,090,212	30,633
Russia	12,000,000	1,700,000 (14%)	4,950,000	2,000,000
Italy	5,615,000	462,391 (8%)	953,886	N/A
United States	4,355,000	50,585 (1%)	205,690	N/A
Belgium	267,000	13,715 (5%)	44,686	30,000
Serbia	707,343	45,000 (6%)	133,148	650,000
Montenegro	50,000	3,000 (6%)	10,000	N/A
Romania	750,000	335,706 (45%)	120,000	275,000
Greece	230,000	5,000 (2%)	21,000	132,000
Portugal	100,000	7,222 (7%)	13,751	N/A
Japan	800,000	300 (less than 1%)	907	N/A
Total:	42,188,810	4,889,090 (12%)	12,809,280	3,157,633
Central Powers				
Germany	11,000,000	1,808,546 (16%)	4,247,143	760,000
Austria-Hungary	7,800,000	922,500 (12%)	3,620,000	300,000
Turkey	2,850,000	325,000 (11%)	400,000	2,150,000
Bulgaria	1,200,000	75,844 (6%)	152,390	275,000
Total:	22,850,000	3,131,889 (14%)	8,419,533	3,485,000
Grand total:	65,038,810	8,020,979 (12%)	21,228,813	6,642,633

Source: Trevor N. Dupuy, *The Harper Encyclopedia of Military History*, Fourth Edition

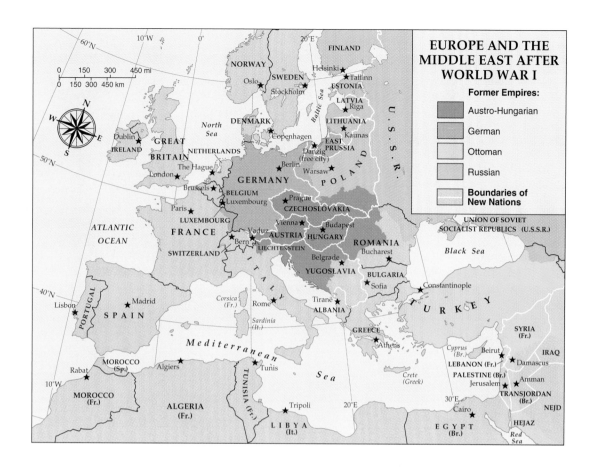

The Versailles Treaty established the League of Nations—the kind of international organization President Wilson had envisioned. To Wilson's great disappointment, however, the United States Senate later refused to ratify the treaty, thus preventing American participation in the League.

Under the terms of the peace treaty, Germany was forced to accept sole responsibility for the war. Germany lost all its colonies and some of its own territory. Alsace-Lorraine was returned to France, and part of the Rhineland was placed under Allied occupation. The German army was limited to 100,000 men and the German navy to a small number of warships. Germany was required to pay reparations of billions of dollars, and much of the country's economic resources were turned over to the Allies.

Other Treaties. World War I destroyed the Austro-Hungarian Empire. In 1919, Austria signed the Treaty of Saint-Germain, recognizing the independence of Czechoslovakia, Poland, Yugoslavia, and Hungary. Other portions of the empire went to Italy and Romania. Among the other Central Powers, Hungary signed the Treaty of Trianon (1919); Bulgaria the Treaty of Neuilly (1919); and Turkey the Treaty of Sèvres (1920).

▶ **THE RESULTS OF THE WAR**

World War I left the nations of Europe, both victors and vanquished, exhausted and impoverished. France and Great Britain owed tremendous war debts. The United States turned away from participation in European affairs to a policy of isolationism. Germany, already close to economic collapse, was burdened with war reparations that it could not pay. In desperation, the Germans would turn to a man who promised to save Germany and avenge its defeat—Adolf Hitler. Within twenty years, a new and more terrible world war would darken Europe.

IRVING WERSTEIN
Author, *1914–1918: World War I*

WORLD WAR II

On September 1, 1939, German armed forces suddenly invaded Poland. Two days later France and Great Britain declared war against Germany, and Europe was swept into a second world war.

World War II was the most wide-spread and the most destructive war in history. It lasted from 1939 to 1945 and eventually involved all the Great Powers and most of the smaller nations of the world. The chief antagonists were Germany,

Italy, and Japan—the Axis Powers—on one side and the United States, Great Britain, the Soviet Union, France, and China—the Allied Powers—on the other. The battlefields of the war stretched from Europe to North Africa and from the islands of the Pacific Ocean to southeastern Asia.

The cost of the war—in death, suffering, and destruction of property—was enormous. Battle deaths alone amounted to about 15 million. Perhaps twice as many civilians lost their lives, and millions more were made homeless. Many of the cities of Europe and Asia were partly or completely destroyed by aerial bombing, and vast areas of land were devastated.

What caused such a terrible conflict? To understand that, it is necessary to go back to 1918, to the end of World War I.

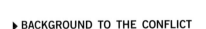

▶ **BACKGROUND TO THE CONFLICT**

World War I had been called the "war to end all wars." When the armistice (truce) was signed on November 11, 1918, people throughout the world believed that lasting peace was at hand. Yet it lasted a mere twenty years. Among the primary reasons for

352

Clockwise from top of opposite page: German dictator Adolf Hitler at a Nazi rally, 1933. An American illustration shows German troops marching to their deaths during the Soviets' successful defense of Stalingrad, 1942. The USS *Shaw* explodes during the Japanese bombing of Pearl Harbor, 1941. Soviet leader Josef Stalin, U.S. president Franklin D. Roosevelt, and British prime minister Winston Churchill meet in Tehran, 1943. U.S. Marines raise the American flag after capturing Iwo Jima, 1945. Magdeburg was one of many German cities destroyed by Allied air raids. The Tuskegee Airmen were among the approximately 1 million African Americans who served in World War II. The Allied supreme commander Dwight D. Eisenhower (left) with British field marshal Bernard Law Montgomery (right), 1944. Survivors in a Nazi concentration camp, 1945.

the short-lived peace were the grave economic and political consequences of the peace treaties signed in 1919 and the subsequent rise to power of several brutal and aggressive dictators.

The Paris Peace Conference

Early in 1919, the leaders of the victorious Allied Powers of World War I met in Paris, France, to negotiate the terms of peace. The decisions were dominated by the United

States, Great Britain, France, and Italy. Neither Germany nor any of the other defeated nations—Austria, Hungary, Bulgaria, and Turkey—were present. The victors simply decided on the terms that the vanquished countries would have to accept. The harshness of the Treaty of Versailles with Germany, and of the various other treaties signed with defeated nations, created severe political and economic frustration in the heart of Europe and crippled the economy of its most productive country, Germany. (For more information, see the article WORLD WAR I on pages 336–51.)

The Rise of the Dictators

The Treaty of Versailles also established the League of Nations, which officially came into being in 1920, although the United States did not join it. Like today's United Nations, the League tried to settle quarrels between nations that might threaten the peace. But the sudden rise of powerful dictators in Italy, Germany, and Japan helped doom the League to failure.

Mussolini and Fascism in Italy. In 1919, Benito Mussolini, a former soldier and professional agitator, founded Italy's Fascist Party, whose members supported an extreme nationalist and anti-Communist program. Using violence to gain their ends, the Fascists won control of the Italian government in the early 1920's, and soon Mussolini's power became absolute.

Hitler and Nazism in Germany. Meanwhile in Germany, another former soldier named Adolf Hitler joined up with other Germans stung by their nation's defeat in World War I. Hitler's group became the nucleus of the National Socialist German Workers' Party, more commonly known as the Nazi Party.

German children hail Nazi dictator Adolf Hitler in 1938. That same year he annexed Austria, occupied part of Czechoslovakia, and signed the Munich Pact, which the British thought would assure "peace for our time."

During the 1920's, the Nazi Party grew in strength, fed by economic despair and bitterness toward the victor nations. In 1932, German president Paul von Hindenburg was persuaded to name Hitler chancellor (prime minister) of Germany. Hitler used his position to crush all opposition to his Nazi Party. In 1933 he suspended the constitution and declared martial law. Thereafter he ruled by decree. With the death of Hindenburg in 1934, Hitler consolidated his power as dictator and aggressively began rebuilding Germany's navy and air force.

The Militarists in Japan. Meanwhile in Japan, the military expanded its influence over the government, and by 1931, the policies of Japan's military leaders had taken hold of the nation. Among them was Tojo Hideki, Japan's future prime minister.

The Dictators Turn to Aggression

Beginning in 1931, Japan, followed by Italy and Germany, embarked on a course of aggression. Their actions were condemned by the League of Nations, but little was done to stop them. In 1935, Germany and Japan quit the League of Nations, and Italy walked out two years later. In 1936, Germany and Italy formed an alliance called the Rome-Berlin Axis, named for their centers of government. In 1940, Japan joined them to form the Rome-Berlin-Tokyo Axis.

Japan Invades China. In 1931 the Japanese army invaded and occupied the Chinese province of Manchuria, which was rich in economic resources. Japanese armies later ad-

vanced deeper into China, and by 1938 they controlled most of eastern China. When the League of Nations failed to halt Japan's unprovoked conquest, the dictators in Europe took notice.

Italy Attacks Ethiopia. In Europe it was Mussolini who struck first. In 1935 he sent troops to crush Ethiopia, a nation in eastern Africa. The League declared Italy an aggressor and voted to impose economic sanctions (restrictions) against it. But France and Great Britain, reluctant to alienate Italy, failed to enforce them.

Germany Extends Its Domination. In 1936, as Mussolini was completing his conquest of Ethiopia, Hitler sent German troops into the Rhineland, which had been made a demilitarized zone under the Treaty of Versailles. France and Great Britain could have stopped this direct violation of the treaty but were reluctant to risk another war. They convinced themselves that if Hitler's demands were met, he would be appeased (satisfied).

Meanwhile, Nazis in Austria were agitating for *Anschluss*, or union, with Germany. In March 1938, Hitler—confident from his success in occupying the Rhineland—sent German troops into Austria and took control of its government.

Hitler's next target was the Sudetenland, a border region of Czechoslovakia populated largely by Germans. Great Britain and

Japanese troops celebrate their victories over China in 1937. By the following year, Japan controlled most of eastern China and all of that country's major cities.

France pressured the Czechs to make concessions to Hitler in order to avert a war. British prime minister Neville Chamberlain twice flew to Germany to try to work out an agreement with Hitler. The Soviet Union stayed silent.

The Munich Pact. In September 1938, Chamberlain and French premier Édouard Daladier met with Hitler and Mussolini in Munich, Germany. Chamberlain and Daladier agreed that Czechoslovakia would have to yield some of its territory to appease Hitler. The Czechs were not permitted a voice in the meeting.

Chamberlain flew back to England, announcing that the Munich Pact had assured "peace for our time." But in March 1939, German troops marched into Prague, the Czech capital, and took what was left of Czechoslovakia. Three weeks later, Italy invaded and conquered the eastern European nation of Albania.

The Spanish Civil War. Meanwhile, in July 1936, Nationalists in the Spanish army launched a rebellion to overthrow Spain's liberal republican government. Germany and Italy promptly came to the aid of the Nationalist rebels, while the Soviet Union supported the Republicans. After three years of bloody civil war, the Nationalists toppled the Republicans, and a Fascist-style government was set up under General Francisco Franco.

The End of Appeasement. In the years following World War I, France and Great Britain had been slow to rebuild their armed forces. But the takeover of Czechoslovakia and the attack on Albania awakened them to the full extent of the danger. They dropped

THE LEND-LEASE ACT

When World War II began, the United States was bound by the Neutrality Act of 1939, which allowed the United States to sell war materials to warring nations, but for cash only—a condition that resulted from the enormous amount of unpaid debt following World War I. But in March 1941, in response to numerous appeals from Britain for economic aid, the U.S. Congress passed the Lend-Lease Act authorizing President Franklin D. Roosevelt to transfer, lease, or lend "any defense article" to "the government of any country whose defense the President deems vital to the defense of the United States." Repayment terms were left to the president's discretion. By Aug. 21, 1945, when the program was terminated, almost $50 billion in Lend-Lease aid had been shipped to Great Britain, the Soviet Union, China, and other Allied nations.

the policy of appeasement and desperately sought to establish an alliance with Poland, Romania, Greece, Turkey, and other nations to form a barrier to German expansion.

Demands on Poland. In March 1939, Hitler turned his attention to Poland. He demanded that the city of Danzig (now Gdańsk), also populated by many Germans, be returned to Germany. He also demanded that Germany be given a corridor, or strip of territory, through Poland to connect the German state of East Prussia with the rest of Germany, which had been separated by the Treaty of Versailles. Poland refused Hitler's demands.

The Russo-German Nonaggression Pact. In late August came the startling news that Germany and the Soviet Union, supposedly sworn enemies, had signed a nonaggression pact. This left Poland at the mercy of Hitler. The world had less than a week of peace remaining as Hitler and his generals made their final preparations for the invasion of Poland.

▶ THE WAR BEGINS, SEPTEMBER 1939

In the morning hours of September 1, 1939, German air and land forces struck swiftly at Poland. The German Luftwaffe (air force) quickly destroyed the small Polish air force before its planes could get off the ground. German planes then bombed Polish cities and destroyed railroads, bridges, and communication lines. At the same time, the German armies, spearheaded by panzer (armored) divisions, advanced into Poland.

Within 17 days, all of Poland's major defenses had been either destroyed or captured. Warsaw, the capital, held out until September 27 and was subjected to ruthless bombing.

On September 17, with victory already assured, Soviet troops invaded Poland from the east. Defeated Poland was then divided between its two conquerors. Then the Soviets forced the Baltic states—Latvia, Lithuania, and Estonia—to sign treaties allowing Soviet military bases in their territory.

The Russo-Finnish War. The Russians made similar demands on Finland. When the Finns refused, the Russians invaded Finland in November 1939. For more than three months, the Finns repelled the Russian attacks. But finally, overwhelmed by sheer numbers, they were compelled to surrender and to give up part of their territory. For its aggression against Finland, the Soviet Union was expelled from the League of Nations.

▶ THE WAR IN WESTERN EUROPE, 1940

Meanwhile in western Europe, only occasional border clashes and dramatic naval action broke the calm. This period, which lasted through the winter of 1939–40, was called the phony war, or *sitzkrieg* ("sitting war"). The French felt secure behind their Maginot Line—a chain of massive fortifications along their frontier with Germany. The British, although they had an army in France, counted on their large navy for safety. Few people outside Germany expected a large-scale war.

The Invasion of Norway and Denmark. The quiet was broken on April 9, 1940, when German troops made surprise landings at the main ports of Norway and Denmark. Denmark, virtually defenseless, was overrun in a single day. Within two days Norway's capital, Oslo, was in German hands. A group of Nor-

The September 1, 1939, edition of *The New York Times* reports the German invasion of Poland, the event that launched World War II in Europe.

wegian Nazi sympathizers aided the German conquest. The most infamous was Vidkun Quisling, who later became head of the German-controlled puppet government of occupied Norway. The name "Quisling" soon became a synonym for "traitor."

The Norwegian government fled to central Norway, where the army continued to fight. British and French troops were sent to support them but were forced to withdraw. On April 30, Norway's King Haakon VII and his ministers escaped to London and established a Norwegian government-in-exile.

The Low Countries. On May 10, Germany invaded the Low Countries—Belgium, the Netherlands, and Luxembourg. (That same

INSET

WORLD WAR II IN
EUROPE AND NORTH
AFRICA (1939–45)

- Allied Powers
- Axis Powers
- Territories Occupied by
  Axis Powers
- Neutral Nations
- ✶ Sites of Major Battles

day, Winston Churchill succeeded Neville Chamberlain as prime minister of Great Britain.) The suddenness of the attack on the Netherlands, together with the bombing of the main Dutch cities, stunned the defenders. Queen Wilhelmina of the Netherlands and members of her government fled to England on May 13. The Dutch army surrendered the next day.

Neighboring Belgium was attacked at the same time. German parachute and glider troops seized key Belgian positions, opening the way for infantry and panzer forces. As British and French troops moved northward to meet this threat, the main German forces struck through Luxembourg into the Ardennes, a partly forested region of southeastern Belgium.

The Invasion of France. The Ardennes were thought to be too mountainous for tanks and were therefore poorly defended. In three days (by May 13) the Germans had crossed

THE HOLOCAUST

From 1933 to 1945, German leader Adolf Hitler and the Nazi Party launched a campaign to exterminate all the people they considered "unworthy of life." The systematic murder of civilians generally focused on Jews and political opponents, but the Nazis also targeted homosexuals and the disabled. It is estimated that 6 million people were executed in the Holocaust, most of them Jews who had been placed in German concentration "work" camps.

the Meuse River into France at Sedan. With one stroke, France's defenses at the Maginot Line had been encircled.

By May 20, panzer forces had reached Abbeville, 12 miles (19 kilometers) from the English Channel. In Belgium, the Germans continued their advance with only occasional resistance. The Belgian Army, cut off from the British and the French, was surrendered by Belgium's King Leopold III on May 28.

Dunkirk. Meanwhile in France, General Lord Gort, commander of the British Expeditionary Force (B.E.F.), prepared to evacuate his men. The British made a fighting retreat to Dunkirk, the only channel port still open to them. With the aid of the Royal Navy and countless civilian ships, more than 300,000 British, French, and Belgian troops were ferried to England.

The Fall of France. On June 10, Italy entered the war on Germany's side and attacked southern France. On June 14, German forces occupied Paris, the French government having fled south to the city of Bordeaux. France's premier, Paul Reynaud, resigned, and Marshal Henri-Philippe Pétain, a military hero of World War I, was called to

succeed him. Pétain asked Hitler for peace terms, and on June 21 an armistice was signed in a railway coach at Compiègne—in the exact place the Germans had surrendered on November 11, 1918.

The Vichy Government. Three-fifths of France was placed under German occupation. The rest of the country was allowed to retain independence in name, although it in fact became an Axis satellite, dominated by Germany. A new French government, under Marshal Pétain and Pierre Laval, was established at Vichy, a resort town in central France. All fighting within France had ceased at the armistice. But outside France there still remained a symbol of resistance in General Charles de Gaulle. He escaped to England and tried to rally the people of France to the Free French movement.

Meanwhile, Japan took advantage of France's collapse to enter French Indochina (now Cambodia, Laos, and Vietnam). The United States, alarmed at the turn of events, began taking measures for the defense of the Western Hemisphere.

The Battle of Britain. Great Britain now faced the threat of invasion, and except for the Royal Air Force (R.A.F.) it was virtually defenseless.

Hitler had expected Great Britain to make peace after the fall of France, and his invasion plans, known as Operation Sea Lion, were vague. Field Marshal Hermann Goering, head of the German Luftwaffe, proposed an air attack against England to soften its defenses and prepare the way for the invasion. His main idea was to draw the R.A.F. into battle and destroy it.

Triumphant German troops in Paris parade down the Avenue Champs-Élysées and through the Arc de Triomphe during the German occupation of France, June 14, 1940.

Above: British prime minister Winston Churchill (center) visits Coventry Cathedral, one of the many places destroyed by German bombs between September 1940 and May 1941.
Above right: English children seek safety in a trench during the Blitz.

Beginning in July 1940, the Luftwaffe hammered England for three months. In London alone, more than 12,000 civilians were killed by bombs in what became known as the Blitz. But eventually the Luftwaffe was beaten back by the R.A.F. fighter squadrons, and Operation Sea Lion was abandoned on October 30.

▶ THE CONFLICT EXPANDS, 1940–41

Africa. While England was under air attack by Germany, Italy launched a campaign against the British in Africa. Mussolini's main objective was Egypt, key to the defense of the eastern Mediterranean and, with the Suez Canal, Great Britain's economic lifeline to the East. The Italians scored easy victories in British Somaliland (now Somalia), the Sudan, and Kenya.

In September 1940, Italian forces invaded Egypt, but a British counterattack threw them back with heavy losses. By February 1941, the British were driving deep into Italian-held Libya. Hitler was now compelled to send aid to his faltering ally in North Africa. He chose one of his ablest and most resourceful generals, Erwin Rommel, to lead the Afrika Korps, the German desert force. Rommel struck swiftly in Libya, and the British were driven back into Egypt.

The Balkans. In October 1940, Mussolini declared war on Greece, and Italian troops invaded that country from Albania. Mussolini had expected an easy victory against the poorly armed Greeks. Instead, his forces suffered bloody defeats in the fierce mountain fighting.

In spite of this setback, Axis domination of the Balkans in eastern Europe steadily increased, and in November, Hungary and Romania joined the Axis partnership. Bulgaria became a member of the Axis early in 1941.

On April 6, 1941, German troops in Bulgaria struck at Yugoslavia and Greece. Within three weeks both countries had been conquered. British troops in Greece were evacuated. A second blow followed quickly. With lightning speed, German airborne troops captured the Greek island of Crete.

The Middle East. The British were also being threatened in the Middle East. German agents in Iraq had fanned Arab resentment of Great Britain into open revolt. At the same time, Germany was seeking bases in Syria, controlled by France since World War I, and the Vichy Government was giving in to its demands. British armored forces drove into Iraq to crush the rebellion. Then they attacked and occupied Syria. But the success of this operation was overshad-

Consult the Index to find more information in *The New Book of Knowledge* about the following people associated with the Allied Powers: U.S. generals Dwight D. Eisenhower, Omar N. Bradley, Douglas MacArthur, George C. Marshall, George S. Patton, Benjamin O. Davis, and Matthew B. Ridgway; British field marshal Bernard Law Montgomery; U.S. presidents Franklin Delano Roosevelt and Harry S. Truman; British prime ministers Neville Chamberlain and Sir Winston Churchill; British Labour Party leader Clement Attlee; Soviet dictator Joseph Stalin; French leader and general Charles De Gaulle; Chinese leader and general Chiang Kai-shek; Yugoslav leader Marshal Tito; Ethiopian emperor Haile Selassie I; Holocaust victim Anne Frank; and humanitarians Oskar Schindler and Raoul Wallenberg.

Henry Harley "Hap" Arnold (1886–1950), born in Gladwyne, Pa., was commanding general of the U.S. Army Air Forces (USAAF) during World War II.

"Hap" Arnold

Mark Clark

Arnold joined the newly formed aviation section of the Army in 1911. He became chief of the Army Air Corps in 1938, and even before the United States' entry into World War II, he began building up American air power. By the end of the war, the USAAF had 80,000 planes and more than 2 million personnel. In 1944, Arnold became general of the army, and in 1949, two years after the U.S. Air Force became an independent military service, he became its first five-star general.

Mark Wayne Clark (1896–1984), born in Madison Barracks, N.Y., commanded the U.S. Fifth Army, which helped defeat the Germans in North Africa (1943) and Italy (1944). A graduate of the U.S. Military Academy (1917), Clark was made chief of staff of U.S. ground forces in Europe in 1942. After the North African and Italian campaigns, he was named Allied commander in Italy. He was promoted to full general in 1945. Clark later served as commander (1952–53) of the United Nations forces during the Korean War (1950–53).

James Harold Doolittle (1896–1993), born in Alameda, Calif., was a U.S. airman who led the first World War II bombing raid over Tokyo, Japan, on April 18, 1942. A pilot instructor in World War I, he became the first man to fly across North America within 24 hours in 1922 and was subsequently known as a racing pilot. Although his famous Tokyo raid was small in scale and did limited damage to the Japanese war effort, its boldness—at a time when U.S. military forces in the Pacific were largely on the defensive—buoyed American morale tremendously. Later in World War II, Lt. Col. Doolittle commanded U.S. air forces elsewhere in the Pacific as well as in North Africa and Europe.

---

owed by an event of far greater importance. On June 22, 1941, Germany invaded the Soviet Union.

The Invasion of the Soviet Union. The German invasion of the Soviet Union, known as Plan Barbarossa, had been scheduled for mid-May 1941, but it was delayed until June. Eventually, the lost month would prove fatal to the whole plan.

Germany attacked on June 22, confident that victory would be won by summer's end. On the fourth day of the campaign, Finland joined Germany. At first, all went according to plan. The northern invasion group, attacking toward Leningrad (now St. Petersburg), swept forward at an astonishing rate. By June 30, the cities of Riga, Grodno (now Hrodna), Brest-Litovsk (now Brest), and Minsk had fallen to the Germans.

In the first six weeks perhaps 500,000 Russian soldiers were captured. Still, the results were not decisive. The main Russian forces stood their ground long enough to slow down the German advance; then they retreated, trading land for time.

Meanwhile, additional German troops advanced toward Moscow. But the Russian capital was still 200 miles (320 kilometers) away when the Germans were forced to halt. They had far outrun their reinforcements and supply lines. In the south, a third invasion group was attacking toward Kiev, the capital of the Ukraine. Kiev was captured, and 600,000 Russian troops were taken prisoner. By then it was late September.

In October, with the harsh northern winter approaching, the Germans resumed their march toward Moscow. They reached Leningrad by early November. Then, immobilized by the weather, they began a siege on Leningrad that was to last two years. For ten weeks the Germans stormed toward Moscow as the great tank battles raged. By the time they reached the outskirts of the capital, their forces were critically depleted. The Russians counterattacked, forcing the Germans to retreat. Thus ended Hitler's bid for Moscow. He had overreached himself at last.

The end of 1941 also saw a German defeat in North Africa, where the Afrika Korps was

William Frederick ("Bull") Halsey (1882–1959), born in Elizabeth, N.J., played a leading role in defeating the Japanese in the Pacific theater. A graduate of the U.S. Naval Academy (1904), Halsey was commander of the U.S. Pacific Fleet's aircraft carriers when Japan attacked Pearl Harbor on December 7, 1941. He directed naval operations in the Solomon Islands campaign (1942) and later became commander of the South Pacific theater. In 1944 Halsey, who reported to Admiral Chester Nimitz, commanded the U.S. Third Fleet, which supported the Allied invasion of the Philippines and defeated the Japanese in the Battle of Leyte Gulf. He became a fleet (five-star) admiral in 1945.

Louis Francis Albert Victor Nicholas Mountbatten (1900–79), born in Windsor, England, served as supreme Allied commander (1943–46) in Southeast Asia and planned the campaign that drove Japanese forces out of Burma. In 1947, Mountbatten became viceroy of India. After supervising the end of British rule there, he served as governor-general of

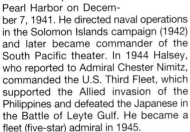
Chester Nimitz

India (1947–48), Britain's first sea lord (1955–59), and chief of the defense staff (1959–67). He was killed in 1979 when Irish Republican Army terrorists fighting for Northern Ireland's independence from Britain blew up his fishing boat.

Chester William Nimitz (1885–1966), born in Fredericksburg, Tex., orchestrated the United States' defeat of the Japanese navy in the Pacific. A graduate of the U.S. Naval Academy (1905), he served with the U.S. submarine force in World War I and thereafter rose steadily in rank. Ten days after the Japanese attack on Pearl Harbor, he was promoted to admiral and named commander in chief of the U.S. Pacific Fleet. Nimitz directed the U.S. victories at the Battle of Midway (1942) and the battles of the Philippine Sea and Leyte Gulf (1944). He was promoted to fleet (five-star) admiral in 1944. In 1945 he was a signer of the Japanese document of surrender. From 1945 to 1947 he was chief of naval operations.

Georgy Konstantinovich Zhukov (1896–1974), born in Strelkovka (near Moscow),

Russia, was named chief of staff of the Soviet Army in 1941. After Germany invaded the Soviet Union in June 1941, he organized the defense of Leningrad (now St. Petersburg) and Moscow. In 1942 he planned the counteroffensive that drove the Germans from the gates of Stalingrad (now Volgograd). Promoted to the rank of marshal in 1943, Zhukov led the Soviet invasion of Germany in 1944 and the capture of Berlin in 1945.

Georgy Zhukov

---

thrown back into Libya with heavy casualties. For the first time, Rommel—known as the Desert Fox—was soundly beaten.

The Battle of the Atlantic. When World War II began, the British navy began a blockade of Germany in an attempt to close its ports to all sea commerce. After the Germans conquered France in 1940, they turned their attention to establishing a counterblockade against Great Britain, hoping to starve the British into surrender. Germany's small navy concentrated most of its efforts in the Atlantic Ocean, seeking to cut Great Britain's vital trade with the United States and Canada. The blockade war unto itself became known as the Battle of the Atlantic.

The most serious threat to the Atlantic lifeline was the German U-boat, or submarine. Shipping losses from U-boat attacks increased steadily, until it seemed as if the British might lose the Battle of the Atlantic. But in time the U-boat menace was overcome, partly through the use of more strongly armed convoys and with the help of the United States.

In September 1940, the United States loaned Great Britain 50 outmoded but serviceable destroyers in exchange for leases on British bases in the Western Hemisphere. In the spring of 1941, United States air and sea forces began patrolling the Atlantic. That summer, American troops arrived in Iceland to relieve the British. Thus the United States, though still a neutral nation, became directly committed to supporting Great Britain.

▶ THE UNITED STATES ENTERS THE WAR, DECEMBER 1941

The Crisis with Japan. Throughout 1941, U.S. forces in the Pacific Ocean had remained in a state of alert, for war with Japan was threatening. Relations between the two countries had declined steadily since 1940, when President Roosevelt had halted the sale of scrap iron and steel to the Japanese.

In the summer of 1941, Japanese forces moved into southern Indochina. President Roosevelt responded by ordering all Japanese assets in the United States frozen and warned Japan against any further advances

Consult the Index to find more information in *The New Book of Knowledge* about the following people associated with the Axis Powers: Italian dictator Benito Mussolini; German dictator Adolf Hitler; and German general Erwin Rommel.

Karl Doenitz (or Dönitz) (1891–1980), born in Grünau (near Berlin), Germany, was commander in chief of the German navy from 1943 to the end of World War II. Prior to that, he directed the German U-boat campaign against Allied shipping. On May 1, 1945, the day after Adolf Hitler committed suicide, Doenitz became chancellor of Nazi Germany. On May 7, he surrendered to the

Karl Doenitz

Allies, thus ending the war in Europe. Found guilty at the Nuremberg war crimes trials, Doenitz was sentenced to ten years in prison. He was released in 1956. His autobiography, *Memoirs*, was published in 1959.

Hermann Goering

Hermann Wilhelm Goering (or Göring) (1893–1946), born in Rosenheim, Germany, was second only to Adolf Hitler in the Nazi regime. A highly decorated World War I pilot, Goering joined the Nazi Party in 1922. In 1928 he was elected to the Reichstag, the German legislature, and became its president in 1932. After Hitler became chancellor of Germany in 1933, Goering became enormously powerful. He organized the Gestapo (secret state police). He built up the German Luftwaffe (air

force) and was its commander. And he directed the growth of Germany's war industry. Hitler promoted him to the rank of field marshal in 1938 and reich marshal in 1940. Captured by the Allies in 1945, he was tried for war crimes at the Nuremberg Trials and condemned to death. He swallowed poison and died before he could be executed.

Tojo Hideki (1884–1948), born in Tokyo, was Japan's most influential militarist and the person most responsible for initiating World War II in the Pacific. In the late 1930's he was chief of staff of the Japanese army that conquered and occupied Manchuria in northern China. And as minister of war in 1940, he brought his country into the Axis alliance with Nazi Germany and Fascist Italy. After becoming prime minister in October 1941, Tojo forced the French to allow Japan to occupy French Indochina. He also ordered the December 7 attack against the U.S. Pacific Fleet at Pearl Harbor. His initial successes made him extremely popular, but in 1944, after Allied forces had turned the tide against Japan, Tojo resigned. Arrested in 1945, he was found guilty of war crimes and hanged.

Emperor Hirohito (1901–89), born in Tokyo, succeeded his father Yoshihito as emperor of Japan in 1926. Although Hiro-

---

into Southeast Asia. Japanese military leaders had already decided that their country had no chance of winning a war with the United States unless the American fleet in Hawaiian waters was destroyed. Accomplishing this became their primary objective.

The Attack on Pearl Harbor. On the morning of Sunday, December 7, 1941—while most of the personnel at the U.S. naval base at Pearl Harbor, Hawaii, slept—a Japanese naval task force approached undetected through the darkness. From the decks of its aircraft carriers, a wave of 189 fighters and bombers took off, then split into two attack groups. One group

bombed the air bases at Hickam Field, Wheeler Field, and Ford Island. The other attacked the American fleet. A second wave of Japanese planes was sent against the islands, then a third.

American planes at Ford Island Naval Station were among the first targets of the Japanese bombs that fell on Pearl Harbor, December 7, 1941.

hito opposed Japan's drift toward war in the 1930's, he was apparently powerless to restrain the military. Only in the Japanese decision to surrender to the Allies in 1945 was he able to influence wartime policy. The new Japanese constitution of 1947 stripped him of all but ceremonial powers, although he remained a symbol of the Japanese state. Hirohito was the first emperor to disavow the traditional claim to imperial divinity. Upon his death in 1989, he was succeeded as emperor by his son, Crown Prince Akihito.

Alfred Jodl (1890–1946), born in Würzburg, Germany, was chief of the Operations Staff of the German Armed Forces High Command. Jodl had become acquainted with Hitler in the early 1920's, and was given this important post shortly before World War II began. During the war, Jodl drafted directives for German military operations under Hitler's supervi-

Tojo Hideki

Alfred Jodl

sion. After Hitler's suicide, Jodl signed the unconditional surrender of the German armed forces at Reims, France, on May 7, 1945, ending the war in Europe. He was found guilty of war crimes at the Nuremberg Trials and hanged.

Henri Philippe Pétain (1856–1951), born at Cauchy-à-la-Tour, France, headed France's Vichy government during World War II. Pétain attained the rank of general during World War I, becoming a hero at the Battle of Verdun in 1916. Rapidly promoted, Pétain became marshal of France in 1918 and held high military and government posts between the world wars. After the Nazi invasion of Paris in 1940, the French government fled to Bordeaux, and Pétain became premier. He concluded an armistice with Germany and became chief of state in the Vichy government of unoccupied France. Although at first he was nominally independent, he found it increasingly difficult to resist German demands. After the liberation of France, the French brought Pétain to trial, where he claimed he had acted only to save France from total destruction. The one-time national hero died in prison in 1951 while serving a life sentence.

Isoroku Yamamoto (1884–1943), born in Nagaoka, Japan, was the admiral who planned and directed the December 7, 1941, Japanese attack on the U.S. Pacific Fleet at Pearl Harbor, Hawaii. The attack crippled the fleet and brought the United States into the war, but it failed to find and destroy the fleet's aircraft carriers. This failure would eventually lead to the defeat of Yamamoto's fleet at the Battle of Midway (1942) and other naval engagements in the Pacific. Yamamoto was killed when his plane was shot down in the South Pacific in April 1943.

In less than two hours, the Japanese destroyed the heart of the U.S. Pacific fleet. Five of its eight battleships were sunk or crippled. In all, 19 warships were hit and 2,086 U.S. naval officers and seamen killed. The U.S. Army lost 237 men, the use of its air bases, and a large part of its air force.

On December 8, the United States declared war against Japan. Three days later, Germany and Italy declared war against the United States. Eventually, the majority of Latin American countries joined the war against the Axis Powers, although only Brazil and Mexico sent troops to assist the Allies.

Japan's Aims. The Japanese plan of conquest called for the takeover of the British colonies of Malaya (now part of Malaysia) and Burma and the islands of Java, Sumatra, and Borneo in the Netherlands East Indies. To hold these conquests, it would also be necessary for Japan to gain control of the Philippines, New Guinea, the Celebes, and the Solomon Islands.

▶ **THE WAR IN THE PACIFIC, 1941–42**

Simultaneously with the Pearl Harbor assault, Japan struck elsewhere. Guam and Wake Island, key American bases in the Central Pacific, were quickly taken by Japanese landing forces. And the Philippines were bombed in preparation for invasion.

Invasion of the Philippines. On December 10, Japanese troops landed on the northern island of Luzon in the Philippines. They quickly captured Manila, the capital, along with much of the rest of the island, then pushed into Mindanao and other southern islands. The outnumbered defending forces, composed of American and Filipino troops under the command of U.S. general Douglas MacArthur, withdrew into a defensive position on the Bataan Peninsula, where they held their ground for three months. A U.S. garrison continued to hold the nearby island fortress of Corregidor.

In February 1942, MacArthur was ordered to Australia to take a new command. He was

U.S. Army nurses arrive at an Allied military base in New Guinea, 1942. During World War II, about 400,000 American women served in uniform. Among those, nearly 60,000 served in the Army Nurse Corps.

From their own bases in the Caroline and Marshall islands in the Central Pacific, Japanese troops had advanced into the Gilbert Islands (now Kiribati), the Solomon Islands, and the Bismarck Archipelago northeast of Australia. Next they landed in New Britain and New Ireland. In March 1942, they began their attempt to conquer New Guinea.

succeeded in the Philippines by Lieutenant General Jonathan M. Wainwright.

Malaya, Hong Kong, and Singapore. Malaya and Hong Kong were also attacked by Japan on December 7, bringing about a declaration of war by Great Britain. The island port of Hong Kong, one of Great Britain's richest possessions, had no air protection and was defended by only six infantry battalions. The Japanese invaded the island on December 18–19, and on Christmas Day, 1941, the garrison surrendered. Then, through supposedly impassable jungle, the Japanese swept through Malaya from the north, and on February 15, 1942, they took Singapore.

Meanwhile, the British had suffered an equally disastrous loss at sea. Two of their major warships, *Repulse* and *Prince of Wales*, were sunk by Japanese aircraft as they retreated from Singapore. Japan now had naval superiority in the Indian Ocean as well as in the western Pacific.

The Conquest of Burma. The Japanese had already occupied Bangkok, the capital of Thailand, and forced that country to sign a treaty of alliance with them. From Thailand, Japanese troops invaded lower Burma. By late May 1942, all of Burma had been occupied, at which time India came under threat.

The Netherlands East Indies. While advancing into the Philippines, Malaya, and Burma, the Japanese were also conquering the islands of the Netherlands East Indies. At the Battle of the Java Sea, an Allied squadron was destroyed by a Japanese naval force. Java fell soon after, and Sumatra fell in the summer of 1942.

THE INTERNMENT OF JAPANESE AMERICANS

On February 19, 1942, a little more than two months after the Japanese bombed Pearl Harbor, U.S. president Franklin D. Roosevelt authorized the forcible removal of approximately 112,000 persons of Japanese ancestry from their homes in the Pacific Coast states to "relocation," or detention, camps. Although about two-thirds of those detained were American citizens, the government feared they would sabotage the American war effort, even though many Japanese American soldiers were fighting bravely in the U.S. Armed Forces. The camps were closed when the war ended in 1945. In 1988 continuing controversy over the forced internments led Congress to pass a bill awarding each of the surviving internees $20,000.

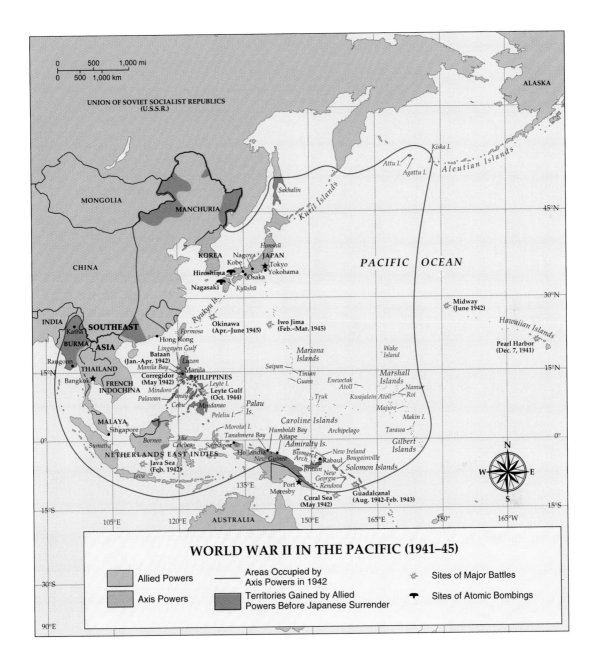

The Fall of the Philippines. At the same time, the Japanese landed in the Philippines to deliver the final blow. In April, Allied defenses in Bataan were smashed, and their forces surrendered. The forced retreat of Allied prisoners to captivity was so severe it became known as the Bataan Death March. Corregidor held out until May, when it, too, was forced to surrender. For six months the Allies had suffered defeat after defeat.

The Tide Begins to Turn. In mid-April 1942, American bombers under the command of Lieutenant Colonel James H. Doolittle took off from the aircraft carrier *Hornet* and bombed Tokyo and other Japanese cities. The raid forced the Japanese to divert fighter planes and anti-aircraft units from the battle areas to guard the home front. It also provided a welcome morale boost to the Allies, especially the Americans.

Battle of the Coral Sea. In May, American and Japanese naval forces clashed in the Coral Sea northeast of Australia. Both sides sustained heavy damage, but the battle was a

Dive bombers launched from the U.S. aircraft carriers *Hornet*, *Enterprise*, and *Yorktown* fly over the coral reefs of Midway Island, June 1942.

The South Pacific. The victory at Midway ended the Japanese threat to Hawaii and Australia. The Allies' next task was to break through the huge triangle of Japanese-held island bases in the South Pacific. In August 1942, U.S. Marines landed at Guadalcanal in the Solomon Islands. Six months of savage fighting followed. The main battles were fought at sea and in the air. U.S. naval and air superiority decided the outcome.

Meanwhile, the Japanese landed troops near Port Moresby, New Guinea. If Port Moresby fell, Australia once again would be open to invasion. A force of Australians and

victory for the United States. For the first time a major Japanese force had suffered crippling losses, and the United States won control of an area desired by the enemy.

Battle of Midway. On June 4, 1942, planes from four Japanese aircraft carriers attacked Midway Island. Torpedo planes and dive bombers from the nearby U.S. aircraft carriers *Hornet*, *Enterprise*, and *Yorktown* put all the Japanese carriers out of action, but at a heavy cost in planes. The next day, American Flying Fortress bombers from Hawaii joined in the attack, and the Japanese were soon in full retreat. Midway was one of the decisive battles of the war. Japan was never able to recover its losses, and the United States regained naval superiority in the Pacific.

At the same time as the Midway attack, Japanese troops attacked and occupied Kiska, Attu, and Agattu in Alaska's Aleutian Islands. This was the only part of North America directly invaded by the enemy during the war. But in the summer of 1943, American forces drove the Japanese out of the Aleutians.

WONDER QUESTION

Who were the Sullivan brothers?

In 1942, five brothers from Waterloo, Iowa—George, Francis, Joseph, Madison, and Albert Sullivan—enlisted in the U.S. Navy on condition they be allowed to serve together. All five were assigned to the USS *Juneau*, a light cruiser on patrol in the South Pacific. On November 13, 1942, during a naval battle for Guadalcanal Island, the Japanese torpedoed the *Juneau*, killing most of its crew, including the five brothers. Many memorials were later erected to the Sullivans, including a Navy destroyer that was named for them.

In the decades following the tragedy, it became widely believed that a Sullivan Law had been enacted to prevent the future possibility of family members perishing together in battle. But there is no basis to this myth, and no law has ever been passed to ensure the separate assignment of family members in wartime. The Military Selective Service Act does include a statute that ensures that no "sole surviving son" may be drafted, although he still may volunteer.

Americans, with strong air support, defeated the Japanese after months of jungle combat.

▶ DEVELOPMENTS IN NORTH AFRICA AND EUROPE, 1942–43

In January 1942, Rommel, recovering from his earlier defeat, struck again at the British in Libya, pushing them back 350 miles (560 kilometers). In May, he attacked again. As tank battles raged across the desert, the British Eighth Army was forced to retreat to El Alamein in Egypt.

The Battle of El Alamein. Two new British commanders had been appointed for North Africa. They were General Sir Harold Alexander, who took command of the theater (area of operation), and Lieutenant General Bernard Law Montgomery, who took command of the Eighth Army. On October 23, Montgomery attacked Rommel at El Alamein. After two weeks of bitter fighting, Rommel's forces had suffered a devastating defeat. By January 1943, they had retreated 1,400 miles (2,250 kilometers), having suffered 59,000 casualties and the loss of hundreds of tanks and guns. It was yet another of the war's decisive battles.

Operation Torch. Meanwhile, to divert some of Germany's strength from the Soviet Union, Allied leaders discussed opening a second front in the West. The American commanders favored an early invasion of western Europe, which the British opposed. Finally, a compromise was reached, calling for an invasion of French North Africa, known as Operation Torch.

On November 8, 1942, a joint British and American force under Lieutenant General Dwight D. Eisenhower landed at Algiers, Oran, Casablanca, and other points in French North Africa. After a brief and irregular resistance, the Vichy French forces went over to the Allies. The Germans then moved into the previously unoccupied portion of France and reinforced their troops in Tunisia.

The Raid on Dieppe. In the summer of 1942, Canadian and British troops made a landing at Dieppe on the northwestern coast of France. The attack was repelled with heavy losses, leading Hitler to believe that he had permanently discouraged the Allies from any large-scale invasion of western Europe.

Allied Attacks from the Air. In 1942, British and American air forces began a massive bombing campaign to destroy Germany's war industries. The steel centers of Essen, Cologne, and Düsseldorf were especially hard hit. But in spite of the terrible destruction, German war industries continued to produce steadily.

The Russian Front. Although the Russians had regained much territory and the German troops had suffered severely the previous winter, Hitler was still able to launch a powerful offensive in the spring of 1942. His target now was the Caucasus, an oil-rich

Below: A British cavalry unit attacks Italian troops in Egypt, 1940. *Right:* Following a series of Axis defeats in North Africa, German general Erwin Rommel was appointed to lead the Afrika Korps, a desert tank force.

mountainous region in southern Russia. A secondary objective was the city of Stalingrad (now Volgograd) on the Volga River. The Germans struck first on the Crimean Peninsula. The port of Sevastopol fell in July after a long siege, and the rest of the Crimea was taken soon after. In August, the Germans reached the foothills of the Caucasus.

The Battle of Stalingrad. Late in August, the Germans turned their attention to Stalingrad. German artillery soon reduced the city to rubble, but the Russians held out, and the siege wore on. In November the Russians counterattacked. The Germans were driven back and then encircled. Their situation was hopeless, but Hitler ordered his soldiers to fight to the last man. The Germans resisted until February 1943, when they at last surrendered, having lost more than 200,000 men. This defeat, the worst ever suffered by a German field army, became another major turning point in the war.

Final Victory in North Africa. Rommel's retreat was closely pursued by Montgomery's Eighth Army into southern Tunisia, where Montgomery came under Eisenhower's command. At the same time, the Germans in northern Tunisia faced the British First Army. In a surprise move, Rommel threw a strong tank force against the U.S. II Corps, breaking through their lines at the vital Kasserine Pass. Driven back by an American counterattack, he made another advance, this time against the British. But again he was driven back. On May 12, the Axis troops in North Africa surrendered.

The Invasion of Italy. The next problem facing the Allies was where to launch the long-awaited invasion of Europe. A decision was finally made to invade Italy.

In July 1943, British and American forces landed on Sicily, completing its occupation by mid-August. On July 25, Mussolini was forced to resign and was immediately imprisoned by the Italians. Six weeks later he was rescued by German troops and placed under protection in northern Italy.

On September 3, Allied forces invaded southern Italy, and the Italian government surrendered. However, the Germans had already rushed reinforcements to Italy, and the country now came under their control.

On September 9 the U.S. Fifth Army, commanded by Lieutenant General Mark W. Clark, landed at Salerno on Italy's southwestern coast. The Americans ran into bitter resistance, but the arrival of air and tank reinforcements saved the day. The Fifth Army soon joined forces with the British Eighth Army, which had advanced easily from the south. On October 1, they took Naples.

▶ DEVELOPMENTS IN THE PACIFIC, 1943–44

Allied Advances in the Pacific. After a year of almost continuous fighting, the Allies, under the command of General MacArthur, had advanced step by step in the Southwest Pacific. The Japanese were pushed back in eastern New Guinea, and the islands of Rendova, New Georgia, and Bougainville were occupied.

Late in 1943, the forces under Admiral Chester W. Nimitz began their offensive in the Central Pacific. Infantry forces landed at Makin Island, while Marines attacked Tarawa, the two main Japanese bases in the Gilbert Islands. Makin was occupied easily. But at Tarawa, in one of the bloodiest battles of the war, the Marines suffered 3,500 casualties before wiping out the Japanese.

Central Pacific. Late in January 1944, American forces struck at three key objectives in the Marshall Islands. Meanwhile, a U.S. battleship and aircraft carrier force continued westward to the Caroline Islands and raided the Japanese naval base of Truk. The next phase of attack was Saipan in the Marianas—only 1,500 miles (2,400 kilometers) from Tokyo.

George S. Patton, nicknamed Old Blood and Guts, was one of the U.S. Army's most successful generals. During the war he led tank forces in North Africa, Sicily, Normandy, Germany, and Czechoslovakia.

Left: American troops land at Anzio, Italy, in an effort to hasten the capture of Rome, January 1944. *Below:* Sacks of flour and other foodstuffs relieve the hungry populace following the liberation of Rome by the Allies, June 1944.

Southwest Pacific. Early in March 1944, the Americans invaded and captured the Admiralty Islands, which lay between Rabaul and Japanese-held Hollandia in New Guinea. Then MacArthur's forces in northeastern New Guinea pushed nearly 600 miles (1,000 kilometers) westward, occupying Aitape, Humboldt Bay, and Tanahmera Bay. This gave the Allies three air bases covering Hollandia and a new naval base.

In May, the Allies continued their advances along the New Guinea coast. In July, Sansapor in northwestern New Guinea was taken. MacArthur's forces had advanced about 1,300 miles (2,100 kilometers) and cut off 140,000 enemy troops. When the Allies took Morotai Island in September, they were near the Philippines. The Japanese position in the far west Pacific was now hopeless.

▶ **PROGRESS IN EUROPE, EARLY 1944**

Anzio. Allied progress northward through Italy had been slow, and the Allied military commanders wanted to push on to Rome as quickly as possible. The Anzio-Nettuno area, 30 miles (50 kilometers) south of Rome, was chosen for the assault. American and British troops began attacking on January 17, 1944. Five days later, a landing was made at Anzio and met little German resistance on the beaches. But in the meantime, the main Allied attack had been stopped by strong German opposition. This gave the Germans enough time to counterattack against the Anzio beachhead, which they soon hemmed in, complicating the Allied problem in Italy.

Cassino. There followed a series of costly Allied attacks on the town of Cassino, dominated by Monastery Hill. Heavy infantry assaults failed to take the hill. The air force then took over, and for two days in mid-February, bomber strength was massed against Monte Cassino. An Allied artillery bombardment followed. But when the Allied infantry attacked again, it was driven back by the Germans. The Allies decided to suspend their assault on Cassino.

Rome Falls. In March, Allied bombers began a systematic pounding of the German supply lines. By mid-May it was so difficult for the Germans to get supplies through that the front was threatened with collapse. They began to pull back on May 16. On the following day, British forces took Cassino, and on June 4, Allied troops entered Rome.

The Russian Front. Following a drive that forced the Germans to fall back behind the Dnieper River, the Russian offensive continued. The severe winter did not slow down the Russian troops. The German siege of Leningrad, which had lasted 2½ years, was finally lifted in January. By spring the Russians had reclaimed almost all of their own country and were pushing into the Balkans and Poland.

▶ THE INVASION OF NORMANDY

D Day. On June 6, 1944, American, British, and Canadian troops under the command of Eisenhower—now the supreme commander of the Allied expeditionary force—made a spectacular amphibious landing on Normandy's Cotentin Peninsula, in France. The far-reaching goal of this long-awaited invasion, code-named Plan Overlord, was to press eastward, overthrow Nazi Germany, and end the war in Europe.

For 60 days before the landing, Allied planes based in England bombed rail lines in France and Belgium. Then they struck at the bridges of northeastern France. Last, they attacked airfields within 130 miles (210 kilometers) of the prospective battle area.

On June 6, shortly after midnight, three airborne divisions—two American and one British—were dropped inland to seize river crossings and exits from the beaches, and to cut enemy communications.

In the early daylight, the Allied seaborne divisions hit the beaches along the southern and western shores of the bay of the Seine River. One American corps formed the center of the landing in the area east of the Vire Estuary (named Omaha Beach in the plan). The forefront of a second American corps landed on the beach of St. Martin de Varreville (named Utah Beach). The British and Canadians composed the left flank in the Bayeux-Caen area, landing on beaches named Gold, Juno, and Sword.

The Allies used a flotilla of more than 5,000 ships to transport the invasion forces and equipment across the English Channel. To move them from the convoy to the beaches in the face of enemy fire required an additional 5,000 landing craft. It was the largest amphibious operation in history.

The American landing at Utah Beach went smoothly from the beginning. British and Canadian forces also got ashore with little difficulty and were dug in by nightfall, when they came under attack.

WONDER QUESTION

What does "D day" mean?

The term "D day" refers to any day that is designated for the launch of a military operation. ("D" stands for the "day" of the offensive.) June 6, 1944—the day the Allies invaded Normandy, France, to begin the liberation of Europe—has itself become known as D Day simply because of the enormity of that specific operation.

But the attack at Omaha Beach, the pivot of the whole landing front, almost failed on the first day and remained imperiled for four days thereafter. The hills overlooking the beach had been strongly fortified by the Germans, and the Americans came under heavy fire. However, the situation began to improve as fresh American troops landed.

When the Allied landings began, the German commanders decided that they were only the first and weaker part of a two-pronged attack. So the German Fifteenth Army was held in place in the Strait of Dover, the narrowest section of the English Channel, for 30 days while the German commanders waited for the remainder of the Allied plan to unfold. Had the Germans used this force to attack the invaders, they could have made the Allies' problems even more difficult.

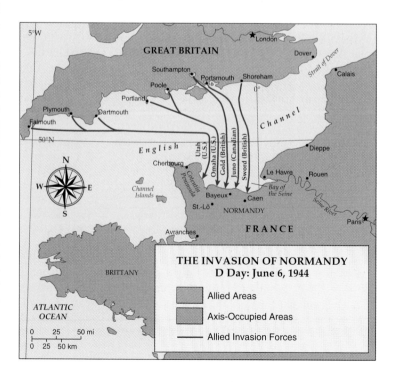

THE INVASION OF NORMANDY
D Day: June 6, 1944

Allied Areas

Axis-Occupied Areas

—— Allied Invasion Forces

The invasion of Normandy was the largest amphibious operation in history. *Right:* An American soldier struggles to get ashore on D Day, June 6, 1944. *Above:* Anti-aircraft balloons protect Allied supply ships from enemy fire at Omaha Beach, off the coast of France.

Conquest of Normandy. By about the eighth day after the invasion of Normandy, the Allied beachhead was secure. Allied troops had gone as far as 20 miles (32 kilometers) inland to Bayeux. Reinforcements and supplies were arriving on schedule. The Allied combat forces outnumbered the Germans in the Normandy area.

Having landed at Utah Beach, the Americans attacked across the Cotentin Peninsula. By June 18, after hard fighting, they isolated the port city of Cherbourg. On June 27, Cherbourg became the first major French port to be taken by the Americans. By that time, 1.5 million Allied troops had already landed on the Normandy beaches. Enough supplies were arriving to support a breakout of troops. But a major supply buildup, enough to assure the advance of Allied troops across France, had to wait until Cherbourg's harbor was cleared. The Germans had done their best to wreck it.

Meanwhile, on June 25, the British had begun a series of attacks along the eastern section of the beachhead, all of them directed toward the city of Caen. But it was not until July 19, after two full-scale assaults preceded by air bombardment, that the British took the city.

Pointing southward, the Americans tried a breakthrough along the road to Brittany. The Germans chose to make their stand at the town of St.-Lô. It became the bloodiest battle to date in the west. However, on July 18, St.-Lô fell to the Americans.

A week later came a major breakthrough. Supported by a gigantic Allied carpet bombing, the Americans tore through the German lines. Victory at St.-Lô ended the struggle for Normandy and lifted the pressure from the

General Charles de Gaulle, leader of the Free French movement and the symbol of French resistance, marches victoriously through Paris, August 26, 1944. The French capital had been liberated by Allied troops the previous day.

British at Caen. It also cleared the path for the American Third Army, under Lieutenant General George Patton, to pass through a narrow gap at Avranches, free Brittany, and swing northeastward on the Seine and outflank Paris on the south. On July 31 the British attacked southward from Caen and cut the road to Avranches.

Allied Advances. The Americans now advanced eastward toward Le Mans and Paris and swung around to the rear of the Germans. Six German divisions were trapped near the town of Falaise.

On August 15, the American Seventh Army landed on the southern coast of France between Cannes and Toulon. Against light German opposition, the Americans advanced 140 miles (225 kilometers) in eight days, moving by way of Marseilles and up the valley of the Rhône. By August 19, German forces in France were in retreat all along the line, except for the garrisons in the southwest. These garrisons were being sealed off rapidly by the Americans.

On August 25, Paris was joyously liberated. Once over the Seine, the Germans' retreat toward their own frontier was orderly. But the German troops now were seriously weakened and very discouraged.

On September 4, British and Canadian troops captured the Belgian city of Antwerp, which, after being cleared of rubble, gave them a major port to supply the Allied troops advancing into Germany. One force of Americans then crossed the Meuse River and swung around the Ardennes. Another group of Americans took Verdun and moved on toward Metz. But then a gasoline shortage hit the Allies and prevented them from receiving new supplies of ammunition and other cargoes. The Allies' enforced wait gave the German army a rest and gave Hitler an opportunity to reorganize his western defenses.

Meanwhile, the invasion of the Netherlands was undertaken on September 17. But a surprisingly strong defense by German artillery and rocket forces stopped the advance short of the Rhine, proving that Germany was not yet on the verge of collapse.

▶ **PROGRESS OF THE WAR, SUMMER OF 1944**

The Russian Front. Four days after the invasion of Normandy, the Russian armies facing Finland attacked along the Karelian Isthmus. The Russians broke through the Mannerheim Line, Finland's defensive line, and on June 20 they captured Viborg. This virtually ended the war between the Soviet Union and Finland. The Russians went on to drive the Germans out of Lithuania, Latvia, and Estonia.

Two weak German armies were still in Romania, and in mid-August the Russians surrounded them. By August 25, the German troops were

U.S. general Douglas MacArthur leads American forces ashore at Leyte to begin the reconquest of the Philippines, October 1944.

defeated. Romania then quit the war, and a popular revolt led by King Michael of Romania threw out the dictator Ion Antonescu.

On August 26, Bulgaria announced its withdrawal from the war, and German forces began to evacuate Greece. The Russians occupied Sofia, Bulgaria, and then got ready to start a campaign up the Danube River to conquer Hungary and Austria.

The Pacific. On June 15, a U.S. Army-Marine amphibious expedition landed on Saipan Island in the western Pacific. The landing at Saipan was an important step in establishing American control of the Mariana Islands and in opening the way to the recapture of the Philippines. Saipan was taken by July 9. Next, the island of Tinian was invaded and conquered. Air and sea forces then turned their attention to Guam. On July 20 it was invaded by a U.S. Army-Marine landing force that conquered it in 20 days.

Following a brief rest in Central Pacific operations, the Americans took the Palau Islands on September 8 and Peleliu Island on September 15. The next step was the liberation of the Philippines. The Far Eastern Air Force and the carrier forces of the United States Third Fleet had already begun (on September 1) major "softening-up" operations. These attacks against the main enemy bases in the southern islands continued through September. In October the aircraft of the Third Fleet hit enemy bases on Luzon in the Philippines. Task Force 58 attacked Japanese airfields and naval bases on Formosa (now Taiwan). By mid-October the Philippines had been cleared of most Japanese aircraft.

On October 20, the United States Sixth Army invaded the island of Leyte, backed up by the Third and Seventh fleets. The Japanese sent in their fleet to counterattack. But their plan ended in disaster. The Americans defeated the Japanese fleet in the Battle of Leyte Gulf, October 23–26. This was the greatest naval battle of the war. After the Battle of Leyte Gulf, the Japanese fleet no longer was strong enough to offer a serious challenge to the Americans.

▶ ATTACK ON GERMANY, 1944–45

The American First Army moved onto German soil at Trier and captured Aachen on October 13. Having taken Nancy in mid-September, they moved northward and took Metz on November 22. The Americans then drove on toward the Saar.

November saw the Allies attacking all along the line in a general effort to reach the Rhine River. The British defeated the Germans still remaining on the western bank of the Waal River in the Netherlands. The Americans attacked west of Düren toward the Roer River, which they reached on December 3.

Battle of the Bulge. On the morning of December 16, 1944, the Germans launched a surprise counterattack against the American front in the Ardennes. Striking directly westward, one German group broke through in two places and raced into Belgium, with the port of Antwerp as their goal. By nightfall,

---

THE HUMAN COST OF WORLD WAR II

	Total Force Mobilized	Military Battle Deaths (approx. % of total troops)	Military Wounded	Civilian Deaths
Allies				
United States	14,900,000	292,100 (2%)	571,822	Negligible
United Kingdom	6,200,000	397,762 (6.5%)	475,000	65,000
France	6,000,000	210,671 (3.5%)	400,000	108,000
Soviet Union	25,000,000	7,500,000 (30%)	14,012,000	10,000,000–15,000,000
China	6,000,000–10,000,000	500,000 (5–8%)	1,700,000	1,000,000
Total:	58,100,000–62,100,000	8,900,533 (14–15%)	17,158,822	11,173,000–16,173,000
Axis Powers				
Germany	12,500,000	2,850,000 (23%)	7,250,000	500,000
Italy	4,500,000	77,500 (2%)	120,000	40,000–100,000
Japan	7,400,000	1,506,000 (20%)	500,000	300,000
Total:	24,400,000	4,433,500 (18%)	7,870,000	840,000–900,000
All Other Participants	20,000,000	1,500,000 (7.5%)	N/A	14,000,000–17,000,000[1]
Grand total:	102,500,000–106,500,000	14,834,033 (14%)	N/A	26,000,000–34,000,000

[1]This includes approximately 6 million Jews of Germany and all occupied European nations and approximately 4,500,000 Poles.

Source: Trevor N. Dupuy, _The Harper Encyclopedia of Military History_, Fourth Edition

American soldiers guard German prisoners captured in Belgium during the Battle of the Bulge, January 1945. The Bulge was Germany's last offensive of the war.

these German forces were well on their way to success. The battle became known as the Battle of the Bulge because, when seen on a map, the battleground had a bulging shape.

The Allied high command thought for the first 24 hours that the advance was a local effort, not part of a greater plan. However, on the second day General Eisenhower realized that this was a major offensive.

Two large towns, Bastogne and St. Vith, not yet reached by the Germans, dominated the mountain roads leading west. An American armored division was rushed to St. Vith. The Americans were soon surrounded by the Germans, and Bastogne was under siege. But the Americans held fast.

The American Third Army troops who had been attacking toward the Saar made a 90-degree turn and struck north toward Bastogne to stop the German advance. Also, clearing skies gave the Allied fliers their first chance to attack the German armor and trains that jammed the roads. Still, the Germans made the Allies fight hard for everything they gained before finally falling back. The Allied columns from north and south met by January 21. The Battle of the Bulge—in which more American troops fought than any other battle of World War II—was Hitler's last gasp.

▶ PROGRESS IN OTHER THEATERS, 1944–45

The Philippines. On January 9, 1945, a convoy of 850 ships carrying troops of the Sixth Army from Leyte arrived at Lingayen Gulf on the island of Luzon. The Americans landed unopposed. Although Japanese naval troops defended the city to the last and died amid its ruins, Manila was taken, and Corregidor was liberated in February. Other American landings were made against the Japanese garrisons on the islands at Palawan, Mindanao, Panay, and Cebu.

While the liberation of Luzon was being completed, a second American attack was staged by the forces from the Central Pacific. This attack was made to take close-by island air bases from which American bombers could make a last crushing offensive against the Japanese home islands. This, they believed, would be followed by an invasion of Japan.

Iwo Jima. The selected target was the island of Iwo Jima, a Japanese military base 775 miles (1,250 kilometers) from the island of Honshū. The expedition landed on February 19. It was made up of 60,000 marines, supported by the Fifth Fleet under Admiral Raymond Spruance. Meeting at first only moderate resistance, the marines advanced rapidly from the beaches to the high ground. There they met the full force of the enemy. The Japanese fought with greater desperation at Iwo Jima than they had in any other battle in the Pacific.

By February 27 the marines had won half the island. The major portion of the fighting ended on March 16.

Okinawa. Okinawa, in the Ryukyu Islands, was supposed to be the last stop for American forces before their direct invasion of Japan. On April 1, in the largest amphibious landing of the war in the Pacific, American soldiers and marines landed on Okinawa.

At first the American advance was scarcely opposed. But on the fifth day it struck a solid wall of resistance. The Japanese garrison of almost 100,000 men had withdrawn to the southern part of the island. Here they had an elaborate system of fortifications cut into the coral rock and limestone cliffs.

U.S. Marines blow up a fortified Japanese outpost on Iwo Jima, 1945. The battle for the small but strategic volcanic island was one of the bloodiest of the war.

For months, Japan had been organizing a corps of kamikaze (suicide) pilots to make up for its dwindling air strength. These pilots were prepared to give their lives to knock out a warship, transport, or some other target. On April 6, 400 Japanese planes from Kyushu struck against the American fleet and shipping. Although the attack was finally beaten off with a loss of 300 planes, 21 of 24 suicide thrusts by kamikazes were successful.

What remained of the Japanese fleet also came out on the night of April 6 for a last strike at American sea power. Planes from the carrier *Essex* were sent against it, and Task Force 58 moved out to intercept it in the East China Sea. In the action on April 7, the Japanese battleship *Yamato*, one cruiser, and four destroyers were sunk. Two other destroyers were left burning. Task Force 58 shot down 54 enemy planes, but a kamikaze pilot crashed on the carrier *Hancock* and put it out of action. Four days later four kamikaze pilots disabled another carrier, the *Enterprise*.

Burma. Early in December 1944, the last step in the reconquest of Burma began. In a double-pronged advance out of India, the British struck at North Burma and made an advance down Burma's western coast. At the same time, five Chinese divisions descended into North Burma. The two forces met on December 16, near Katha on the Irrawaddy River. They had restored overland communications between India and China and opened the Burma Road to Allied convoys by the end of January. After a long and hard campaign, the British reconquered all of Burma. By May 2, Rangoon (now Yangon), Burma's capital, was again in British hands.

The Soviet Union Against Germany. The Russian winter campaign opened on November 29 with an advance against Budapest, which was taken on February 13 after a desperate struggle. In mid-January the Russians attacked East Prussia, Poland, and Upper Silesia. The Germans abandoned Warsaw on January 17, and the Russians crossed into

Germany on January 20. By mid-February, Russian troops were within 60 miles (100 kilometers) of Berlin. In East Prussia, 20 German divisions were strenuously resisting the Russians. It was not until April 9 that Königsberg was taken by storm and East Prussia was conquered.

After the failure of a German counterattack against the Russian forces west of the Danube River, the Russians launched their general counteroffensive on March 18. By the end of March, the German front had collapsed, and the Russians had crossed into Austria. They reached Vienna on April 7. Within a week the capital was in Russian hands.

▶ **VICTORY IN EUROPE**

Throughout February 1945, American troops cleared the Saar Basin and moved to the Rhine between Düsseldorf and Mainz. They also built up their strength in the area from Mainz to the Swiss border. By March 6, the western bank of the Rhine was largely in Allied hands. Cologne was about to fall.

At the same time, American troops were pursuing the Germans near the town of Remagen. On March 7, the Americans seized the Remagen Bridge over the Rhine before the Germans could demolish it. Weeks later the bridge, weakened by artillery fire, collapsed. But it had remained in use just long enough to threaten the German position on the eastern bank of the Rhine.

On the night of March 22, a division of the American Third Army crossed the Rhine

375

B-17 Flying Fortresses of the U.S. Air Force drop their bombs over Germany, 1944. Allied bombing raids damaged or destroyed many German cities.

south of Mainz. Naval forces and naval craft were already in place to stage the main Rhine crossing at Wesel. The assault was preceded by heavy Allied artillery fire, following which a vast swarm of small boats started across the Rhine. Two parachute divisions were dropped on the eastern bank. The operation was successful.

From the Wesel bridgehead, the American First Army turned south behind the Ruhr, Germany's industrial center. By April 1 it had joined the Third Army and together they surrounded the Germans. On April 18 the German survivors—30 general officers and about 325,000 men—surrendered. After these and many other defeats the defense of western Germany collapsed.

The Russians attacked Berlin from their Oder River positions on April 17, and on April 25 they had the city surrounded. Hitler had chosen to remain in Berlin. On April 30 he committed suicide and was soon followed by his propaganda minister, Joseph Goebbels, and several high military advisers. Two days later the Berlin garrison surrendered.

In Italy the Allies crossed the Po River on April 25. The Germans in Italy were in full retreat. Three days later the war ended in Italy. Italian partisans had killed Benito Mussolini on the previous day while he was attempting to escape to Switzerland.

Before his death, Hitler made Admiral Karl Doenitz leader of Germany. On May 4 Doenitz offered to surrender all German forces in northern Germany, the Netherlands, and Denmark. Marshal Montgomery accepted this offer on May 5 and ordered his troops to cease fire. On May 7 the official document of surrender was signed at Eisenhower's Supreme Allied Headquarters in Reims, France. On May 8, V-E (Victory in Europe) Day was celebrated.

▶ **VICTORY OVER JAPAN**

When the fighting ended in Europe, the war in the Pacific was still in progress. The Battle of Okinawa was the final land battle of World War II—and it was extremely costly. Between April 1 and June 21, Americans suffered 49,151 casualties, of which 12,250 were killed or missing. Approximately 110,000 Japanese were killed during the Okinawa campaign, and 7,400 taken prisoner.

A Soviet soldier plants his nation's flag atop the damaged Reichstag (Parliament) building in Berlin, the war-ravaged capital of Nazi Germany, April 1945.

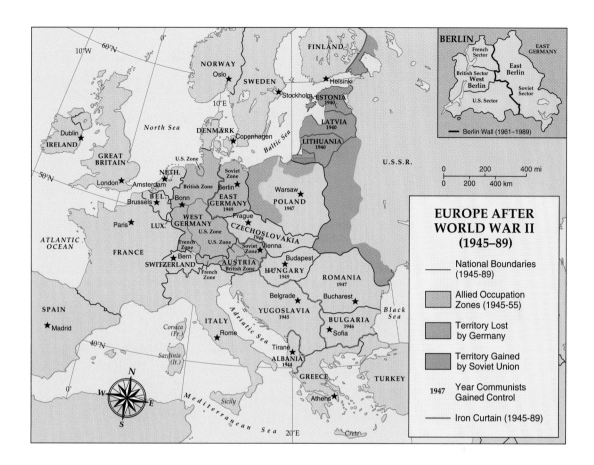

EUROPE AFTER WORLD WAR II (1945–89)

National Boundaries (1945-89)

Allied Occupation Zones (1945-55)

Territory Lost by Germany

Territory Gained by Soviet Union

1947   Year Communists Gained Control

Iron Curtain (1945-89)

BERLIN

French Sector

British Sector West Berlin

U.S. Sector

East Berlin

Soviet Sector

EAST GERMANY

— Berlin Wall (1961–1989)

Strategic Bombing of Japan. Long-distance bombing of Japan's interior had been started in the fall of 1943 by American bombers based in China. With the capture of the islands of Guam, Saipan, and Tinian one year later, the Japanese home islands came under direct air attack.

However, it was not until the spring of 1945—after the conquest of the Philippines and the fall of Iwo Jima—that the Americans began night bombing operations against Japan's main cities. In all, more than 100,000 tons of firebombs were dropped on Japan. Because of the large amount of wood construction in Japanese cities, the bombs did great damage. Tokyo, Yokohama, Nagoya, Kobe, Osaka, and other cities were in large part destroyed by fire.

The Atomic Bomb. The first atomic bomb was tested at White Sands, New Mexico, on July 16, three months after the death of President Roosevelt. It was decided by Roosevelt's successor, Harry S. Truman, and his secretary of war, Henry Stimson, to use two of the bombs against Japan in an effort to force a quick surrender and save the lives of hundreds of thousands of Allied troops.

THE NUREMBERG WAR CRIMES TRIALS

From November 1945 to October 1946, the victorious Allied Powers, acting through an International Military Tribunal, established a court in Nuremberg, Germany. The Nuremberg Trials resulted in the sentencing to death of twelve German military leaders for "crimes against humanity." Chief among them was Reich Marshal Hermann Goering.

From June 1946 to November 1948, the United States held similar trials in Japan. Seven Japanese leaders, including former prime minister Tojo Hideki, were sentenced to death.

THE MANHATTAN PROJECT

The Manhattan Project was the code name for the U.S. effort during World War II to produce the atomic bomb. The program was organized after nuclear fission was discovered by German scientists in 1938, and many U.S. scientists expressed the fear that Hitler would attempt to build a fission bomb.

The project began in 1942 under the direction of physicist J. Robert Oppenheimer. A successful test explosion took place at White Sands Proving Grounds, in New Mexico, on July 16, 1945, two months after Germany surrendered. But the war against Japan was still in progress. Fearing that many thousands of American lives would be lost if Allied forces had to invade Japan, U.S. president Harry S. Truman ordered the use of atomic bombs, resulting in the destruction of the Japanese cities of Hiroshima on August 6 and Nagasaki on August 9. The Japanese surrendered on September 2.

On July 26, without mentioning the atomic bomb, the United States joined with Britain and China in making a surrender demand upon Japan in the form of an ultimatum. Because the ultimatum did not mention the status of their emperor, the Japanese rejected it.

In the early morning of August 6, a lone American B-29 appeared over Hiroshima, Japan, released a projectile, and sped away. An atomic bomb exploded moments later. Its blast killed or maimed or otherwise injured more than half the city's population of 320,000. Not only Japan but the whole world was morally and politically rocked. Three days later, another atomic bomb was dropped on Nagasaki, killing about 40,000 people. The Soviet Union, realizing that Japan was near collapse, declared war and invaded Manchuria, which was still held by the Japanese.

On August 10, the Japanese government announced that it was ready to accept the terms the Allies had proposed on July 26, provided that acceptance did not compromise "the prerogatives of the Emperor as a sovereign ruler." The Allies replied the following day that the authority of the emperor would be "subject to the Supreme Commander of the Allied Powers."

On August 14 the emperor accepted this condition, and all forces were directed to cease fighting. American forces prepared to enter Japan. On September 2, the final surrender was signed aboard the U.S. battleship *Missouri*. World War II had ended.

▶ THE RESULTS OF THE WAR

Peace Treaties. After the war, Germany and Austria were divided into four occupation zones to be administered by the United States, Great Britain, France, and the Soviet Union. A formal peace treaty, however, was not agreed upon until 1955. In 1946, the Allies signed peace treaties with Italy, Romania, Bulgaria, Hungary, and Finland. All were required to pay reparations to the Allies, and all but Bulgaria lost territory.

In the Pacific, the United States alone occupied Japan. In 1947, the Japanese adopted a new constitution that reduced the powers of the emperor and guaranteed democracy. A formal peace treaty was signed in 1951.

The United Nations. During World War II, four of the Allied Powers—the United States, Great Britain, the Soviet Union, and China—agreed to establish an international peacekeeping organization to replace the failed League of Nations. Thus the United Nations, the world's leading mediator of international disputes, was formed in 1945.

The Cold War. World War II permanently changed the global balance of power. The United States and the Soviet Union emerged as the world's two lone superpowers, each with the terrifying ability to wage atomic war. The vast political and economic differences between them led to a Cold War that lasted 50 years.

S. L. A. MARSHALL
Brigadier General, U.S. Army Reserve (Ret.)
Former Chief Combat Historian, Central Pacific;
Chief Historian, European Theater

Reviewed by JOHN SD EISENHOWER
Author, *The Bitter Woods, Allies*

SUPPLEMENT

Deaths

Independent Nations of the World

The United States

    Senate

    House of Representatives

    Cabinet

    Supreme Court

    State Governors

Canada and Its Provinces and Territories

DEATHS

Allen, Steve. American entertainer; died on October 30, at the age of 78. The bespectacled Allen, pioneer of the late-night television talk show, hosted the original *Tonight Show* (1953–56). During his more than 50 years in show business, he was widely regarded as a talented comedian, actor, and songwriter.

Bandaranaike, Sirimavo. Former prime minister of Sri Lanka; died on October 10, at the age of 84. Bandaranaike was the first woman in the world elected prime minister. She held that office three times—from 1960 to 1965, 1970 to 1977, and 1994 to 2000.

Carnahan, Mel. Governor of Missouri; died in a plane crash on October 16, at the age of 66. Carnahan, a Democrat, had served as governor since 1993. Widely respected for his integrity, Carnahan was known for his strong commitment to education.

Cartland, Barbara. British novelist; died on May 21, at the age of 98. Queen of the romance novel, the prolific Cartland was often cited as the world's best-selling author. Her

Barbara Cartland

723 novels sold about a billion copies worldwide. She routinely turned out more than 20 books a year—which she usually dictated to a secretary while reclining on a sofa.

Coverdell, Paul. U.S. Senator from Georgia; died on July 18, at the age of 61. Coverdell, a Republican, served in the Senate since 1993. He was noted for his quietly influential leadership on such issues as education, Social Security, and drug prevention.

Gielgud, Sir John. British actor; died on May 21, at the age of 96. Hailed as one of the greatest actors of the 20th century, Gielgud's eloquent voice and regal manner transfixed audiences for more than 70 years. Although he was especially celebrated for his theater work in the Shakespearean roles of Hamlet, Macbeth, Romeo, and King Lear, Gielgud also worked in radio, television, and film. He won an Academy Award in 1982 for his role as the proper butler in *Arthur*.

Gorey, Edward. American writer and illustrator; died on April 15, at the age of 75. Gorey entertained readers with his ghoulish illustrations and morbidly funny texts in more

Steve Allen

than 100 books. One of his best-known works was *The Gashlycrumb Tinies* (1963), a macabre alphabet book that begins with: "A is for Amy who fell down the stairs."

Guinness, Sir Alec. British actor; died on August 5, at the age of 86. During his 60-year career, the versatile Guinness played a wide range of dramatic and comic roles—winning acclaim for his chameleonlike ability to disappear into his characters. He won an Academy Award as best actor for his role as a mad British army officer in *The Bridge on the River Kwai* (1957). In recent years, he was best known for portraying Obi-Wan Kenobi in *Star Wars* (1977) and its two sequels.

Henning, Doug. Canadian-born magician; died on February 7, at the age of 52. A master of the art of illusion, the curly-maned Henning amazed audiences with his incredible magic tricks. At the peak of his career in the 1970's and 1980's, he starred in three Broadway shows and made numerous appearances on television.

Lamarr, Hedy. Austrian-born actress; died on January 19, at the age of 86. Famed for her exotic beauty, Lamarr was one of Hollywood's top screen sirens of the 1930's and 1940's. Her best-remembered role was as Delilah in

Sir Alec Guinness

Walter Matthau

the biblical epic *Samson and Delilah* (1949). During World War II, she helped to invent a radio-signal device that's still used today.

Linville, Larry. American actor; died on April 10, at the age of 60. Linville played the role of the sniveling Major Frank Burns on the popular television series *M*A*S*H*. He appeared on the show for five seasons (1972–77).

Marchand, Nancy. American actress; died on June 18, at the age of 71. A distinguished character actress, Marchand won four Emmy Awards for her portrayal of the autocratic newspaper publisher Mrs. Pynchon on the television series *Lou Grant* (1977–82). She also gained notice as the wicked Mafia matriarch in the television series *The Sopranos* (1998–2000).

Matthau, Walter. American actor; died on July 1, at the age of 79. With his hangdog looks and curmudgeonly manner, Matthau created unforgettable comic characters. His signature role was as the hopeless slob Oscar Madison in *The Odd Couple,* a hit on Broadway in 1965 and in the movies in 1968. In the movie version, he played opposite Jack Lemmon, who portrayed Felix Unger, his fussy roommate. Matthau teamed up with Lemmon in several

Cardinal John J. O'Connor

Puente, Tito. American bandleader and percussionist; died on May 31, at the age of 77. Called *El Rey* (the king), the fiery Puente gained renown with his blending of Latin dance rhythms with traditional jazz. He was instrumental in launching the mambo and cha-cha crazes of the 1940's and 1950's. In his six-decade career, he recorded nearly 120 albums and won five Grammy Awards, and made Latin music part of American pop culture.

Rampal, Jean-Pierre. French-born classical flutist; died on May 20, at the age of 78. A world-renowned virtuoso, Rampal was credited with restoring the flute to popularity as a solo instrument for the first time since the eighteenth century. Though best known for his performances of music from the Baroque era, Rampal played everything from jazz to folk on his 14-karat-gold flute.

Richard, Maurice. Canadian hockey player; died on May 27, at the age of 78. As a forward for the Montreal Canadiens (1942–60), Richard earned the nickname the "Rocket" for his speed and goal-scoring ability. He helped the Canadiens win eight Stanley Cups, including five in a row from 1956 to 1960. Richard was the first hockey player to score 50 goals in a season, and the first to score more than 500 goals in a career.

other hit comedies, including *The Fortune Cookie* (1966)—for which Matthau won an Academy Award—*Grumpy Old Men* (1993) and its 1995 sequel, and *The Odd Couple* sequel in 1998.

Merrick, David. American theatrical producer; died on April 25, at the age of 88. From the 1950's to the 1980's, Merrick dominated Broadway with a series of long-running hit shows, including *Gypsy* (1959), *Hello Dolly!* (1964), and *42nd Street* (1980). Notorious for his tyrannical temperament, Merrick often garnered publicity for his productions by staging elaborate promotional stunts and engaging in constant feuds.

O'Connor, Cardinal John J. American Roman Catholic archbishop; died on May 3, at the age of 80. During his tenure as archbishop of New York (1984–2000), O'Connor became the leading spokesman for the Roman Catholic Church in the United States. A charismatic leader, he was known for his eloquent and forceful stands on many social issues.

Tito Puente

Trudeau, Pierre Elliott. Prime minister of Canada from 1968 to 1979 and 1980 to 1984; died on September 28, at the age of 80. Trudeau was a politician of great charm, wit, and flair. He attracted many youthful followers. And their energetic, sometimes frenzied support—known as "Trudeaumania"—gave Trudeau's Liberal Party a landslide victory in his first election as prime minister in 1968.

Trudeau's popularity wasn't always as great as it was in 1968. But he accomplished a great deal during his 15½ years in office. Many people in the French-speaking province of Quebec wanted to form a separate nation. But Trudeau helped keep Canada united. United States influence in Canada was far too strong, he said. So he fought to take Canada out from under the shadow of its giant neighbor. Trudeau also took control of Canada's Constitution away from Britain, Canada's former colonial ruler. But he felt that his greatest achievement was Canada's Charter of Rights and Freedoms. It guaranteed all Canadians such rights as freedom of speech, freedom of worship, and the right to due process of the law.

Schulz, Charles M. American cartoonist; died on February 12, at the age of 77. Schulz was the creator of *Peanuts,* the most widely read comic strip in history. Readers in 75 countries followed the adventures of the lovable loser Charlie Brown, his dog Snoopy, and the rest of the *Peanuts* gang each day. The strip, which first appeared in 1950, inspired a number of animated films and television shows, and the Broadway musical *You're a Good Man, Charlie Brown* (1967). (See also pages 244–47.)

Segal, George. American sculptor; died on June 9, at the age of 75. Segal molded life-sized plaster casts of real people and grouped them with ordinary objects like chairs, tables, and even traffic signs to create snapshots of contemporary life. Critics said that his ghostly Pop Art sculptures convincingly portrayed a sense of human alienation in modern society.

Young, Loretta. American actress; died on August 12, at the age of 87. A glamorous leading actress of the 1930's and 1940's, Young won an Academy Award for her performance in *The Farmer's Daughter* (1947). She later starred in her own television drama series, *The Loretta Young Show* (1953–63). A trademark of the popular weekly show was Young's twirling entrance onto the set wearing a designer gown.

Loretta Young

INDEPENDENT NATIONS OF THE WORLD

NATION	CAPITAL	AREA (in sq mi)	POPULATION (estimate)	GOVERNMENT
Afghanistan	Kabul	250,000	26,700,000	The Taliban—Muslim fundamentalist group
Albania	Tirana	11,100	3,400,000	Rexhep Mejdani—president Ilir Meta—premier
Algeria	Algiers	919,595	31,500,000	Abdelaziz Bouteflika—president
Andorra	Andorra la Vella	175	100,000	Marc Forne Molne—premier
Angola	Luanda	481,354	12,900,000	José Eduardo dos Santos—president
Antigua and Barbuda	St. John's	171	100,000	Lester Bird—prime minister
Argentina	Buenos Aires	1,068,297	37,000,000	Fernando de la Rúa—president
Armenia	Yerevan	11,500	3,800,000	Robert Kocharyan—president
Australia	Canberra	2,967,895	19,200,000	John Howard—prime minister
Austria	Vienna	32,374	8,100,000	Thomas Klestil—president Wolfgang Schüssel—chancellor
Azerbaijan	Baku	33,500	7,700,000	Heydar A. Aliyev—president
Bahamas	Nassau	5,380	300,000	Hubert A. Ingraham—prime minister
Bahrain	Manama	240	700,000	Hamad bin Isa al-Khalifa—head of state
Bangladesh	Dhaka	55,598	128,100,000	Shahabuddin Ahmed—president Sheik Hasina Wazed—prime minister
Barbados	Bridgetown	168	300,000	Owen Arthur—prime minister
Belarus	Minsk	80,154	10,000,000	Aleksandr Lukashenko—president
Belgium	Brussels	11,781	10,200,000	Albert II—king Guy Verhofstadt—premier
Belize	Belmopan	8,867	300,000	Said Musa—prime minister
Benin	Porto-Novo	43,484	6,400,000	Mathieu Kerekou—president
Bhutan	Thimbu	18,147	900,000	Jigme Singye Wangchuck—king
Bolivia	La Paz Sucre	424,165	8,300,000	Hugo Banzer Suarez—president
Bosnia and Herzegovina	Sarajevo	19,800	3,800,000	3-member presidency
Botswana	Gaborone	231,804	1,600,000	Festus Mogae—president
Brazil	Brasília	3,286,478	170,100,000	Fernando Henrique Cardoso—president
Brunei Darussalam	Bandar Seri Begawan	2,226	300,000	Hassanal Bolkiah—head of state
Bulgaria	Sofia	42,823	8,200,000	Petar Stoyanov—president Ivan Kostov—premier
Burkina Faso	Ouagadougou	105,869	11,900,000	Blaise Compaoré—president
Burma (Myanmar)	Rangoon (Yangon)	261,218	48,900,000	Than Shwe—head of government
Burundi	Bujumbura	10,747	6,100,000	Pierre Buyoya—president

NATION	CAPITAL	AREA (in sq mi)	POPULATION (estimate)	GOVERNMENT
Cambodia	Phnom Penh	69,898	12,100,000	Norodom Sihanouk—king Hun Sen—prime minister
Cameroon	Yaoundé	183,569	15,400,000	Paul Biya—president
Canada	Ottawa	3,851,809	30,800,000	Jean Chrétien—prime minister
Cape Verde	Praia	1,557	400,000	Antonio Mascarenhas Monteiro—president
Central African Republic	Bangui	240,535	3,500,000	Ange-Felix Patasse—president
Chad	N'Djamena	495,754	8,000,000	Idriss Deby—president
Chile	Santiago	292,257	15,200,000	Ricardo Lagos Escobar—president
China	Beijing	3,705,390	1,264,500,000	Jiang Zemin—communist party secretary Zhu Rongji—premier
Colombia	Bogotá	439,736	40,000,000	Andrés Pastrana Arango—president
Comoros	Moroni	838	600,000	Azaly Assoumani—president
Congo (Zaire)	Kinshasa	905,565	52,000,000	Laurent Kabila—president
Congo Republic	Brazzaville	132,047	2,800,000	Denis Sassou-Nguesso—president
Costa Rica	San José	19,575	3,600,000	Miguel Angel Rodríguez—president
Croatia	Zagreb	21,829	4,600,000	Stipe Mesic—president
Cuba	Havana	44,218	11,100,000	Fidel Castro—president
Cyprus	Nicosia	3,572	900,000	Glafcos Clerides—president
Czech Republic	Prague	30,469	10,300,000	Vaclav Havel—president Milos Zeman—premier
Denmark	Copenhagen	16,629	5,300,000	Margrethe II—queen Poul Nyrup Rasmussen—premier
Djibouti	Djibouti	8,494	600,000	Ismail Omar Guelleh—president
Dominica	Roseau	290	100,000	Roosevelt Douglas—prime minister
Dominican Republic	Santo Domingo	18,816	8,400,000	Hipólito Mejía Dominguez —president
Ecuador	Quito	109,483	12,600,000	Gustavo Noboa Bejarano—president
Egypt	Cairo	386,660	68,300,000	Mohammed Hosni Mubarak—president Atef Mohamed Ebeid—premier
El Salvador	San Salvador	8,124	6,300,000	Francisco Flores Pérez—president
Equatorial Guinea	Malabo	10,831	500,000	Teodoro Obiang Nguema Mbasogo—president
Eritrea	Asmara	45,405	4,100,000	Isaias Afeworki—president
Estonia	Tallinn	17,413	1,400,000	Lennart Meri—president
Ethiopia	Addis Ababa	426,372	64,100,000	Negasso Ghidada—president
Fiji	Suva	7,055	800,000	Ratu Josefa Iloilo—president
Finland	Helsinki	130,120	5,200,000	Tarja Halonen—president Paavo Lipponen—premier
France	Paris	213,000	59,400,000	Jacques Chirac—president Lionel Jospin—premier
Gabon	Libreville	103,346	1,200,000	Omar Bongo—president
Gambia	Banjul	4,361	1,300,000	Yahya Jammeh—head of state
Georgia	Tbilisi	27,000	5,500,000	Eduard Shevardnadze—president

NATION	CAPITAL	AREA (in sq mi)	POPULATION (estimate)	GOVERNMENT
Germany	Berlin	137,744	82,100,000	Johannes Rau—president Gerhard Schröder—chancellor
Ghana	Accra	92,099	19,500,000	Jerry Rawlings—president
Greece	Athens	50,944	10,600,000	Costis Stefanopoulos—president Costas Simitis—premier
Grenada	St. George's	133	100,000	Keith Mitchell—prime minister
Guatemala	Guatemala City	42,042	12,700,000	Alfonso Portillo Cabrera—president
Guinea	Conakry	94,926	7,500,000	Lansana Conté—president
Guinea-Bissau	Bissau	13,948	1,200,000	Kumba Yala—president
Guyana	Georgetown	83,000	700,000	Bharrat Jagdeo—president
Haiti	Port-au-Prince	10,714	6,400,000	Jean-Bertrand Aristide—president
Honduras	Tegucigalpa	43,277	6,100,000	Carlos Flores Facusse—president
Hungary	Budapest	35,919	10,000,000	Ferenc Madl—president Viktor Orban—premier
Iceland	Reykjavik	39,768	300,000	Olafur Grimsson—president David Oddsson—premier
India	New Delhi	1,269,340	1,002,100,000	Kocheril Raman Narayanan—president Atal Bihari Vajpayee—prime minister
Indonesia	Jakarta	735,358	212,200,000	Abdurrahman Wahid—president
Iran	Tehran	636,293	67,400,000	Ayatollah Ali Khamenei—religious leader Mohammed Khatami—president
Iraq	Baghdad	167,925	23,100,000	Saddam Hussein—president
Ireland	Dublin	27,136	3,800,000	Mary McAleese—president Bertie Ahern—prime minister
Israel	Jerusalem	8,019	6,200,000	Moshe Katsav—president Ehud Barak—prime minister
Italy	Rome	116,303	57,800,000	Carlo Azeglio Ciampi—president Giuliano Amato—premier
Ivory Coast	Yamoussoukro	124,503	16,000,000	Laurent Gbagbo—president
Jamaica	Kingston	4,244	2,600,000	Percival J. Patterson—prime minister
Japan	Tokyo	143,751	126,900,000	Akihito—emperor Yoshiro Mori—premier
Jordan	Amman	35,475	5,100,000	Abdullah II—king Ali Abu al-Ragheb—prime minister
Kazakhstan	Almaty	1,049,000	14,900,000	Nursultan A. Nazarbayev—president
Kenya	Nairobi	224,959	30,300,000	Daniel arap Moi—president
Kiribati	Tarawa	264	100,000	Teburoro Tito—president
Korea (North)	Pyongyang	46,540	21,700,000	Kim Jong II—president Kim Yong Nam—premier
Korea (South)	Seoul	38,025	47,300,000	Kim Dae Jung—president Lee Han Dong—premier
Kuwait	Kuwait	6,880	2,200,000	Jabir al-Ahmad al-Sabah—head of state
Kyrgyzstan	Bishkek	76,641	4,900,000	Askar Akayev—president
Laos	Vientiane	91,429	5,200,000	Khamtai Siphandon—president Sisavat Keobounphan—premier
Latvia	Riga	24,600	2,400,000	Vaira Vike-Freiberga—president

NATION	CAPITAL	AREA (in sq mi)	POPULATION (estimate)	GOVERNMENT
Lebanon	Beirut	4,015	4,200,000	Emile Lahoud—president Selim al-Hoss—premier
Lesotho	Maseru	11,720	2,100,000	Letsie III—king Pakalitha Mosisili—premier
Liberia	Monrovia	43,000	3,200,000	Charles G. Taylor—president
Libya	Tripoli	679,362	5,100,000	Muammar el-Qaddafi—head of government
Liechtenstein	Vaduz	61	30,000	Hans Adam II—prince
Lithuania	Vilnius	25,174	3,700,000	Valdas Adamkus—president
Luxembourg	Luxembourg	998	400,000	Henri—grand duke Jean-Claude Juncker—premier
Macedonia	Skopje	9,928	2,000,000	Boris Trajkovski—president
Madagascar	Antananarivo	226,657	14,900,000	Didier Ratsiraka—president
Malawi	Lilongwe	45,747	10,400,000	Bakili Muluzi—president
Malaysia	Kuala Lumpur	127,317	23,200,000	Jaafar bin Abdul Rahman—king Mahathir bin Mohamad—prime minister
Maldives	Male	115	300,000	Maumoon Abdul Gayoom—president
Mali	Bamako	478,765	11,200,000	Alpha Oumar Konare—president
Malta	Valletta	122	400,000	Guido De Marco—president Eddie Fenech Adami—prime minister
Marshall Islands	Majuro	70	100,000	Kessai Note—president
Mauritania	Nouakchott	397,954	2,700,000	Maaouya Ould Sid Ahmed Taya—president
Mauritius	Port Louis	790	1,200,000	Cassam Uteem—president Anerood Jugnauth—premier
Mexico	Mexico City	761,602	99,600,000	Vicente Fox Quesada—president
Micronesia	Colonia	271	100,000	Leo Falcom—president
Moldova	Kishiniev	13,000	4,300,000	Petru Lucinschi—president
Monaco	Monaco-Ville	0.6	30,000	Rainier III—prince
Mongolia	Ulan Bator	604,248	2,500,000	Natsagiin Bagabandi—president
Morocco	Rabat	172,413	28,800,000	Mohammed VI—king Abderrahmane Youssoufi—premier
Mozambique	Maputo	309,494	19,100,000	Joaquím A. Chissano—president
Namibia	Windhoek	318,260	1,800,000	Sam Nujoma—president
Nauru	Yaren District	8	10,000	Bernard Dowiyogo—president
Nepal	Katmandu	54,362	23,900,000	Birendra Bir Bikram Shah Deva—king Girija Prasad Koirala—premier
Netherlands	Amsterdam	15,770	15,900,000	Beatrix—queen Willem Kok—premier
New Zealand	Wellington	103,736	3,800,000	Helen Clark—prime minister
Nicaragua	Managua	50,193	5,100,000	Arnoldo Alemán Lacayo—president
Niger	Niamey	489,190	10,100,000	Mamadou Tandja—president
Nigeria	Abuja	356,667	123,300,000	Olusegun Obasanjo—president
Norway	Oslo	125,056	4,500,000	Harold V—king Jens Stoltenberg—premier

NATION	CAPITAL	AREA (in sq mi)	POPULATION (estimate)	GOVERNMENT
Oman	Muscat	82,030	2,400,000	Qaboos bin Said Al Said—sultan
Pakistan	Islamabad	310,404	150,600,000	Pervez Musharraf—head of government
Palau	Koror	192	20,000	Tommy Remengesau—president
Panama	Panama City	29,761	2,900,000	Mireya Moscoso de Grubar—president
Papua New Guinea	Port Moresby	178,260	4,800,000	Mekere Morauta—prime minister
Paraguay	Asunción	157,047	5,500,000	Luis González Macchi—president
Peru	Lima	496,222	27,100,000	Valentin Paniagua—president
Philippines	Manila	115,830	80,300,000	Joseph Estrada—president Gloria Macapagal-Arroyo—vice-president
Poland	Warsaw	120,725	38,600,000	Aleksander Kwasniewski—president Jerzy Buzek—premier
Portugal	Lisbon	35,553	10,000,000	Jorge Sampaio—president Antonio Guterres—premier
Qatar	Doha	4,247	600,000	Hamad bin Khalifa al-Thani—head of state
Romania	Bucharest	91,700	22,400,000	Ion Iliescu—president Mugur Isarescu—premier
Russia	Moscow	6,600,000	145,200,000	Vladimir V. Putin—president
Rwanda	Kigali	10,169	7,200,000	Paul Kagame—president
St. Kitts and Nevis	Basseterre	105	40,000	Denzil Douglas—prime minister
St. Lucia	Castries	238	200,000	Kenny Anthony—prime minister
St. Vincent and the Grenadines	Kingstown	150	100,000	James F. Mitchell—prime minister
San Marino	San Marino	24	30,000	Gabriele Gatti—head of state
São Tomé and Príncipe	São Tomé	372	200,000	Miguel Trovoada—president
Saudi Arabia	Riyadh	830,000	21,600,000	Fahd bin Abdul-Aziz al-Saud—king
Senegal	Dakar	75,750	9,500,000	Abdoulaye Wade—president
Seychelles	Victoria	107	100,000	France Albert René—president
Sierra Leone	Freetown	27,700	5,200,000	Ahmad Tejan Kabbah—president
Singapore	Singapore	224	4,000,000	S. R. Nathan—president Goh Chok Tong—prime minister
Slovakia	Bratislava	18,933	5,400,000	Rudolf Schuster—president
Slovenia	Ljubljana	7,819	2,000,000	Milan Kucan—president
Solomon Islands	Honiara	10,983	400,000	Manasseh Sogavare—prime minister
Somalia	Mogadishu	246,200	7,300,000	Abdiqassim Salad Hassan—president
South Africa	Pretoria Cape Town Bloemfontein	471,444	43,400,000	Thabo Mbeki—president
Spain	Madrid	194,896	39,500,000	Juan Carlos I—king José María Aznar—premier
Sri Lanka	Colombo	25,332	19,200,000	C. Bandaranaike Kumaratunga—president
Sudan	Khartoum	967,500	29,500,000	O. Hassan Ahmed al-Bashir—president

NATION	CAPITAL	AREA (in sq mi)	POPULATION (estimate)	GOVERNMENT
Suriname	Paramaribo	63,037	400,000	Jules Wijdenbosch—president
Swaziland	Mbabane	6,704	1,000,000	Mswati III—king
Sweden	Stockholm	173,731	8,900,000	Carl XVI Gustaf—king Göran Persson—premier
Switzerland	Bern	15,941	7,100,000	Moritz Leuenberger—president
Syria	Damascus	71,498	16,500,000	Bashar al-Assad—president Mohammed Mustafa Miro—premier
Taiwan	Taipei	13,885	22,300,000	Chen Shui-bian—president Chang Chun-hsiung—premier
Tajikistan	Dushanbe	55,250	6,400,000	Oqil Oqilov—premier
Tanzania	Dar es Salaam	364,898	35.300,000	Amani Karume—president
Thailand	Bangkok	198,457	62,000,000	Bhumibol Adulyadej—king Chuan Leekpai—premier
Togo	Lomé	21,622	5,000,000	Gnassingbe Eyadema—president
Tonga	Nuku'alofa	270	100,000	Taufa'ahau Tupou IV—king Lavaka ata Ulukalala—premier
Trinidad & Tobago	Port of Spain	1,980	1,300,000	A.N.R. Robinson—president Basdeo Panday—prime minister
Tunisia	Tunis	63,170	9,600,000	Zine el-Abidine Ben Ali—president
Turkey	Ankara	301,381	65,300,000	Ahmet Necdet Sezer—president Bulent Ecevit—prime minister
Turkmenistan	Ashkhabad	188,455	5,200,000	Saparmurad Niyazov—president
Tuvalu	Funafuti	10	10,800	Ionatana Ionatana—prime minister
Uganda	Kampala	91,134	23,300,000	Yoweri Museveni—president
Ukraine	Kiev	231,990	49,500,000	Leonid M. Kuchma—president
United Arab Emirates	Abu Dhabi	32,278	2,800,000	Zayed bin Sultan al-Nuhayyan—president
United Kingdom	London	94,226	59,800,000	Elizabeth II—queen Tony Blair—prime minister
United States	Washington, D.C.	3,618,467	275,600,000	George W. Bush—president-elect Richard Cheney—vice-president-elect
Uruguay	Montevideo	68,037	3,300,000	Jorge Batlle—president
Uzbekistan	Tashkent	172,750	24,800,000	Islam A. Karimov—president
Vanuatu	Vila	5,700	200,000	John Bani—president
Vatican City	Vatican City	0.17	1,000	John Paul II—pope
Venezuela	Caracas	352,143	24,200,000	Hugo Chávez—president
Vietnam	Hanoi	128,402	78,700,000	La Kha Phieu—communist party secretary Phan Van Khai—premier
Western Samoa	Apia	1,097	200,000	Malietoa Tanumafili II—head of state
Yemen	Sana	203,849	17,000,000	Ali Abdullah Saleh—president Abd al-Karim Iryani—premier
Yugoslavia	Belgrade	39,390	10,700,000	Vojislav Kostunica—president Momir Bulatovic—premier
Zambia	Lusaka	290,585	9,600,000	Frederick Chiluba—president
Zimbabwe	Harare	150,333	11,300,000	Robert Mugabe—president

THE CONGRESS OF THE UNITED STATES

UNITED STATES SENATE
(50 Republicans, 50 Democrats)

Alabama
Richard C. Shelby (R)
Jefferson B. Sessions (R)

Alaska
Ted Stevens (R)
Frank H. Murkowski (R)

Arizona
John S. McCain III (R)
Jon Kyl (R)**

Arkansas
Tim Hutchinson (R)
Blanche L. Lincoln (D)

California
Barbara Boxer (D)
Dianne Feinstein (D)**

Colorado
Ben Nighthorse Campbell (R)
Wayne Allard (R)

Connecticut
Christopher J. Dodd (D)
Joseph I. Lieberman (D)**

Delaware
Joseph R. Biden, Jr. (D)
Thomas Carper (D)*

Florida
Robert Graham (D)
Bill Nelson (D)*

Georgia
Max Cleland (D)
Zell Miller (D)*

Hawaii
Daniel K. Inouye (D)
Daniel K. Akaka (D)**

Idaho
Larry E. Craig (R)
Mike Crapo (R)

Illinois
Richard J. Durbin (D)
Peter Fitzgerald (R)

Indiana
Richard G. Lugar (R)**
Evan Bayh (D)

Iowa
Charles E. Grassley (R)
Thomas R. Harkin (D)

Kansas
Sam Brownback (R)
Pat Roberts (R)

Kentucky
Mitch McConnell (R)
Jim Bunning (R)

Louisiana
John B. Breaux (D)
Mary Landrieu (D)

Maine
Olympia J. Snowe (R)**
Susan Collins (R)

Maryland
Paul S. Sarbanes (D)**
Barbara A. Mikulski (D)

Massachusetts
Edward M. Kennedy (D)**
John F. Kerry (D)

Michigan
Carl Levin (D)
Deborah A. Stabenow (D)*

Minnesota
Paul Wellstone (D)
Mark Dayton (D)*

Mississippi
Thad Cochran (R)
Trent Lott (R)**

Missouri
Christopher S. Bond (R)
Jean Carnahan (D)*

Montana
Max S. Baucus (D)
Conrad Burns (R)**

Nebraska
Chuck Hagel (R)
Ben Nelson (D)*

Nevada
Harry Reid (D)
John Ensign (R)*

New Hampshire
Judd Gregg (R)
Robert C. Smith (R)

New Jersey
Robert G. Torricelli (D)
Jon S. Corzine (D)*

New Mexico
Pete V. Domenici (R)
Jeff Bingaman (D)**

New York
Charles E. Schumer (D)
Hillary Rodham Clinton (D)*

North Carolina
Jesse A. Helms (R)
John Edwards (D)

North Dakota
Kent Conrad (D)**
Byron L. Dorgan (D)

Ohio
Mike DeWine (R)**
George Voinovich (R)

Oklahoma
Don L. Nickles (R)
James M. Inhofe (R)

Oregon
Gordon Smith (R)
Ron Wyden (D)

Pennsylvania
Arlen Specter (R)
Rick Santorum (R)**

Rhode Island
Lincoln D. Chafee (R)**
John Reed (D)

South Carolina
Strom Thurmond (R)
Ernest F. Hollings (D)

South Dakota
Thomas A. Daschle (D)
Tim Johnson (D)

Tennessee
Bill Frist (R)**
Fred D. Thompson (R)

Texas
Phil Gramm (R)
Kay Bailey Hutchinson (R)**

Utah
Orrin G. Hatch (R)**
Robert F. Bennett (R)

Vermont
Patrick J. Leahy (D)
James M. Jeffords (R)**

Virginia
John W. Warner (R)
George F. Allen (R)*

Washington
Patty Murray (D)
Maria Cantwell (D)*

West Virginia
Robert C. Byrd (D)**
John D. Rockefeller IV (D)

Wisconsin
Herbert H. Kohl (D)**
Russell D. Feingold (D)

Wyoming
Craig Thomas (R)**
Michael Enzi (R)

(D) Democrat
(R) Republican

* elected in 2000
** re-elected in 2000

UNITED STATES HOUSE OF REPRESENTATIVES
(221 Republicans, 211 Democrats, 2 Independents, 1 Vacancy)

Alabama
1. H. L. Callahan (R)
2. T. Everett (R)
3. B. Riley (R)
4. R. Aderholt (R)
5. B. Cramer (D)
6. S. Bachus (R)
7. E. Hilliard (D)

Alaska
D. E. Young (R)

Arizona
1. J. Flake (R)*
2. E. Pastor (R)
3. B. Stump (R)
4. J. Shadegg (R)
5. J. Kolbe (R)
6. J. D. Hayworth (R)

Arkansas
1. M. Berry (D)
2. V. F. Snyder (D)
3. A. Hutchinson (R)
4. M. A. Ross (D)*

California
1. M. Thompson (D)
2. W. Herger (R)
3. D. Ose (R)
4. J. T. Doolittle (R)
5. R. T. Matsui (D)
6. L. Woolsey (D)
7. G. Miller (D)
8. N. Pelosi (D)
9. B. Lee (D)
10. E. Tauscher (D)
11. R. Pombo (R)
12. T. Lantos (D)
13. F. H. Stark (D)
14. A. Eshoo (D)
15. M. Honda (D)*
16. Z. Lofgren (D)
17. S. Farr (D)
18. G. Condit (D)
19. G. Radanovich (R)
20. C. Dooley (D)
21. W. Thomas (R)
22. L. Capps (D)
23. E. Gallegly (R)
24. B. Sherman (D)
25. H. McKeon (R)
26. H. L. Berman (D)
27. A. Schiff (D)*
28. D. Dreier (R)
29. H. A. Waxman (D)
30. X. Becerra (D)
31. H. L. Solis (D)*
32. Vacant***
33. L. Roybal-Allard (D)
34. G. Napolitano (D)
35. M. Waters (D)
36. J. Harman (D)*
37. J. Millender-McDonald (D)
38. S. Horn (R)
39. E. Royce (R)
40. J. Lewis (R)
41. G. Miller (R)
42. J. Baca (D)
43. K. Calvert (R)
44. M. Bono (R)
45. D. Rohrabacher (R)
46. L. Sanchez (D)
47. C. C. Cox (R)
48. D. Issa (R)*
49. S. A. Davis (D)*
50. B. Filner (D)
51. R. Cunningham (R)
52. D. Hunter (R)

Colorado
1. D. DeGette (D)
2. M. Udall (D)
3. S. McInnis (R)
4. R. W. Schaffer (R)
5. J. Hefley (R)
6. T. Tancredo (R)

Connecticut
1. J. Larson (D)
2. R. R. Simmons (R)*
3. R. DeLauro (D)
4. C. Shays (R)
5. J. H. Maloney (D)
6. N. L. Johnson (R)

Delaware
M. N. Castle (R)

Florida
1. J. Scarborough (R)
2. A. Boyd, Jr. (D)
3. C. Brown (D)
4. A. Crenshaw (R)*
5. K. Thurman (D)
6. C. B. Stearns (R)
7. J. Mica (R)
8. R. Keller (R)*
9. M. Bilirakis (R)
10. C. W. Young (R)
11. J. Davis (D)
12. A. Putnam (R)*
13. D. Miller (R)
14. P. J. Goss (R)
15. D. Weldon (R)
16. M. Foley (R)
17. C. Meek (D)
18. I. Ros-Lehtinen (R)
19. R. Wexler (D)
20. P. Deutsch (D)
21. L. Diaz-Balart (R)
22. E. C. Shaw, Jr. (R)*
23. A. L. Hastings (D)

Georgia
1. J. Kingston (R)
2. S. Bishop (D)
3. M. Collins (R)
4. C. McKinney (D)
5. J. Lewis (D)
6. J. Isakson (R)*
7. B. Barr (R)
8. S. Chambliss (R)
9. N. Deal (R)
10. C. Norwood (R)
11. J. Linder (R)

Hawaii
1. N. Abercrombie (D)
2. P. T. Mink (D)

Idaho
1. C. L. Otter (R)*
2. M. Simpson (R)

Illinois
1. B. Rush (D)
2. J. Jackson, Jr. (D)
3. W. O. Lipinski (D)
4. L. V. Gutierrez (D)
5. R. R. Blagojevich (D)
6. H. J. Hyde (R)
7. D. K. Davis (D)
8. P. M. Crane (R)
9. J. Schakowsky (D)
10. M. Kirk (R)*
11. G. Weller (R)
12. J. F. Costello (D)
13. J. Biggert (R)
14. J. D. Hastert (R)
15. T. V. Johnson (R)*
16. D. Manzullo (R)
17. L. Evans (D)
18. R. LaHood (R)
19. D. Phelps (D)
20. J. M. Shimkus (R)

Indiana
1. P. J. Visclosky (D)
2. M. Pence (R)*
3. T. Roemer (D)
4. M. Souder (R)
5. S. Buyer (R)
6. D. L. Burton (R)
7. B. D. Kearns (R)*
8. J. Hostettler (R)
9. B. Hill (D)
10. J. Carson (D)

Iowa
1. J. A. Leach (R)
2. J. Nussle (R)
3. L. L. Boswell (D)
4. G. Ganske (R)
5. T. Latham (R)

Kansas
1. J. Moran (R)
2. J. Ryun (R)
3. D. Moore (D)
4. T. Tiahrt (R)

Kentucky
1. E. Whitfield (R)
2. R. Lewis (R)
3. A. Northup (R)
4. K. Lucas (D)
5. H. Rogers (R)
6. E. Fletcher (R)

Louisiana
1. D. Vitter (R)
2. W. J. Jefferson (D)
3. W. J. Tauzin (R)
4. J. McCrery (R)
5. J. Cooksey (R)
6. R. H. Baker (R)
7. C. John (D)

Maine
1. T. Allen (D)
2. J. Baldacci (D)

Maryland
1. W. T. Gilchrest (R)
2. R. L. Ehrlich, Jr. (R)
3. B. L. Cardin (D)
4. A. Wynn (D)
5. S. H. Hoyer (D)
6. R. Bartlett (R)
7. E. E. Cummings (D)
8. C. A. Morella (R)

Massachusetts
1. J. Olver (D)
2. R. E. Neal (D)
3. J. McGovern (D)
4. B. Frank (D)
5. M. Meehan (D)
6. J. F. Tierney (D)
7. E. J. Markey (D)
8. M. Capuano (D)
9. J. J. Moakley (D)
10. W. D. Delahunt (D)

Michigan
1. B. Stupak (D)
2. P. Hoekstra (R)
3. V. Ehlers (R)
4. D. Camp (R)
5. J. Barcia (D)
6. F. S. Upton (R)
7. N. Smith (R)
8. M. J. Rogers (R)*
9. D. E. Kildee (D)
10. D. E. Bonior (D)
11. J. Knollenberg (R)
12. S. M. Levin (D)
13. L. Rivers (D)
14. J. Conyers, Jr. (D)
15. C. C. Kilpatrick (D)
16. J. D. Dingell, Jr. (D)

Minnesota
1. G. Gutknecht (R)
2. M. Kennedy (R)*
3. J. Ramstad (R)
4. B. McCollum (D)*
5. M. O. Sabo (D)
6. W. Luther (D)
7. C. C. Peterson (D)
8. J. L. Oberstar (D)

Mississippi
1. R. Wicker (R)
2. B. Thompson (D)
3. C. W. Pickering, Jr. (R)
4. R. Shows (D)
5. G. Taylor (D)

Missouri
1. W. L. Clay, Jr. (D)*
2. T. Akin (R)*
3. R. A. Gephardt (D)
4. I. Skelton (D)
5. K. McCarthy (D)
6. S. B. Graves (R)*
7. R. Blunt (R)
8. J. A. Emerson (R)
9. K. Hulshof (R)

Montana
D. Rehberg (R)*

Nebraska
1. D. K. Bereuter (R)
2. L. Terry (R)
3. T. W. Osborne (R)*

Nevada
1. S. Berkley (D)
2. J. Gibbons (R)

New Hampshire
1. J. E. Sununu (R)
2. C. Bass (R)

New Jersey
1. R. E. Andrews (D)
2. F. LoBiondo (R)
3. H. J. Saxton (R)
4. C. H. Smith (R)
5. M. Roukema (R)
6. F. Pallone, Jr. (D)
7. M. A. Ferguson (R)*
8. W. J. Pascrell, Jr. (D)
9. S. R. Rothman (D)
10. D. M. Payne (D)
11. R. Frelinghuysen (R)
12. R. Holt (D)
13. R. Menendez (D)

New Mexico
1. H. Wilson (R)
2. J. R. Skeen (R)
3. T. Udall (D)

New York
1. F. J. Grucci, Jr. (R)*
2. S. J. Israel (D)*
3. P. T. King (R)
4. C. McCarthy (D)
5. G. L. Ackerman (D)
6. G. Meeks (D)
7. J. Crowley (D)
8. J. Nadler (D)
9. A. Weiner (D)
10. E. Towns (D)
11. M. R. Owens (D)
12. N. Velazquez (D)
13. V. J. Fossella (R)
14. C. Maloney (D)
15. C. B. Rangel (D)
16. J. E. Serrano (D)
17. E. L. Engel (D)
18. N. M. Lowey (D)
19. S. W. Kelly (R)
20. B. A. Gilman (R)
21. M. R. McNulty (D)

22. J. E. Sweeney (R)
23. S. L. Boehlert (R)
24. J. McHugh (R)
25. J. T. Walsh (R)
26. M. Hinchey (D)
27. T. M. Reynolds (R)
28. L. M. Slaughter (D)
29. J. J. LaFalce (D)
30. J. Quinn (R)
31. A. Houghton, Jr. (R)

North Carolina
1. E. Clayton (D)
2. B. R. Etheridge (D)
3. W. Jones, Jr. (R)
4. D. E. Price (D)
5. R. Burr (R)
6. J. H. Coble (R)
7. M. McIntyre (D)
8. R. Hayes (R)
9. S. Myrick (R)
10. T. C. Ballenger (R)
11. C. H. Taylor (R)
12. M. Watt (D)

North Dakota
E. Pomeroy (D)

Ohio
1. S. Chabot (R)
2. R. Portman (R)
3. T. P. Hall (D)
4. M. G. Oxley (R)
5. P. E. Gillmor (R)
6. T. Strickland (D)
7. D. L. Hobson (R)
8. J. A. Boehner (R)
9. M. Kaptur (D)
10. D. Kucinich (D)
11. S. T. Jones (D)
12. P. J. Tiberi (R)*
13. S. Brown (D)
14. T. C. Sawyer (D)
15. D. Pryce (R)
16. R. S. Regula (R)
17. J. A. Traficant, Jr. (D)
18. B. Ney (R)
19. S. LaTourette (R)

Oklahoma
1. S. Largent (R)
2. B. Carson (D)*
3. W. Watkins (R)
4. J. C. Watts (R)
5. E. J. Istook (R)
6. F. Lucas (R)

Oregon
1. D. Wu (D)
2. G. Walden (R)
3. E. Blumenauer (D)
4. P. DeFazio (D)
5. D. Hooley (D)

Pennsylvania
1. R. Brady (D)
2. C. Fattah (D)
3. R. A. Borski (D)
4. M. A. Hart (R)*
5. J. E. Peterson (R)

6. T. Holden (D)
7. W. C. Weldon (R)
8. J. Greenwood (R)
9. E. G. Shuster (R)
10. D. L. Sherwood (R)
11. P. E. Kanjorski (D)
12. J. P. Murtha, Jr. (D)
13. J. M. Hoeffel (D)
14. W. J. Coyne (D)
15. P. Toomey (R)
16. J. R. Pitts (R)
17. G. W. Gekas (R)
18. M. Doyle (D)
19. T. R. Platts (R)*
20. F. Mascara (D)
21. P. English (R)

Rhode Island
1. P. Kennedy (D)
2. J. R. Langevin (D)*

South Carolina
1. H. E. Brown, Jr. (R)*
2. F. Spence (R)
3. L. Graham (R)
4. J. DeMint (R)
5. J. M. Spratt, Jr. (D)
6. J. Clyburn (D)

South Dakota
J. Thune (R)

Tennessee
1. W. Jenkins (R)
2. J. J. Duncan, Jr. (R)
3. Z. Wamp (R)
4. V. Hilleary (R)
5. B. Clement (D)
6. B. J. Gordon (D)
7. E. Bryant (R)
8. J. S. Tanner (D)
9. H. E. Ford, Jr. (D)

Texas
1. M. Sandlin (D)
2. J. Turner (D)
3. S. Johnson (R)
4. R. M. Hall (D)
5. P. Sessions (R)
6. J. Barton (R)
7. J. A. Culberson (R)*
8. K. Brady (R)
9. N. Lampson (D)
10. L. Doggett (D)
11. C. Edwards (D)
12. K. Granger (R)
13. W. Thornberry (R)
14. R. Paul (R)
15. R. Hinojosa (D)
16. S. Reyes (D)
17. C. W. Stenholm (D)
18. S. Jackson-Lee (D)
19. L. Combest (R)
20. C. Gonzalez (D)
21. L. S. Smith (R)
22. T. D. DeLay (R)
23. H. Bonilla (R)
24. J. M. Frost (D)
25. K. Bentsen (D)
26. D. Armey (R)

27. S. P. Ortiz (D)
28. C. Rodriguez (D)
29. G. Green (D)
30. E. B. Johnson (D)

Utah
1. J. V. Hansen (R)
2. J. D. Matheson (D)*
3. C. Cannon (R)

Vermont
B. Sanders (I)

Virginia
1. J. S. Davis (R)*
2. E. L. Schrock (R)*
3. R. C. Scott (D)
4. N. Sisisky (D)
5. V. H. Goode, Jr. (I)**
6. R. Goodlatte (R)
7. E. I. Cantor (R)*
8. J. P. Moran, Jr. (D)
9. F. C. Boucher (D)
10. F. R. Wolf (R)
11. T. Davis III (R)

Washington
1. J. Inslee (D)
2. R. R. Larsen (D)*
3. B. Baird (D)
4. D. Hastings (R)
5. G. Nethercutt (R)
6. N. D. Dicks (D)
7. J. McDermott (D)
8. J. Dunn (R)
9. A. Smith (D)

West Virginia
1. A. B. Mollohan (D)
2. S. M. Capito (R)*
3. N. J. Rahall II (D)

Wisconsin
1. P. Ryan (R)
2. T. Baldwin (D)
3. R. Kind (D)
4. G. D. Kleczka (D)
5. T. Barrett (D)
6. T. E. Petri (R)
7. D. R. Obey (D)
8. M. Green (R)
9. F. J. Sensenbrenner, Jr. (R)

Wyoming
B. Cubin (R)

(D) Democrat
(R) Republican
(I) Independent

* elected in 2000
  all others: re-elected in 2000
** switched parties in 2000
*** due to death of J. Dixon, in
    December

UNITED STATES SUPREME COURT

Chief Justice: William H. Rehnquist (1986)
Associate Justices:
John Paul Stevens (1975)
Sandra Day O'Connor (1981)
Antonin Scalia (1986)
Anthony M. Kennedy (1988)
David H. Souter (1990)
Clarence Thomas (1991)
Ruth Bader Ginsburg (1993)
Stephen G. Breyer (1994)

UNITED STATES CABINET

(President-elect G. W. Bush's Cabinet
nominations, as of January 1, 2001)

Secretary of Agriculture: Ann M. Veneman
Attorney General: John D. Ashcroft
Secretary of Commerce: Donald L. Evans
Secretary of Defense: Donald H. Rumsfeld
Secretary of Education: Roderick R. Paige
Secretary of Energy: Spencer Abraham
Secretary of Health and Human Services: Tommy G. Thompson
Secretary of Housing and Urban Development: Mel Martinez
Secretary of Interior: Gale A. Norton
Secretary of Labor: Linda Chavez
Secretary of State: Colin L. Powell
Secretary of Transportation: Norman Y. Mineta
Secretary of the Treasury: Paul H. O'Neill
Secretary of Veteran Affairs: Anthony J. Principi

Missouri Governor Mel Carnahan had been running for the U.S. Senate when he was killed in a plane crash in October. Nevertheless, he won the election, and his wife, Jean (*above*), was appointed to fill the seat.

STATE GOVERNORS

Alabama	Donald Siegelman (D)
Alaska	Tony Knowles (D)
Arizona	Jane Dee Hull (R)
Arkansas	Mike Huckabee (R)
California	Gray Davis (D)
Colorado	Bill Owens (R)
Connecticut	John Rowland (R)
Delaware	Ruth Ann Minner (D)*
Florida	Jeb Bush (R)
Georgia	Roy Barnes (D)
Hawaii	Ben Cayetano (D)
Idaho	Dirk Kempthorne (R)
Illinois	George H. Ryan (R)
Indiana	Frank O'Bannon (D)**
Iowa	Tom Vilsack (D)
Kansas	Bill Graves (R)
Kentucky	Paul Patton (D)
Louisiana	Mike Foster (R)
Maine	Angus King (I)
Maryland	Parris Glendening (D)
Massachusetts	Paul Cellucci (R)
Michigan	John Engler (R)
Minnesota	Jesse Ventura (RF)
Mississippi	Ronnie Musgrove (D)
Missouri	Bob Holden (D)*
Montana	Judy Martz (R)*
Nebraska	Mike Johanns (R)
Nevada	Kenny Guinn (R)
New Hampshire	Jeanne Shaheen (D)**
New Jersey	Christine Todd Whitman (R) [1]
New Mexico	Gary Johnson (R)
New York	George Pataki (R)
North Carolina	Mike Easley (D)*
North Dakota	John Hoeven (R)*
Ohio	Bob Taft (R)
Oklahoma	Frank Keating (R)
Oregon	John Kitzhaber (D)
Pennsylvania	Thomas J. Ridge (R)
Rhode Island	Lincoln Almond (R)
South Carolina	Jim Hodges (D)
South Dakota	William Janklow (R)
Tennessee	Don Sundquist (R)
Texas	Rick Perry (R) [2]
Utah	Mike Leavitt (R)**
Vermont	Howard Dean (D)**
Virginia	James S. Gilmore III (R)
Washington	Gary Locke (D)**
West Virginia	Robert E. Wise, Jr. (D)*
Wisconsin	Tommy G. Thompson (R) [3]
Wyoming	Jim Geringer (R)

*elected in 2000   **re-elected in 2000   (D) Democrat   (R) Republican   (I) Independent   (RF) Reform

[1] nominated by G. W. Bush to head the U.S. Environmental Protection Agency
[2] succeeded G. W. Bush
[3] nominated by G. W. Bush to become Secretary of Health and Human Services

CANADA

Capital: Ottawa
Head of State: Queen Elizabeth II
Governor General: Adrienne Clarkson
Prime Minister: Jean Chrétien (Liberal)
Leader of the Opposition: Stockwell Day (Canadian Alliance)
Population: 30,800,000
Area: 3,851,809 sq mi (9,976,185 km²)

PROVINCES AND TERRITORIES

Alberta
Capital: Edmonton
Lieutenant Governor: Lois E. Hole
Premier: Ralph Klein (Progressive Conservative)
Leader of the Opposition: Nancy MacBeth (Liberal)
Entered Confederation: Sept. 1, 1905
Population: 2,997,000
Area: 255,285 sq mi (661,188 km²)

British Columbia
Capital: Victoria
Lieutenant Governor: Garde Gardom
Premier: Ujjal Dosanjh (New Democratic Party)
Leader of the Opposition: Gordon Campbell (Liberal)
Entered Confederation: July 20, 1871
Population: 4,063,700
Area: 366,255 sq mi (948,600 km²)

Manitoba
Capital: Winnipeg
Lieutenant Governor: Peter M. Liba
Premier: Gary Albert Doer (New Democratic Party)
Leader of the Opposition: Stuart Murray
   (Progressive Conservative)
Entered Confederation: July 15, 1870
Population: 1,147,900
Area: 251,000 sq mi (650,090 km²)

New Brunswick
Capital: Fredericton
Lieutenant Governor: Marilyn Trenholme Counsell
Premier: Bernard Lord (Progressive Conservative)
Leader of the Opposition: Camille Thériault (Liberal)
Entered Confederation: July 1, 1867
Population: 756,600
Area: 28,354 sq mi (73,436 km²)

Newfoundland
Capital: St. John's
Lieutenant Governor: Arthur Max House
Premier: Beaton Tulk (Liberal)
Leader of the Opposition: Ed Byrne
   (Progressive Conservative)
Entered Confederation: March 31, 1949
Population: 538,800
Area: 156,185 sq mi (404,517 km²)

Nova Scotia
Capital: Halifax
Lieutenant Governor: Myra A. Freeman
Premier: John F. Hamm (Progressive Conservative)
Leader of the Opposition: Helen MacDonald (New
   Democratic Party)
Entered Confederation: July 1, 1867
Population: 941,000
Area: 21,425 sq mi (55,491 km²)

Ontario
Capital: Toronto
Lieutenant Governor: Hilary M. Weston
Premier: Mike Harris (Progressive Conservative)
Leader of the Opposition: Dalton McGuinty (Liberal)
Entered Confederation: July 1, 1867
Population: 11,669,300
Area: 412,582 sq mi (1,068,582 km²)

Prince Edward Island
Capital: Charlottetown
Lieutenant Governor: Gilbert R. Clements
Premier: Patrick Binns (Progressive Conservative)
Leader of the Opposition: Ron MacKinley (Liberal)
Entered Confederation: July 1, 1873
Population: 138,900
Area: 2,184 sq mi (5,657 km²)

Quebec
Capital: Quebec City
Lieutenant Governor: Lise Thibault
Premier: Lucien Bouchard (Parti Québécois)
Leader of the Opposition: Jean Charest (Liberal)
Entered Confederation: July 1, 1867
Population: 7,372,400
Area: 594,860 sq mi (1,540,700 km^2)

Saskatchewan
Capital: Regina
Lieutenant Governor: Lynda M. Haverstock
Premier: Roy Romanow (New Democratic Party)
Leader of the Opposition: Elwin Hermanson
    (Saskatchewan Party)
Entered Confederation: Sept. 1, 1905
Population: 1,023,600
Area: 251,700 sq mi (651,900 km^2)

Yukon
Capital: Whitehorse
Premier: Pat Duncan (Liberal)
Leader of the Opposition: Eric Fairclough (New
    Democratic Party)
Commissioner: Jack Cable
Organized as a Territory: June 13, 1898
Population: 30,700
Area: 186,299 sq mi (482,515 km^2)

Northwest Territories
Capital: Yellowknife
Commissioner: Glenna Hansen
Government Leader: Stephen Kakfwi
Reconstituted as a Territory: Sept. 1, 1905
Population: 42,100
Area: 468,000 sq mi (1,170,000 km^2)

Nunavut
Capital: Iqaluit
Commissioner: Peter Irniq
Government Leader: Paul Okalik
Organized as a Territory: April 1, 1999
Population: 27,700
Area: 797,600 sq mi (1,994,000 km^2)

INDEX

A

Academy Awards 248–49, *pictures* 248–49
Accidents and disasters
  avalanches and landslides 332–33
  cable-car fire (Austria) 38
  Carnahan, Mel, death of 36
  Cole explosion 36, 60
  ferry sinking (Indonesia) 28
  fires (western United States) 26, 127–28
  floods (India and Bangladesh) 32
  oil spill (South Africa) 129
  submarine accident (Russia) 32
Accounting, careers in 225–26
Acela Express (train), *picture* 38
Adams, Abigail (American First Lady) 217
Adams, John (president of the United States) 217, 258
Adams, John Quincy (president of the United States) 48
Adoption, stamps commemorating 139
Adventures of Rocky and Bullwinkle, The (movie) 267
Afghanistan 384
Africa
  endangered primates 35
  lovebirds 90–91
  political turmoil 52–55
African Americans
  census predictions 197
  young people's literature 292, 295
African gray parrots 91
African wildcats, *picture* 92
Agassi, Andre (American athlete) 190
Aged, the *see* Old age
Agriculture
  genetically modified foods 104–7
Aguilera, Christina (American singer) 270, *picture* 271
Ahtisaari, Martti (president of Finland) 21
AIDS 54
Alaska
  auroras 132
  caribou 335
  census count begun in 195
  Inuit 318–22
  moose 334
Albania 384
Alberta (province, Canada) 394
Albright, Madeleine (United States Secretary of State) 56, 205
Alex (African gray parrot) 91
Alferov, Zhores I. (Russian scientist) 37
Algeria 384
Aliki (American author)
  William Shakespeare & the Globe (book) 294
Allen, Steve (American entertainer) 380, *picture* 380
Almost Famous (movie) 267, *picture* 267
Altman, Scott (American astronaut) 34

Amanar, Simona (Romanian athlete) 164
Amato, Giuliano (premier of Italy) 25
Amazon parrots 90, 91
American Beauty (movie), *picture* 248
American Museum of Natural History (New York City) 108–9, 211, 213
America Online (AOL) 18
Amistad (ship) 30
Amtrak train, *picture* 38
Andorra 384
Andrews, Jessica (American singer) 274
Angola 53, 384
Animals
  balance of natural ecosystems 100
  carnivorous plants eat insects 82–85
  chameleons 70–73, *picture* 68–69
  cloning 22, *picture* 22
  commemorative coins and stamps 140–41, 159
  dinosaur fossil discoveries 74–75
  elk and moose 334
  endangered primates 35
  genetically modified foods 104–5, 106
  Hawaii 241
  newsmakers, *pictures* 92–95
  Olympic mascots, *picture* 167
  pandas at National Zoo 40
  parrots 88–91
  protection of young 76–81
  reindeer and caribou 335
  rhythms of life 120, 122
  sea stars 86–87
  word puzzle 142
Animation 265, 267
  Looney Tunes stamps 139
Anniversaries
  Hubble Space Telescope, 10th anniversary of 97, 119
  Library of Congress, 200th anniversary of, *pictures* 158, 258
  Peanuts comic strip, 50th anniversary of 159, *picture* 159
  Saint-Exupéry, Antoine de, 100th anniversary of birth of, *picture* 259
  Silly Putty, 50th anniversary of, *picture* 236
  Vietnam War, 25th anniversary of end of 202, 205
  Vikings' arrival in North America, 1000th anniversary of 212–13
  White House, 200th anniversary of 216–19
  Wonderful Wizard of Oz, 100th anniversary of, *picture* 235
Antarctic 126, 127
Antibiotics 25, 124–25
Antigua and Barbuda 384
Antiope (asteroid) 116
Antitrust laws 24
Apes 35
Aquarius Underwater Laboratory (Florida), 241, *picture* 239
Arafat, Yasir (Palestinian leader) 30, 62, 63
Archeology
  time capsules 208–11
Archery 170
Arctic 126, 132, 318–22
Argentina 384
Aristide, Jean-Bertrand (president of Haiti) 38
Arizona
  census and congressional seats 196

Arkansas
Whitewater investigation 35
Armenia 141, 384
Armstrong, Lance (American cyclist) 30, *picture* 30
Army, United States
missing in action, search for 204
Arthur, Chester (president of the United States) 218
Arts *see also* Sculpture
fireworks 199–201
left-handed artists in history 112
Puppy (floral sculpture by Jeff Koons), *picture* 262
Rockwell, Norman, *pictures* 261
traditional crafts at EXPO 2000 207
Viking objects, *pictures* 213, 215
Arzu Irigoyen, Alvaro (president of Guatemala) 19
Asian Americans
census predictions 197
Mineta, Norman Y., first Asian-American Cabinet member 28
Assad, Bashar al- (president of Syria) 28, 62, *picture* 62
Assad, Hafez al- (president of Syria) 28, 62
Asset managers 228–29
Asteroids 116–17
Astronomy
auroras 130–33
Hayden Planetarium 108–9
Hubble Space Telescope, view from, *picture* 96–97
space programs 20, 27, 34, 36, 114–16
Atlantis (space shuttle) 27, 34
Atmosphere, ozone hole in 127
Auroras (polar lights) 130–33
Australia 384
animals as Olympic mascots, *picture* 167
boomerangs, origin of 144–45
brave cat, *picture* 94
coins 159
millennium celebrations 19, 198
Olympic Games (Sydney) 36, 162–73, *pictures* 164, 165
parrots 89, 90
Austria 21, 38, 384
Avalanches 332–33
Aviation
Carnahan, Mel, death of 36
Saint-Exupéry, Antoine de 259
Awards *see* Prizes and awards
Azerbaijan 384

B

Babbitt, Natalie (American author)
Ouch! (book) 294
Babysitter, The (painting by Norman Rockwell), *picture* 261
Backstreet Boys (music group) 270, *picture* 272
Bacteria, drug-resistant 25, 124–25
Badminton 170
Bahamas 384
Bahrain 384
Ballard, Robert (American oceanographer) 238, 240, 241, *picture* 240

Bamboo (plant) 122
Bandaranaike, Sirimavo (prime minister of Sri Lanka) 380
Bangladesh 32, 384
Banking, careers in 224–25, 231
Barak, Ehud (prime minister of Israel) 30, 41, 62, 63
Barbados 163, 384
Barenaked Ladies (music group) 270–71
Barrymore, Drew (American actress) 266
Baseball 174–76
left-handed players 112
Little League 177
Olympic Games 167, 170
Basketball 178–80
Olympic Games 167–68, 170
Bats (animals) 81
Baum, L. Frank (American author)
Wonderful Wizard of Oz, The, picture 235
Beach volleyball 168, 170
Beaks (of parrots) 88
Bears 78, 126
Beatles (music group) 275
Beautiful (movie) 267
Beavers 78
Bédié, Henri Konan (president of the Ivory Coast) 55
Belarus 384
Belgium 384
Belize 384
Bell, Jamie (British actor) 266
Benin 384
Berg, Laura (American athlete), *picture* 167
Best in Show (movie) 267
Beverly Hills, 90210 (television program), *picture* 257
Bhattarai, Krishna Prasad (premier of Nepal) 22
Bhutan 206, 384
Bicentennial Wagon Train Time Capsule 210
Bicycling *see* Cycling
Billy Elliot (movie) 266
Bin Laden, Osama (international terrorist) 60
Biodiversity (variety of life on Earth) 98–101
Biology
biodiversity 98–101
emotions 323–24
genetically modified foods 104–7
handedness 110–13
human genome 102–3
rhythms of life 120–23
Birchbark House, The (book by Louise Erdrich) 295
Birds
kookaburra as Olympic mascot 167
parrots 88–91
penguin rescue 129
peregrine falcon, *picture* 101
protection of young 76, 77–78, 79–80, 80–81
rhythms of life 120, 122
Woodstock (comic-strip character) 245
Bizimungu, Pasteur (president of Rwanda) 25
Björk (Icelandic singer) 273
Bladderworts (carnivorous plants) 84–85
Blanton, Dain (American athlete) 168
Bloomfield, Michael (American astronaut) 40
Bolivia 384
Bondevik, Kjell Magne (premier of Norway) 22

Books see Literature; Young people's literature
Boomerangs 144–49
Bosnia and Herzegovina 61, 384
Botswana 54, 141, 384
Boxing 168, 170–71
Boy bands 272
Boys Don't Cry (movie), *picture* 249
Boyz II Men (music group) 270
Bradley, Bill (American political figure) 43
Brain 110–11, 323–24
Brazil 19, 35, 90, 198, 384
Bridges, Ruby (American author)
   Through My Eyes (book) 295
British Columbia (province, Canada) 394
Brown, Charlie (comic-strip character) 244–47,
   pictures 244, 246
Brown, Sally (comic-strip character) 245
Bruijn, Inge de (Dutch athlete) 166
Brunei Darussalam 384
Bud, Not Buddy (book by Christopher Paul
   Curtis) 292
Budgerigars (parakeets) 90
Buffalo 81
Buffett, Warren (American investor) 228
Bulgaria 207, 384
Burbank, Daniel (American astronaut) 34
Burkina Faso 384
Burma (Myanmar) 384
Burton, Richard (British actor) 253
Burundi 53, 384
Bush, George (president of the United States) 110,
   picture 110
Bush, George W. (president of the United States)
   32, 40–41, 42–48, *pictures* 12–13, 32, 42, 46
Bush, Laura (wife of George W. Bush) 47,
   picture 32
Business
   America Online-Time Warner merger 18
Butterflies 106, *picture* 107
Butterworts (carnivorous plants) 84

C

Cabinet, United States 393
Caesar, Julius (Roman ruler) 21
Caine, Michael (British actor), *picture* 249
Cairo (Egypt) 198
Caldecott Medal (children's literature) 279, 293
Calendars
   leap year 21
   perpetual calendar, how to make a 156
California
   bulletproof vests for police dogs, *picture* 233
   census and congressional seats 196
   Democratic Party's national convention 32
Caligula (Roman emperor) 251
Cambodia 385
Cameroon 168, 385
Camouflage (of animals) 70–71, 80
Campaign finances 44, *picture* 66
Canada 385
   auroras 132
   caribou 335
   children's literature awards 293

coins 158–59, *pictures* 159
elections 39
elk and moose 334
football 182
global warming 126
Group of Eight summit meeting 30
Inuit 318–22
moose statues in Toronto 256
oil prices 51
Olympic Games 166, 168–69, *picture* 168
provinces and territories 394–95
recipe 152
space program 40, 114
stamps 138, 139, 141
Trudeau, Pierre Elliott, death of 383
Viking settlement remains 214–15,
   picture 214
Canoeing 171
Cape Verde 385
Capitol, United States 210
Careers in the financial industry 224–31
Carey, Mariah (American singer) 271
Caribou 335
Carlsson, Arvid (Swedish scientist) 37
Carnahan, Jean (United States Senator), *picture*
   183
Carnahan, Mel (governor of Missouri) 36, 380
Carnivorous plants 82–85
Carolina parakeets (extinct birds) 88
Carpenter, John (American quiz-show winner),
   picture 263
Carrey, Jim (Canadian actor) 267
Carrington, Richard (English astronomer) 131
Carter, Aaron (American singer) 270
Carter, Cris (American football player),
   picture 181
Cartland, Barbara (British novelist) 380,
   picture 380
Cassini (spacecraft) 118
Castro, Fidel (president of Cuba) 29
Catfish 78
Cats
   brave Australian cat, *picture* 94
   commemorative stamps 141
   International Cat Show winner, *picture* 93
   predators should be kept from roaming 101
   protection of young 79
   "test-tube" wildcat kitten, *picture* 92
Cayman Islands 141
Celera Genomics (company) 103
Cells (basic units of life) 122
Census, United States (official count of the
   population) 194–97, *picture* 192–93
Central African Republic 385
Century Safe, The (time capsule) 210
Chad 385
Chameleons (lizards) 70–73, *picture* 68–69
Chang Chun-hsiung (premier of Taiwan) 37
Charlie Brown (comic-strip character) 244–47,
   pictures 244, 246
Charlie Brown Christmas, A (television program)
   246
Charlie's Angels (movie) 266
Chechnya (Russian province) 59
Chemistry, Nobel Prize in 37
Cheney, Lynne (wife of Richard Cheney), *picture*
   32

Cheney, Richard B. (vice president of the United States) 32, 43, 47, *picture* 32, 44
Chen Shui-bian (president of Taiwan) 23, 57–58
Chiao, Leroy (American astronaut) 36
Chicago (Illinois)
    Field Museum dinosaur display 74
    millennium celebrations 198
Chickadees 79
Chicken Run (movie) 265, *picture* 265
Chickens 79
Children *see* Youth
Chile 18, 385
China 385
    coins 159
    cultured pearls 255
    endangered primates 35
    EXPO 2000 pavilion 207
    fireworks, invention of 199
    millennium celebrations 19
    Olympic Games 36, 163, 164, 166, 167
    pandas loaned to United States 40
    Taiwan, relations with 56–58
    United States, relations with 34, 58
Chinese New Year
    commemorative coins and stamps 139, 159
Chlorofluorocarbons (CFC's) 127
Chrétien, Jean (prime minister of Canada) 39, *picture* 39
Chromatophores (chameleon's color cells) 71
Chronobiology (study of biological rhythms) 120–23
Cider House Rules, The (movie), *picture* 249
Circadian rhythms (daily rhythms of life) 120
Civil War, United States
    Hunley, raising of the 33
"Claymation" (animation method) 265
Cleary, Beverly (American author)
    Ramona's World (book) 295
Clement, Gary (Canadian author)
    Great Poochini, The (book) 293
Cleopatra (queen of Egypt) 251
Climate and global warming 126
Clinton, Hillary Rodham (American First Lady and United States Senator), 34–35, 49, *pictures* 65, 208
Clinton, William Jefferson (Bill) (president of the United States), *pictures* 18, 25, 55, 110, 208
    final State of the Union address 18
    Giant Sequoia National Monument 25
    Hawaiian nature preserve 40
    left-handedness 110
    Middle East peace talks 30, 62, 63
    OpSail 2000 address 30
    trip to Africa 52
    trip to India and Pakistan 22
    trip to Russia 59
    trip to Vietnam 38, 205
    Whitewater investigation 34–35
Clocks, floral 123
Clocks, internal 122–23
Cloning (genetic replication) 22
Clooney, George (American actor) 265, *picture* 266
Close, Glenn (American actress) 267
Clothing and fashion
    high-tech sports gear 169
Cloud swifts (birds) 77
Cockatoos (parrots) 90, 91, *picture* 89

Cohen, William (United States Defense Secretary) 205
Coin collecting 158–59
Cole, USS (United States Navy destroyer) 36, 60
Colombia 207, 385
Color
    auroras 131–32
    chameleons 70–71, 73
    fiddler crabs 120
    pearls 254
Colorado
    census and congressional seats 196
Comic strips 244–47
    cartoon characters on coins 159
    Schulz, Charles, death of 383
Communication, animal 78–79, 91
Communism 202–5
Comoros 385
Compact discs (CD's) 276
Computers *see also* Internet
    Hayden Planetarium 109
    keyboard, left-handed, *picture* 110
    Love Bug virus 26
    Microsoft monopoly ruling 24
    music distribution on Internet 276–77
    video games 316–17
    Y2K bug 18
Confederate flag 24
Congo (Zaire) 52–53, 385
Congo Republic 385
Congress of the United States 390–92 *see also* House of Representatives; Senate
Connecticut
    census and congressional seats 196
Constantinescu, Emil (president of Romania) 41
Cook Islands 159
Copyright laws 277
Coral reefs 40
Coretta Scott King Author award 292
Corn, genetically modified 105, 106, *pictures* 105, 107
Cornerstones (of buildings) 209
Costa Rica 385
Country music 274
Coverdell, Paul (United States Senator) 380
Cows, fiberglass statues of, *picture* 242–43
Crabs 120, 122, *picture* 98
Crafts *see* Arts; Hobbies, handicrafts, and projects
Creed (music group) 270
Crime *see also* Terrorism
    Internet hacking attack 20
    left-handed criminals in history 112
    Love Bug computer virus 26
Croatia 385
Crocodiles 79
Crowe, Cameron (American film director) 267
Crowe, Russell (Australian actor) 266
Crudup, Billy (American actor) 267
Cruise, Tom (American actor) 266
Crypt of Civilization 210, *picture* 209
Cuba 385
    González, Elián 29
    Olympic Games 166, 167, 168
Cults, religious 22
Cultured pearls 253–54, 255
Curtis, Christopher Paul (American author)
    Bud, Not Buddy (book) 292

Cycling 30, 171
Cyprus 385
Czech Republic 385

D

D'Alema, Massimo (premier of Italy) 25
Daley, William M. (United States Secretary of Commerce) 28
Dallas Stars (hockey team) 185–87
Davenport, Lindsay (American athlete) 190, 191
Day, Stockwell (Canadian politician) 39
Deaths 380–83
  Carnahan, Mel 36
  Richard, Maurice 187
  Schulz, Charles 244
Deer
  elk and moose 334
  protection of young 79, 80, 81
  reindeer and caribou 335
Dementieva, Elena (Russian athlete) 168
Demirel, Suleyman (president of Turkey) 27
Democratic Party (of the United States) 32, 42–49
Demonstrations and protests
  genetically modified foods, *pictures* 104, 107
  Haddock, Doris, cross-country walk protesting campaign finance system, *picture* 66
  high oil prices in Europe 51
  Yugoslavia 61, *picture* 60
De Niro, Robert (American actor) 264, 266
Denmark 385
De Paola, Tomie (American author)
  26 Fairmount Avenue (book) 295
Destiny's Child (music group), *picture* 273
Diaz, Cameron (American actress) 266
Dinosaur (movie) 267
Dinosaurs, fossil discoveries of 74–75
Diouf, Abdou (president of Senegal) 23
Disasters *see* Accidents and disasters
Discovery (space shuttle) 36, 115
Diving 165, 166, 172, *picture* 166
Dixie Chicks (music group) 274
Djibouti 385
DNA (Deoxyribonucleic acid) 102–3, 105
"Dog-bone" asteroid 117
Dogs
  bulletproof vests for police dogs, *picture* 233
  commemorative stamps 141
  dogsled, *picture* 195
  litter of sixteen Saint Bernard puppies, *picture* 94
  motion pictures 266, 267
  predators should be kept from roaming 101
  protection of young 79
  Puppy (floral sculpture by Jeff Koons), *picture* 262
  Snoopy (comic-strip character) 245
  star of the movie *My Dog Skip*, *picture* 95
  Westminster Kennel Club Show winner, *picture* 93
Dolphins 81
Dominica 18–19, 141, 385
Dominican Republic 27, 385
Douglas, Roosevelt (prime minister of Dominica) 18–19
"Doves" (opponents of the Vietnam War) 203
Dragila, Stacy (American athlete), *picture* 189

Dre, Dr. (American singer) 274, 277
Driver, Minnie (British actress) 267
Drug abuse (at Olympic Games) 164
Ducks 80–81
Duffy, Brian (American astronaut) 36
Duvall, Clea (American actress), *picture* 249

E

Eagles 77
Earth (planet) 118–19
Eastwood, Clint (American actor) 265, *picture* 266
E-books, *picture* 260
Echidnas (mammals) 167
Echinoderms (animals) 86–87
Ecology *see* Environment
Economics
  Group of Eight summit meeting 30
  Nobel Prize in 37
  presidential election issues 44
  United States economic boom 50–51
Ecosystems (plants and animals in a habitat) 98
Ecuador 19, 385
Education
  JASON Project 238–41
  presidential election issues 44–45
Egypt 19, 198, 207, 385
Eiffel Tower (Paris, France) 198, *picture* 199
Eisenberg, Hallie Kate (American actress) 267
Elections *see also* Presidents (of the United States)
  campaign finances 44, *picture* 66
Electoral College (of the United States) 42, 45, 48, 49
Electric trains, *picture* 38
Electronic publishing, *picture* 260
Electronics 37
Elizabeth (Queen Mother of Britain), *picture* 64
Elizabeth I (queen of England), *picture* 251
Elk 334
Elliott, Alecia (American singer) 274
El Salvador 385
E-mail viruses 26
Eminem (American singer) 274
Emmy Awards 268–69, *pictures* 268, 269
Emotions (feelings) 323–24
Endangered species
  carnivorous plants 83, 85
  commemorative stamps 140–41
  pandas 40
  parrots 89
  primates 35
  protection 100–101
  "test-tube" method of reproduction 92
Endeavour (space shuttle) 20, 40, 114, 118
England *see* United Kingdom
Environment
  biodiversity 98–101
  biological rhythms and 122
  EXPO 2000 exhibits 206–7
  global warming 126
  Hawaiian nature preserve 40
  penguin rescue 129
  presidential election issues 45
  wildfires 127–28

Equatorial Guinea 385
Equestrian events 171
Erdrich, Louise (American author)
    Birchbark House, The (book) 295
Ericson, Leif (Norse explorer) 214, 215
Eric the Red (Viking chieftain) 214
Erin Brockovich (movie) 264
Eritrea 54, 385
Eros (asteroid) 116
Eskimos see Inuit
Estonia 385
Ethics and corruption
    African political turmoil 52
    Clinton, Bill, and Whitewater affair 34–35
Ethiopia 54, 165, 206, 385
Europa (moon of Jupiter) 118
Europa stamps 139–40
Europe
    genetically modified foods 106
    Middle Ages 325–31
    oil price increases 51
    World War I 336–51
    World War II 352–61, 367–76, 378
European Space Agency 114
Everybody Loves Raymond (television program),
    picture 269
Exploration and discovery
    JASON Project 238–41
    Vikings 212–15
Explosions
    Cole, USS 36, 60
    Russian submarine accident 32
EXPO 2000 (world's fair in Germany) 206–7
Extinct species 100
    biodiversity 98, 99
    Carolina parakeets 88
    primates 35
Extrasolar planets 119
Eyes (of animals)
    chameleons 73
    sea stars 86

F

Faeroe Islands 213–14
Falcons (birds), *picture* 101
Fanning, Shawn (American student) 277
Fantasia (movie) 267
Fast foods 107
Federal Bureau of Investigation (FBI) 20
Federal Reserve Board 50, 51
Feet (of animals)
    parrots 88
    sea stars 86–87
Fencing (sport) 171
Fernandez Reyna, Leonel (president of the
    Dominican Republic) 27
Ferry accident (Indonesia) 28
Fiberglass statues, *pictures* 242–43, 256
Fiddler crabs 120, 122
Field hockey 171
Field Museum of Natural History (Chicago,
    Illinois) 74
Fiji 30, 141, 385

Finance, careers in 224–31
Financial planners 229–30
Finland 21, 385
Fioravanti, Domenico (Italian athlete) 166
Fire
    cable-car fire (Austria) 38
    wildfires (western United States) 26, 127–28
Fireworks 198–201
Fish 78, 99–100
Flag, American, Web site on 222
Flag, Confederate 24
Fleming, Alexander (Scottish scientist) 124
Floods (in India and Bangladesh) 32
Floral clocks 123
Florida
    auroras 132
    census and congressional seats 196
    González, Elián 29
    housing development in Everglades, *picture* 100
    presidential election (2000) 40–41, 47–49
Flowers
    Puppy (floral sculpture by Jeff Koons), *picture* 262
    rhythms of life 120, 123
Fonoimoana, Eric (American athlete) 168
Food
    genetically modified foods 104–7
    recipes 152–53
Food and Drug Administration, United States 106
Football 181–83
Ford, Gerald (president of the United States) 110
Fossils *see* Paleontology
Foster, Jodie (American actress) 109
Fourth of July 30, 200
Fox, Michael J. (Canadian actor), *picture* 269
Fox Quesada, Vicente (president of Mexico) 30
France 385
    Group of Eight summit meeting 30
    Louis, son of Louis XVI and Marie Antoinette,
        picture 65
    millennium celebrations 198, *picture* 199
    stamps 140
    Vietnam War, background of 202
Freaks and Geeks (television program), *picture*
    220–21
Freeman, Cathy (Australian athlete) 163, 165,
    pictures 162, 164
Frito-Lay, Inc. 107
Frogs, Web site on 223
Fugit, Patrick (American actor) 267, *picture* 267
Fujimori, Alberto (president of Peru) 39
Fu Mingxia (Chinese athlete), *picture* 166
Fungi, *picture* 99

G

Gabon 385
Galaxy Quest (movie) 266–67
Galileo (spacecraft) 116, 118, *picture* 117
Gambia 385
Gannon, Rich (American football player), *picture*
    182
Gao Xinjian (Chinese-born French author) 37
Gardner, Rulon (American athlete) 168
Garfield (cartoon character) 159, *picture* 159

Garland, Judy (American actress), *picture* 235
Garneau, Marc (Canadian astronaut) 40
Garner, James (American actor) 265, *picture* 266
Gates, Bill (American entrepreneur), *picture* 24
Gbagbo, Laurent (president of the Ivory Coast) 37, 55
Geese 81
Genes 98–99, 102–3
Genetic engineering 22, 104–7
Geography
    National Geographic Bee winner, *picture* 234
    word puzzle 150–51
Georgia (republic) 385
Georgia (U.S. state)
    census and congressional seats 196
    Crypt of Civilization 210
Germany 20, 30, 206–7, 386
Ghana 35, 141, 386
Giambi, Jason (American baseball player) 175
Gibbons 35
Gibson, Mel (American actor) 264, 265
Gidzenko, Yuri (Russian cosmonaut) 114
Gielgud, Sir John (British actor) 380
Gilman, Billy (American singer) 274, *picture* 274
Gilmore, Rachna (Canadian author)
    Screaming Kind of Day, A (book) 293
Giraffes 81
Girl, Interrupted (movie), *picture* 249
Gladiator (movie) 266
Global warming 126, 127
Gober, Hershel W. (American public official) 30
Golf 184
Gomez, Scott (American athlete) 187
Goncz, Arpád (president of Hungary) 28
González, Elián (Cuban boy) 29
Gooding, Cuba, Jr. (American actor) 264
Gore, Al (vice president of the United States) 32, 40–41, 42–49, *pictures* 32, 42, 46, 110
Gore, Tipper (wife of Al Gore), *picture* 32
Gorey, Edward (American writer and illustrator) 380–81
Gorie, Dominic (American astronaut) 20
Gorillas 35
Gou Jingjing (Chinese athlete), *picture* 166
Governors of the states of the United States 393
Grammy Awards 275
"Granny D" (American protest walker) *see* Haddock, Doris
Gray, Macy (American singer) 273, *picture* 273
Great Britain *see* United Kingdom
Great Poochini, The (book by Gary Clement) 293
Grebes (birds) 80
Greece 165, 386
Greene, Maurice (American athlete) 164
Greengard, Paul (American scientist) 37
Greenhouse effect 126
Greenland 318–22
Grenada 386
Grint, Rupert (British actor), *picture* 232
Group of Eight summit meeting 30
Guatemala 19, 386
Gueï, Robert (president of the Ivory Coast) 37, 55
Guernsey (one of the Channel Islands, Great Britain) 138
Guinea 386
Guinea-Bissau 21, 386
Guinness, Sir Alec (British actor) 381, *picture* 381

Gun control 27, 45
Guyana 386
Gymnastics 163–64, 169, 171

H

Hackers (people who use computers to break the law) 20
Haddock, Doris (American protest walker), *picture* 66
Haiti 38, 207, 386
Halonen, Tarja (president of Finland) 21
Halsell, James, Jr. (American astronaut) 27
Hampton, Mike (American baseball player) 174
Handball 171
Handedness 110–13
Hanging parrots 90
Hanks, Tom (American actor) 109
Hanson (music group) 272
Harris, Emmylou (American singer) 274
Harrison, Benjamin (president of the United States) 48
Harry Potter and the Goblet of Fire (book by J. K. Rowling) 292, 295
Harry Potter and the Sorcerer's Stone (book by J. K. Rowling) 232
Hassan, Abdiqassim Salad (president of Somalia) 33
Hausas (African people) 55
Hawaii
    JASON Project 241
    nature preserve 40
Hawks (birds) 79
"Hawks" (supporters of the Vietnam War) 203
Hayden Planetarium (New York City) 108–9
Hayes, Rutherford B. (president of the United States) 48
Hayes, Sean (American actor), *picture* 268
Health *see* Medicine and health
Health insurance 45
Hearts (of dinosaurs) 75
Heaton, Patricia (American actress), *picture* 269
Heckman, James J. (American economist) 37
Heeger, Alan J. (American scientist) 37
Helms, Susan (American astronaut) 27
Hendrickson, Sue (American fossil hunter) 74
Henning, Doug (Canadian-born magician) 381
Henri (Grand Duke of Luxembourg) 37
Hibernation (winter sleep) 120, 122
Hill, Faith (American singer) 274
Hingis, Martina (Swiss athlete) 190, 191
Hip-hop music 273–74
Hispanic Americans 197
History
    census, United States 194–97, *picture* 192–93
    EXPO 2000, world's fair 206–7
    fireworks 199–200
    left-handed people in history 111–12
    Louis, son of Louis XVI and Marie Antoinette, *picture* 65
    Middle Ages 325–31
    pearls 251–53
    time capsules 208–11
    Vietnam War 202–5

Vikings 212–15
White House 216–19
World War I 336–51
World War II 352–78
Hoban, James (Irish-born architect) 217
Hobbies, handicrafts, and projects
  bags decorated to hold gifts 134–35
  beaded collages 155
  boomerangs 144–49
  braided paper wreaths 154–55
  coin collecting 158–59
  collage cards 136–37
  cooking 152–53
  note boards 155–56
  perpetual calendars 156
  stamp collecting 138–41
  word puzzles 142–43, 150–51
Ho Chi Minh (Vietnamese political leader) 202, 203
Hockey 185–87
  Richard, Maurice, death of 382
Holidays, stamps commemorating 139
Holm, Jennifer L. (American author)
  Our Only May Amelia (book) 295
Holocaust commemorative sculpture, *picture* 257
Holy Land (in present-day Israel and Jordan) 23
Holy Year (of the Roman Catholic Church) 23
Honduras 386
Hong Kong 19
Hoogenband, Pieter van den (Dutch athlete) 166
Horowitz, Scott (American astronaut) 27
Hostages
  United Nations peacekeepers 26, 53, 54
Houphouët-Boigny, Félix (president of the Ivory Coast) 55
Housatonic, **USS** (Union ship in the Civil War) 33
House of Representatives, United States 391–92
  apportioning congressional seats 194, 196
  election 38, 49
Houses, snow 320
Houston, Whitney (American singer) 19
How the Grinch Stole Christmas (movie) 267
Hubble Space Telescope 119
  view from, *picture* 96–97
Hudson, Kate (American actress) 267, *picture* 267
Hummingbirds 80
Hungary 28, 386
Hunt, Helen (American actress) 264, *picture* 265
Hutu (African people) 52, 53
Hyacinth macaws (parrots) 90, 91

I

Iceland 213–14, 386
Ice skating 188
Ida (asteroid) 116
Idaho
  wildfires 128
Igloos (houses of the Inuit) 320
Iliescu, Ion (president of Romania) 41
Illinois *see also* Chicago
  census and congressional seats 196
  Holocaust commemoration sculpture, *picture* 257
Iloilo, Ratu Josefa (president of Fiji) 30
Image (satellite) 133

Impeachment (legal action against a public official) 35
Independence Day 30, 200
India 22, 32, 386
Indiana Pacers (basketball team) 178–80
Indians, American *see* Native Americans
Indonesia 386
  endangered primates 35
  EXPO 2000 pavilion 207
  ferry sinking 28
  recipe 153
Inflation (of prices) 51
Insects
  carnivorous plants eat insects 82–85
  monarch butterflies 106
Institute for Exploration (Mystic, Connecticut) 240
Intelligence, animal 91
Intel Science Talent Search winner, *picture* 236
International Cat Show winner, *picture* 93
International Space Station (ISS) 27, 34, 36, 40, 114–16
International Time Capsule Society 210
Internet (network of on-line services)
  America Online-Time Warner merger 18
  aurora predictions 133
  cool Web sites 222–23
  hacking attack 20
  JASON Project 238–41
  Microsoft monopoly ruling 24
  music distribution 276–77
  securities industry 227–28
Inuit (people formerly known as Eskimos) 131, 318–22
Investment banking 231
Io (moon of Jupiter) 118, *picture* 117
Iran 63, 386
Iraq 386
Ireland 386
Irish Republican Army (IRA) 20
Islam *see* Muslims
Israel 386
  EXPO 2000 pavilion 207
  fighting with Palestinian Arabs 36, 61–63
  leadership change 30, 41
  Middle East peace talks 30
  Pope John Paul II's Holy Land visit 23
  stamps 141
  Syria, relations with 62
  withdrawal of forces from Lebanon 26
Italy 386
  Group of Eight summit meeting 30
  leadership change 25
  millennium celebrations 19
  Olympic Games 166
Ivory Coast 35, 37, 55, 386

J

Jackson, Andrew (president of the United States) 217
Jagr, Jaromir (Czech athlete) 187
Jamaica 386
James, Edison (prime minister of Dominica) 19
Janney, Allison (American actress), *picture* 269

Japan 386
  cultured pearls 255
  EXPO 2000 pavilion 206
  Group of Eight summit meeting 30
  leadership change 25
  Olympic Games 165, 166, 167
  space program 20, 114
Jarrett, **USS** (guided-missile frigate) 66
JASON Project (educational science program) 238–41
Jean (Grand Duke of Luxembourg) 37
Jefferson, Thomas (president of the United States) 217, *picture* 258
Jerusalem (Israel) 62
Jeter, Derek (American baseball player) 175, *picture* 174
Jet lag 123
Jett, Brent (American astronaut) 40
Jewelry
  pearls 254–55, *pictures* 252–53
Jews
  Lieberman, Joseph, first Jewish vice-presidential candidate of a major party 43
John Paul II (pope) 19, 23, *picture* 23
Johnson, Lyndon (president of the United States) 204
Johnson, Michael (American athlete) 165, *picture* 164
Johnson, Randy (American baseball player) 175, *picture* 175
Johnson Space Center (Texas), *picture* 238
Jolie, Angelina (American actress), *picture* 249
Jones, Marion (American athlete) 164, *picture* 160–61
Jones, Tommy Lee (American actor) 265, *picture* 266
Jordan 23, 28, 386
Joseph Had a Little Overcoat (book by Simms Taback) 292–93, *picture* 278–79
Judo 171–72
Jugnauth, Aneerood (premier of Mauritius) 35
Jungle fowl, *picture* 78
Jupiter (planet) 118
Justice, David (American baseball player) 174
Justice, United States Department of 24

K

Kabila, Laurent (president of the Democratic Republic of the Congo) 52, 53
Kafelnikov, Yevgeny (Russian athlete) 168
Kagame, Paul (president of Rwanda) 25
Kakas (parrots) 89–90
Kandel, Eric R. (Austrian-born American scientist) 37
Karavaeva, Irina (Russian athlete) 169
Karelin, Aleksander (Russian athlete) 168
Karume, Amani (president of Tanzania) 39
Kashmir 22
Katie and the Mona Lisa (book by James Mayhew) 293
Katsav, Moshe (president of Israel) 30
Kavandi, Janet (American astronaut) 20
Kayaking 169

Kazakhstan 168, 386
Keas (parrots) 89–90
Kelly, Moira (American actress), *picture* 269
Kennedy, Jacqueline (American First Lady) 218
Kent, Jeff (American baseball player) 175
Kenteris, Konstantinos (Greek athlete) 165
Kenya 165, 386
Khamenei, Ayatollah Ali (spiritual leader of Iran) 63
Khatami, Mohammed (president of Iran) 63
Kidnapping
  United Nations peacekeepers 26, 53, 54
Kilauea (volcano in Hawaii) 241
Kilby, Jack S. (American scientist) 37
Kim Dae Jung (president of South Korea) 28, 37, 56, *picture* 28
Kim Jong Il (president of North Korea) 28, 56, *picture* 28
Kim Jong Pil (premier of South Korea) 19
King, Martin Luther, Jr. (American civil-rights leader), *picture* 66
King, Stephen (American author), *picture* 260
Kipling, Rudyard (English writer)
  Rikki-Tikki-Tavi 280–89
Kiribati 19, 141, 386
Kleopatra (asteroid) 117
Klima, Viktor (chancellor of Austria) 21
Koirala, Girija Prasad (premier of Nepal) 22
Kookaburras (birds) 167
Koons, Jeff (American artist)
  Puppy (floral sculpture), *picture* 262
Korea, North 28, 56, 163, 386
Korea, South 386
  Kim Dae Jung and Nobel Peace Prize 37
  leadership change 19, 27
  Olympic Games 163
  summit with North Korea 28, 56
Kosovo (region in Serbia) 61
Kostunica, Vojislav (president of Yugoslavia) 37, 60, 61, *picture* 59
Krayzelburg, Lenny (American athlete) 166, *picture* 165
Kregel, Kevin (American astronaut) 20
Krikalev, Sergei (Russian cosmonaut) 114
Kroemer, Herbert (German-born American scientist) 37
Kuerten, Gustavo (Brazilian athlete) 190–91
Kursk (Russian submarine) 32
Kuwait 163, 386
Kwan, Michelle (American athlete), *picture* 188
Kyoto Protocol (on global warming) 45, 126
Kyrgyzstan 163, 386

L

Lamarr, Hedy (Austrian-born actress) 381
Lamm, C. Drew (American author)
  Prog Frince, The (book) 293
Landslides 332–33
Language, parrots' use of 91
Langurs (animals) 35
L'Anse aux Meadows (Newfoundland) 214–15, *picture* 214

Laos 386
Lareau, Sebastien (Canadian athlete) 168
Laser shows 109
Latvia 386
Lazio, Rick (United States Representative) 65
Leap year 21
Lebanon 26, 387
Lee, Jason (American actor) 267
Lee Han Dong (premier of South Korea) 27
Lee Teng-hui (president of Taiwan) 23, 57
Left-handedness 110–13
Lefthanders International (organization) 112
Lemurs (animals) 35
L'Enfant, Pierre Charles (French architect) 217
Leonardo da Vinci (Italian artist), *picture* 112
Lesotho 387
Lewinsky, Monica (American former White
    House intern) 35
Liberal Party (Canada) 39
Liberia 387
Library of Congress
    200th birthday, *picture* 258
    commemorative coins 158, *picture* 158
    Wonderful Wizard of Oz exhibit 235
Libya 387
Lieberman, Hadassah (wife of Joseph Lieberman),
    picture 32
Lieberman, Joseph I. (United States Senator) 32,
    43, *picture* 32, 44
Liechtenstein 387
Lie detectors 324
Light and biological rhythms 123
Linnaeus, Carolus (Swedish botanist) 123
Linus (comic-strip character) 245, *picture* 245
Linville, Larry (American actor) 381
Lions 77
Literature *see also* Young people's literature
    Cartland, Barbara, death of 380
    electronic publishing, *picture* 260
    Gorey, Edward, death of 380–81
    Nobel Prize in 37
Lithuania 387
Little League baseball 177
Little Prince, The (book by Antoine de Saint-
    Exupéry), *picture* 259
Little Wildrose (story) 308–14
Liu, Lucy (American actress) 266
Livestock feed 125
Lizards 70–73, *picture* 68–69
Loan officers (in banks) 225
Lopez-Alegria, Michael (American astronaut) 36
Lories (parrots) 90
Lorikeets (parrots) 90, *picture* 89
Los Alamos (New Mexico) 26, 128
Los Angeles (California)
    Democratic Party's national convention 32, 43
Los Angeles Lakers (basketball team) 178–80
Louis (son of Louis XVI and Marie Antoinette),
    picture 65
Lovebirds (parrots) 90–91, *picture* 88
Love Bug (computer virus) 26
Lowe, Rob (American actor), *picture* 269
Lu, Edward (American astronaut) 34
Lucy (comic-strip character) 244–45,
    pictures 244, 246
Lucy (fossil skeleton) 206
Luxembourg 37, 140, 387

M

M2M (music group) 270
Macaws (parrots) 90, 91, *picture* 89
MacDiarmid, Alan G. (American scientist) 37
Macedonia 387
Madagascar 35, 73, 387
Madison, Dolley (American First Lady) 219
Madison, James (president of the United States)
    217, 219
Madl, Ferenc (president of Hungary) 28
Madonna (American singer) 271
Magic
    Henning, Doug, death of 381
Magnetic field (of the Earth) 131, 133
Maguire, Tobey (American actor), *pictures* 249,
    262
Mahuad Witt, Jamil (president of Ecuador) 19
Maine
    electoral votes 45
Mairan, Jean Jacques d'Ortous de (French
    astronomer) 122
Malawi 387
Malaysia 387, *picture* 100
Malcolm in the Middle (television program),
    picture 237
Maldives 387
Malenchenko, Yuri (Russian cosmonaut) 34
Mali 387
Malnutrition, *picture* 54
Malta 140, 387
Mammals, protection of young by 76
Man, Isle of 159
Mandela, Nelson (president of South Africa) 53
Mangabeys (animals) 35
Manitoba (province, Canada) 394
Mapping, radar 118–19
Mara, Kamisese (president of Fiji) 30
Marcellino, Fred (American illustrator)
    Ouch! (book by Natalie Babbitt) 294
Marchand, Nancy (American actress) 381
Mars (planet) 117, *picture* 116
Mars Global Surveyor (spacecraft) 117
Marshall Islands 387
Marsh hawks 79
Marsh wrens 80
Martin, Ricky (Puerto Rican singer) 271
Martinez, Pedro (Dominican baseball player) 175
Maryland
    commemorative coin 158, *picture* 158
*M*A*S*H* (television program) 210
Masked lovebirds (parrots), *picture* 88
Massachusetts
    commemorative coin 158, *picture* 158
Mastracchio, Rick (American astronaut) 34
Matchbox Twenty (music group) 273
Matthau, Walter (American actor) 381–82,
    picture 381
Mauritania 387
Mauritius 35, 387
Mayhew, James (British author)
    Katie and the Mona Lisa (book) 293
Mayi-Mayi (African people) 53
McArthur, William, Jr. (American astronaut) 36

McCain, John (United States Senator) 43
McClintock, Barbara (American illustrator)
  Prog Frince, The (book by C. Drew Lamm) 293
McCormack, Eric (American actor), *picture* 268
McDonald's Corporation 107
McDormand, Frances (American actress) 267
McFadden, Daniel L. (American economist) 37
McGrath, Kathleen (United States Navy captain),
  picture 66
McMahon, Brigitte (Swiss athlete) 169
Medicine and health
  AIDS 54
  antibiotic, new type of 25
  emotions 323–24
  health insurance 45
  human genome 103
  microbes, drug-resistant 124–25
  Nobel Prize in 37
  parrots carry psittacosis 91
  wild species as sources of medicine 100
Meet the Parents (movie) 266
Mei Xiang (panda) 40
Mejía Dominguez, Hipólito (president of the
  Dominican Republic) 27
Melanin (dark brown pigment) 71
Melroy, Pam (American astronaut) 36
Mendel, Gregor (Austrian monk and scientist) 105
Men of Honor (movie) 264
Mergers (of companies)
  America Online and Time Warner 18
Merrick, David (American theatrical producer) 382
Messing, Debra (American actress), *picture* 268
Metallica (music group) 277
Mexico 30, 387
Mice 76–77, *picture* 105
Microbes, drug-resistant 124–25
Micronesia 387
Microsoft Corporation 24
Middle Ages 325–31
Middle East
  breakdown of peace talks 30
  fighting between Israelis and Palestinian Arabs
    36, 61–63
  Pope John Paul II's Holy Land visit 23
Mikimoto, Kokichi (Japanese jewelry designer) 253
Military *see also* Navy, United States
  left-handed people in history 111
Millennium celebrations 19, 198–99
  commemorative stamps 141, *pictures* 140–41
  time capsules 211
Millennium Summit (of the United Nations) 34
Million Mom March 27
Million Paws Walk (Brisbane, Australia) 94
Milosevic, Slobodan (president of Yugoslavia)
  37, 60–61
Mineta, Norman Y. (United States Secretary of
  Commerce) 28
Minnesota
  fiberglass Snoopy statues in St. Paul 256
Mint, United States 158
Missing in action 204
Mission: Impossible 2 (movie) 266
Mississippi
  census and congressional seats 196
Missouri
  Carnahan, Mel, death of 36, 380
Miss Waldron's red colobus (extinct monkey) 35

Mr. Potato Head statues, *picture* 256
Mkapa, Benjamin (president of Tanzania) 39
Mobutu Sese Seko (president of Zaire) 52
Mohri, Mamoru (Japanese astronaut) 20
Moldova 387
Monaco 387
Mona Lisa (painting by Leonardo da Vinci) 293
Monarch butterflies 106, *picture* 107
Money
  coin collecting 158–59
  finance, careers in 224–31
Mongolia 206, 387
Monkeys 35, 78, 79, *picture* 76
Monopoly (in law) 24
Montana
  census and congressional seats 196
  wildfires 128
Montminy, Anne (Canadian athlete) 166
Monuments and memorials
  proposed Martin Luther King, Jr. memorial,
    picture 66
Moons (of planets) 117–18
Moose 334
  fiberglass statues 256
Mori, Yoshiro (premier of Japan) 25
Morocco 387
Morukov, Boris (Russian cosmonaut) 34
Moskalenko, Aleksandr (Russian athlete) 169
Moths (insects) 85
Motion pictures
  Academy Awards 248–49
  Guinness, Sir Alec, death of 381
  Harry Potter and the Sorcerer's Stone, picture 232
  Lamarr, Hedy, death of 381
  left-handed actors and actresses 112
  Maguire, Tobey, *picture* 262
  Matthau, Walter, death of 381–82
  My Dog Skip 237, *picture* 95
  Young, Loretta, death of 383
Mountain goats 81
Mountain gorillas 35
Mourning, Alonzo (American athlete) 180
**Movement for the Restoration of the Ten
  Commandments of God** 22
Mozambique 387
MP3 (audio format) 276, 277
Mugabe, Robert (president of Zimbabwe) 55
Mullally, Megan (American actress), *picture* 268
Muniz, Frankie (American actor) 266, *picture* 237
Murder
  Ugandan cult killings 22
Museums
  American Museum of Natural History 108–9
  Field Museum dinosaur display 74
  North Carolina Museum of Natural Sciences 75
  Rockwell touring show 261
Music 270–75
  fireworks shows 200, 201
  Internet distribution 276–77
  left-handed musicians in history 112
  Puente, Tito, death of 382
  Rampal, Jean-Pierre, death of 382
Muslims 55, 63
Mutation
  drug-resistant bacteria 125
Myanmar *see* Burma
My Dog Skip (movie) 237, 266, *picture* 95

N

Nader, Ralph (American activist) 46
Nakamura, Kuniwo (president of Palau) 39
Namibia 53, 387
Napster (Internet service to download music) 276–77
National Aeronautics and Space Administration (NASA) 133
National Archives (United States) 211
National Millennium Time Capsule 211, *picture* 208
National monuments (United States)
    Giant Sequoia National Monument 25
National Museum of Natural History (Washington, D.C.) 212–13
National Oceanic and Atmospheric Administration (NOAA) 133
National Park Service 26
National Zoo (Washington, D.C.) 40
Native Americans *see also* Inuit
    pearls 252
    Sacagawea, commemorative coin of 158
    throw sticks 149
    Vikings, conflict with 215
Nauru 387
Navy, United States
    Cole explosion 36, 60
    McGrath, Kathleen, first woman to command a warship at sea, *picture* 66
NEAR (Near Earth Asteroid Rendezvous) 116
Nebraska
    electoral votes 45
Nelson, Willie (American singer) 274
Nemov, Aleksei (Russian athlete) 163–64
Nepal 22, 387
Nestor, Daniel (Canadian athlete) 168
Nests (of birds) 77–78, 80, 89
Netherlands 165, 166, 206, 387
Nevada
    census and congressional seats 196
Newbery Medal (children's literature) 292
New Brunswick (province, Canada) 394
Newfoundland (province, Canada) 394
    L'Anse aux Meadows 214–15, *picture* 214
New Hampshire
    commemorative coin 158, *picture* 158
New Jersey Devils (hockey team) 185–87
New Mexico
    Los Alamos wildfire 26, 128
New York
    census and congressional seats 196
    Clinton, Hillary Rodham, United States Senator, *picture* 65
New York City
    fiberglass cow statues, *picture* 242–43
    Hayden Planetarium 108–9
    millennium celebrations 19, 198
    OpSail 2000, *picture* 30
    Puppy (floral sculpture by Jeff Koons), *picture* 262
    time capsules 210–11
New York Mets (baseball team) 174–75
New York World's Fair (1939-40) 210–11, 296–307, *picture* 209

New York World's Fair (1965) 211
New York Yankees (baseball team) 174–75
New Zealand 89–90, 141, 387
Ngeny, Noah (Kenyan athlete) 165
Ngo Dinh Diem (president of South Vietnam) 203
Nicaragua 387
Niger 387
Nigeria 52, 53, 55, 387
98° (music group) 272
Niue (Pacific island) 159
Nixon, Richard (president of the United States) 204
Nobel Prizes 37
Noboa Bejarano, Gustavo (president of Ecuador) 19
Noriega, Carlos (American astronaut) 40
North Carolina
    Museum of Natural Sciences 75
    Venus's-flytrap 83
North Dakota, University of
    hockey championship 187
Northern Ireland 20
North Korea *see* Korea, North
Northwest Territories (Canada) 395
Norway 22, 168, 206, 387
Notebook, left-handed, *picture* 110
Nova Scotia (province, Canada) 394
'N Sync (music group) 270, 272, *picture* 270
Nuclear weapons 22, 26
Nunavut (territory in Canada) 395

O

Obasanjo, Olusegun (president of Nigeria) 55, *picture* 55
Obuchi, Keizo (premier of Japan) 25
Ocean
    JASON Project 238–41
    sea stars 86–87
    South African oil spill 129
O'Connor, Cardinal John J. (American Roman Catholic archbishop) 382, *picture* 382
Ohio
    census and congressional seats 196
    Cincinnati pig statues, *picture* 256
Oil spills 129
Oklahoma
    census and congressional seats 196
Old age
    census predictions 197
    Elizabeth (Queen Mother of Britain) turns 100 years old, *picture* 64
    Haddock, Doris, walked across United States at age 90, *picture* 66
Olympic Games (2000) 36, 162–73
    boomerang exhibition 149
    commemorative coins and stamps 141, 159
    Dragila, Stacy, winning pole vault, *picture* 189
    Jones, Marion, winning sprint, *picture* 160–61
Oman 388
O'Neal, Shaquille (American athlete) 178, 179, 180, *picture* 178
102 Dalmatians (movie) 267
Ontario (province, Canada) 394
OpSail 2000 (procession of ships), *picture* 30

Orangutans 35
Organic foods 106
Organization of African Unity 54
Organization of Petroleum Exporting Countries (OPEC) 51
Osama bin Laden (international terrorist) 60
Osment, Haley Joel (American actor) 264, *picture* 265
Ouattara, Alassane D. (Ivory Coast political figure) 55
Ouch! (book by Natalie Babbitt) 294
Our Only May Amelia (book by Jennifer L. Holm) 295
Owl parrots 89
Oysters (mollusks) 250–51, 255
Ozone hole (in the atmosphere) 127

P

Pakistan 22, 206, 207, 388
Palau (island nation, Pacific Ocean) 38–39, 388
Paleontology 74–75
Palestinian Arabs 30, 36, 61–63
Palm cockatoos (parrots) 91
Panama 388
Pandas 40
Paniagua, Valentin (president of Peru) 39
Papua New Guinea 207, 388
Paraguay 388
Parakeets 90, 91
Park Tae Joon (premier of South Korea) 19, 27
Parrots 88–91, *picture* 98
Patriot, The (movie) 264
Pay It Forward (movie) 264, *picture* 265
Peace, Nobel Prize in 37
Peanuts (comic strip) 244–47
    commemorative coins 159, *picture* 159
    fiberglass Snoopy statues 256
    Schulz, Charles, death of 383
Pearls 250–55
Peng, Felix (American student), *picture* 234
Penguins 129
Penicillin 124
Pennsylvania
    census and congressional seats 196
    Little League World Series (Williamsport) 177
    Republican Party's national convention 32
Pentathlon 172
Pepperberg, Irene (American biologist) 91
Peppermint Patty (comic-strip character) 245, *pictures* 244, 245
Peregrine falcons (birds), *picture* 101
Perfect Storm, The (movie) 265, *picture* 266
Peru 39, 388
Petroleum (Oil) 51
Pets
    cats and dogs are predators 101
    chameleons 73
    parrots and people 91
Philadelphia (Pennsylvania)
    first true time capsule 209–10
    Republican Party's national convention 32, 43
Philbin, Regis (American quiz-show host), *picture* 263

Philippines 26, 388
Physics, Nobel Prize in 37
Physiology, Nobel Prize in 37
Pierce, Mary (French athlete) 190
Pig Pen (comic-strip character) 245
Pigs
    cloning 22
    fiberglass statues, *picture* 256
    genetically modified 106
Pink cockatoos (parrots), *picture* 89
Pitcher plants (carnivorous plants) 85, *picture* 85
Planetariums 108–9
Planets, extrasolar 119
Plant, The (book by Stephen King) 260
Plants
    balance of natural ecosystems 100
    carnivorous plants 82–85
    genetically modified foods 104–7
    Hawaii 241
    rhythms of life 120
Platypuses (mammals) 167
Plovers (birds) 81
Poetry 290–91
Poland 388
Polar bears 126
Polar ice pack 126
Police dogs, *picture* 233
Pollution *see* Environment
Polo, Teri (American actress) 266
Population
    census, United States 194–97
    nature, effect on 99–100
Portillo Cabrera, Alfonso (president of Guatemala) 19
Portugal 388
Potter, Harry (fictional character) 232, 292, 295
Poverty
    Africa 52
    poor countries and conservation 101
Prairie dogs 79
Presidents (of the United States)
    election (2000) 38, 40–41, 42–49
    left-handedness 110, 112
    nominating conventions 32
    White House 216–19
Préval, René (president of Haiti) 38
Prince Edward Island (province, Canada) 394
Prizes and awards
    Academy Awards 248–49
    Caldecott Medal 279, 293
    Canadian Governor General's children's literature awards 293
    Coretta Scott King Author award 292
    Emmy Awards 268–69
    Grammy Awards 275
    Intel Science Talent Search winner, *picture* 236
    National Geographic Bee winner, *picture* 234
    National Spelling Bee winner, *picture* 234
    Newbery Medal 292
    Nobel Prizes 37
Prog Frince, The (book by C. Drew Lamm) 293
Pronger, Chris (Canadian athlete) 187, *picture* 186
Protests *see* Demonstrations and protests
Proverbs
    Madagascar's sayings about chameleons 73
Psittacosis (disease spread from parrots to humans) 91

Public accountants 225
Publishing, electronic, *picture* 260
Puente, Tito (American bandleader and percussionist) 382, *picture* 382
Pull tabs (from soda cans) 257
Puppy (floral sculpture by Jeff Koons), *picture* 262
Putin, Vladimir (president of Russia) 23, 58–59
Pygmy parrots 90

Q-R

Qatar 388
Quebec (province, Canada) 39, 395
Quiz shows 263
Rabbits 78
Raccoons 80
Radar mapping of Earth 118–19
Radcliffe, Daniel (British actor), *picture* 232
Raducan, Andreea (Romanian athlete) 164
Ragheb, Ali Abu al- (prime minister of Jordan) 28
Railroads
  high-speed electric train, *picture* 38
Rainbow lorikeets (parrots), *picture* 89
Rain forests 99
Rallies
  Million Mom March 27
Ralph, Shea (American athlete), *picture* 180
Ramgoolam, Navinchandra (premier of Mauritius) 35
Ramona's World (book by Beverly Cleary) 295
Rampal, Jean-Pierre (French-born flutist) 382
Rap music 274
Rawabdeh, Abdoul Raouf al- (prime minister of Jordan) 28
Recipes 152–53
Recycling (of waste materials) 101
Refugees
  Congo 53, *picture* 52
  Eritrea 54
  González, Elián 29
Reindeer 335
Religion *see also* Roman Catholic Church
  Ugandan cult killings 22
Remember the Titans (movie) 264, *picture* 264
Remengesau, Tommy (president of Palau) 38–39
Reproduction 22, 92, 120
Republican Party (of the United States) 32, 42–49
Rhode Island
  fiberglass Mr. Potato Head statues, *picture* 256
Rhymes, Busta (American singer) 274
Rhythm and blues music 273–74
Richard, Maurice (Canadian athlete) 187, 382
Riding the Bullet (book by Stephen King), *picture* 260
Rikki-Tikki-Tavi (story by Rudyard Kipling) 280–89
Risca, Viviana (American student), *picture* 236
Roberts, Julia (American actress) 264
Rock and Roll Hall of Fame 274–75
Rockets
  fireworks 200, 201
Rock music 272–73, 274–75
Rockwell, Norman (American artist), *pictures* 261
Roman Catholic Church
  O'Connor, Cardinal John J., death of 382

Pope John Paul II's Holy Land visit 23
Pope John Paul II's millennium blessing 19
Romania 41, 164, 388
Romano, Ray (American actor), *picture* 269
Rome, ancient
  leap year 21
  parrots 91
  pearls 251
Roosevelt, Theodore (president of the United States) 218
Rose (ship), *picture* 30
Rose Center (American Museum of Natural History, New York City) 108–9
Rosolino, Massimiliano (Italian athlete) 166
Rowing 169, 172
Rowling, J. K. (British author)
  Harry Potter and the Goblet of Fire (book) 292, 295
  Harry Potter and the Sorcerer's Stone (book) 232
Ruler, left-handed, *picture* 110
Russia 388
  Group of Eight summit meeting 30
  Inuit 318–22
  leadership change 23, 58–59
  millennium celebrations 19
  Olympic Games 36, 163–64, 168, *picture* 163
  reindeer 335
  space program 27, 34, 114–16
  submarine accident 32
Ruth, Babe (American athlete), *picture* 111
Rwanda 25, 52, 53, 388

S

Sacagawea (Shoshone Indian guide)
  commemorative coin 158, *picture* 158
Safety of genetically modified foods 106–7
Safin, Marat (Russian athlete), *picture* 191
Saint-Exupéry, Antoine de (French author), *picture* 259
St. Kitts and Nevis 388
St. Louis Rams (football team) 181–82
St. Lucia 388
St. Paul (Minnesota)
  fiberglass Snoopy statues 256
St. Vincent and the Grenadines 388
Sally Brown (comic-strip character) 245
Salmon, genetically modified 106
Samoa 141
Sampras, Pete (American athlete) 191
Sanha, Malan Bacai (president of Guinea-Bissau) 21
Sankoh, Foday (Sierra Leone rebel leader) 53–54
San Marino 388
Santana, Carlos (Mexican guitarist) 273, *picture* 275
São Tomé and Príncipe 388
Saskatchewan (province, Canada) 395
Satellites, artificial 133
Saturn (planet) 117–18
Saudi Arabia 163, 388
Savage Garden (music group) 271, *picture* 271
Sawalha, Julia (British actress) 265
Scarlet macaws (parrots), *picture* 89

Schiff, Richard (American actor), *picture* 269
Schools *see* Education
Schrier, Jeffrey (American artist) 257
Schroeder (comic-strip character) 245, *pictures* 245
Schulz, Charles M. (American cartoonist) 244–47, 383, *picture* 247
Schüssel, Wolfgang (chancellor of Austria) 21
Science
  auroras 130–33
  avalanches and landslides 332–33
  biodiversity 98–101
  boomerangs' flight 145–46
  cloning 22
  dinosaur fossil discoveries 74–75
  drug-resistant bacteria 124–25
  fireworks 200–201
  genetically modified foods 104–7
  global warming 126
  Hayden Planetarium 108–9
  Hubble Space Telescope, view from, *picture* 96–97
  human genome 102–3
  Intel Science Talent Search winner, *picture* 236
  JASON Project 238–41
  left-handedness 110–13
  ozone hole 127
  penguin rescue 129
  rhythms of life 120–23
  wildfires 127–28
Scissors, left-handed, *picture* 110
Scooters, *picture* 233
Scotland
  Norse settlements 213–14
Screaming Kind of Day, A (book by Rachna Gilmore) 293
Sculpture
  fiberglass statues, *pictures* 242–43, 256
  Segal, George, death of 383
  Wings of Witness, picture 257
Sea levels 126
Seasonal affective disorder (SAD) 123
Sea stars (Starfish) 86–87
Secretary birds 77
Securities dealers 226–28
Segal, George (American sculptor) 383
Selective breeding (of plants and animals) 104–5
Seles, Monica (American athlete), *picture* 112
Senate, United States 390
  Chinese trade restrictions, vote on ending 34
  Clinton, Hillary Rodham, *picture* 65
  Coverdell, Paul, death of 380
  election 38, 49
Senegal 23, 207, 388
Sequoias, giant (trees) 25
Sesame Street (television program)
  commemorative stamps 141
Seychelles 388
Sezer, Ahmet Necdet (president of Turkey) 27
Shakespeare, William (English playwright) 294
Sharon, Ariel (Israeli politician) 62–63
Sheen, Martin (American actor), *picture* 269
Sheep, *picture* 78
Shepherd, William (American astronaut) 114
Ships *see also* Submarines
  Cole explosion 36, 60
  McGrath, Kathleen, first woman to command an American warship at sea, *picture* 66

OpSail 2000, *picture* 30
  Tall Ships 2000 commemorative stamps 139
  Treasure sinking and oil spill 129
Shirakawa, Hideki (Japanese scientist) 37
Shooting (sport) 172
Sierra Leone 26, 53–54, 159, 388
Siew, Vincent (premier of Taiwan) 23
Silly Putty, *picture* 236
Singapore 159, 207, 388
Skating *see* Hockey; Ice skating
Skiing 188
  cable-car fire (Austria) 38
Skunks 77
Slovakia 388
Slovenia 140, 388
Smithsonian Institution (Washington, D.C.)
  Viking exhibition 212–13
Snoopy (comic-strip character) 245, 256, *pictures* 245, 247
"Snoopy vs. the Red Baron" (song) 246
Snow houses (of the Inuit) 320
Soap, antibacterial 125
Soccer 168, 172
Social Security 45–46
Softball 166–67, 172
Solomon Islands 159, 388
Somalia 33, 388
South Africa 54, 129, 388
South Carolina
  commemorative coin 158, *picture* 158
  Confederate flag controversy 24
  Hunley, raising of the 33
  Venus's-flytrap 83
South Dakota
  dinosaur fossil discoveries 74, 75
South Korea *see* Korea, South
Space Cowboys (movie) 265–66, *picture* 266
Space programs 114–19
  aurora study 133
  biological rhythm experiment 122
  missions 20, 27, 34, 36, 40
Space shuttles 20, 27, 34, 36, 40, 114, 115
Space stations 114–16
Spacey, Kevin (American actor) 264, *picture* 248
Spain 206, 388
Spears, Britney (American singer) 270
Spelling Bee, National, winner, *picture* 234
Spencer, John (American actor), *picture* 269
Spider webs, *picture* 99
Spin City (television program), *picture* 269
Sports
  baseball 174–76
  basketball 178–80
  commemorative coins 159
  football 181–83
  golf 184
  hockey 185–87
  ice skating 188
  Jones, Marion, winning Olympic sprint, *picture* 160–61
  left-handed athletes 111–12
  Little League baseball 177
  Olympic Games 36, 162–73, *picture* 160–61
  skiing 188
  tennis 190–91
  track and field 189
Squirrels 77, 79, 81

Sri Lanka 388
  Bandaranaike, Sirimavo, death of 380
Stamp collecting 138–41
Staphylococcus bacteria, *picture* 124
Starfish *see* Sea stars
Star-Spangled Banner (historic flag)
  Web site 222
State of the Union address 18
Stevens, Scott (Canadian athlete) 187, *picture* 185
Stiller, Ben (American actor) 266
Sting (British singer) 271
Stock market 50, 51, 226–28
Stoltenberg, Jens (premier of Norway) 22
Streptococcus bacteria, *picture* 124
Stuart Little (movie) 267
Submarines 32, 33
Sudan 388
Sue (dinosaur fossil) 74
Sun
  auroras caused by solar storms 131, 132, 133
Sundews (carnivorous plants) 83–84, *picture* 83
Supreme Court, United States 393
  presidential election (2000) 40–41, 42, 48
Suriname 389
Sutherland, Donald (Canadian actor) 265, *picture*
  266
Swank, Hilary (American actress), *picture* 249
Swaziland 54, 389
Sweden 141, 335, 389
Swimming 165–66, 169, 172
Switzerland 140, 169, 389
Swords, Viking, *picture* 213
Synchronized swimming 172
Syria 28, 62, 389

T

Taback, Simms (American author)
  Joseph Had a Little Overcoat (book) 293,
    picture 278–79
Table tennis 172
Tae kwon do 172
Taiwan 23, 37, 56–58, 389
Tajikistan 389
Takahashi, Naoko (Japanese athlete) 165
Tall Ships 2000 139, *picture* 30
Tamarins (animals) 35
Tang Fei (premier of Taiwan) 23, 37
Tanner, Joseph (American astronaut) 40
Tanzania 389
  Clinton's visit 52, 53
  EXPO 2000 pavilion 207
  leadership change 39
  turmoil in Africa 53
Taylor, Elizabeth (American actress) 253
Taylor, Stephanie (American student), *picture* 233
Technology
  high-tech sports gear 169
  video games 316–17
  World of Tomorrow (story) 296–307
Teenagers *see* Youth
Television
  Allen, Steve, death of 380
  Beverly Hills, 90210, picture 257
  Emmy Awards 268–69
  Freaks and Geeks, picture 220–21
  JASON Project field trip broadcasts 238–39
  Linville, Larry, death of 381
  Marchand, Nancy, death of 381
  Muniz, Frankie, *picture* 237
  Peanuts specials 246
  Who Wants to Be a Millionaire, picture 263
  Young, Loretta, death of 383
Tellers (in banks) 224
Tennessee Titans (football team) 181–82
Tennis 190–91
  Olympic Games 168, 173
Terrorism
  Cole explosion 36, 60
Texas
  auroras 132
  census and congressional seats 196
Thailand 389
Thampy, George Abraham (American student),
    picture 234
Theater
  Gielgud, Sir John, death of 380
  Merrick, David, death of 382
  You're a Good Man, Charlie Brown 246
Thescelosaurus (dinosaur) 75
Thiele, Gerhard (German astronaut) 20
Thompson, Jenny (American athlete) 166, *picture*
  165
Thorpe, Ian (Australian athlete) 165–66, *picture* 165
Through My Eyes (book by Ruby Bridges) 295
Tian Tian (panda) 40
Tilden, Samuel J. (American political figure) 48
Time capsules 208–11
Times Capsule (American Museum of Natural
    History) 211
Time Warner Inc. 18
Titanic (ship) 240
Togo 389
Tonga 389
Tour de France (bicycle race) 30
Toys and games
  boomerangs 144–49
  scooters, *picture* 233
  Silly Putty, *picture* 236
  video games 316–17
Track and field 189
  Jones, Marion, winning Olympic sprint, *picture*
    160–61
  Olympic Games 164–65, 169, 173
Trade, international
  China and the United States 34, 58
  United States and Vietnam 205
Trains *see* Railroads
Trampoline 169
Transportation
  high-speed electric train, *picture* 38
  scooters, *picture* 233
Trees
  giant sequoias 25
Triathlon 168–69, 173
Trinidad & Tobago 389
Tropical rain forests 99
Trudeau, Pierre Elliott (prime minister of Canada)
  383, *picture* 383
Truman, Harry S. (president of the United States)
  218

Trust officers (in banks) 225
Tuberculosis bacteria, *picture* 124
Tunisia 389
Turkey 27, 389
Turkeys (birds) 80
Turkmenistan 389
Tutsi (African people) 52, 53
Tuvalu 389
26 Fairmount Avenue (book by Tomie de Paola) 295
Tyrannosaurus rex (dinosaur) 74

U

U2 (music group) 273
Uganda 22, 53, 207, 389
Ukraine 389
Unita (rebel group in Angola) 53
United Arab Emirates 389
United Kingdom 389
  Group of Eight summit meeting 30
  millennium celebrations 19, 198, *picture* 199
  Northern Ireland 20
  royal family, *pictures* 64
  time capsule, *picture* 209
United Nations
  Millennium Summit 34
  peacekeepers 26, 53, 54
  stamps 140–41
United States 389
  census 194–97, *picture* 192–93
  China, relations with 34, 58
  Clinton's final State of the Union address 18
  coins 158, *picture* 158
  economic boom 50–51
  environmental protection 100–101
  government 390–93
  Group of Eight summit meeting 30
  Olympic Games 36, 163, 164–65, 166–67, 167–68, *pictures* 164, 165, 167
  political parties' conventions 32
  presidential election 38
  space program 20, 27, 34, 36, 40, 114–19
  stamps 138–39
  Vietnam War 202–5
  wildfires 127–28
Unity (space station module) 114
Uranus (planet) 117–18
Uruguay 207, 389
Usachev, Yuri (Russian cosmonaut) 27
Uzbekistan 389

V

Vaccines 106
Van Pelt, Linus (comic-strip character) 245, *picture* 245
Van Pelt, Lucy (comic-strip character) 244–45, *pictures* 244, 246
Vanuatu 389
Vatican City 389
Venezuela 206–7, 389

Venture capital firms (investors in new businesses) 231
Venus's-flytrap (carnivorous plant) 83, *picture* 82
Veterans Affairs, United States Department of 30
Victoria (queen of Great Britain), *picture* 111
Video games 316–17
Vietnam 389
  Clinton, Bill, trip to 38
  endangered primates 35
  EXPO 2000 pavilion 207
  Olympic Games 163
  Vietnam War 202–5
Vietnam Veterans Memorial (Washington, D.C.), *picture* 205
Vietnam War 202–5
Vikings (Scandinavian seafarers) 212–15
Vinland (Viking name for America) 215
Violence *see* Crime; Terrorism
Virginia
  auroras, *picture* 132
  commemorative coin 158, *picture* 158
Virtual reality 108–9, 238–41
Viruses, computer 26
Vitamin C (music group) 271
Viva Rock Vegas (movie) 267
Volcanoes
  Io 118, *picture* 117
  JASON Project 241
Volleyball 168, 173
Voss, James (American astronaut) 27
Voss, Janice (American astronaut) 20
Vulturine parrots 89

W

Wade, Abdoulaye (president of Senegal) 23
Wakata, Koichi (Japanese astronaut) 36
War of 1812 217, 219, 258
Washington (D.C.)
  millennium celebrations 198
  Million Mom March 27
  National Millennium Time Capsule 211
  pandas at National Zoo 40
  proposed Martin Luther King, Jr. memorial, *picture* 66
  White House 216–19
Washington (state)
  Centennial Capsule 211
Washington, Denzel (American actor) 264
Washington, George (president of the United States) 216–17
Washington Monument (Washington, D.C.) 198
Water on Mars, possibility of 117
Water polo 173
Watson, Emma (British actress), *picture* 232
Weber, Mary Ellen (American astronaut) 27
Weight lifting 173
Weinke, Chris (American football player), *picture* 183
Weizman, Ezer (president of Israel) 30
West, Togo D., Jr. (American public official) 30
Western Samoa 389
Westminster Kennel Club Show winner, *picture* 93

412

West Wing, The (television program), *picture* 269
White House (Washington, D.C.)
  200th anniversary of 216–19
  word puzzle 142
Whitewater affair (in U.S. history) 34–35
Whitfield, Simon (Canadian athlete) 168–69
Whitford, Bradley (American actor), *picture* 269
Who Wants to Be a Millionaire (television
  program), *picture* 263
Wilcutt, Terrence (American astronaut) 34
Wildcats, *picture* 92
Wildebeest 80
Wilkinson, Laura (American athlete) 166
Will & Grace (television program), *picture* 268
William (prince of Great Britain), *pictures* 64, 111
  commemorative stamps 140
Williams, Jeffrey (American astronaut) 27
Williams, Serena (American athlete) 168, 191
Williams, Venus (American athlete) 168, 191,
  picture 190
William Shakespeare & the Globe (book by Aliki)
  294
Willo (dinosaur fossil) 75
Wilson, Roger (governor of Missouri) 36
Windows (computer operating system) 24
Winfrey, Oprah (American entertainer),
  picture 112
Wings of Witness (sculpture), *picture* 257
Wisconsin
  census and congressional seats 196
Wisoff, Jeff (American astronaut) 36
Wizard of Oz, The (movie), *picture* 235
Wobbling (of stars) 119
Wolves 77
Women
  basketball 180
  Jones, Marion, first woman to win five track
    medals in same Olympics 161
  McGrath, Kathleen, first woman to command an
    American warship at sea, *picture* 66
  Olympic Games 164, 165, 166–67, 168
  record thirteen female Senators after 2000
    election 49
Wonderful Wizard of Oz, The (book by L. Frank
  Baum), *picture* 235
Woodbridge, Todd (Australian athlete) 191
Woodchucks 78
Woodcocks 79
Woodforde, Mark (Australian athlete) 191
Woodpeckers 78
Woods, Tiger (American athlete), *picture* 184
Woodstock (comic-strip character) 245, *picture* 245
World Health Organization (WHO) 124, 125
World Series (baseball) 174–75
  Little League 177
World's fairs
  EXPO 2000 (Hanover, Germany) 206–7
  time capsules 210–11, *picture* 209
  World of Tomorrow (story) 296–307
World War I 336–51
World War II 352–78
  Saint-Exupéry, Antoine de 259
World Wide Web (system of documents on the
  Internet)
  cool Web sites 222–23
  Library of Congress web site for kids 258
Wrestling 168, 173

X-Y-Z

Y2K bug (of computers) 18
Yachting 173
Yahoo.com 20
Yala, Kumba (president of Guinea-Bissau) 21
Yeltsin, Boris (president of Russia) 23, 58
Yemen 36, 60, 389
Yoruba (African people) 55
Young, Loretta (American actress) 383, *picture* 383
Young people's literature
  Birchbark House, The (book by Louise Erdrich)
    295
  Bud, Not Buddy (book by Christopher Paul
    Curtis) 292
  Great Poochini, The (book by Gary Clement) 293
  Harry Potter and the Goblet of Fire (book by
    J. K. Rowling) 295
  Harry Potter and the Sorcerer's Stone (book by
    J. K. Rowling) 232
  Joseph Had a Little Overcoat (book by Simms
    Taback) 292–93, *picture* 278–79
  Katie and the Mona Lisa (book by James
    Mayhew) 293
  Little Prince, The (book by Antoine de Saint-
    Exupéry), *pictures* 259
  Little Wildrose (story) 308–14
  Ouch! (book by Natalie Babbitt) 294
  Our Only May Amelia (book by Jennifer L. Holm)
    295
  poetry 290–91
  Prog Frince, The (book by C. Drew Lamm) 293
  Ramona's World (book by Beverly Cleary) 295
  Rikki-Tikki-Tavi (story by Rudyard Kipling) 280–89
  Screaming Kind of Day, A (book by Rachna
    Gilmore) 293
  Through My Eyes (book by Ruby Bridges) 295
  26 Fairmount Avenue (book by Tomie de Paola)
    295
  William Shakespeare & the Globe (book by Aliki)
    294
  Wonderful Wizard of Oz, The (book by L. Frank
    Baum), *picture* 235
  World of Tomorrow (story) 296–307
You're a Good Man, Charlie Brown (play) 246
Youth
  cool Web sites 222, 223
  finance, careers in 224–31
  Freaks and Geeks (television program), *picture*
    220–21
  González, Elián, Cuban refugee 29
  JASON Project 238–41
  music scene 270, 274
  newsmakers, *pictures* 232–37
  stamp-design contest 138
Yugoslavia 37, 60–61, 168, 389, *pictures* 59
Yukon (territory, Canada) 395
Zambia 53, 389
Zarya (space station module) 114
Zedillo Ponce de León, Ernesto (president of
  Mexico) 30
Zimbabwe 53, 54, 55, 389
Zvezda (space station module) 114
Zyvox (antibiotic) 25

ILLUSTRATION CREDITS AND ACKNOWLEDGMENTS

The following list credits or acknowledges, by page, the source of illustrations and text excerpts used in this work. Illustration credits are listed illustration by illustration—left to right, top to bottom. When two or more illustrations appear on one page, their credits are separated by semicolons. When both the photographer or artist and an agency or other source are given for an illustration, they are usually separated by a slash. Excerpts from previously published works are listed by inclusive page numbers.

6 © Andrew J. Martinez/Photo Researchers, Inc.; © John Pack; © Fabian Bimmer/AP/Wide World Photos

7 © Renee Lynn/Photo Researchers, Inc.; © Pascal Tour-naire/Liaison Agency; Illustration by Mary GrandPré © 2000/Warner Bros. By permission of Scholastic Inc.

12– © Rick Wilking/Reuters Newmedia Inc./Corbis
13

14 © Stephan Savoia/AP/Wide World Photos; © U.S. Navy/AP/Wide World Photos

15 © Alexei Kondrashkin/AP/Wide World Photos; © Rick Bowmer/AP/Wide World Photos

16 Courtesy of PPL Therapeutics/Newsmakers; © Mikhail Metzel/AP/Wide World Photos

17 © Bongart/SportsChrome; *The News Times*/Photo by Linda B. Koonz

18 Corbis-Sygma

19 © Peter Morgan/Reuters/Archive Photos; © Chris Hondros/Liaison Agency

20 © Peter Morrison/AP/Wide World Photos

22 Courtesy of PPL Therapeutics/Newsmakers

23 © Arturo Mari/AP/Wide World Photos

24 © Bob Gorrell/Creators Syndicate

25 © Susan Walsh/AP/Wide World Photos

26 © Michael Caulfield/AP/Wide World Photos

27 © Larry Downing/Reuters/Archive Photos

28 © Yonhap, Pool/AP/Wide World Photos

29 © Ricardo Mazalan/AP/Wide World Photos

30 © Laurent Rebours/AP/Wide World Photos

31 © K. Meyers/*The New York Times*

32 © Stephan Savoia/AP/Wide World Photos; © Charles Rex Arbogast/AP/Wide World Photos

33 © Paula Illingworth/AP/Wide World Photos

34 United Nations Photo by Terry Deglau/Eastman Kodak

35 © F. W. Frohawk

36 © U.S. Navy/AP/Wide World Photos

37 © Ahn Young-joon/AP/Wide World Photos

38 © Stephen J. Boitano/AP/Wide World Photos

39 © Fred Chartrand, CP/AP/Wide World Photos

40 © Jeff Tinsley/The Smithsonian National Zoo/AP/Wide World Photos

41 Artist, Natasha Lessnick Tibbott

42 © Dennis O'Clair/Stone; © Rick Wilking/Liaison Agency; © Mark Wilson/Liaison Agency

44 © Joel Page/AP/Wide World Photos; © David Zalubowski/AP/Wide World Photos

46 © Luke Frazza/AFP/Corbis

49 © Newsmakers/Liaison Agency; © Rhona Wise/AFP/Corbis

50 © Chris Gardner/AP/Wide World Photos

51 © Claude Paris/AP/Wide World Photos

52 © David Guttenfelder/AP/Wide World Photos

53 © Brennan Linsley/AP/Wide World Photos

54 © Celine Amiot/Corbis-Sygma; © Denis Farrell/AP/Wide World Photos

55 © Rick Bowmer/AP/Wide World Photos

56 © Lee Jae-won/AP/Wide World Photos

57 © Dave Smith/AP/Wide World Photos; © Vincent Yu/AP/Wide World Photos

58 © Alexei Kondrashkin/AP/Wide World Photos

59 © Darko Vojinovic/AP/Wide World Photos; © Zeljko Safar/AP/Wide World Photos

60 © U.S.M.C., Sgt. Don L. Maes/AP/Wide World Photos

61 © Lefteris Pitarakis/AP/Wide World Photos

62 © Syrian Arab News Agency/AP/Wide World Photos

63 © Enric Marti/AP/Wide World Photos

64 © Ian Jones/AP/Wide World Photos; © Rebecca Naden/AP/Wide World Photos

65 © Bebeto Matthews/AP/Wide World Photos; © The Granger Collection

66 © Ed Kashi; © Martin Luther King, Jr. National Memorial Project Foundation Inc./AP/Wide World Photos

67 © Leslie E. Kossoff/AP/Wide World Photos

68– © Art Wolfe/Art Wolfe, Inc.
69

70 © Frans Lanting/Minden Pictures

71 © Art Wolfe/Art Wolfe, Inc.; © Dwight R. Kuhn; © Dwight R. Kuhn

72 © Nuridsany et Perennou/Photo Researchers, Inc.; © Art Wolfe/Art Wolfe, Inc.; Frans Lanting/Minden Pictures

73 © Wolfgang Kaehler/Corbis

74 © Charlie Bennett/AP/Wide World Photos

75 © Ed Heck/North Carolina Museum of Natural Sciences; © Karen Tam/AP/Wide World Photos

76 © Art Wolfe/Art Wolfe, Inc.

77 © Steve Maslowski/Photo Researchers, Inc.; SuperStock

78 © Patti Murray/Animals Animals; © Johnny Johnson/Animals Animals

79 © Wolfgang Bayer/Bruce Coleman Inc.

80 © Bob & Clara Calhoun/Bruce Coleman Inc.

81 © W. Gregory Brown/Animals Animals

82 © Howard Miller/Photo Researchers, Inc.

83 © Ken W. Davis/Tom Stack & Associates

84 © James R. Fisher/Photo Researchers, Inc.; © Breck P. Kent/Earth Scenes; © Norm Thomas/Photo Researchers, Inc.

85 © Joe McDonald/Bruce Coleman Inc.; © John Shaw/Bruce Coleman Inc.

86 © Darrell Gulin/DRK Photo

86– © Gregory Ochocki/Photo Researchers, Inc.; © Steve
87 Wolper/DRK Photo

87 © L. Newman and A. Flowers/ Photo Researchers, Inc.; © Fred Bavendam; © Andrew J. Martinez/Photo Researchers, Inc.

88 © Hans Reinhard/Bruce Coleman Inc.

89 © Renee Lynn/Photo Researchers, Inc.; © Fritz Pren-zel/Animals Animals; © Fritz Prenzel/Animals Animals

90 © Hans Reinhard/Bruce Coleman Inc.; © Jane Burton/Bruce Coleman Inc.

91 © David Carter

92 © Bill Haber/AP/Wide World Photos

93 © Hillside Studio/Courtesy, Pamela J. Bassett; © Mark Lennihan/AP/Wide World Photos

94 © Jimmy Pozarik/Liaison Agency; © Allison Leach/*People* Weekly

95 Courtesy, Warner Bros.

96– © NASA, The Hubble Heritage Team (AURA/STScI)
97

98 © Mark Smith/Photo Researchers, Inc.; © Maresa Pryor/Animals Animals

99 © M. H. Black/Bruce Coleman Inc.; © Hans Reinhard/Bruce Coleman Inc.

100 © Kevin Fleming/Corbis; © Sally A. Morgan; Ecoscene/Corbis

101 © Richard Sheinwald/AP/Wide World Photos; © Earl & Nazima Kowall/Corbis

102 © Digital Art/Corbis

103 © Elise Amedola/AP/Wide World Photos

104 © Charles Bennett/AP/Wide World Photos

105 © Keith Weller/AP/Wide World Photos; © Bob Child/AP/Wide World Photos

106 © Stephen Saks/Photo Network

107 © J. Scott Applewhite/AP/Wide World Photos

108 © Denis Finnin/American Museum of Natural History/AP/Wide World Photos; © Digital Galaxy Project/American Museum of Natural History/National Center for Supercomputing Applications (NCSA)/ University of Illinois

109 © Denis Finnin/American Museum of Natural History

110 © Greg Gibson/AP/Wide World Photos; © Doug Mills/AP/Wide World Photos; © Dirck Halstead/ Liaison Agency

111 © Leonard Lessin, FBPA

112 © The Granger Collection; © Dave Caulkin/AP/Wide World Photos; Bettmann-UPI/Corbis

113 © Kevin Frayer/AP/Wide World Photos; The Granger Collection; © Mitchell Gerber/Corbis

114 © Mikhail Metzel/AP/Wide World Photos

115 © Scott Audette/AP/Wide World Photos

116 © JHUAPL/NASA; © JHUAPL/NASA; © NASA/JPL/Malin Space Science Systems

117 © NASA/JPL; © NASA/JPL/University of Arizona; © NASA/JPL/CALTECH/AP/Wide World Photos

118 © STS-99/NASA; © DLR/NASA

119 © STS-103/NASA; © A. Fruchter and the ERO team (STScI)/NASA

120– © John Pack
122

123 Courtesy, Don Pavey/Micro Academy

273 © Gilbert Flores/Celebrity Photo; © Reuters
NewMedia Inc./Corbis
274 © Kevork Djansezian/AP/Wide World Photos
275 © Reed Saxon/AP/Wide World Photos
276 © Laura Rauch/AP/Wide World Photos
277 © Eric Risberg/AP/Wide World Photos; © Katsumi
Kasahara/AP/Wide World Photos
278– From *Joseph Had a Little Overcoat* by Simms Taback,
279 copyright © 1999 by Simms Taback. Used by
permission of Viking Penguin, a division of Penguin
Putnam Inc.
280– Artist, Betsy Feeney
289
290– Artist, Michele A. McLean
291
292 © 2000 Delacorte Press. Permission by Random
House Children's Books, a division of Random House,
Inc.; © James Mayhew. Illustrations by James Mayhew.
Reproduced by permission of Orchard Books, A
Grolier Company
293 Illustration from *The Great Poochini.* Copyright
© 1999 by Gary Clement. First published in Canada
by Groundwood Books/Douglas & McIntyre.
Reprinted by permission of the publisher.
294 © 1999 by C. Drew Lamm. Illustrations © 1999 by
Barbara McClintock. Reproduced by permission of
Orchard Books, A Grolier Company.; Illustrations
Copyright © 1998 by Fred Marcellino. Used by
permission of HarperCollins Publishers.
295 Used by permission of HarperCollins Publishers.;
Illustration by Mary GrandPré © 2000/Warner Bros.
By permission of Scholastic Inc.
296– Artist, Gary Torrisi (based on work by Bob Scott)
307
308– Artist, Anne Feiza
314
316 © Michael S. Yamashita/Corbis
317 © Eriko Sugita/Reuters/Archive Photos
318 © Lawrence Migdale/Photo Researchers, Inc.; © Wolfgang Kaehler; © John Eastcott/Yva Momatiuk/Photo
Researchers, Inc.; © Bryan & Cherry Alexander
319 ©Bryan & Cherry Alexander; © Lowell Georgia/Corbis
320 ©Bryan & Cherry Alexander
321 © Wolfgang Kaehler/Corbis
322 © David Hiser/Photographers/Aspen/PictureQuest

323 © Jose Luis Pelaez Inc./The Stock Market; © Michael
Grecco/Stock, Boston
325 © Wood River Gallery/PictureQuest
326 © Giraudon/Art Resource, New York
327 © Art Resource, New York
328 The Granger Collection
329 © Masters of the Osservanza Tript/Wood River
Gallery/PictureQuest
330 The Bridgeman Art Library International Ltd.
331 © Alinari/Art Resource, New York; The Bridgeman
Art Library International Ltd.; The Bridgeman Art
Library International Ltd.
332 © William Bacon/Photo Researchers, Inc.
333 © Grantpix/Photo Researchers, Inc.
334 © Ken N. Johns/Photo Researchers, Inc.
335 © Herve Donnezan/Photo Researchers, Inc.
336 The Art Archive; © IWM/Camera Press/Retna Ltd.
U.S.A.; Hulton Getty/Liaison Agency; Hulton
Getty/Liaison Agency
337 Corbis-Bettmann; King Features Syndicate; Hulton
Getty/Liaison Agency; © L'Illustration/Sygma; King
Visual Technology
338 Corbis-Bettmann
339 SuperStock; © IWM/Camera Press/Retna Ltd. U.S.A.
341 © Imperial War Museum; © Roger Viollet/Liaison
Agency; Hulton Getty/Liaison Agency
342 Popperfoto/Archive Photos; Corbis-Bettmann; The
Art Archive
343 © Imperial War Museum
344 ©Hulton Getty/Liaison Agency; The Art Archive;
Corbis-Bettmann
345 © Imperial War Museum; TimePix
346 Culver Pictures; Art Staff, Inc.
347 Art Staff, Inc.; TimePix
348 Archive Photos/PictureQuest
349 Tass/Sovfoto/Eastfoto
350 Underwood & Underwood
352 © ILN/Camera Press/Retna; Margaret Bourke-
White/*Life* Magazine/© Time Inc.; UPI/Corbis;
UPI/Corbis
353 The Granger Collection; Photo Researchers, Inc.;
© Hulton-Deutsch Collection/Corbis; Courtesy of
the National Archives/Woodfin Camp & Associates;
© AP/Wide World Photos/Courtesy of the National
Archives/Woodfin Camp & Associates

354 Hulton Getty/Liaison Agency
355 © Charles P. Cushing
356 *New York Times*
358 Liaison Agency
359 Corbis-Bettmann; © Topham/The Image Works
360 The Granger Collection; Topham Picuturepoint/
The Image Works, Inc.
361 Archive Photos; Sovfoto/Eastfoto
362 © Topham/The Image Works; © Popperfoto/Archive
Photos; © National Archives/King Features Syndicate
363 Corbis-Bettmann; © Keystone Paris/Corbis-Sygma
364 © Hulton-Deutsch Collection/Corbis; © National
Archives/Photo Researchers, Inc.
366 © Frank Scherschel/TimePix; © National
Archives/King Features Syndicate
367 © Hulton Getty/Liaison Agency; © IWM/Camera
Press/Retna
368 Culver Pictures
369 © IWM/NYF 74459/Camera Press/Retna; Hulton
Getty Picture Library
371 © U.S. Coast Gaurd; © Robert Capa/Magnum Photos
372 Archive Photos; © National Archives/King Features
Syndicate
374 © John Florea/TimePix
375 © W. Eugene Smith/TimePix
376 Archive Photos; © Evgeny Khaldey/TS/RBO/Camera
Press/Retna
378 © National Archives/King Features Syndicate
380 © David Reed/Corbis; © Bettmann/Corbis
381 © Julie Markes/AP/Wide World Photos; AP/Wide
World Photos
382 © Michael Russo/Liaison Agency; © Mike
Albans/AP/Wide World Photos
383 © Ryan Remiorz/Canadian Press/AP/Wide World
Photos; © Bettmann/Corbis
393 © Orlin Wagner/AP/Wide World Photos